Richard Hooker

T&T Clark Studies in English Theology

Series editors
Karen Kilby
Michael Higton
Stephen R. Holmes

Richard Hooker

The Architecture of Participation

Paul Anthony Dominiak

t&tclark

LONDON • NEW YORK • OXFORD • NEW DELHI • SYDNEY

T&T CLARK
Bloomsbury Publishing Plc
50 Bedford Square, London, WC1B 3DP, UK
1385 Broadway, New York, NY 10018, USA

BLOOMSBURY, T&T CLARK and the T&T Clark logo
are trademarks of Bloomsbury Publishing Plc

First published in Great Britain 2020
Paperback edition first published 2021

Copyright © Paul Anthony Dominiak, 2020

Paul Anthony Dominiak has asserted his right under the Copyright,
Designs and Patents Act, 1988, to be identified as Author of this work.

For legal purposes the Acknowledgements on p. vi constitute
an extension of this copyright page.

Cover design: Terry Woodley
Cover image: claireviz/iStock

All rights reserved. No part of this publication may be reproduced or
transmitted in any form or by any means, electronic or mechanical,
including photocopying, recording, or any information storage or retrieval
system, without prior permission in writing from the publishers.

Bloomsbury Publishing Plc does not have any control over, or responsibility for,
any third-party websites referred to or in this book. All internet addresses given
in this book were correct at the time of going to press. The author and publisher
regret any inconvenience caused if addresses have changed or sites have
ceased to exist, but can accept no responsibility for any such changes.

A catalogue record for this book is available from the British Library.

Library of Congress Control Number: 2019949296

ISBN: HB: 978-0-5676-8507-0
PB: 978-0-5676-9892-6
ePDF: 978-0-5676-8508-7
eBook: 978-0-5676-8510-0

Typeset by Newgen KnowledgeWorks Pvt. Ltd., Chennai, India

To find out more about our authors and books visit
www.bloomsbury.com and sign up for our newsletters.

Contents

Acknowledgements		vi
Note on the text		vii
List of abbreviations		viii
1	'The participation of God himselfe': Hooker and the retrieval of participation	1
2	'Most abundant vertue': Hooker's metaphysical architecture of participation	35
3	'A drop of that unemptiable fountain of wisdom': Cognitive participation in God	89
4	'Politique societie': The politics of participation	149
5	'To resolve the conscience': Revisiting the architecture of participation	191
Bibliography		199
Index		217

Acknowledgements

The practical, intellectual and moral support of numerous people supported the production of this book. I am thankful for the funding provided by the Arts and Humanities Research Council, as well as generous book grants from the Cleaver Trust. The gentle, calm and wise guidance of Professor Christopher Insole of Durham University as he supervised my doctoral work (of which this book is a revision) encouraged me during times when I felt torn between multiple commitments. I could not have asked for a better supervisor. Any errors in this work reflect my own inadequacy. Other people have, at various times, greatly cheered me by showing an interest in my research, giving me a much-needed sense that I did have something to say. In this regard, I am especially indebted to the following: Dr Bradford Littlejohn, Professor Torrance Kirby, Professor Sarah Coakley, Dr Charles Drummond and Dr Ashley Cocksworth. Throughout my career to date, I have received constant friendship, encouragement, care and good cheer from the Rev. Mark Eminson, his wife Elise, and their children, Grace, Martha, Joseph and Beatrice. Groups of people have also shown me great love and support, especially the following: the parish of St Francis of Assisi, Ingleby Barwick; the Richard Hooker Society; the ordinands and staff of Westcott House; and the fellows, staff and students of Trinity College and Jesus College, Cambridge. Above all else, however, I am grateful for the love, understanding and encouragement of my wife, Kaitlin, and for the wonderful distractions provided by our children, Sophia and Eleanor. It is to my family, then, that I dedicate this book.

Note on the text

All quotations from Hooker are taken from the modern, seven-volume *Folger* edition of Hooker's works: W. Speed Hill, gen. ed., *The Folger Library Edition of the Works of Richard Hooker* (vols 1–5, Cambridge: Belknap Press, 1977–90; vol. 6, Binghamton: Belknap Press, 1993; vol. 7, Tempe: Medieval and Renaissance Texts and Studies, 1998). This book uses a dual reference system for the *Laws* designed to aid those readers who only have access to Keble's widely available nineteenth-century edition, and takes the following format: volume number in the *Folger* edition followed by page and line numbers, plus Hooker's note number, where relevant; followed by Keble's reference numbers of book, chapter and section. For example: *Laws*, 1:73.8–10; I.5.2 refers to the first volume of the *Folger* edition, page 73, lines 8 through 10, corresponding with Book One of the *Laws*, fifth chapter, second section in Keble's edition.

Abbreviations

This book uses the following abbreviations for Hooker's works and contemporaneous responses to Hooker:

A Christian Letter	A Christian Letter of Certaine English Protestantes . . . unto that Reverend and Learned Man Maister R. Hoo[ker]
Autograph Notes	Autograph Notes to the Christian Letter
Answer	Answer to the Supplication
Certaintie	A Learned and Comfortable Sermon of the Certaintie and Perpetuitie of Faith in the Elect
Dublin Fragments	The Dublin Fragments. Grace and Free Will, the Sacraments, and Predestination
FLE	Folger Library Edition
Jude	The Sermons Upon Part of S. Judes Epistle
Justification	A Learned Discourse of Justification, Workes, and How the Foundation of Faith is Overthrowne
Laws	Of the Laws of Ecclesiastical Polity
Predestination	Notes toward a Fragment on Predestination
Pride	A Learned Sermon of the Nature of Pride

References to other theological works give the full reference in the first use, followed by an indicative shortened version thereafter.

1

'The participation of God himselfe': Hooker and the retrieval of participation

Introduction

Every political vision assumes an epistemology, a way of looking at and understanding the world, in turn buttressed by some kind of ontology, a claim about what, how and why the world is. The vision of Richard Hooker's *Of the Laws of Ecclesiastical Polity*, a late sixteenth-century apology for the Elizabethan Church, is no different. In the *Laws*, Hooker moves from 'general meditations' to the 'particular decisions'[1] that govern the Elizabethan Religious Settlement but which have proved contentious. In his initial general meditations, 'law' acts as Hooker's controlling image, an architectural blueprint through which Hooker will parse subsequent particular points of controversy over the role and interpretation of Scripture, the Book of Common Prayer, and ultimately the nature of the Elizabethan Church. For Hooker, all things 'do work, after a sort, according to law', and such laws direct creatures to their perfective formal end.[2] Hooker perceives that the root issue underneath the religious and political controversy of his age is whether the Elizabethan Religious Settlement has the character of such law. In the move from the general to the particular, then, Hooker's apology for the political structures of the Elizabethan Church assumes a particular epistemology undergirded by a legal ontology. Early on within his general account of law, Hooker crucially claims that, through formal laws, 'all things in the worlde are saide in some sort to seeke the highest, and to covet more or lesse the participation of God himselfe'.[3] For Hooker, the metaphysics of participation describe how creation relates to the divine Creator: creation consists of participatory and teleological bodies, both physical and social, ordered within a cosmic hierarchy of laws and which desire to share analogically in the divine nature. If 'law' lays out a formal metaphysical blueprint, 'participation in God' emerges as its living, dynamic architecture that generates and illuminates the entire edifice of Hooker's subsequent rebuttal of 'them that seeke (as they tearme it) the reformation of Laws, and orders Ecclesiastical, in the Church of England'.[4] As this

---

[1] Hooker, *Laws*, 1:57.29–32; I.1.2.
[2] Ibid., 1:58.32–3; I.2.1.
[3] Ibid., 1:73.8–10; I.5.2.
[4] Ibid., 1:1.2–4; Pref.1.1.

work will show, the concept of participation rests behind every major argument in the *Laws*. A study of Hooker's architecture of participation opens up new horizons both for understanding the internal coherence of his work and for grasping how, far from representing an arcane museum piece, the *Laws* illuminates modern theological, ecumenical and political discussions around the concept of participation and the closely related idea of deification.

The meaning, architecture and retrieval of participation

When the modern reader hears Hooker claim that law and the sacraments draw people into 'the participation of divine nature',[5] and that in the Incarnation 'God hath deified our nature',[6] it begs the question about what Hooker takes these closely related terms to mean, as well as how his use might relate to recent ecumenical retrievals. In order to grasp the interconnected quality of Hooker's thought, it is necessary to define participation and deification, explore how these terms relate to each other, draw out a heuristic 'architecture of participation', and finally, examine why and how there have been modern ecumenical rediscoveries of such concepts.

The concept of participation has a double register – the philosophical and the scriptural – each of which will be important for Hooker, especially as they converge on the closely related idea of deification. Unpacking this double register eventually generates the heuristic 'architecture of participation' that this study will use to explore Hooker's thought.

At first glance, participation seems to have a straightforward Latin etymology: as Thomas Aquinas puts it, 'to participate [*participare*] is, as it were, to take a part [*partem capere*]'.[7] For Aquinas, however, such Latin also renders an older Greek philosophical notion of participation as *methexis*. Unlike *methexis*, the Latin etymology of *participare* seems to suggest that participation divides some simple quality into discrete parts (*partem capere*). To avoid this suggestion, Aquinas quickly extends his definition also to state that, 'when something receives in particular fashion that which belongs to another in universal fashion, the former is said to participate in the latter.' Accordingly, Aquinas shifts the still familiar, quotidian notion of participation (as taking a part in or of something) towards a more philosophical sense of *methexis*, which involves an asymmetrical relationship between something restricted and contingent with some donating, universal source.

Aquinas hereby accommodates a Platonic notion of participation. Plato was the first philosopher to use participation (*methexis*) in a precise philosophical sense in relation to the problem of the many and the one, namely, how a contingent phenomenological multiplicity relates to some metaphysically simple, unitive, formal source.[8] For Plato,

---

[5] Ibid., 1:73.8–10; 2:238.18; I.5.2; V.56.7.
[6] Ibid., 2:224.14–15; V.54.5.
[7] Thomas Aquinas, *Expositio libri Boetii de Hebdomadibus*, 2.24; hereafter abbreviated as *In De Heb*. English translation in *An Exposition of the 'On the Hebdomads' of Boethius*, trans. J. Schultz and E. Synan (Washington: Catholic University of America Press, 2001), 14–29.
[8] See M. Annice, 'Historical Sketch of the Theory of Participation', *New Scholasticism* 26 (1952): 49–79.

participation (*methexis*) expresses the way in which many things can warrant the same name without dividing some simple quality into separate parts. The etymology of *methexis* (μέθεξις from μετέχω) indicates that things in the world have an ontological dependency on higher spiritual, intellectual realities, and implies plurality, similarity, relation and asymmetry all at once.[9] Indeed, participation becomes an attempt to see the world as, in some sense, saturated with divinity. The root of the term, ἔχω ('to have') when used with a genitive object indicates the 'having of', in the sense of 'sharing in' a whole rather than 'taking' a part. Thus, many things share limited possession of a whole without dividing it into many discrete, separate parts. Meanwhile, the prefix, μετά, means 'amidst' and, in compositional words, 'after' or 'in pursuit of' something else. *Methexis* is therefore a compound construction suggesting that one thing has its own reality only by virtue of sharing in something other than itself and by dynamically tending towards that other. Accordingly, Charles Bigger defines Plato's use of *methexis* in this manner: '"Participation" is the name of the "relation" which accounts for the togetherness of elements of diverse ontological type in the essential unity of a single instance. In this sense it is a real relation, one constitutive of the nexus qua nexus which arises from it.'[10] For example, one calls something 'beautiful' insofar as it participates in the exemplary form of beauty. In participatory metaphysics, there exists a real, constitutive (if asymmetrical) relation between an exemplary, heavenly, participable form and the temporal, embodied participant of that same form. Plato uses a host of other terms in addition to *methexis* in order to describe this asymmetrical relationship: *mixis* (mixture), *symplokē* (interweaving), *koinōnia* (coupling) and *mimesis* (copying). Yet, *methexis* has had the most enduring and wide-ranging impact.

The attendant Platonic idea of imitating God connects the metaphysics of participation with ideas about deification, or becoming godlike through assimilation (*homoiōsis theōi*) in some regard.[11] Plato understands the 'divine' in diverse ways throughout his writings, including the gods of mythology, the soul of the world, the intellect that orders all things and the formal philosophical notion of 'the Good' as the fullness of being.[12] In the dialogue 'Timaeus', for example, Plato describes how an intelligent Maker produces the sensible world, describing this intelligent Maker as God, Father, Craftsman, One or Mind.[13] For Plato, both human beings and the cosmos exhibit a likeness to the divine, a similarity making possible the participation (*methexis*) and imitation (*mimesis*) of God, the dynamic ensoulment of the exemplary

---

[9] See Fritz-Gregor Hermann, 'μετέχειν, μεταλαμβάνειν and the Problem of Participation in Plato's Ontology', *Philosophical Inquiry* 25, nos 3–4 (2003): 19–56. See also David C. Schindler, 'What's the Difference? On the Metaphysics of Participation in a Christian Context', *The Saint Anselm Journal* 3, no. 1 (2005): 1–27.

[10] Charles P. Bigger, *Participation: A Platonic Inquiry* (Baton Rouge: Louisiana State University Press, 1968), 7.

[11] See Paul M. Collins, *Partaking in Divine Nature: Deification and Communion* (London: T&T Clark, 2012), 18–27.

[12] As commentators often point out, the English word 'god' therefore remains an inadequate translation of the Greek word. See G. M. Grube, *Plato's Thought*, 2nd edn (London: Athlone Press, 1980); and J. P. Kenney, *Mystical Monotheism: A Study in Ancient Platonic Theology* (Hanover and London: Brown University Press, 1991).

[13] Plato, 'Timaeus', 28–9 in *Plato: Complete Works*, ed. John M. Cooper (Indianapolis, Cambridge: Hackett, 1997), 1234–6; hereafter *Works*.

Good, Beautiful and True.[14] The end goal of such imitation of and participation in God is assimilation, which Plato sees as the development and growth of divine characteristics, and which some later Neoplatonists more strongly (and evocatively) parse as ontological union (*henosis*), the ecstatic mingling of the many with the one.[15]

Early Christian thinkers either baptized Greek thought with the exigencies of Christian soteriology or developed the ideas of participation in God and deification on strictly scriptural terms.[16] As such, whether on a philosophical or scriptural register (or with the integration of both), participation in God and deification soon assumed great importance in patristic scriptural exegesis and theology.[17] In the New Testament, the word often translated into English as 'participation' renders a host of terms other than (but not contrary to) the philosophical register of *methexis*. These scriptural terms echo the philosophical problem of the many and the one, but cast it in terms of how the multitude of diverse believers relate to God and Christ. The scriptural terms for participation include: *metechō* (sharing in something), *metalambanō* (receiving a share), *koinōnia* (inward fellowship or communion) and *menō* (abiding, indwelling). The final two terms are particularly significant: *koinōnia* expresses the unitive and constitutive relationship of the believer to Christ (1 Cor. 1.9; 1 Jn 1.3), especially in the Eucharist (1 Cor. 10.16) and so through the Church as Christ's Body (1 Cor. 12.27); and *menō* again alludes to Eucharistic participation and union with Christ (Jn 6.56). The idea of becoming 'participants [*koinōnoi*] of the divine nature [*theias . . . physeōs*]' becomes explicitly mooted in 2 Pet. 1.3–4. There, Paul links knowledge (*epignōsis*) of Christ as the doorway to sharing in God's 'divine power' and 'divine nature'.[18]

The idea of 'becoming participants of the divine nature' found in 2 Pet. 1.4 stood alongside a number of other scriptural and philosophical themes and texts that became important for early Christian ideas about deification as a form of participation in God. Gregory of Nazianzus in the fourth century coined *theōsis* to describe the deiform transformation of believers through their participation in God, although earlier periods also used a number of other terms, the most significant of which is *theopoiēsis*, and earlier patristic writers similarly placed deification as a central theme.[19] In terms of etymology, *theōsis* (formed from the verb *theoō*, 'to make god') means 'becoming god', while *theopoiēsis* (from the verb *theopoieō*, 'to deify') means 'making divine' or 'making

---

[14] See Plato, 'Phaedo', 100b-d; 'Theaetetus', 176a; 'Republic', 476a; 'Timaeus', 29e; and 'Laws', 716b-c; in *Works*, 86; 195; 1102; 1236; 1402–3.

[15] For example, see Plato, 'Theaetetus', 176b; in *Works*, 195. Compare Plotinus, 'Enneads', I.6.6; VI.9.9 in *The Enneads*, trans. Stephen MacKenna (London: Penguin, 1991), 51–2; 545–6; hereafter Mackenna.

[16] See Grant Macaskill, *Union with Christ in the New Testament* (Oxford: Oxford University Press, 2013), esp. 42–76 and 305–7 for a nuanced account highlighting how the patristic adoption of Platonic categories took place in the specific context of Alexandria, but also how the categories were radically reconfigured by their Christian recipients.

[17] See Mark Edwards and Elena Ene D-Vasilescu (eds), *Visions of God and Ideas on Deification in Patristic Thought* (Oxford: Routledge, 2016).

[18] See Stephen Finlan, 'Second Peter's Notion of Divine Participation', in *Theōsis: Deification in Christian Theology*, ed. Stephen Finlan and Vladimir Kharlamov (Eugene: Princeton Theological Monograph Series, 2006), 32–50.

[19] Stephen Finlan and Vladimir Kharlamov (eds), *Theōsis: Deification in Christian Theology* (Eugene: Princeton Theological Monograph Series, 2006), 5–8. For a comprehensive overview, see Norman Russell, *The Doctrine of Deification in the Greek Patristic Tradition* (Oxford: Oxford University Press, 2006), 'Appendix 2: The Greek Vocabulary of Deification', 333–44.

into a god', but the terms remained imprecise and broad in early usage. Despite such imprecision, early Christian writers drew careful lines around the terms. Typically, early Christian writers took *theōsis* to refer to the transformation of believers into the likeness of God, rather than the pagan notion of *apotheōsis*, the literal making of a god, an idea that would have violated Christian monotheism. Gregory of Nazianzus used this nuanced version of *theōsis*, then, to circumscribe the whole economy of salvation: the self-emptying of God in the Incarnation, the assumption of Christ's resurrected body into the divine life, the sharing in deified humanity through baptism, the ascent of the believer to God through contemplation, and the eschatological fulfilment of human nature in heaven. Although ideas about deification formed a central theme for patristic writers of the second to fourth centuries, Pseudo-Dionysius in the sixth century was the first to attempt a definition of *theōsis*. He defines it as 'being as much as possible like and in union with God',[20] an intellectual union with the essential divine attributes such as truth, goodness and oneness through participation in the Eucharist. Pseudo-Dionysius's definition remained general and inexact, covering a wide range of ideas. All told, however, deification worked on two broad levels in the early Christian period, one theological and another pedagogical.[21] At a theological level, deification referred to the Incarnation, the 'exchange formula' of Athanasius (echoing Irenaeus of Lyons and recapitulated by many others) that Christ 'became human that we might become divine'.[22] On a pedagogical level, it referred to the teaching that the purpose of human life was to become like God as far as is possible, especially through the participation of Christ.

The constitutive ideas of such *theōsis* varied immensely, then, but incorporated a wide semantic field of scriptural motifs that contained the embryonic notion of deification as a form of participation in God. These motifs included: being made in God's image and likeness (Gen. 1.26, 27); divine filiation or adoption (Ps. 82.6; Gal. 4.5; Rom. 8.15; Eph. 1.5); taking on God's nature (2 Pet. 1.4; Jn 10.34); imitation of holiness or divine perfection (Mt. 5.48; Jn 14.12; Eph. 5.1); being reformed by God (Jn 3.6; Rom. 12.2; 2 Cor. 5.17); being conformed or united to Christ (Jn 17.21–23; Phil. 2.5–11, 3.21; Rom. 8.29; 1 Jn 3.2); and the transformation of the universe through God's action (Hab. 2.14; 1 Cor. 15.28).[23] Stephen Finlan and Vladimir Kharlamov helpfully suggest that the influence of scriptural images, Greek philosophical terms and popular ideas about deification meant that the ocean of conceptual equivalents for *theōsis* therefore

---

[20] Pseudo-Dionysius, *The Ecclesiastical Hierarchy*, 1.3, in *Pseudo-Dionysius: The Complete Works*, trans. Colm Luibheid (New York: Paulist Press, 1987), 198; hereafter *Pseudo-Dionysius: Complete Works*.

[21] See Norman Russell, *Fellow Workers with God: Orthodox Thinking on Theosis* (New York: St Vladimir's Seminary Press, 2009), 23–7.

[22] Athanasius, 'De Incarnatione Verbi Dei', 54, English translation in *Nicene and Post-Nicene Fathers*, ed. Philip Schaff and Henry Wace, second series, 14 vols (Peabody: Hendrickson, 1994), vol. 4, 65. See also Athanasius, 'Orationes contra Arianos IV', 1.38; 1.48; 2.61; ibid., 329; 335; 381. Compare Irenaeus, 'Adversus Hareseses', 5 (praef.), in *Irenaeus of Lyons*, ed. Alexander Roberts and James Donaldson, 10 vols. Vol. 1 trans. Robert M. Grant (London: Routledge, 1997), 164.

[23] See Basil Studer, 'Divinization', in *Encyclopedia of the Early Church*, ed. Angelo Di Beradina, 2 vols (New York: Oxford University Press, 1992), vol. 1, 242; Stephen Thomas, *Deification in the Eastern Orthodox Tradition: A Biblical Perspective* (Piscataway: Gorgias Press, 2008); M. David Litwa, *We Are Being Transformed: Deification in Paul's Soteriology* (Berlin: Walter de Gruyter, 2012); and Macaskill, *Union with Christ*, esp. 219–308.

included the following: 'union, participation, partaking, communion/partnership, divine filiation, adoption, recreation, intertwined with the divine, similitude with God, transformation, elevation, transmutation, commingling, assimilation, intermingling, rebirth, regeneration, transfiguration.'[24] Accordingly, Norman Russell provides a useful typology of nominal, analogical, ethical and realistic uses of *theōsis*, all of which indicate just how polyvalent the term was in early Christian thought.[25] In this typology, 'deification' could refer to a title of honour (nominal), the gift of grace that gives to human beings what belongs properly to Christ's nature (analogical), imitation of divine moral attributes (ethical) or the complete transformation of human nature through participation in God (realistic). The possible meanings of 'deification' remained broad and overlapped considerably, then, with the philosophical and scriptural registers of participation, even if they remained conceptually distinct. The most important virtual synonyms for *theōsis* in the patristic period are, however, 'participation', 'union' and 'adoption'. As Anna N. Williams puts it, 'without one of these three concepts ... we are speaking of some form of sanctification that is not specifically deification.'[26] As the later part of this chapter shows, these typologies will prove helpful in charting out precisely what Hooker takes deification as a form of participation to mean.

Theōsis developed over later centuries in Eastern theology, however, from such broad and allusive themes to a more tightly controlled doctrine. In the fourteenth century, Gregory Palamas developed the distinction coined by Maximus the Confessor in the sixth century between God's essence and energies: *theōsis* involves participation in the latter rather than the former, protecting the utter transcendence of God, while allowing for the ontological transformation of the believer.[27] Gösta Hallonsten's proposal that studies must therefore distinguish between a doctrine and a theme of *theōsis* proves useful here. Deification as a doctrine means 'a rather well-defined complex of thought that centers [sic] on one or more technical terms'.[28] Such

[24] Finlan and Kharlamov, *Theōsis*, 6.
[25] Russell, *Doctrine of Deification* 1–3. See Ivan V. Popov, 'The Idea of Deification in the Early Eastern Church', trans. Boris Yakim, in *Theōsis: Deification in Christian Theology, Volume Two*, ed. Vladimir Kharlamov, trans. Boris Yakimin (Cambridge: James Clarke, 2012), 42–82. In this classic essay, Popov develops a twofold typology of 'realistic' and 'idealistic' forms of deification, the former stressing popular and palpable aspects of deification, and the latter stressing elitist and mystical aspects.
[26] Anna N. Williams, *The Ground of Union: Deification in Aquinas and Palamas* (New York: Oxford University Press, 1999), 32. See also Anna N. Williams, 'Deification in the *Summa Theologiae*: A Structural Interpretation of the Prima Pars', *Thomist* 61, no. 2 (1997): 219–55.
[27] See Vladimir Lossky, *The Mystical Theology of the Eastern Church* (Crestwood: St. Vladimir's Seminary Press, 1973), esp. 67–90; G. I. Mantzaridis, *The Deification of Man: St. Gregory Palamas and the Orthodox Tradition* (Crestwood: St. Vladimir's Seminary Press, 1984); Melchisedec Törönen, *Union and Distinction in the Thought of St Maximus the Confessor* (Oxford: Oxford University Press, 2007); Emil Bartos, *Deification in Eastern Orthodox Theology* (Eugene: Wipf and Stock, 2007), esp. 57–94; David Bradshaw, *Aristotle East and West. Metaphysics and the Division of Christendom* (Cambridge: Cambridge University Press, 2008), esp. 153–86; Torstein Theodor Tollefsen, *Activity and Participation in Late Antique and Early Christian Thought* (Oxford: Oxford University Press, 2012), esp. 159–220; and Jean-Claude Larchet, 'The Mode of Deification', in *The Oxford Handbook of Maximus the Confessor*, ed. Pauline Allen and Bronwen Neil (Oxford: Oxford University Press, 2015), 341–59.
[28] Gösta Hallonsten, '*Theōsis* in Recent Research: A Renewal of Interest and a Need for Clarity', in *Partakers of the Divine Nature: The History and Development of Deification in the Christian Traditions*, ed. M. J. Christensen and Jeffrey A. Wittung (Grand Rapids, MI: Baker, 2007), 281–93 (283-7).

a complexity of thought encompasses a particular Orthodox synergistic anthropology, soteriology and understanding of the divine nature (with the distinction between essence and energies) uncommon in the Western tradition. Andrew Louth labels this the 'cosmic dimension of *theōsis*', an 'arch stretching from creation to deification' since 'the doctrine of deification preserves this sense that God created the world to unite it to himself'.[29] Here, the end of participation in God is most commonly 'Christification', namely becoming the image of Christ. The doctrine of *theōsis* does not simply equate with Western notions of sanctification, then, but rather, Eastern theology sees it as 'the *telos* (goal) of salvation and existence'.[30] In contrast, deification as a theme loosely contains ideas of participation in the divine nature, adoption and union with God or Christ, often derived from biblical sources and therefore commonly found across ecclesial traditions.[31] Indeed, the language of deification as a form of participation in God occurs in figures such as Augustine of Hippo, Aquinas, Luther, Calvin, Charles Wesley and Jonathan Edwards, but reflects biblical themes of adoption, participation and union rather than Palamite doctrine directly as such.[32] Again, the distinction

---

[29] Andrew Louth, 'The Place of *Theōsis* in Orthodox Theology', in *Partakers of the Divine Nature: The History and Development of Deification in the Christian Traditions*, ed. M. J. Christensen and Jeffrey A. Wittung (Grand Rapids, MI: Baker, 2007), 32–46 (34–6).

[30] Finlan and Kharlamov, *Theōsis*, 5. Compare D. Reid, *Energies of the Spirit: Trinitarian Models in Eastern Orthodox and Western Theology* (Oxford: Oxford University Press, 2000); and Veli-Matti Karkkainen, *One with God: Salvation as Deification and Justification* (Collegeville: Liturgical Press, 2004).

[31] Collins, *Partaking in Divine Nature*, similarly writes that 'there is no equivalent in the West' of the Orthodox doctrine of deification, but that 'within Western traditions there are constant traces of the metaphor of deification' (111). On Anglican uses of participation and deification, see Paul M. Collins, 'An Investigation of the Use of the Metaphor of Deification in the Anglican Tradition', *Studia Theologia Orthodoxa* 1 (2010): 205–17. On the broad Catholic use of participation and deification, see David Meconi and Carl E. Olson, *Called to Be the Children of God: The Catholic Theology of Human Deification* (San Francisco: Ignatius Press, 2016). For early Latin accounts, see Jared Ortiz (ed), *Deification in the Latin Patristic Tradition* (Washington: Catholic University of America Press, 2019).

[32] On Augustine: Gerald Bonner, 'Deification, Divinization', in *Augustine Through the Ages: An Encyclopedia*, ed. Allan D. Fitzgerald (Grand Rapids, MI: Eerdmans, 1999), 265–6; and David Vincent Meconi, *The One Christ: St. Augustine's Theology of Deification* (Washington: Catholic University of America Press, 2013). On Aquinas: Daria Spezzano, *The Glory of God's Grace: Deification According to St. Thomas Aquinas* (Washington: Catholic University of America Press, 2015); and Williams, *The Ground of Union*. Williams argues, of course, for an ecumenical accord between the theologies of Palamas and Aquinas. Others remain sceptical of such an accord: see Hallonsten, '*Theōsis* in Recent Research', 282–3. On Luther: Carl E. Braaten, and Robert W. Jenson (eds), *Union with Christ: The New Finnish Interpretation of Luther* (Grand Rapids, MI: Eerdmans, 1998). The New Finnish School is not without its critics: see, for example, Robert Kolb, *Martin Luther: Confessor of the Faith* (Oxford: Oxford University Press, 2009). On Calvin: J. Todd Billings, *Calvin, Participation, and the Gift: The Activity of Believers in Union with Christ* (Oxford: Oxford University Press, 2007); and Carl Mosser, 'The Greatest Possible Blessing: Calvin and Deification', *Scottish Journal of Theology* 55, no. 1 (2002): 36–57. Other scholars disagree that deification is present in Calvin's thought. See Frederick W. Norris, 'Deification: Consensual and Cogent', *Scottish Journal of Theology* 49, no. 4 (1996): 411–28; and Jonathan Slater, 'Salvation as Participation in the Humanity of the Mediator in Calvin's Institutes of the Christian Religion: A Reply to Carl Mosser', *Scottish Journal of Theology* 58, no. 1 (2005): 39–58. On Wesley: Michael J. Christensen, 'John Wesley: Christian Perfection as Faith Filled with the Energy of Love', in *Partakers of the Divine Nature : The History and Development of Deification in the Christian Traditions*, ed. M. J. Christensen and Jeffrey A. Wittung (Grand Rapids, MI: Baker, 2007), 219–33; S. T. Kimbrough, 'Theosis in the Writings of Charles Wesley', *St. Vladimir's Theological Quarterly* 52 (2008): 199–212; and S. T. Kimbrough, *Partakers of the Life Divine: Participation in the Divine Nature in the Writings of Charles Wesley* (Eugene: Cascade, 2016).

between deification as a theme and as a doctrine will provide a useful safeguard against misrepresenting Hooker's usage, as the later part of this chapter will develop.

Having explored how protean the philosophical and scriptural registers of participation can be, it is now possible to draw out what the 'architecture of participation' looks like, meaning the intellectual material, joists and structures which buttress the background to Hooker's idea of 'participation in God'. This architecture emerges out of a cumulative genealogy of participation, or what Jacob Sherman labels as the three historical iterations of the concept: the formal (regularly associated with Plato); the existential (exemplified in the thought of Thomas Aquinas); and the creative (emerging out of Christian Neoplatonism and finding full expression in certain Baroque and Romantic modes of thought).[33] To these three turns we might add a fourth between the formal and existential – the unitive, especially as seen in Neoplatonism. Each of these iterations add elements to what the 'architecture of participation' looks like, as well as what theological claims it informs, buttresses or enlightens.

For Sherman, the first participatory turn comes out of Platonic accounts of *methexis* as a response to the philosophical problem of the many and the one. As noted earlier, Plato's account of participation revolves around formality: *methexis* describes how the divine realm of forms constitutes embodied and temporal things; the manifest realm of becoming dynamically receives its variety of forms through participation in divine forms. Such participation is real but analogical. On the one hand, the participated forms are ontologically different from their particular, contingent participants. Forms are immutable, eternal, incorporeal, sensually imperceptible but intellectually apprehensible.[34] On the other hand, forms are the constitutive cause of being and truly relate to the particular beings that participate in them, even if not in a univocal sense. As such, particular beings share in the whole of the eternal, transcendent form, but they do not exhaust it, meaning that particular beings exhibit the divine form in an embodied, temporal and contingent fashion.[35] Such a formal turn in participatory metaphysics addresses the 'what-ness' of temporal things and establishes a relationship of causality or existential constitution from the divine realm as an architectural mark of participation. The hallmarks of such formal participation are analogy, real relation, asymmetry and the immanent saturation of the world with the divine, all of which preserves the priority of transcendence.

The second participatory turn for Sherman is existential, the question of 'why' anything exists at all. Aquinas fulfils this participatory turn to the existential for

---

On Jonathan Edwards: Richard B. Steel, 'Transfiguring Light: The Moral Beauty of the Christian Life According to Gregory Palamas and Jonathan Edwards', *St. Vladimir's Theological Quarterly* 52 (2008): 403–39; Kyle Strobel, 'Jonathan Edwards and the Polemics of Theosis', *Harvard Theological Review* 105, no. 3 (2012): 259–79; and Brandon G. Withrow, *Becoming Divine: Jonathan Edwards's Incarnational Spirituality within the Christian Tradition* (Cambridge: Lutterworth, 2017).

[33] Jacob H. Sherman, 'A Genealogy of Participation', in *The Participatory Turn: Spirituality, Mysticism, Religious Studies*, ed. Jorge N. Ferrer and Jacob H. Sherman (Albany: State University of New York Press, 2008), 81–112.

[34] Plato, 'Phaedo', 78c; 79a; 79d; 80a-b; in *Works*, 68–70.

[35] Plato, 'Phaedo', 100c; and 'Timaeus', 28a; in *Works*, 86; 1234. See R. E. Allen, 'Participation and Predication in Plato's Middle Dialogues', *Philosophical Review* 69 (1960): 147–83.

Sherman by emphasizing how formal participation establishes existence. Participation becomes a claim, then, about divine agency in creation: just as a Platonic form causes everything named after that form, so too, for Aquinas, God as self-subsistent being itself (*ipsum esse subsistens*) must cause by emanation everything that participates in the first perfection of being (*esse*). Indeed, Thomas describes creation as 'the issuing of the whole of being from the universal cause [*emanatio totius entis universalis a primo principio*]'.[36] Aquinas explicates creaturely being (*esse*) in both Aristotelian terms of act-as-perfection, and in Platonic terms of participation. In Aristotelian fashion, Aquinas argues that being is 'first thing conceived by the intellect' and thus has priority over the other transcendentals.[37] 'Being' precedes all other notions and acts as the basis for all other perfections: 'being' involves act (*actus essendi*) and act is perfection. Aquinas then adds to this Aristotelian framework the Platonic notion of participation as a sharing in something that belongs to another more properly. Aquinas argues that all beings (*enta*) are substantial unities of 'essence' (*essentia*) and 'existence' (*esse*).[38] Yet, no contingent being (*ens*) is identical with being (*esse*): whatever does not exist by eternal necessity only exists by participating in being (*esse*), which means participating in God as *ipsum esse subsistens* (self-subsisting being).[39] Each created being (*ens*) receives existence to the extent to which it participates in God's self-subsistent being. The particular capacity of an essence determines the degree to which a creature participates in being, as potency to act.[40] Aquinas argues that God's ideas act as the exemplary cause of created things.[41] The diversity of creatures stems from the diverse ways in which creation relates to God's exemplarity. The first exemplary cause of things remains the principle of distinct multiplicity: the divine essence contains all the various perfections of things in its simple unity. The multitude of things reflects God's goodness more perfectly: one creature alone cannot represent adequately God's perfection or exemplify all of the ways in which a creature can participate in God's exemplarity.[42] God, therefore, freely wills a hierarchy of being, proceeding from less to more perfect forms: 'the universe would not be perfect if only one grade of goodness were found in things', as Aquinas puts it.[43] Multiplicity in creation reveals what Rudi Te Velde calls 'a multiplicity of an intelligible order' in which created diversity represents its cause 'not in the manner of

---

[36] Thomas Aquinas, *Summa Theologiae*, I.45.1 resp.; hereafter *ST*. English translation in Thomas Aquinas, *Summa Theologiae. Latin and English dual text* (New York: Blackfriars, 1964–81).
[37] Thomas Aquinas, *De Veritate*. 1.1 resp.; hereafter *De Ver*. English translation in Thomas Aquinas, *Truth*, trans. N. T. Bourke (Chicago: University of Chicago Press, 1952–4). Compare *ST*, I.5.2 resp. and I.11.1 resp.
[38] Thomas Aquinas, *Summa contra Gentiles* I.c.32 & 34; hereafter *ScG*. English translation in Thomas Aquinas, *Summa contra Gentiles*, trans. A. Pegis and V. Bourke (Notre Dame, IN: University of Notre Dame Press, 1975).
[39] Thomas Aquinas, *In octo libros Physicorum expositio*, 21, 1153; hereafter *In Phys*. English translation in *Commentary on Aristotle's Physics*, trans. R. J. Blackwell, Richard J. Spath and W. Edmund Thirlkel (Notre Dame: Dumb Ox, 1999). Compare *ST*, I.II.26.4.
[40] See C. Fabro, 'The Intensive Hermeneutics of Thomistic Philosophy: The Notion of Participation', *Review of Metaphysics* 27 (1947): 465–9.
[41] Aquinas, *ST*, I.44.3 resp.
[42] Ibid., I.47.1 resp.
[43] Ibid., I.47.2 resp.

the cause itself, but in its own distinct manner as intended and preconceived by the cause'.[44]

John Rziha describes four implications of Aquinas's existential account of participation.[45] First, creation depends totally on God for all perfections, which God alone possesses as a self-subsistent being, and which creatures possess only by participation in God. In participation, creation is a gift. Second, participation defines creatureliness, simultaneously setting creation apart from the self-subsistent Creator but also yoking creation to God through the *creatio continua* (continuous creation). Third, existential claims in participatory metaphysics are therefore analogical: creatures exist by participation (*per participationem*) and God simply and essentially (*per essentiam*). Finally, participation explains both the primary perfection of being and all further, secondary perfections, including the cognitive participation in divine knowledge.

The third participatory turn for Sherman is creative, a more numinous turn involving diverse thinkers and still underway in some modern philosophy and theology. Here, participation expresses the contingent, historical sharing in divine creativity through human imagination and skill, the discovery of creative abilities such that the human being becomes *homo creator*. Sherman sees John Scotus Eriugena in the ninth century as the first theologian to place the 'theme of *homo creator* central, defining the human being as essentially both *created* and *creating* (*natura creata* and *natura creans*) and making the human central to the eschatological re-creation of all things'.[46] Sherman traces in the later Meister Eckhart, Nicholas of Cusa and Tommaso Campanella similar ideas that human creativity shares in divine artisanship and expresses divine knowledge, eliding the distinction between heaven and earth as human inventiveness echoes, and unfolds the eternal Word in creation. Although Sherman does not draw the consequence, the creative turn also flows out of Aquinas's existential understanding of participation, where all secondary acts and perfections (and so all activities properly human, whether cultural, linguistic, artistic or work) can be said to participate in God just as much as our existence. Formal participation remains dynamic, the move from becoming to being. The hallmark of creative participation is indeed to see the human participant as a divine gift, an ongoing work and a co-worker with the divine, rendering human beings as homo faber (the fabricating human).

The final, additional participatory moment (a fruitful addition to Sherman's genealogy) revolves around a unitive turn somewhere between the formal and existential, namely, the Platonic and Neoplatonic emphasis on union and assimilation with the divine through participation. The Platonic notion of 'likeness to God' as the telos of human life became elevated into religious mysticism in later Platonists such as Plotinus, for whom the final stage of the soul's ascent to God was to become one with the divine (*henosis*) without losing individuation through a process of virtuous

---

[44] Rudi Te Velde, *Participation and Substantiality in Thomas Aquinas* (New York: Brill Press, 1995), 97–106.

[45] John Rziha, *Perfecting Human Actions: St. Thomas Aquinas on Human Participation in Eternal Law* (Washington: Catholic University of America Press, 2009), 12–15.

[46] Sherman, 'A Genealogy of Participation', 94. See John Scotus Eriugena, *Periphyseon: the Division of Nature*, trans. John O'Meara (Montreal: Bellarmin, 1987), esp. Bk II.

purification.⁴⁷ Plotinus imaged such union as ecstatic (even erotic) vision, touch, blending or mingling with divine unity.⁴⁸ The deiform nature of the soul indicated a complementary aspect of participatory henology, namely, the idea, developed by Neoplatonic thinkers, of the cyclical emanation of the universe from (and reversion to) the divine Creator, which modern scholars often label as the *exitus-reditus* (exit-return).⁴⁹ Proclus describes, for example, how 'every effect remains in its cause, proceeds from it, and reverts upon it', relating the multiplicity of an intelligible order to its unitary causal source.⁵⁰ As such, 'participation in God' is the hallmark of creation and the engine driving both its existence from and its formal end in (re)union with the divine. The exit from the divine is deiform, and so the return to the divine is deificatory. Yet, far from emptying agency from the created 'middle' between exit and reversion, Neoplatonists like Proclus imagine a triadic structure of *monē-proodos-epistrophē* that honours the suspended middle between exit and return.⁵¹ The *monē* (rest, remaining) describes how God remains supereminently identical with itself as the unitive source of emanation (*monos*). The *proodos* (proceeding, emanating) identifies the rise of every being into its own determinate being. The *epistrophē* (return) describes the reversion of the *proodos* (the created being) to the *monos*. As such, the *proodos* circumscribes the creative agency engendered in determinate beings by their emanation, a dynamic sharing in the productive capacity of the *monos* through participation that yields what Proclus calls 'a likeness of the secondary to the primary'.⁵²

Then, these four participatory moments cumulatively produce an 'architecture of participation', which exhibits something like what Kathryn Tanner calls a 'weak' and 'strong' sense of participation, but which might be better phrased as an 'extensive' and an 'intensive' sense, or even better as an 'exit' and 'return' (*exitus-reditus*).⁵³ In a weak, extensive, or exiting sense, the architecture of participation revolves around the dynamic sphere of ontological becoming: it images the becoming of creation as it shares in the self-diffusive plenitude of God's perfect being. This weak sense encompasses both the formal and the existential modes of participation. Here, insofar as things exist, they exist by participation in God as self-subsistent being itself; and, according to the degree to which they share in participated being, things move from potentiality to actuality. In this weak sense, the focus remains on how things receive their formal and efficient reality dynamically from God. The weak form of participation constitutes

---

⁴⁷ Plotinus, *Enneads*, IV.4.2; IV.8.1; V.5.4; in MacKenna, 287; 334–5; 395–6. See Pierre Hadot, *Plotinus or the Simplicity of Vision*, trans. Michael Chase (Chicago: University of Chicago Press, 1993), esp. 64–73.
⁴⁸ Plotinus, *Enneads*, I.2.6; I.4.16; I.6.9; III.8.10; IV.8.1; V.3.17; VI.7.31; VI.9.9; VI.9.4; VI.9.11; in MacKenna, 21; 44; 54–5; 245–7; 334–5; 385–6; 499–500; 539–40; 545–9.
⁴⁹ See Andrew Louth, *The Origins of the Christian Mystical Tradition* (Oxford: Clarendon Press, 1981), 38.
⁵⁰ Proclus, *The Elements of Theology*, Proposition 35, trans. E. R. Dodds (Oxford: Clarendon Press, 2004), 39; hereafter Dodds.]
⁵¹ Proclus, *Elements*, Propositions 25–39; in Dodds, 29–43. My thanks to Professor Andrew Davison and Professor Brendan Sammon for pointing out this triadic structure. See Brendan Thomas Sammon, *The God Who Is Beauty: Beauty as a Divine Name in Thomas Aquinas and Dionysius the Areopagite* (Eugene: Pickwick Publications, 2013), esp. 56–88.
⁵² Proclus, *Elements*, Proposition 29; in Dodds, 35.
⁵³ Kathryn Tanner, *Christ the Key* (Cambridge: Cambridge University Press, 2009), 1–57.

identity as created by, through and for God, echoing the scriptural idea that in God 'we live and move and have our being' (Acts 17.28). In effect, the weak, extensive or exiting, sense of participation in our heuristic architecture establishes creation as a diminished likeness of the divine, diffuses divinity throughout the universe, and occurs almost as a commonplace image in a variety of Christian thinkers.

In a strong, intensive or returning sense, however, the architecture of participation describes the telos (end) of created being: a creature experiences the final perfection of being through an intense (re)union with the divine nature, and so finally becomes what it is not, namely godlike. This strong sense of 'participation in God' encompasses the other two participatory turns: the creative and unitive. Accordingly, this strong sense of participation often corresponds with what Norman Russell calls the analogy and metaphor of deification discussed earlier.[54] Deification as analogy entails that people are 'godlike' through grace such that they enjoy the status that properly belongs to Christ through sharing in his nature. In turn, the metaphor of deification has two distinct approaches, the ethical and the realistic. The extrinsic, ethical approach 'takes deification to be the attainment of likeness to God through ascetic and philosophical endeavour, believers reproducing some of the divine attributes in their own lives by imitation', as Russell puts it. The more intrinsic, realistic approach 'assumes that human beings are in some sense ontologically transformed by deification', either directly by virtue of the Incarnation or through participation in the sacraments. In either approach, deification images the teleological aspect of participation. It often includes the weak version of participation in God but stresses the end of participation as a (re)union with the self-diffusive plenitude of God's subsistent, perfect being, elevating the creature so that it becomes (whether analogically, ethically or realistically) 'godlike', that is, a fulfilled (even if diminished) similitude of divinity as it shares in the divine nature.

Both the weak and strong versions of participation in God do not evacuate creation, however, of its own agency. Much like Proclus's notion of the *proodos,* both versions appeal to the Neoplatonic concept of influence (*influentia*) in which the highest cause resides within its effects, endowing even the secondary acts of creatures with divinity. The weak version of participation in God typically revolves around the metaphysical becoming of creation through created forms that participate in their original cause. In the strong version of participation in God, deification images the perfection of created things according to their form, most typically human beings. Such perfection therefore encompasses human making as well as divine creativity, the co-creative aspect of participation. Human work shares in the self-diffusive generosity of God's nature: it is a theonomous participation emanating from our formal nature as a diminished similitude of divinity bound up in, and made for, communion with God.

As such, rather than being two divergent versions of participation in God, these 'weak/extensive/exiting' and 'strong/intensive/returning' senses often penetrate and complement each other. Indeed, Tanner argues that Christ acts as the key who unlocks both senses of 'participation in God'. On one hand, 'the paradigms for created things exist in the second person [of the trinity], God's own Word or Wisdom',[55] making

---

[54] Russell, *Doctrine of Deification,* 1–2.
[55] Tanner, *Christ the Key,* 9.

created things images of the eternal Logos. On the other hand, Christ's Incarnation means that 'perfect human imaging of God is achieved by perfect unity with what is perfectly and properly the image of God, the second person of the trinity'.[56] As such, participation in Christ (as both eternal and incarnate Word) often forms the basis of participation in God for both weak and strong senses. In the weak aspects of the architecture of participation, Christ acts as the divine giver of the gift of form and existence. In the strong aspect of the architecture of participation, Christ reorients the participant as an image of the divine, capable of similitude to divine creativity, that is to say, a participant of God's own self-diffusive nature.

This architecture of participation will be an important foil for tracing the idea of participation as found in Hooker's *Laws*. A further prolegomenon, however, is why and how modern studies and ecumenism have had to recover participation and deification, as this unveils the tensions and possibilities for how a study of Hooker might contribute to the contemporary retrievals of these concepts. When Hooker alludes to 'the participation of divine nature', he cites 2 Pet. 1.4, a key biblical text (as we have seen) for those who have historically claimed that human beings are 'participants' (*koinōnoi*) in divinity, even to the point of becoming like God (*theōsis*). Yet, such claims suffered from neglect and opprobrium for a long period in certain quarters of Western theology, making such an ecumenical retrieval of participation and deification seem unlikely. Rowan Williams argues that the root of the antipathy came as a 'result of the claims of medieval and sixteenth-century sectarian and apocalyptic groups to be united in essence with God (and so incapable of sin)'.[57] Others trace the problem concerning deification as a form of participation to another source. One of the most severe and influential attacks on such language came from Adolf von Harnack, a nineteenth-century Protestant scholar. Harnack claimed that the early Church had subverted the original Gospel with pagan and 'Hellenistic' ideas such that

> when the Christian religion was represented as the belief in the incarnation of God as the sure hope of the deification of man, a speculation that had originally never got beyond the fringe of religious knowledge was made the central point of the system and the simple content of the Gospel was obscured.[58]

While Jules Gross's seminal study of Patristic thought on deification in 1938 subsequently showed that Harnack misrepresented the Greek Fathers, the suspicion that deiform participation obscured the Christian *kerygma* remained commonplace in scholarship.[59] Protestant writers in particular expressed theological concern that

---

[56] Ibid., 13.
[57] Rowan Williams, 'Deification', in *A Dictionary of Christian Spirituality*, ed. Gordon S. Wakefield (London: SCM Press, 1983), 106–8.
[58] Adolf von Harnack, *History of Dogma*, 7 vols (London: Williams & Norgate, 1896-9), vol. 3, 318.
[59] Jules Gross, *The Divinisation of the Christian According to the Greek Fathers*, trans. Paul A. Onica (Anaheim: A & C Press, 2002). On the negative reaction to deification, see H. Rashdall, *The Idea of Atonement in Christian Theology* (London: Macmillan, 1919); J. Lawson, *The Biblical Theology of Saint Irenaeus* (London: The Epworth Press, 1948), 154; E. Underhill, *Mysticism: A Study in the Nature and Development of Man's Spiritual Consciousness* (London: Methuen, 1949), 99; M. Werner, *The Formation of Christian Dogma* (New York: Harper, 1957), 168; W. Bousset, *Kyrios Christos: A History of the Belief in Christ from the Beginnings of Christianity to Irenaeus* (Nashville, TN: Abingdon,

any exegesis of 2 Pet. 1.4 that entertained notions of deification ended up eliding the distinction between creatures and their Creator, or between nature and grace, and so violated monotheism. For example, Karl Barth instead interpreted the Petrine passage only to mean 'the practical fellowship of Christians with God and on this basis the conformity of their acts with the divine nature'.[60] Western thought commonly saw, therefore, the idea that participation in God might mean deification as an aberrant, exotic and suspicious feature of Eastern theology, a fall into pantheism. Even within Orthodox Christianity, until recently *theōsis* 'was a technical term familiar only to monks and patristic scholars'.[61]

The past few decades witnessed, however, a slow but steady retrieval in both Eastern and Western theology of deification alongside participation that has revealed both the protean complexity and profound ecumenical possibility of these related concepts.[62] The impetus came from the confluence of several streams, each of which proved to be tributaries to an ever-increasing sea of retrieval. Gross's seminal study noted earlier was the first to comprehensively analyse deification, taking into account its varied Christian and non-Christian sources. Gross showed that early Christian theology transcended the pagan notion of *apotheōsis* and rooted the idea of *theōsis* within a biblical matrix. Partly as a result of Gross's work, the study of participation in God, along with the attendant idea of *theōsis*, eventually regained currency across theological traditions. Norman Russell argues that, from within Orthodox Christianity, there were four crucial factors to the popular re-reception of deification.[63] First, there was an apologetic rediscovery of Gregory Palamas in response to claims that his teachings on *theōsis* were 'near to heresy'. Second, Russian religious philosophers like Myrrha Lot-Borodine, Vladimir Lossky and John Meyendorff influenced both Eastern and Western thought by placing *theōsis* as the goal of Christian life and the crowning theological achievement of Orthodoxy. Third, the spirituality of the *Philokalia* (an anthology of Byzantine texts) was recovered when it was translated into various languages. Finally, Orthodox scholars re-engaged with the early Greek Fathers and their emergent thought on *theōsis*. A similar retrieval of deification as a form of participation occurred in Roman Catholic thought through figures like Reginald Garrigou-Lagrange, Karl Rahner and Henri de Lubac, all of whom 'explicitly grounded their soteriology using the traditional conceptual instruments and vocabulary of *theosis* or graced participation in the intra-Trinitarian intimacy of divine life'.[64] As will be shown in the later part of the chapter, scholars trace a comparable resurgence of interest in participation and deification in the Anglican tradition too, including in Hooker's thought.

1970), 420–53; B. Drewery, 'Deification', in *Christian Spirituality: Essays in Honour of Gordon Rupp*, ed. Peter Brooks (London: SCM, 1975), 49–62; and Bruno Burnhart, 'One Spirit, One Body: Jesus' Participatory Revolution', in *The Participatory Turn: Spirituality, Mysticism, Religious Studies*, ed. Jorge N. Ferrer and Jacob H. Sherman (Albany: State University of New York Press, 2008), 265–91.

[60] Karl Barth, *The Christian Life: Church Dogmatics, IV, 4, Lecture Fragments*, trans. G. W. Bromiley (Grand Rapids, MI: Eerdmans, 1981), 28.

[61] Russell, *Fellow Workers with God*, 13.

[62] See Roger E. Olson, 'Deification in Contemporary Theology', *Theology Today* 64 (2007): 186–200.

[63] Russell, *Fellow Workers with God*, 13–31.

[64] Adam G. Cooper, *Naturally Human, Supernaturally God: Deification in Pre-conciliar Catholicism* (Minneapolis, MN: Fortress Press, 2014), 4.

In turn, these rediscoveries of deification became a springboard for modern ecumenical dialogue and study. Hallonsten's distinction between the doctrinal and thematic aspects of deification confirms that studies cannot see deification per se as the sole preserve of Eastern theology. The biblical images of participation, union and adoption (which together act as virtual synonyms for deification in patristic thought) form a theme in Western thought as much as Eastern, even if the narrower doctrinal formulations of deification are absent. Accordingly, the number of scholarly works and collections about the idea of participation and deification have proliferated in recent years, tracing both the historical development of the idea as well as contemporary reconstructions, placing it firmly on the theological agenda. In addition to official ecumenical dialogues that have considered, in part at least, participation and deification, there have been many academic attempts to trace the idea within particular thinkers or use them within different traditions, both Western and Eastern, Protestant and Catholic.[65]

The most relevant modern ecumenical conversation for this study remains, of course, Anglican and Eastern Orthodox dialogue. Over the past four decades, there have been four phases of Anglican-Orthodox ecumenical dialogues, producing four reports.[66] In each phase, references to participation and deification are few in number and scattered throughout numerous theological topics. While participation in the life of God constitutes the basis of Christian life and the Church in all four Anglican-Orthodox dialogues, there also remains some deep-seated ambivalence over the language of *theōsis*. For example, the *Moscow Agreed Statement* of 1976 briefly casts faith in terms of participation in and union with God, but also marks out *theōsis* as a difficult ecumenical idiom:

> To describe the fullness of man's sanctification and the way in which he shares in the life of God, the Orthodox Church uses the patristic term *theosis kata*

---

[65] For lists of such studies, see Paul L. Gavrilyuk, 'The Retrieval of Deification: How a Once-Despised Archaism Became an Ecumenical Desideratum', *Modern Theology* 25, no. 4 (2009): 647–59. See also Finlan and Kharlamov, *Theōsis*, 10–11 (nn. 30–1); and Vladimir Kharlamov (ed.), *Theōsis: Deification in Christian Theology, Volume Two* (Cambridge: James Clarke, 2012), 2–14. Recent examples appropriating or retrieving the idea of deification as a form of participation in Western traditions include Daniel Keating, *Deification and Grace* (Washington: Catholic University of America Press, 2007); Michael J. Gorman, *Inhabiting the Cruciform God: Kenosis, Justification, and Theosis in Paul's Narrative Soteriology* (Grand Rapids, MI: Eerdmans, 2009); Jordan Cooper, *Christification: A Lutheran Approach to Theosis* (Eugene: Wipf & Stock, 2014); and John Arblaster and Rob Faesen (eds), *Mystical Doctrines of Deification: Case Studies in the Christian Tradition* (Oxford: Routledge, 2018). There are also, of course, the various official ecumenical dialogues that at times deal with participation and deification. For an exhaustive collection of such dialogues between 1972 and 2005, see World Council of Churches, *Growth in Agreement*, 3 vols (Geneva: WCC 2000–2007).

[66] Anglican-Orthodox Joint Doctrinal Commission, *Anglican-Orthodox Dialogue 1976: Moscow Agreed Statement* (London: SPCK, 1977); Anglican-Orthodox Joint Doctrinal Commission, *Anglican-Orthodox Dialogue 1984: Dublin Agreed Statement* (London: SPCK, 1985); International Commission for Anglican-Orthodox Theological Dialogue, *Church of the Triune God: Cyprus Statement Agreed by the International Commission for Anglican-Orthodox Theological Dialogue 2006* (London: Anglican Communion Office, 2006); International Commission for Anglican-Orthodox Theological Dialogue, *In the Image and Likeness of God: A Hope-Filled Anthropology. The Buffalo Statement Agreed by the International Commission for Anglican-Orthodox Theological Dialogue* (London: Anglican Communion Office, 2015).

charin (divinisation by grace). Once again such language is not normally used by Anglicans, some of whom regard it as misleading and dangerous.[67]

Here, the *Moscow Agreed Statement* affirms participatory language as acceptable to both Anglican and Orthodox theology, but sees the Orthodox doctrine of *theōsis* as exotic, even aberrant, to some (unidentified) Anglican thinkers. Even though the doctrinal language of *theōsis* remains problematic, the report admits, however, that 'Anglicans do not reject the underlying doctrine [i.e., the fullness of sanctification as a sharing in the life of God] which this language seeks to express; indeed, such teaching is to be found in their own liturgies and hymnody'.[68]

At the same time as the rediscovery of participation as deification, Western interest in participatory metaphysics has also witnessed an unlikely renaissance in recent decades.[69] Participatory thought in Western philosophical and religious study suffered a steady decline from the seventeenth century onwards, largely as a result of what Walter Capps calls the advent of a 'Cartesian-Kantian temper'.[70] If participation suspends creatures from the creative divine nature in which they share, then the 'Cartesian-Kantian temper' or 'paradigm' brackets off or denies the existence of any religious or metaphysical source: such sources are either cognitively inaccessible as 'noumenal' realities, or are produced by 'subjective' imagination and cultural-linguistic invention. The 'Cartesian-Kantian temper' metaphysically flattened and disenchanted the world, overtaking participatory metaphysics as the cultural assumption about how the world was constituted.

Some scholars argue that this modern disenchantment has genealogical roots in late medieval ideas of univocity and nominalism, which Hans Boersma claims 'serve as the two blades of a pair of scissors that cut the tapestry [of heavenly participation] by severing the participatory link between earthly sacrament (*sacramentum*) and heavenly reality (*res*)'.[71] On the one hand, Duns Scotus introduced the idea that 'being' (*esse*) is univocal: both creatures and God exist in the same way or in the same sense. For Boersma, univocity snipped the participatory cord: in participatory metaphysics, creatures exist only insofar as they participate in 'being-itself', namely, God's self-subsistent nature; the univocity of being instead unhooks creatures from God and places them together onto a flattened ontological spectrum. On the other hand, late medieval nominalism 'was the seedbed for modern individualism', being 'predicated on the notion that each person was, as it were, a self-subsistent entity, whose being was, in principle, unrelated to the being of other persons'.[72] Whereas 'participation in God'

---

[67] Anglican-Orthodox Joint Doctrinal Commission, *Moscow Agreed Statement*, 1.1–3.
[68] Ibid., 1.3.
[69] For an overview, see Andrew Davison, *Participation in God: A Study in Christian Doctrine and Metaphysics* (Cambridge: Cambridge University Press, 2019).
[70] Walter Capps, *Religious Studies: The Making of a Discipline* (Minneapolis, MN: Fortress Press, 1995), 2–12.
[71] Hans Boersma, *Heavenly Participation: The Weaving of a Sacramental Tapestry* (Grand Rapids, MI: Eerdmans, 2011), 69. Such readings, often influenced by Radical Orthodoxy, have provoked controversy over how accurately they read figures like Duns Scotus. See Robert Sweetman, 'Univocity, Analogy, and the Mystery of Being According to John Duns Scotus', in *Radical Orthodoxy and the Reformed Tradition: Creation, Covenant, and Participation*, ed. James K. A. Smith and James H. Olthuis (Grand Rapids, MI: Baker, 2005), 73–87.
[72] Boersma, *Heavenly Participation*, 89.

implied real relations (transcendentally with God and laterally with all other creatures who participate in God), nominalism bred atomism and voluntarism, the separation of creatures from one another and God, who becomes inscrutably Other and relates to creation through the arbitrary fiat of the divine will. The separation of the natural and supernatural sphere seemed to make the latter, in a sense, intellectually dispensable. As Boersma puts it, 'heavenly participation gave way to a celebration of the natural ends of earthly realities',[73] a paradigmatic shift which shaped modernity and seemed to relegate participatory metaphysics.

Yet, several tributaries emerged and converged to revivify the metaphysical potential of participation in modern Western theology. Diverse thinkers such as Owen Barfield, Henri Bergson, Pierre Teilhard de Chardin, Sergei Bulgakov, Gilles Deleuze and Alfred North Whitehead (among others) appropriated, in widely different ways, the language of participation. From another direction, the central role of participation in Thomistic thought was rediscovered (or uncovered) by the work of Fabro, Geiger, Te Velde and Wippel.[74] Despite internal differences, these scholars illustrate how participation allows Aquinas to show how creation depends upon God for the perfection of 'being' (*esse*). Partly out of this Thomistic recovery, other scholars have called for an ethical and political return to participatory thought since participation images both the first perfection of creatures (the act of being, *actus essendi*) and also the secondary acts of creatures (such as directed by natural law) as participations in the providential ordering of the universe.[75] Studies of the links between participatory metaphysics, the language of deification and biblical ideas of union with Christ have also helped place participation back on the scholarly agenda.[76]

Elsewhere, a number of contemporary religious studies scholars identify themselves with a 'participatory turn' away from the 'Cartesian-Kantian paradigm'. This turn argues for an '*enactive* understanding of the sacred, seeking to approach religious phenomena, experiences, and insights as cocreated events' which emerge from 'the interaction of all human attributes and a nondetermined spiritual power or creative dynamism of life'.[77] Kathryn Tanner and Hans Boersma also turn to participation, but as an ecumenical and ecclesial offering. Tanner uses participation as part of her continued development of a 'Christ-centered theological vision' that can 'be productively used to talk about almost anything of Christian interest in an integrated way', thereby giving Christians 'sufficient confidence about its fruitfulness to employ [the vision] themselves'.[78] Boersma even more strongly hopes that a '*ressourcement*' of participatory metaphysics

---

[73] Ibid., 82.
[74] See L. B. Geiger, *La participation dans la philosophie de Thomas d'Aquin* (Paris: J. Vrin, 1953); C. Fabro, *Participatio et causalité selon S. Thomas d'Aquin* (Paris: Louvain, 1961); Te Velde, *Participation and Substantiality in Thomas Aquinas*; and J. Wippel, *The Metaphysical Thought of Thomas Aquinas: From Finite Being to Uncreated Being* (Washington: Catholic University of America Press, 2000).
[75] See J. Rziha, *Perfecting Human Actions*; and Adrian Pabst, *Metaphysics: The Creation of Hierarchy* (Grand Rapids, MI: Eerdmans, 2012).
[76] For an excellent summary, see Macaskill, *Union with Christ*, 1–99.
[77] Ferrer and Sherman, *The Participatory Turn*, 34; emphasis in the original. See also, Jacob H. Sherman, *Partakers of the Divine: Contemplation and the Practice of Theology* (Minneapolis, MN: Fortress Press, 2014) in which Sherman sees participatory metaphysics as intimately related with contemplative practice.
[78] Tanner, *Christ the Key*, vii.

'will, as a matter of course, lead to genuine rapprochement between evangelicals and Catholics' against 'the onslaught of a desacralized modernity'.[79]

Finally, Radical Orthodoxy constitutes the most significant contemporary English retrieval of participation. In brief, Radical Orthodoxy politically retrieves participation in order to challenge the privileging of 'autonomy' as a fundamental value within secular liberalism:

> The central theological framework of radical orthodoxy is 'participation' as developed by Plato and reworked in Christianity, because any alternative configuration perforce reserves a territory independent of God. The latter can only lead to nihilism (though in different guises). Participation, however, refuses any reserve of created territory, while allowing things their finite integrity.[80]

Radical Orthodoxy histories describe a 'theological fall' from participation to nominalism beginning with the univocal ontology of Duns Scotus and the voluntarism of late scholasticism, a story with which, as we have seen, Hans Boersma concurs. Such a fall creates both a secular space evacuated of the divine and also a vision of the 'absolutely autonomous free individual', who forms the basis for the 'subtle growth of a totalitarian politics' (of which, it is claimed, political liberalism is one variant) through 'the promotion of a cold will-to-power'.[81] As James K. A. Smith suggests, the histories of Radical Orthodoxy attempt to unpick how 'behind the *politics* of modernity (liberal, secular) is an *epistemology* (autonomous reason), which is in turn undergirded by an *ontology* (univocity and the denial of participation)'.[82] Radical Orthodox histories construct a pejorative view, then, of the political consequences developed out of a Scotist univocal ontology. Unhooked from participation in God, social order became seen as merely a collection of autonomous individuals, especially in such philosophers like Thomas Hobbes and Adam Smith. The origin of society becomes essentially violent: competition and self-interest mark social relations, mediated by social contract in a supposedly neutral public space. Radical Orthodoxy calls for an ecclesial return to a participatory worldview that begins with 'the ontological priority of peace over conflict'.[83] Indeed, Christianity contains 'the precise opposite of nihilism – a creed which vigorously excludes all violence from its picture of the original, intended, and final state of the cosmos'.[84] Participation in God therefore constitutes the political essence of Radical Orthodoxy: the doctrine

---

[79] Boersma, *Heavenly Participation*, 10–11.
[80] John Milbank, Catherine Pickstock and Graham Ward (eds), *Radical Orthodoxy: A New Theology* (London: Routledge, 1999), 3.
[81] John Milbank and Simon Oliver, 'Radical Orthodoxy', in *God's Advocates: Christian Thinkers in Conversation*, ed. Rupert Shortt (London: Darton, Longman & Todd, 2005), 116.
[82] James K. A. Smith, *Introducing Radical Orthodoxy: Mapping a Post-Secular Theology* (Grand Rapids, MI: Baker, 2004), 99–100. Compare John Milbank, 'Materialism and Transcendence', in *Theology and the Political: The New Debate*, ed. Creston Davis, John Milbank and Slavoj Žižek (Durham: Duke University Press, 2005), 393–426.
[83] John Milbank, *Theology and Social Theory: Beyond Secular Reason* (Oxford: Blackwell, 1990), 390.
[84] Ibid., 288.

of the Trinity expresses 'a multiple which is not set dialectically over against the one, but itself manifests a unity', an analogate in which the analogue of creation shares.[85] Radical Orthodoxy opens up an antagonistic dualism, then, between participatory Christianity as 'the true politics, the true polity', and Western modernity.[86] The recovery of participation has turned into an ecumenical call to arms.[87] It is into this contested context, full of possibility but also peril, which this study of the architecture of participation in the thought of Richard Hooker speaks.

Retrieving participation in Hooker's thought

Having set out the heuristic architecture of participation and contemporary retrievals of participation, we can now turn to the presence, promise and problems of Hooker's use of that term. As will be shown, while the central claim of this book is that participation structures and enlightens every substantial claim in the *Laws*, there are significant challenges to the idea that Hooker's thought represents either a coherent or systematic whole at all. These challenges require, therefore, some guidelines as to what these terms might mean in association with the architecture of participation holding his work together.

At first sight, the presence of participatory language in Hooker's thought seems incontestable but unpromising. Indeed, within the *Laws*, the idea of participation only explicitly occurs in Books One and Five. In Book One, Hooker refers to participation directly only twice, and both times in relation to the pursuit of the Good within a legal ontology. First, when he considers 'the law wherby man is in his actions directed to the imitation of God', Hooker appeals to two scholastic ideas with roots in Aristotle and Neoplatonism: that God is perfect actuality ('conteyned under the name of *Goodnesse*') while creatures are a mixture of potentiality and actuality; and that effects contain something of (and desire to become like) their causes. Hooker concludes that 'every effect doth after a sort conteine, at least wise resemble the cause from which it proceedeth: all things in the world are saide in some sort to seeke the highest, and to covet more or lesse the participation of God himselfe'.[88] Second, Hooker casts goodness in more Platonic terms later on in Book One as he discusses the human pursuit of perfection: 'No good is infinite but only God: therefore he our felicitie and blisse.

---

[85] Ibid., 376.
[86] Daniel Bell, *Liberation Theology after the End of History: The Refusal to Cease Suffering* (London: Routledge, 2001), 4.
[87] The reception of Radical Orthodoxy in Catholic, Protestant and Orthodox traditions itself represents a form of ecumenism, but not one without criticism of Radical Orthodoxy as a loose sensibility. See Laurence Paul Hemming (ed.), *Radical Orthodoxy? A Catholic Enquiry* (Aldershot: Ashgate, 2000); James K. A. Smith and James H. Olthuis (eds), *Radical Orthodoxy and the Reformed Tradition*; Wayne J. Hankey and Douglas Hedley (eds), *Deconstructing Radical Orthodoxy: Postmodern Theology, Rhetoric, and Truth* (Abingdon: Routledge, 2005); Rosemary Radford Ruether and Marian Grau (eds), *Interpreting Postmodernity: Responses to Radical Orthodoxy* (New York: T&T Clark, 2006); and Adrian Pabst and Christoph Schneider (eds), *Encounter between Eastern Orthodoxy and Radical Orthodoxy: Transfiguring the World through the Word* (Farnham: Ashgate, 2009).
[88] Hooker, *Laws*, 1.72.27–73.10; I.5.1–2.

Moreover desire tendeth unto union with that it desireth. If then in him we be blessed, it is by force of participation and conjunction with him'.[89] Both of these references to participation in Book One stand clearly within a Thomistic tradition of participation (*participare, methexis*) which combines Aristotelian causality with Neoplatonic metaphysics. The remaining direct uses of participation happen in Book Five from the fiftieth chapter onwards. Here, Hooker discusses sacramental participation and union with God, considering 'how God is in Christ, then how Christ is in us, and how the sacramentes doe serve to make us pertakers of Christ'.[90] Within these chapters, Hooker parses participation through biblical idioms, especially of abiding (*menō*) and inward fellowship (*koinōnia*): sacramental and ecclesial participation in Christ's hypostatic union constitutes the restoration and fulfilment of human nature in (re)union with God. Accordingly, these later references to participation root the notion in the Trinity and our share in divine life through Christ. As such, Hooker offers in Book Five his only real definition of participation as 'that mutuall inward hold which Christ hath of us and wee of him, in such sort that ech possesseth other by waie of speciall interest propertie and inherent copulation'.[91] As he elaborates this definition, Hooker paraphrases 2 Pet. 1.4 ('the *participation of divine nature*') as a participatory chain from Christ to the Trinity where 'wee are therefore adopted sonnes of God to eternall life by participation of the onlie begotten Son of God, whose life is the wellspringe and cause of oures'.[92]

In these passages, although Hooker variously uses philosophical and scriptural registers to explore participation, he consistently employs the verb in a singularly transitive and reciprocal manner.[93] Thus, Hooker will always use 'participation of' (the objective genitive) rather than 'participation in' in order to show what would have been the grammatical object of 'participate'. As such, Christ and the believer mutually participate in one another through an asymmetric pattern of salvific transformation in the sacraments, just as all things participate in God through God's creation of all things and God's act resides in his effects as the First Cause. Hooker's transitive and reciprocal use of participation, whatever the biblical idioms that also shroud it, ultimately recalls Proclus's Neoplatonic use of *metechein*. Indeed, after Hooker defines participation in Book Five, he immediately outlines two principles to unpack the nature of reciprocity within participation: 'that every original cause imparteth itself unto those things which come of it'; and 'whatsoever taketh being from any other, the same is after a sort in that which giveth it being'.[94] These principles of reciprocity recapitulate the account of participatory causality set out by Proclus in his *Elements of Theology*, discussed earlier. These Proclean principles were mediated to Hooker via Pseudo-Dionysius and Aquinas, and they help Hooker describe participation as the pattern of causality

---

[89] Ibid., 1:112.12–15; I.11.3.
[90] Ibid., 2:208.24–209.2; V.50.3.
[91] Ibid., 2:234.29–31; V.56.1.
[92] Ibid., 2:238.15–239.13; V.56.7.
[93] On the grammatical form of participation in Hooker's work and its similarity to Proclus, see David Neelands, 'The Theology of Grace of Richard Hooker' (Unpublished PhD thesis, Toronto: Trinity College, University of Toronto, 1988), 340–3.
[94] Hooker, *Laws*, 2:235.1–3; V.56.1.

through which God's utter transcendence causes, sustains and redeems creation as its effect.

Yet, while these direct references to participation may seem relatively brief given the length and scope of the *Laws*, they form the metaphysical architecture for the whole work. The earlier discussion showed just how polyvalent the concept of participation could be. The broad semantic field around participation means that, if the architectural connections of Hooker's *Laws* are laid bare (as this study hopes to do), then the subject of every part may be said to be participation, even if direct references are only made in Books One and Five. Indeed, though apparently unpromising, participation acts as an architectural principle that generates, informs, coheres and illuminates the entirety of the *Laws*: it is the principle behind and implied in every argument; and all of Hooker's claims must be read in light of his commitment to participation.

Despite the relatively sparse direct references to participation in Hooker's *Laws*, modern scholars have indeed increasingly recognized its key generative role within Hooker's thought as part of a broader *ressourcement* of participatory metaphysics in Anglican thought. Yet, these accounts have not fully developed the generative and systematic architecture of participation in God strictly in relation to the polemical particulars of the *Laws* itself, namely, the move from ontology to epistemology and finally to politics hinted at earlier. Neither do studies agree on what participation means for Hooker, nor how it relates to deification, not to mention the meta-questions of what constitutes coherency and systematicity in the first place. We must first, then, address the retrieval of participation in the Anglican tradition, and in Hooker's thought, before exploring the challenges faced by it.

F. L. Cross and E. A. Livingstone locate the modern recovery of participation (especially parsed as deification) in English thought to the patristic revival of the Oxford Movement.[95] A. M. Allchin's work on the idea of participation in Anglican thought from the late sixteenth through to the nineteenth centuries attempted to demonstrate an even earlier persistence of such thought, a persistence in which the Oxford Movement also stood.[96] Allchin saw the ecumenical possibilities behind such *ressourcement* of participation and deification, especially as found in the Oxford Movement, writing:

> It was as if there was a veritable epiphany of patristic spirituality and theology in the midst of our divided western Christendom, an epiphany which would draw together into new possibilities of reconciliation elements of the Reformation heritage and elements of the continuing tradition of the churches in communion with Rome. Here again there is much unfinished business, much in the original vision of the Oxford Movement which has not yet been realised and appropriated.[97]

---

[95] F. L. Cross and E. A. Livingstone, 'Deification', in *The Oxford Dictionary of the Christian Church*, ed. F. L. Cross and E. A. Livingstone (Oxford and New York: Oxford University Press, 2005), 465.
[96] A. M. Allchin, *Participation in God: A Forgotten Strand in Anglican Tradition* (London: Darton, Longman & Todd, 1988).
[97] Ibid., 49.

If the Oxford Movement for Allchin looked to Rome, then the contemporaneous study of E. C. Miller on deification in the Anglican tradition claims that Anglicanism might stand as a kind of 'Western Orthodoxy'.[98] With studies such as those of Allchin and Miller, participation and deification seemed academically ripe for ecumenism, even as official Anglican-Orthodox dialogue counselled (as mentioned earlier) that *theōsis* was largely alien and problematic for Anglicans, at least in its Orthodox formulation.

Yet, the broad claims about participation and deification are controversial when applied to Hooker. For Allchin, Hooker was the earliest key representative who makes participation in God the central feature of theology, the 'forgotten strand in Anglican tradition'. Allchin coins the phrase 'theocentric humanism' to describe how Hooker's use of participation provides 'a vision of man which finds its fulfilment in God', a cosmic arc from creation through to salvation.[99] Taking into account Books One and Five of the *Laws*, Allchin provocatively argued that Hooker's language of participation in God implies a doctrine of deification. For Allchin, the *Laws* describes how 'not only that God has come down to be where we are, in our human mess, but that he has lifted us up to where he is in his divine splendour'.[100] Allchin accordingly aligns Hooker's thought with 'the doctrine of man's *theosis*' which 'can only make sense when seen in relation to a world filled, or rather drenched, with God'.[101] Participation in the life of God therefore entails 'a constant growth into the three theological virtues or powers of faith, hope, and love, a growth which leads us slowly from this world of time into the great world which lasts for ever'.[102] For Allchin, Hooker (along with selected others) accordingly represents an Anglican reception of the Orthodox doctrine of 'deification'. David Neelands follows Allchin in seeing that Hooker was 'informed by the Patristic notion of *theosis* or divinization'.[103]

Other scholars challenge, however, the link that Allchin draws between participation and *theōsis*. For example, while John Booty affirms that participation is the key to Hooker's theology, he suggests that Hooker does not intend the term to signify *theōsis*. Booty translates *theōsis* as 'fusion, absorption, or deification' and claims that Hooker clearly rejects such an idea.[104] Instead, Booty claims, Hooker only uses biblical idioms to describe participation rather than the Orthodox idea of deification. For Booty, rather than ontological union with God, 'the spirituality of participation is fundamentally social . . . restoring us to relationship with God and with one another'.[105]

---

[98] E. C. Miller, *Toward a Fuller Vision: Orthodoxy and the Anglican Experience* (Wilton: Morehouse Barlow, 1984).
[99] Allchin, *Participation in God*, 9.
[100] Ibid., 16.
[101] Ibid., 9.
[102] Ibid., 11.
[103] David Neelands, 'Hooker on Divinization: Our Participation of Christ', in *From Logos to Christos: Essays in Christology in Honour of Joanne McWilliam*, ed. Ellen Leonard and Kate Merriman (Waterloo: Wilfrid Laurier University Press, 2010), 137.
[104] John E. Booty, 'Book V', in *The Folger Library Edition of the Works of Richard Hooker*, ed. W. Speed Hill, 7 vols (vols 1–5, Cambridge: Belknap Press, 1977–90; vol. 6, Binghamton: Belknap Press, 1993; vol. 7, Tempe: Medieval and Renaissance Texts and Studies, 1998), 6 (1): 183–231 (198). See also John E. Booty, 'Richard Hooker', in *The Spirit of Anglicanism*, ed. William J. Wolf, John E. Booty and Owen C. Thomas (Wilton: Morehouse Barlow, 1979), 1–45.
[105] John E. Booty, 'The Spirituality of Participation in Richard Hooker', *Sewanee Theological Review* 38, no. 1 (1994): 9–20 (12).

Of course, Allchin, Neelands and Booty are all problematic in their readings. Allchin talks loosely of a 'doctrine' of participation and deification in Hooker's thought, but draws no immediate relationship to the doctrinal particulars of deification within Orthodox thought. Similarly, Neelands spends too little attention on what constitutes the patristic idea of deification, while Booty's definition of *theōsis* seems weak, if not misleading or even incorrect.

Beyond such exegetical problems, however, the metaphysical role of participation in Hooker's thought has gained steady currency. The most significant study, which Allchin uses, comes from Olivier Loyer, who places participation as the key that unlocks 'not only the economy of creation, but also the economy of the Trinity and salvation'.[106] Loyer continues that in Books One and Five of the *Laws*:

> Participation, in fact, emphasizes at the same time both transcendence and divine immanence. At the level of creation, God is in us, hidden in the depths of our being, precisely because he has created this being from nothing and, therefore, he is infinitely external. On the plane of redemption, God is also in us, precisely because he gave us his grace and, by it, reveals his entire sovereignty.[107]

For Loyer, participation forms an ontological chain in Hooker's thought, as it were, from the first gift of creation (in Book One) through to the final gift of adoption and union with the divine (developed in Book Five). Participation in Christ is the turning point from ontological becoming in Book One towards ontological being as believers share in the life of the Trinity. As Olivier Loyer writes of Hooker's participatory account in Book Five, 'the mystery of Trinitarian life and our participation in Christ is the origin and the end of any reflection, of any religious practice.'[108]

Following from Loyer's seminal study, a number of studies have paid attention to one or more aspects of how participation relates to other aspects of Hooker's thought in the *Laws*. Bryan D. Spinks and Charles Irish trace how Hooker uses participation in relation to the sacraments.[109] Spinks notes how Hooker's discussion of law in Book One paves the way for the later discussion of the *ordo salutis* in Book Five. Spinks draws the arc in this way: for Hooker, 'the created universe itself, with its laws, allows participation in the divine . . . [E]lection through Christ, justification, and the society of the church allows this participation to be achieved.'[110] Irish similarly traces how Hooker's account of participation in Book One combines Neoplatonic and Aristotelian ideas to create a legal entelechy; after sin frustrates such legal desire for perfection, the divine law (co-identical with Christ) restores and fulfils human nature, leading to

---

[106] Olivier Loyer, *L'Anglicanisme de Richard Hooker: Thèse Presentée devant l'université de Paris III*, 2 vols (Paris: Université de Paris, 1979), 378; translation mine.
[107] Ibid., 476; translation mine.
[108] Ibid., 476; translation mine.
[109] Bryan D. Spinks, *Two Faces of Elizabethan Anglican Theology: Sacraments and Salvation in the Thought of William Perkins and Richard Hooker* (Lanham, MD and London: Scarecrow Press, 1999); Charles Irish, '"Participation of God himselfe": Law, the mediation of Christ, and sacramental participation in the thought of Richard Hooker', in *Richard Hooker and the English Reformation*, ed. W. J. T. Kirby (Dordrecht: Kluwer Academic Publishers, 2003), 165–84.
[110] Spinks, *Two Faces of Elizabethan Anglican Theology*, 133.

Hooker's discussion in Book Five of sacramental participation in Christ. Other writers, like Egil Grislis, Robert Schwarz, Robert Slocum and Edmund Newey, variously see participation as a cornerstone in Hooker's theological system in relation to topics as diverse as Christology, creation, anthropology and soteriology.[111] J. V. Fesko likewise sets Hooker's 'doctrines of union and communion' within the idea of participation in God and Christ, arguing that they rest 'within the mainstream of Reformation views' about salvation, a sentiment echoed by André Gazal.[112] Andrea Russell suggests that 'participation can be discerned in the *Lawes*, not just as a theological theme but also in its very structure', with the style and rhetoric of Hooker's prose inviting 'a participation not just in the text but also . . . in God'.[113] Generally, however, such works do not move beyond Books One and Five, and avoid or do not focus on Hooker's language of deification. Accordingly, the illuminating potential of participation for the entirety of the *Laws* goes largely unexplored, especially related to Hooker's polemical purpose to defend the 'particular decisions' that govern the Elizabethan Religious Settlement.

The cumulative works of the Canadian scholar W. J. T. Kirby form the most helpful exception to this lacuna. Kirby's studies of participation in Hooker's thought range from close, analytical readings of the idea, particularly in Book One, through to exploring the governing role that participation plays both to extol and limit the royal ecclesiastical dominion. Kirby's work consistently shows how Hooker combines participatory metaphysics with the concrete political and constitutional issues of the Elizabethan period. As such, Kirby insists that the *Laws* acts as 'political theology' where particular theological commitments determine the shape of political claims. Participation remains the most significant theological commitment in the *Laws*, according to Kirby, that in turn significantly shapes Hooker's political vision. In particular, Kirby argues that Hooker's participatory exposition of Chalcedonian Christology (especially in the fifty-third chapter of Book Five) shapes his polemical defence of lay ecclesiastical supremacy in Book Eight:

> The Christological categories of person and nature, of subject and accident, are deployed throughout Hooker's examination .... By his studied use of these categories, Hooker invoked a powerful and traditional theological model for his defence of the Tudor constitution and, by implication, impugned the Disciplinarian opposition to the union of Church and Commonwealth as itself doctrinally unsound.[114]

---

[111] Egil Grislis, 'Jesus Christ – The Centre of Theology in Richard Hooker's *Of the Lawes of Ecclesiastical Polity*, Book V', *Journal of Anglican Studies* 5, no. 2 (2007): 227–51; Robert C. Schwarz, 'Dignified and Commodious: Richard Hooker's 'Mystical Copulation' Metaphor', *Sewanee Theological Review* 43, no. 1 (1999): 16–30; Robert B. Slocum, 'An Answering Heart: Reflections on Saving Participation', *Anglican Theological Review* 84, no. 3 (2002): 1009–15; and Edmund Newey, 'The Form of Reason: Participation in the work of Richard Hooker, Benjamin Whichcote, Ralph Cudworth, and Jeremy Taylor', *Modern Theology* 18, no. 1 (2002): 1–26.

[112] J. V. Fesko, 'Richard Hooker and John Owen on Union with Christ', in *Richard Hooker and Reformed Orthodoxy*, ed. Scott Kindred-Barnes and W. Bradford Littlejohn (Göttingen, Bristol: Vandenhoeck & Ruprecht, 2017), 255–72 (256); André Gazal, '"By force of participation and conjunction with him": John Jewel and Richard Hooker on Union with Christ', *Perichoresis* 12, no. 1 (2014): 39–56.

[113] Andrea Russell, *Richard Hooker, Beyond Certainty* (Abingdon: Routledge, 2017), 104–5.

[114] W. J. T. Kirby, *Richard Hooker's Doctrine of the Royal Supremacy* (Leiden: Brill, 1990), 8. Kirby's other works will be discussed throughout this study and so are not listed here.

Accordingly, this work intends to build upon that of Kirby and take it one step further. Kirby's insight that a particular ontology generates the shape of politics remains true, but misses out the intervening epistemology that connects the two as a kind of flying buttress. Indeed, the participatory structures of Books One and Five generate Hooker's epistemological claims in Books Two through Five just as much as his later political apologetics.

The claim that participation systematically forms the architectural *ratio* that makes the parts of the *Laws* cohere together as a whole begs, of course, two questions: namely, whether or not the *Laws* actually is both systematic and coherent.

The idea of Hooker being a coherent systematic thinker at all causes difficulty in certain circles. On one side, William Haugaard claims that 'no theologian before Richard Hooker had given [emerging Anglicanism] systematic or coherent theological expression',[115] and Lee Gibbs proclaims that 'Hooker saw his work as a logically consistent whole'.[116] Likewise, according to Aidan Nichols, it is in Hooker's *Laws* that 'Anglicanism first achieved a relatively coherent form', while Paul Avis thinks that Hooker 'laid the foundations of Anglican ecclesiology' since he was 'great with the greatness of Shakespeare'.[117] Similarly, Dionisio De Lara, J. S. Marshall, George Morrel, Olivier Loyer, A. S. McGrade, Lee W. Gibbs and A. J. Joyce all argue that Hooker's works reveal a coherent, systematic unity, although only Marshall, Morrel and Loyer see participation as a constituent part of such harmony.[118] Indeed, Marshall guardedly writes that the *Laws* 'is not a systematic theology', by which he means a systematic arrangement of doctrinal topics, but rather represents 'a system of unique comprehensiveness of design and fullness of interpretation' and 'an organic scheme'.[119]

Yet, on the other hand, some writers cast doubt on Hooker's status as a systematic theologian or as a coherent thinker at all. James Cargill Thompson describes the *Laws* merely as a piece of polemical writing: 'Hooker was continually arguing to a brief, and he cannot easily be acquitted of the charge of subordinating his political ideas

---

[115] William Haugaard, 'The Preface', in *The Folger Library Edition of the Works of Richard Hooker*, ed. W. Speed Hill, 7 vols (vols 1–5, Cambridge: Belknap Press, 1977–90; vol. 6, Binghamton: Belknap Press, 1993; vol. 7, Tempe: Medieval and Renaissance Texts and Studies, 1998), 6 (1): 1–80 (2–3).

[116] Lee Gibbs, 'Book I', in *The Folger Library Edition of the Works of Richard Hooker*, ed. W. Speed Hill, 7 vols (vols. 1–5, Cambridge: Belknap Press, 1977–90; vol. 6, Binghamton: Belknap Press, 1993; vol. 7, Tempe: Medieval and Renaissance Texts and Studies, 1998), 6 (1): 81–124 (87).

[117] Aidan Nichols, *The Panther and the Hind: A Theological History of Anglicanism* (Edinburgh: T & T Clark, 1993), 43; Paul Avis, *Anglicanism and the Christian Church* (Edinburgh: T & T Clark, 1989), 47.

[118] Dionisio De Lara, 'Richard Hooker's Concept of Law', *Anglican Theological Review* 44 (1962), 380–9; J. S. Marshall, *Hooker and the Anglican Tradition: An Historical and Theological Study of Hooker's Ecclesiastical Polity* (London: Adam and Charles Black, 1963); George Morrel, 'The Systematic Theology of Medieval Richard Hooker' (Unpublished Th.D. thesis, Pacific School of Religion, 1969); Loyer, *L'Anglicanisme de Richard Hooker*, 664–70; A. S. McGrade, 'The Coherence of Hooker's Polity: The Books on Power', *Journal of the History of Ideas* 24 (1963): 163–82; Lee Gibbs, 'Richard Hooker's Via Media Doctrine of Justification', *Harvard Theological Review* 74, no. 2 (1981): 211–20; and A. J. Joyce, *Richard Hooker and Anglican Moral Theology* (Oxford: Oxford University Press, 2012), esp. 40–4.

[119] Marshall, *Hooker and the Anglican Tradition*, 81.

to the immediate needs of the controversy.'[120] The logical unity of Hooker's thought was, according to Cargill Thompson, a product of political necessity rather than theological commitment. In a similar vein, Diarmaid MacCulloch witheringly writes of Book Five, 'one feels that if the parliamentary legislation of 1559 had prescribed that English clergy were to preach standing on their heads, then Hooker would have found a theological reason for justifying it.'[121] Other scholars, like William Bouwsma and Charles Miller, argue that to classify the *Laws* as a theological system would be misleading, even inappropriate.[122] For Bouwsma and Miller, the *Laws* do not fit the genre of systematic theology where philosophical systems or theological categories determine the shape, content or order of a work.[123] Despite this reservation, however, Miller affirms, however, that 'we can, nevertheless, see across Hooker's writings a coherence' that comes out of 'a core of concepts' such as rationality, hierarchy and participation.[124] Spinks likewise stresses the coherent structure of the *Laws* that allows Hooker to move from general philosophical principles to a defence of the Elizabethan Religious Settlement.[125]

Other scholars attack the coherency of Hooker's *Laws*, whether in its political, epistemological or ontological claims, or in the relation between them. First, a series of scholars argue that Hooker's political vision in the later parts of the *Laws* fails to cohere with his ontological commitments in Book One. For example, H. F. Kearney argues that Hooker remains unable to reconcile rationalist and voluntaristic conceptions of law across the *Laws*.[126] Likewise, Peter Munz suggests that Hooker fails to reconcile Thomistic principles of the reasonableness of law with the realities of the Tudor political situation, the latter of which called for appeals to Marsilius of Padua and the implication that the state was purely voluntaristic and secular.[127] Other scholars challenge Hooker's coherency in terms of how his epistemological claims relate to his ontology. Gunnar Hillerdal writes that 'Hooker's philosophical failure is evident' since he fails to join an Aristotelian-Thomist philosophy of reason, which evaluates nature in a positive light, with a Protestant theology of grace and predestination.[128] Joseph Devine similarly challenges the integrity of Hooker's thought when he concludes that Hooker 'scholastic theology broke down' when it fails to explain in satisfactory terms the Reformation soteriological principle of *sola fide* (faith alone) alongside the Thomistic idea that

---

[120] W. D. J. Cargill Thompson, 'The Philosopher of the Politic Society: Richard Hooker as a Political Thinker', in *Studies in Richard Hooker*, ed. W. Speed Hill (Cleveland and London: Case Western Reserve University Press, 1972), 3–76 (12).

[121] Diarmaid MacCulloch, 'Richard Hooker's Reputation', in *A Companion to Richard Hooker*, ed. W. J. T. Kirby (Leiden: Brill, 2008), 563–612 (570).

[122] William J. Bouwsma, 'Hooker in the Context of European Cultural History', in *Richard Hooker and the Construction of Christian Community*, ed. A. S. McGrade (Tempe: Medieval and Renaissance Texts and Studies, 1997), 41–58; Charles Miller, *Richard Hooker and the Vision of God: Exploring the Origins of 'Anglicanism'* (Cambridge: James Clarke, 2013), 30–1.

[123] Bouwsma, 'Hooker in the Context of European Cultural History', 44.

[124] Miller, *Vision of God*, 30.

[125] Spinks, *Two Faces of Elizabethan Anglican Theology*, ch. 6.

[126] H. F. Kearney, 'Richard Hooker: A Reconstruction', *Cambridge Journal* 5 (1952): 300–11.

[127] Peter Munz, *The Place of Hooker in the History of Thought* (London: Routledge & Kegan Paul, 1952).

[128] Gunnar Hillerdal, *Reason and Revelation in Richard Hooker* (Lund: Gleerup, 1962), 148.

grace perfects nature.[129] As A. S. McGrade looks over scholarly studies of Hooker's epistemology, then, he observes that Hooker 'has the unusual distinction of being severely criticised for both hypo- and hyper-rationalism', of either subsuming reason under the activity of irrational grace or extolling reason at the expense of revelation, and in either case running the risk of incoherency.[130] In turn, Rory Fox claims that 'Hooker's ecclesiastical polity is muddled, incomplete, and quite simply incoherent'.[131] For Fox, tradition is the only warrant Hooker can employ against the arguments of his radical puritan opponents for further reform, and yet Hooker rejects this same warrant when he considers the arguments put forward against the English Reformation by his Roman Catholic opponents. Elsewhere, W. J. Torrance Kirby points to how 'two Christian Platonisms' found in Hooker's legal ontology causes broad and perhaps irreconcilable tensions. Kirby describes the two Christian Platonisms as Augustinian immediacy (immediate participation through Christ) and Dionysian hierarchy (the mediation of participation through created orders). The two traditions of participation here appear contradistinctive: if one has immediate participation in Christ, then a mediatory system of created orders would seem gratuitous. For Kirby, 'the continuing debate over the logical cohesiveness of Hooker's thought might be illuminated by further reflection on these two Christian Platonisms'.[132]

Both praise and criticism of Hooker's status as a systematic thinker, and of the coherency of the *Laws*, have lacked clear definition of what exactly constitutes these things in the first place. The final duty of this chapter, then, is to outline four hermeneutical principles in relation to the terms 'participation' and 'deification', as well as 'systematic' and 'coherency', which will guide the exploration of the architecture of participation in Hooker's thought through the remainder of this book.

The first principle comes from the heuristic 'architecture of participation' developed earlier. This heuristic device will inform what Hooker means when he refers directly to participation in Books One and Five, as well as the wider semantic field around participation as it occurs throughout the *Laws*. As the architecture of participation shows, participation works as a polyvalent term, covering philosophical and scriptural registers. The participatory architecture has two non-competitive and overlapping cadences: the 'weak/extensive/exiting' and the 'strong/intensive/returning'. The language of creation describes the former, while the language of deification (itself capable of multiple meanings) exists as a possibility in the latter cadence.

The second principle relates to the first and upholds Hallonsten's distinction between a theme and a doctrine of deification developed earlier. The doctrine of deification remains unique to Eastern Orthodoxy, while the theme of deification holds possibilities for modern ecumenical discourse since it describes the broad and commonly held exegetical set of biblical images, especially participation, union and adoption. A theme of deification does not necessarily entail, of course, a doctrine,

---

[129] Joseph G. Devine, 'Richard Hooker's Doctrine of Justification and Sanctification in the Debate with Walter Travers, 1585–1586' (PhD thesis, Hartford: Hartford Seminary Foundation, 1976), 299.
[130] McGrade, 'The Coherence of Hooker's Polity', 166.
[131] Rory Fox, 'Richard Hooker and the Incoherence of "Ecclesiastical Polity"', *Heythrop Journal* 44, no. 1 (2003): 43–59 (57).
[132] W. J. T. Kirby, *Richard Hooker, Reformer and Platonist* (Aldershot: Ashgate, 2005), 37.

especially not in its Orthodox formulation. Accordingly, this study will explore Hooker's thematic account of participation and deification without assuming its direct equivalence to doctrinal uses in Eastern theology.[133] In order to describe and classify precisely Hooker's thematic account of *theōsis*, this study employs Russell's salutary fourfold typology of nominal, analogical, ethical and realistic aspects of deification, also referenced earlier.

The third and fourth principles concern what constitutes coherence and system, but require some more explanation. The two terms share, of course, some common ground. 'Coherency' suggests something about the logical arrangement and connection of parts. Similarly, 'system' suggests the causal relation of parts in a whole.[134] Indeed, W. V. Quine and J. S. Ullian suggest that system, coherence, truth and logic remain intimately nestled together, implying one another through a web of connected gestures.[135] Yet, both terms come with intellectual baggage and claims that they obfuscate either the indeterminacy or the clarity of Christian kerygma. Quentin Skinner, for example, writes about the 'myth of coherence' in which later exegetes impose a unified reading of particular thinkers, giving them a false 'coherence, and an air generally of a closed system', which they may never have attained or ever been meant to attain'.[136] As mentioned earlier, William Bouwsma wonders whether 'system' acts as a useful lens at all through which to view thinkers like Hooker. In a different vein, Paul Holmer attacks the 'scandal' of some academic theologians and their 'senseless system-mongering' that looks like idle speculation.[137] Hooker faces his own critics, of course, in this regard too. The anonymous conforming puritan authors of *A Christian Letter* in 1599 accuse Hooker of writing in a style in which he would show himself 'another Aristotle by a certain metaphisicall and crupticall method [in order] to bring men into a maze'.[138] The anonymous authors of *A Christian Letter* here allege that Hooker obscures his heterodoxy with abstract speculation far removed from apostolic and kerygmatic simplicity. If either coherence or system are going to be useful terms, then, it needs to be clear what these terms will mean in this study of Hooker's participatory thought.

As Robert Audi notes, there are many varying philosophical accounts of 'coherency', and the term raises the wider issues of justification and truth.[139] Justification involves a vertical relation between basic propositions to those they justify. A claim is justified if it corresponds with contiguous claims in a broader network of belief. In contrast, claims of truthfulness either involve horizontal relations between propositions within a web that demonstrate their truthful coherence or a comparison between the beliefs (or

[133] Other recent studies in Reformed thought similarly take Hallonsten's distinction as axiomatic, for example, Billings, *Calvin, Participation, and the Gift*, 55–6.
[134] See Gale Heide, *Timeless Truth in the Hands of History. A Short History of System in Theology* (Cambridge: James Clarke, 2012), 1–8.
[135] W. V. Quine and J. S. Ullian, *The Web of Belief*, 2nd edn (New York: Random House, 1978), 40–1.
[136] Quentin Skinner, 'Meaning and Understanding in the History of Ideas', *History and Theory* 8, no. 1 (1969): 3–53 (17).
[137] Paul Holmer, *The Grammar of Faith* (San Francisco, CA: Harper and Row, 1978), x.
[138] *A Christian Letter*, in *The Folger Library Edition of the Works of Richard Hooker*, ed. W. Speed Hill, 7 vols (vols 1–5, Cambridge: Belknap Press, 1977–90; vol. 6, Binghamton: Belknap Press, 1993; vol. 7, Tempe: Medieval and Renaissance Texts and Studies, 1998), 4:72.14–17.
[139] Robert Audi, *The Architecture of Reason: The Structure and Substance of Rationality* (Oxford: Oxford University Press, 2001), 24.

judgements) and the world as it is commonly experienced. Such comparison demands correspondence in order to claim veracity. Unlike correspondence theories of truth, then, philosophical coherentism in its most stringent forms therefore holds that, 'the epistemic justification of an empirical belief derives entirely from its coherence with the believer's overall system of empirical beliefs and not at all from any sort of factor outside that system.'[140] Likewise, philosophical coherentism stresses that the harmonious horizontal relation of propositions marks the truthfulness of a system of beliefs: a statement coheres (and so is true) if it follows logically from, or implies, some other statement.

While questions of justification and truth (as well as the philosophical shortcomings of coherentism) are beyond the concerns of this work on Hooker, three useful aspects about coherency come to the fore. First, at a basic level, coherency suggests the relation of ideas within a web, where ideally each belief in the web entails or gestures towards all the others. Second, coherency assumes that the logical principle of non-contradiction must hold for these relations to have structural integrity: one proposition cannot contradict another within the web. As such, coherence also involves the stronger notion of logical implication already indicated in the first aspect: a statement coheres either if it follows on from, or implies, another statement.[141] Third, as Laurence BonJour admits, 'since actual human systems of belief seem inevitably to fall short of perfect coherence, however that is understood, their truth is usually held to be approximate at best.'[142]

Anna Williams points out that theological and secular epistemology diverge on a number of points, but converge nevertheless in a number of significant ways regarding what constitutes coherency, as well as the provisionality and epistemic limits of truth claims.[143] Unlike propositions in some coherentist accounts, theological claims do not exist in a self-contained propositional system, but rather act as a way to describe how creation relates to God and so how creatures relate to one another. As Anna Williams writes, theology 'never claimed its plausibility rested solely on the compatibility of propositions within a system, but only that coherence is the goal and by-product of correct interpretation of its recognized warrants', especially Scripture.[144] While the divine subject and origin of theology remains certain, theological claims are not indubitable but rather reflect the provisional understanding of their human participants in the divine act of self-disclosure. Williams notes that 'the provisionality of Christian belief does not, however, distinguish it from non-theological claims' since current philosophical epistemologies rarely argue that certitude remains attainable, as seen in the third aspect of philosophical coherency mentioned earlier.[145]

---

[140] Laurence BonJour, *The Structure of Empirical Knowledge* (Cambridge: Harvard University Press, 1985), 101. Other coherentists have suggested that external factors do play an important role too in justification.

[141] Paul K. Moser, Dwayne H. Mulder and J. D. Trout, *The Theory of Knowledge: A Thematic Introduction* (Oxford: Oxford University Press, 1998), 69.

[142] Laurence BonJour, 'Coherence Theories of Truth', in *The Cambridge Dictionary of Philosophy*, ed. Robert Audi (Cambridge: Cambridge University Press, 2001), 153–4.

[143] Anna N. Williams, *The Architecture of Theology: Structure, System & Ratio* (Oxford: Oxford University Press, 2011), 23–78.

[144] Ibid., 13.

[145] Ibid., 48.

Texts from Hooker seem to lend support to a nuanced account of coherency. On the one hand, for Hooker in the *Laws* sacred doctrine is a *scientia*, a way of knowledge, rather than simply a propositional set: 'Theologie, what is it but the science of thinges divine? What science can be attained unto without the help of natural discourse and reason?'[146] As Peter Candler shows in relation to Aquinas, the medieval notion of theology as a *scientia* involves the manuduction (*manuductio*) of believers as it 'leads them by the hand' to participate in the life of God.[147] Similarly for Hooker, since human beings grow 'by steppes and degrees', theology aims to help them grow and participate in God. In the *Laws*, such participation occurs especially through embodied worship, the edifying liturgical acts that serve as a 'hand to lead and a way to direct'.[148] As Andrea Russell argues, the *Laws* might indeed be said itself to be an exercise in manuduction given its emphasis on participation, an attempt to lead his theological opponents 'by the hand' to conformity and 'the participation of God himselfe'.[149]

On the other hand, Hooker elsewhere describes the provisionality of faith as an intellectual habit. Hooker remains aware of the apophatic limits of theological enquiry, writing how 'dangerous it were for the feeble brain of man to wade farre into the doings of the Most High ... [Y]et our soundest knowledge is to know that we know him not as in deed he is, neither can know him'.[150] Indeed, Hooker declares that human attempts to understand perfectly the relationship between God and creation are limited by the incommensurability of human limitation and divine transcendence.[151] For Hooker, theology retains the capacity for self-critiquing because it understands the limits of human understanding and the debilitating effects of sin.

In light of Hooker's stress on theology as provisional and *in via*, the third hermeneutical principle of this study will be the following: 'coherency' refers to the web of claims that, although less than indubitable, exhibits as few internal inconsistencies as possible while seeking to imitate the divine self-disclosure and draw people into divine participation. The degree to which the web coheres lends it internal strength and credibility. Yet, because the web remains provisional, such coherence does not thereby involve a zero-sum game in which any inconsistency or tension necessarily makes the whole structure collapse. While many studies show an unspoken hermeneutic preference for suspicion and the unveiling of what they attack as indissoluble dilemmas in Hooker's thought, this nuanced form of coherency lends to this study a spoken preference to discern deeply ordered complexity around the concept of participation. Indeed, it opens up an interpretation of Hooker's texts that is expansive, extensive, simple (without being simplistic), unified and explanatory. Participation implies the web of claims made in the *Laws*, its own architectural gestures making these claims cohere together, and to which other claims themselves gesture back. Giving priority

---

[146] Hooker, *Laws*, 1:230.1–3; III.8.11.
[147] Peter Candler, *Theology, Rhetoric, Manuduction, or Reading Scripture Together on the Path of God* (London: SCM Press, 2011), 41–51, 90–107. See Hooker, *Laws*, 1:112.17–20; 2:237.23–5; 2:241.5–11; I.11.2; V.56.5; V.56.9; and *Pride*, I, in *FLE*, 5:329.10.
[148] Hooker, *Laws*, 1:275.21–4; IV.1.3.
[149] Russell, *Beyond Certainty*, 92–102 on Candler's account of manuduction in relation to Hooker's thought.
[150] Hooker, *Laws*, 1:59.12–16; I.2.1.
[151] Ibid., 1:68.2–6; I.3.4.

to a generous hermeneutic opens up the possibility to unveil Hooker's architecture of order that bears and distributes the load of metaphysical, epistemological, and political tensions evident in his context into a stable edifice. As such, Hooker's thought will be coherent to the degree that the ontological, epistemological and political claims of the *Laws* exhibit mutuality and avoid blatant contradiction but not necessarily tension. Indeed, for Hooker such tensions are endemic to the human search for knowledge and arise because 'every cause admit not such infallible evidence of profe, as leaveth no possibilitie of doubt or scruple behind it'.[152]

This third principle about coherency leads to the fourth principle about what counts as systematic. The relational nature of propositions indicates a system in which they operate. W. V. Quine and J. S. Ullian write:

> Nearly any body of knowledge that is sufficiently organized to exhibit appropriate evidential relationships among its constituent claims has at least some claim to be seen as scientific. What makes for science is a system, whatever its subject.[153]

As shown earlier, Hooker sees theology as a science, a body of knowledge about 'thinges divine'. As such, as an exercise in theology, the *Laws* must involve system in some regard. Anna Williams provides a helpful distinction here between two senses of what 'systematic theology' might mean.[154] The term can refer to 'a body of prose intended to give a reasonably comprehensive account of Christian doctrine, ordered locus by locus', a tendency which Williams labels as 'Type1'. Yet, the term can also refer to 'theological writing in which the treatment of any one locus indicates, at least in some measure, how it is informed by other loci or how it will itself determine the shape of others', a tendency which Williams labels as 'Type 2'. The fourth hermeneutical principle turns on whether Hooker's *Laws* exhibits a Type 1 or Type 2 form of system.

Some scholars claim, as noted earlier, that Hooker's *Laws* work is in some regard a Type 1 systematic theology. Marshall argues, for example, that Hooker's *Laws* largely parallels the structure of Aquinas's *Summa Theologiae*, while De Lara exclaims that 'Richard Hooker is the St Thomas Aquinas of Anglicanism . . . with his powers for systematic thinking'.[155] Yet, these claims are fraught with almost intractable difficulties over the theological identity of Hooker, not to mention the structural implausibility that the *Laws* in any meaningful sense maps onto the *Summa Theologiae*. Recent Hookerian scholarship traces the influence of Reformed thought on Hooker,[156] as well as Reformed uses of Aquinas,[157] making it difficult for modern scholars to reach

---

[152] Ibid., 1:146.13–14; II.1.3.
[153] Quine and Ullian, *The Web of Belief*, 3.
[154] Williams, *The Architecture of Theology*, 1–4.
[155] Marshall, *Hooker and the Anglican Tradition*, ch. 8; De Lara, 'Richard Hooker's Concept of Law', 388.
[156] For a taxonomy of approaches to Hooker's theological tradition, see the following: Corneliu Simut, *Richard Hooker and His Early Doctrine of Justification: A Study of His Discourse on Justification* (Aldershot: Ashgate, 2005), 1–12; and W. Bradford Littlejohn, 'The Search for a Reformed Hooker: Some Modest Proposals', *Reformation and Renaissance Review* 16, no. 1 (2015): 68–82.
[157] Manfred Svensson and David VanDrunen (eds), *Aquinas among the Protestants* (Chichester: Wiley-Blackwell, 2018), esp. 27–48, 91–108. See also Paul Dominiak, 'Hooker, Scholasticism, Thomism, and Reformed Orthodoxy', in *Richard Hooker and Reformed Orthodoxy*, ed. Scott Kindred-Barnes and W. Bradford Littlejohn (Göttingen, Bristol: Vandenhoeck & Ruprecht, 2017), 101–26.

a consensus about how to identify Hooker's theology. Furthermore, the contingent polemical concerns determine the structure of the *Laws*, rather than any Type 1 systematic genre. Yet, while it excludes the *Laws* as a Type 1 systematics, Hooker's polemicist position actually frames the *Laws* within Type 2. Hooker scholars have noted the rhetorical side of Hooker's work, in terms of style, strategy and polemic.[158] Brain Vickers convincingly argues that 'Hooker's use of rhetoric is ultimately subordinate to, and dependent upon, logical argument'.[159] For Vickers, Hooker appeals to a particular *genus* of Aristotelian rhetoric – the judicial oratory – through which he hopes to establish the justice or injustice of certain actions and beliefs in relation to the Elizabethan Religious Settlement and lay ecclesiastical supremacy. The genre of the judicial oratory implies settling a dispute through logical demonstration and thus depends more upon cumulative reason and judgement rather than persuasive guile. Vickers focuses here on Hooker's logical and orderly attempt to provide a coherent account of the disputed ontological, epistemological and political aspects of the Elizabethan Religious Settlement. As such, 'it is abundantly clear that Hooker has structured his work using the terms and techniques of formal logic' which 'soon develops strands or filaments that reach out to make other connection'.[160] The notes here of logic and the generative relation between ideas that mutually gesture towards each other in Hooker's *Laws* sound out something like Williams' Type 2 form of system.

Even though Hooker does not consider an exhaustive set of doctrinal loci in the *Laws*, this work will show how Hooker's participatory metaphysics gesture towards, shape and knit together his epistemological and political claims into a coherent whole. As such, Hooker's participatory metaphysics act like a jigsaw piece: though a complete doctrinal puzzle may be absent, 'a solitary piece displays by its very shape its trajectory towards linkage', as Anna Williams phrases it.[161] Hooker indeed sees the *Laws* as constituting a whole whereby each element adds strength to what follows, and each former part gestures back and illuminates what has gone before. Of this purpose, Hooker writes:

> For as much help whereof as may be in this case, I have endeavoured throughout the bodie of this whole discourse, that every former part might give strength unto all that followe, and every later bring some light unto all before. So that if the judgements of men doe but holde themselves in suspence as touching these first

---

[158] Brian Vickers, 'Introduction 2: Hooker's Prose Style', in *Of the Laws of Ecclesiastical Polity: An Abridged Edition*, ed. A. S. McGrade and Brian Vickers (London: Sidgwick & Jackson, 1975), 41–59; John N. Wall, 'Hooker's "Faire Speeche". Rhetorical Strategies in the *Lawes of Ecclesiastical Polity*', in *This Sacred History. Anglican Reflections for John Booty*, ed. Donald S. Armentrout (Cambridge: Cowley, 1990), 125–43; Rudolph Almasy, 'The Purpose of Richard Hooker's Polemic', *Journal of the History of Ideas* 39, no. 2 (1978): 251–70.

[159] Brian Vickers, 'Public and Private Rhetoric in Hooker's *Lawes*', in *Richard Hooker and the Construction of Christian Community*, ed. A. S. McGrade (Tempe: Medieval and Renaissance Texts and Studies, 1997), 95–145 (113). Compare William P. Haugaard, 'The Preface', in *FLE*, 6 (1): 62–80.

[160] Vickers, 'Public and Private Rhetoric in Hooker's *Lawes*', 129–30.

[161] Williams, *The Architecture of Theology*, 1.

more general meditations, till in order they have perused the rest that ensue: what may seeme darke at the first will afterwards be founde more plaine, even as the later particular decisions will appeare, I doubt not more strong, when the other have beene read before.[162]

Thus, Hooker works through the most significant metaphysical claim – participation – to specific epistemological and political consequences since 'in all parts of knowledge rightly so termed things most general are most strong' and 'the certaintie of our perswasion touching particulars dependeth altogether upon the credite of those generalities out of which they growe'.[163] The final hermeneutical principle, then, accords with Williams' Type 2 account of systematic theology. This final principle acts as the litmus test for the presence of system in Hooker's thought, understood not as a genre but as an orderly relation of gestures that portray or suggest comprehensiveness, either explicitly or tacitly.

Using these four hermeneutical principles, this book considers in turn Hooker's ontology, epistemology and political vision, tracing out the architectural role of participation in each area, as well as suggesting how it overcomes or diffuses alleged problems over the coherency of the *Laws*. As such, this order follows Hooker's aim to move from the 'general' to the 'particular' in the *Laws*. The second chapter considers the architecture of participation as it occurs in two metaphysical mini-treatises in Books One and Five of the *Laws*. It argues that Hooker explores an extensive and an intensive mode of participation to explore the metaphysical distinction and relationship between nature and grace in creation and redemption. The third chapter then explores how Hooker constructs in Books Two through Five of the *Laws* two modes of cognitive participation in God derived from and corresponding with these two modes of metaphysical participation, namely the natural and the supernatural. The fourth chapter explores how the architecture of participation evident in Hooker's argument generates a 'grammar of participation' in the closing 'books of power' of the *Laws* that structures his political vision. The closing chapter returns to the provocations of this opening chapter, addressing how Hooker's architecture of participation accordingly unites the *Laws* as a whole, lending to it a sense of system and coherence.

A serious and in-depth study of the architectural framework of participation in Hooker's *Laws* promises two benefits, then – one particular and the other general. On the one hand, this study addresses particular debates within contemporary Hookerian study over the coherency of his various ontological, epistemological and political claims, laying out how the architecture of 'participation in God' informs, illuminates, connects and coheres these claims together. On the other hand, it offers Hooker's model of participation and deification as a salutary resource for both Anglican-Orthodox dialogue and for those who are interested in or involved with the modern theological *ressourcement* of participatory metaphysics.

---

[162] Hooker, *Laws*, 1:57.24–33; I.1.2.
[163] Ibid., 1:146.9–12; II.1.3.

2

'Most abundant vertue': Hooker's metaphysical architecture of participation

Introduction

If every political vision assumes an epistemology that is in turn buttressed by some kind of ontology, then the first task in establishing the systematic homology between these aspects in Hooker's thought is to explicate the metaphysical claims of the *Laws*. Here, participation forms the central concept that shapes Hooker's metaphysical discourse. The previous chapter offered the heuristic 'architecture of participation'. Participation describes the ordering of individuals and communities towards the perfection found most properly in God. Architecturally, participation has two non-competitive and complementary motifs. On the one hand, participation (*methexis*) images a 'weak/extensive/exiting' paradigm, namely the divine influence within creation. An intrinsic pattern of divine causality renders all that exists as a divine gift and similitude, a sharing in God's 'most glorious and most abundant vertue', as Hooker puts it.[1] On the other hand, participation can also image a 'strong/intensive/returning' paradigm, namely, the final perfection of creatures through an intense (re)union with the divine nature such that they become (as far as their forms allows) what they are not, namely godlike (*theōsis*). Hooker appeals to both architectural motifs in two metaphysical mini-treatises within the *Laws*.[2] First, in chapters two through fifteen of Book One, he uses participation to describe how creatures generally participate in (and desire union with) God through a legal ontology that circumscribes creation and redemption. Later, in chapters fifty through sixty-eight of Book Five, he renders sacramental participation in Christ as a form of deification. This chapter examines in turn, then, these two participatory moments.

The presence in Books One and Five of the two aspects found in the heuristic architecture of participation occasions, however, the first challenge to the coherency of the *Laws*. These two aspects loosely correlate with what Wayne Hankey labels as

---

[1] Hooker, *Laws*, 1:60.1–2; 1:61.6–8; I.2.3–4.
[2] Gibbs, 'Book I', in *FLE*, 6 (1): 81, 86 who describes Book One as a 'treatise within a treatise' since 'while Book I functions as the general introduction to a sustained polemic, it also lays the foundations for a coherent philosophical theology'. Similarly, see John Booty, 'Book V', in *FLE*, 6 (1): 192–9 who sees chapters fifty to sixty-eight on sacramental participation as the metaphysical centre of Book Five.

'Dionysian mediation' and 'Augustinian immediacy'[3] both Platonic in origin, or what Kirby calls 'hierarchy' and 'grace'[4] respectively. First, Hooker appeals to 'Dionysian mediation' with his use of the Neoplatonic, hierarchical *lex divinitatis* (law of divine power), the system of laws that participate in eternal law and mediate between creation and the utterly transcendent, creative and unitary principle of God's own being.[5] Such a participatory system of mediating hierarchies flows through the work of thinkers like Pseudo-Dionysius and Aquinas into Hooker's *Laws*. Second, however, Hooker also appeals to the idea that, since God creates human beings in the divine image, they are also made capable of God and can immediately participate in the grace of Christ's union of human and divine natures through faith, especially within the dominical sacraments. Hankey labels this participatory dynamic as 'Augustinian immediacy' since it derives from Augustine of Hippo, whose work heavily influenced the sixteenth-century Reformers and led to their emphasis on salvation by grace, faith and Christ alone (the triumvirate of *sola gratia*, *sola fide* and *solus christus*).[6] These claims about immediacy flow out of the confluence between early Christianity with middle and late Neoplatonism as they are commonly concerned with the soul's mystical ascent to immediate union with God. Whatever the parallel presence of Dionysian mediation, such arguments remained influential within the medieval period with, for example, Aquinas also defending the possibility of immediate union with God. For Aquinas, God creates the rational soul immediately, and the rational soul cannot attain its ultimate perfection until it returns to God in the same manner, that is without creaturely mediation.[7]

W. J. T. Kirby questions the logical cohesiveness of these two 'Christian Platonisms' when Hooker tries to hold them together in the *Laws*.[8] These two manners of mediation seem to stand in strong contrast to one another: the first mediates through a complex legal hierarchy of being; and the second mediates immediately through Christ. On one hand, Dionysian mediation seems to render Augustinian immediacy as insufficient in some way. On the other hand, Augustinian immediacy seems to render Dionysian mediation as superfluous. Indeed, for the anonymous authors of *A Christian Letter* in 1599, the Dionysian aspects of Hooker's account appear to overthrow the Reformed doctrine of the Church of England. For these authors, Hooker's appeal to the natural law tradition, the light of reason and the authority of pagan philosophy (especially

---

[3] Wayne Hankey, 'Augustinian Immediacy and Dionysian Mediation in John Colet, Edmund Spenser, Richard Hooker and the Cardinal de Bérulle', in *Acts of the 1996 Kolloquium Augustinus in der Neuzeit*, ed. Kurt Flasch and Dominique de Courcelles (Turnhout: Editions Brepols, 1998), 125–60.
[4] Kirby, *Reformer and Platonist*, 29–44.
[5] On this translation, see Kirby, *Reformer and Platonist*, 32, n. 16. On the *lex divinitatis*, see Pseudo-Dionysius, *Ecclesiastical Hierarchy*, 5.4, 504c and *Celestial Hierarchy*, 1.3, 124a; in *Pseudo-Dionysius: Complete Works*, 146–7; 235–6.
[6] See Augustine, *De civitate Dei*, 9.15, in *Nicene and Post-Nicene Fathers*, ed. Philip Schaff and Henry Wace, first series, 14 vols (Peabody: Hendrickson, 1994), vol. 2, 173–4.
[7] Aquinas, *De Ver*, 8.1; and *ST*, I.12.1 and 2 resp. On the presence and synthesis of Augustinian and Dionysian theologies of union, see Damien Boquet and Piroska Nagy, *Medieval Sensibilities. A History of Emotions in the Middle Ages*, trans. Robert Shaw (Cambridge: Polity, 2018), 14–16.
[8] Kirby, *Reformer and Platonist*, 32–44. See also W. J. T. Kirby, 'Grace and Hierarchy: Richard Hooker's Two Platonisms', in *Richard Hooker and the English Reformation*, ed. W. J. T. Kirby (Dordrecht: Kluwer Academic Publishers, 2003), 25–39, esp. 29–33.

Aristotle) breach the emphasis of the *Articles of Religion* on Reformation principles about the sufficiency of Christ, faith and Scripture such that 'almost all the principall pointes of our English creed [are] greatlie shaked and contradicted'.[9] While Kirby argues that Hooker successfully combines a Neoplatonic ontology with Protestant assumptions about nature and grace, he also states that 'the continuing debate over the logical cohesiveness of Hooker's thought might be illuminated by further reflection on these two Christian Platonisms'.[10]

The burden of this chapter, then, is to unpack in turn the complexity of Hooker's two metaphysical accounts of participation in Books One and Five of the *Laws*. Such unpacking unveils the presence of the extensive and the intensive modes of participation in both of these two accounts. It also manifests how, for Hooker, Christ acts as the key who unlocks both participatory orders (mediatory hierarchy and immediate grace), distinguishing between but also uniting nature and grace as complementary acts of the same divine influence. As such, Hooker's two Platonisms form a productive tension where nature and grace cohere as aspects of one divine knowing and gift, that is to say, as differing but related intensities of participation in God through Christ. Indeed, in Hooker's architecture of participation, Christ forms the influential principle behind the mediating hierarchies, while their work remains his such that he personally perfects and elevates them in the immediacy of the hypostatic union shared in as a gift by believers.

'The father of lights': Extensive participation in God and law

Lee Gibbs points out that Book One of the *Laws* 'is not an abstract essay in philosophical theology or political theory' but that Hooker's 'systematic examination' of law 'has to be considered in terms of its polemical overtones and implications'.[11] Hooker's defence of the Elizabethan Church rested on distinguishing between necessary matters of faith determined by scriptural authority and 'things indifferent' left open to human discretion (such as external forms of worship and government). This distinction was crucial to make in Hooker's polemical context with the radical puritans.[12] The

---

[9] *A Christian Letter*, 20, in *FLE*, 4:65.16–68.19.
[10] Kirby, *Reformer and Platonist*, 37; 57–78.
[11] Gibbs, 'Book I', in *FLE*, 6 (1): 82. On the wider context for Hooker's work, see W. B. Patterson, 'Elizabethan Theological Polemics', in *A Companion to Richard Hooker*, ed. W. J. T. Kirby (Leiden: Brill, 2008), 89–120.
[12] Peter Lake, *Anglicans & Puritans? Presbyterian and English Conformist Thought from Whitgift to Hooker* (London: Unwin Hyman, 1988), 4–8, 25–6 argues that the term 'puritan' covers a wide variety of opinions and attitudes, preferring the term 'Presbyterian' to refer to puritans who 'espoused or defended the Presbyterian platform of government' (7). Others prefer the contemporaneous term 'precisian' to name the advanced protestant tendency towards seeking a precise biblical mandate for all human actions, such as Theodore Dwight Bozeman, *The Precisianist Strain: Disciplinary Religion and Antinomian Backlash in Puritanism to 1638* (Chapel Hill: University of North Carolina Press, 2004), 3–10. Yet, the term 'puritan' remains almost ubiquitous in scholarly use, as recognized by William Haugaard, 'Preface', in *FLE*, 6 (1): 10 n.13. This study therefore retains the term 'puritan', but appends the adjective 'radical' to denote the radical degree of religious zeal within a looser puritan sensibility exhibited by those to whom Hooker responds, especially Thomas Cartwright and Walter

radical puritans saw Scripture as normative and prescriptive in all matters, including in matters of church governance. Hooker determines from the beginning of the *Laws* to demonstrate that this radical puritan emphasis on what William Haugaard labels 'scriptural omnicompetence'[13] was theologically deficient (in mischaracterizing Scripture and in abrogating any other form of law), as well as politically dangerous (in undermining the lay ecclesiastical supremacy established by human positive law).[14]

The architecture of participation plays a key theological and polemical role in this endeavour. While Hooker only explicitly mentions participation twice in this general account of law, Book One puts law in analogical terms. Analogy indicates the omnipresence of participatory metaphysics: the various laws derive from God as the 'father of lights' and so intrinsically frame creation as a participatory analogue of eternal law.[15] Casting the 'several kindes' of law as analogues which participate in eternal law opens up a place for natural and supernatural laws to cohere. Indeed, as these various laws dispose creation to perfective ends, they thereby reveal how all things 'covet more or lesse the participation of God himselfe' as the source and site of perfection. Such participation begins with the first 'weak/extensive/exiting' paradigm (namely, creation and natural law). It also sets the end of creation as the second 'strong/intensive/returning' pattern of (re)union with God (or redemption and supernatural law). As later chapters will develop, this architecture of participation eventually allows Hooker to deflate radical puritan objections to the Elizabethan Religious Settlement, casting them as setting up their own private judgement above the authority of the Church.[16]. It also allows Hooker to frame positively the possibilities and limits of the established Church of England in promoting godliness. This part, however, explores as prolegomena how Hooker's account of law in Book One balances Dionysian mediation and Augustinian immediacy through establishing an architecture of participation in the first place.

In Book One, Hooker immediately proposes that

> because the point about which we strive is the qualitie of our *Lawes*, our first entrance hereinto cannot better be made, then with consideration of the nature of lawe in general, and of that lawe which giveth life unto all the rest, which are commendable just and good, namely the lawe whereby the Eternall himselfe doth worke. Proceeding from hence to the lawe first of nature, then of scripture, we shall

---

Travers. The term 'radical puritan' recognizes both their intense biblicism and their advocacy for presbyteral governance in ways that implicitly threatened the legal basis and established practices of the Elizabethan ecclesiastical polity.

[13] William P. Haugaard, 'Books II, III, & IV', in *The Folger Library Edition of the Works of Richard Hooker*, ed. W. Speed Hill, 7 vols (vols 1–5, Cambridge: Belknap Press, 1977–90; vol. 6, Binghamton: Belknap Press, 1993; vol. 7, Tempe: Medieval and Renaissance Texts and Studies, 1998), 6 (1): 163.

[14] See Alexander S. Rosenthal, *Crown under Law: Richard Hooker, John Locke, and the Ascent of Modern Constitutionalism* (Lanham: Lexington Books, 2008), 15–6.

[15] Hooker, *Laws*, 1:135.11–13; I.16.1.

[16] Ibid., 1:183.13–8; II.7.6. See Cargill Thompson, 'The Philosopher of the Politic Society: Richard Hooker as a Political Thinker', in *Studies in Richard Hooker*, ed. W. Speed Hill (Cleveland and London: Case Western Reserve University Press, 1972), 14. More widely on Hooker's polemicist position, see Rudolph P. Almasy, 'Rhetoric and Apologetics', in *A Companion to Richard Hooker*, ed. W. J. T. Kirby (Leiden: Brill, 2008), 121–50; and Joyce, *Anglican Moral Theology*, 45–68.

have easier accesse unto those things which come after to be debated, concerning the particular cause and question which wee have in hand.[17]

Hooker here distinguishes in effect between three *summa genera* related to law that he will develop in Book One through an essentially Thomistic lens: eternal law; natural law (covering the law of nature, angelic law and the law of reason); and divine law.[18] In order to see what might connect them, Hooker initially turns to the 'nature of lawe in general' that binds them together. Hooker gives a general definition of law (very similar to that of Aquinas) as 'that which doth assigne unto each thing the kinde, that which doth moderate the force and power, that which doth appoint the forme and measure of working, the same we terme a *Lawe*'.[19] In other words, as it is for Aquinas, law is a rule of action appropriate to the thing it directs. 'Law' here acts as a conceptual lynchpin in Hooker's teleological account of reality as inherently ordered within a universal entelechy that participates in diminished fashion in God's own perfection. For Hooker, 'all things therefore do worke after a sort according to lawe'.[20] The phrase 'after a sort' indicates an analogical relationship across types of law. On the one hand, then, law binds God and creation into a non-contrastive community. Both God and all of creation are or have such an intrinsic *ratio* or *nomos* shaping the kinds of actions appropriate to their specific natures. Yet, on the other hand 'law' also separates God and creation since it acts as an analogical (rather than univocal) term that describes the actions of created things and 'even of God himselfe' but only 'after a sort'.[21] In relation to law, Hooker notes an asymmetry in the analogy between God and creation. Creation experiences the differentiated kinds of law as either the author of law or (more commonly) as the subject of law's direction. Yet, in contrast, 'the workes and

---

[17] Hooker, *Laws*, 1:58.11–19; I.1.3.

[18] On Hooker's Thomism, see Dominiak, 'Hooker, scholasticism, Thomism, and Reformed orthodoxy', 111–19. On Hooker's complication of Aquinas's system of laws, see Daniel Westberg, 'Thomistic Law and the Moral Theology of Richard Hooker', *Catholic Philosophical Quarterly* 68 (1994): 203–14. Compare W. J. T. Kirby, 'Richard Hooker and Thomas Aquinas on defining Law', in *Aquinas Among the Protestants*, ed. Manfred Svensson and David VanDrunen (Chichester: Wiley-Blackwell, 2018), 91–108. See also: Gibbs, 'Book I', *FLE*, 6 (1): 92; Munz, *History of Thought*, 49–57; A. P. D'Entrèves, *The Medieval Contribution to Political Thought: Thomas Aquinas, Marsilius of Padua, Richard Hooker* (Oxford: Oxford University Press, 1939; repr. New York: Humanities Press, 1959), chs 5–6; David Neelands, 'Hooker on Scripture, Reason and Tradition', in *Richard Hooker and the Construction of Christian Community*, ed. A. S. McGrade (Tempe: Medieval and Renaissance Texts and Studies, 1997), 76–89; and Newey, 'Form of Reason', 5–6.

[19] Hooker, *Laws*, 1:58.26–9; I.2.2. Aquinas sees law as 'a certain rule and measure [*regula et mensura*] of acts' in *ST*, I.II.90.1 resp. Compare Hooker, *Pride*, I, in *FLE*, 5:312.8–9 in which Hooker defines law as 'an exact rule wherby humane actions are measured. The rule to measure and judge them by is the law of God'.

[20] Hooker, *Laws*, 1:58.33–59.1; I.2.3.

[21] For more on Hooker's use of analogy, see Neelands, *The Theology of Grace*, 316–25. Neelands points out that Hooker rarely uses the term 'analogy' although that does not mean he does not describe a universe analogically related to God. Hooker more commonly prefers the term 'proportion' to 'analogy', recalling Aquinas's analogy of proportionality where two or more terms are linked by a proportional relationship. Yet, Hooker's use of participation suggests a relationship different to proportionality. Since there is a causal connection between the two terms of a participatory relationship, Hooker implicitly suggests an analogy of intrinsic attribution where a perfection found in creatures exists pre-eminently in God as its source. Compare Aquinas, *ST*, I.13.5–6 for his account and defence of analogy as the proper way to predicate perfections of God and creatures.

operations of God have him both for their worker, and for the lawe whereby they are wrought'.²² Hooker locates the ontological nature of law perfectly and simply in God's self-mediated identity since the 'being of God is a kinde of lawe to his working'. In Thomist terms, God simply is co-identical to law (*per essentiam*), whereas creation has laws which participate as analogues in eternal law (*per participationem*).²³

Hooker's use of analogy strongly echoes Aquinas's thought and plays a comparable structural role in building a participatory relationship through law between God and creatures in which every separation constitutes a link.²⁴ Aquinas understands that participation has three elements.²⁵ First, a source (the analogate) possesses some perfection in a total and unrestricted fashion. Second, a subject (the analogue) possesses the same perfection, but in a limited and restricted way. Third, the subject depends on the donating source of the perfection to receive that perfection, as an effect from a cause (the suspension of the analogue from the analogate). In terms of the primary perfection of being (*esse*), for example, we can only predicate it analogically: as the primary analogate, God self-subsists and simply is (*per essentiam*) whereas creation exists as an analogue by participating in God (*per participationem*), the donating source of participated being. Aquinas appeals to participation again in his account of humankind's natural law: 'natural law is nothing other than the sharing (*participatio*) in the eternal law by intelligent creatures'.²⁶ Here, Aquinas suspends the intrinsic character of natural law (formally disposed to perfective ends) from the perfect eternal law. Natural law accordingly acts as a diminished similitude of divine government (providence, the *ratio* of eternal law).²⁷ The eternal law expresses, for Aquinas, the rational order (*ordo rationis*) of creation in the divine mind which human reason then participates in and mediates through acts of the will and through particular actions.²⁸ Aquinas sees divine law both as a remedial aid for sin, but also as a new form of participation in eternal law. Indeed, divine law acts as the supernatural revelation of God's providence, equated with the eternal law, in moral matters. It also charitably gifts the grace of the Holy Spirit, and the light of grace illuminates the created intellect such

---

²² Hooker, *Laws*, 1:58.22–59.4; I.2.1.
²³ See Kirby, 'The Neoplatonic Logic of Richard Hooker's Generic Division of Law', *Renaissance et Réforme* 22, no. 4 (1998): 49–67, esp. 56: 'God himself *is* Law, both to himself and to all other things besides.'
²⁴ See Aquinas, *ST*, I.II.90–108 for the treatise on law; and *In De Heb*, lect. 2, n.24 for a discussion of the types and structure of participation. See also Aquinas, *In duodecim libros Metaphysicorum expositio*, IV, lect.1, n. 535–543 (hereafter *In IV Met*.). English translation in *Commentary on Aristotle's Metaphysics*, trans. John P. Rowan (Notre Dame: Dumb Ox, 1995). Compare *ST*, I.13.5 resp., and *ScG*, I. c. 34, for discussions of analogical predication. On Hooker's similarity to contemporary Reformed orthodoxy, see Bradford Littlejohn, 'Hooker, Junius, and a Reformed Theology of Law', in *Richard Hooker and Reformed Orthodoxy*, ed. Scott Kindred-Barnes and W. Bradford Littlejohn (Göttingen, Bristol: Vandenhoeck & Ruprecht, 2017), 221–40. More broadly on the reclamation of scholasticism in Reformed Orthodox thought relating to the doctrine of God, see Richard A. Muller, *Post-Reformation Reformed Dogmatics*, 4 vols (Grand Rapids, MI: Baker, 2003), vol. 3, 101–15.
²⁵ W. N. Clarke, 'The Meaning of Participation in St. Thomas', *Proceedings of the American Catholic Philosophical Association* 26 (1952): 150–2.
²⁶ Aquinas, *ST*, I.II. 91.2 resp.
²⁷ Ibid., I.II. 90.1 ad.1; I-II.91.2 resp.
²⁸ M. Rhonheimer, *Natural Law and Practical Reason: A Thomist View of Moral Autonomy*, trans. Gerald Malsbary (New York: Fordham University Press, 2000), 64–70.

that the creature becomes deiform (*deiformis*).²⁹ Divine law, especially the new law of Christ, has the greatest participation in eternal law because 'nothing can approach nearer to the last end than that which is the immediate cause of our being brought to the last end'.³⁰ As will be shown, Hooker's account of law, whatever the differences of terminology, recapitulates a Thomistic architecture of participation to describe both creation and redemption as modes of participation in eternal law.

Two other features in Hooker's definition of law also echo Aquinas and compound their similarity. Like Aquinas, Hooker couches the definition of law within Aristotelian ideas of causality that emphasize the non-coercive and teleological nature of law.³¹ Hooker leads up to his general definition of law with the Aristotelian ideas that 'all things that are have some operation not violent or causall', and that 'neither doth any thing ever begin to exercise the same without some foreconceaved ende for which it worketh'. Since Hooker appeals to the Aristotelian-Thomist dictum that all things work towards some perfective telos, law acts as an internal principle of action that ensures that agents are 'made suteable fit and correspondent unto their end'.³² As a concept, law accordingly has a non-coercive character because it operates as a natural or voluntary principle that directs all things towards the perfective ends proper to their natures. Second, Hooker's definition emphasizes the essential rationality of law, akin to Aquinas's insistence that law is grounded in reason (*aliquid rationis*) and acts as a rule and measure for action (*regula et mensura*).³³ Hooker here betrays his suspicion of a crude and unmitigated voluntarism that portrays the inscrutable will of God as the root of all action and obligation, an attitude he thinks common in those advocating further ecclesiastical reform.³⁴ For Hooker, 'they erre therefore who thinke that of the will of God to do this or that, there is no reason besides his will.'³⁵ Similarly, in *A Learned Sermon of the Nature of Pride*, Hooker insists that 'a law simplie commanding or forbidding is but dead in comparison of that which expresseth the reason why it doth the one or the other.'³⁶ Against such crude voluntarism, Hooker construes law as an inherent and rational pattern that directs all things to 'the means whereby they tende to their owne perfection'.³⁷

---

[29] Aquinas, *ST*, I.12.5 resp.
[30] Ibid., I.II.106.4 resp.
[31] For Aristotle, 'violent' is opposed to 'natural' operation. Hooker casts law as an intrinsic, natural principle rather than as the external, coercive mandate of an imposing force. See Aristotle, *Nicomachean Ethics*, 1135a-1136b. English translation in *The Complete Works of Aristotle*, ed. Jonathan Barnes, 2 vols (Princeton, NJ: Princeton University Press, 1995), vol. 2, 1791-3; hereafter *Complete Works*. On Hooker's non-coercive account, see Paul E. Forte, 'Richard Hooker's Theory of Law', *Journal of Medieval and Renaissance Studies* 12 (1982): 135-41; and Joyce, *Anglican Moral Theology*, 156 following Gibbs, 'Book I', *FLE*, 6 (1): 88, who both (erroneously) see this emphasis as parting company with Reformed thought.
[32] See Aquinas, *ST*, I.44.4 resp: 'every agent acts for an end: otherwise one thing would not follow more than another from the action of an agent, unless it were by chance.'
[33] Ibid., I.II.90.1 resp.
[34] On Hooker's equivalence in this regard with other first and second-generation reformers, see Littlejohn, 'Hooker, Junius, and a Reformed Theology of Law', 223-4.
[35] Hooker, *Laws*, 1:61.18-19; I.2.5.
[36] Hooker, *Pride*, I, in *FLE*, 5:309.11-13.
[37] Hooker, *Laws*, 1:69.10; I.3.5. Hooker does not ignore, however, the importance of the divine will in moving God to action. Since rational law directs creative action, it also involves the Scotist and Thomist idea of willing most rationally (*rationabilissime*), even where the divine reason may be

For Hooker, then, the analogical concept of law forms a first principle that both unites and distinguishes the divine nature and the participatory created order. Law is a non-coercive, mediatory principle: the rational essence of law instils an intrinsic ordo directing things to their own perfection, found in God. Such a notion can be asymmetrically applied to God as well as creatures: in God, law is found *simpliciter*; and in creatures, law works through participation. Indeed, the variety of laws in creation analogously expresses the participation of the cosmos in its perfect Creator since 'for that perfection which God is, geveth perfection to that he doth'.[38] The analogical link between God and creation militates against seeing creation as an autonomous space evacuated of God. Indeed, the source and root of all law is the being of God, entailing that all creation by its very nature theonomously participates in the divine nature.[39] The gratuity of God's self-giving undergirds the mediating hierarchy of law. In other words, Dionysian mediation presupposes the priority of Augustinian immediacy. In casting law in such terms, Hooker describes what Charles Irish calls 'a process of participation' where law 'has a mediating role, in which the emanation of being through [secondary] causes results in a return to the First and Final Cause, God.'[40]

Hooker moves, then, in chapters two and three of Book One from this general, teleological definition of law into a more detailed and specific consideration of the different legal genera distinguished and held together through analogy, beginning with the eternal law co-identical with God's nature. As already noted, participation implies that some quality exists in unrestricted fashion in a primary analogate, exists in some diminished manner in an analogue, and that the analogue is causally suspended from the analogate. In legal terms, then, eternal law represents the primary analogate, 'her voice the harmony of the world', as Hooker phrases it.[41] Accordingly, Hooker determines to show 'in what maner as every good and perfect gift, so this very gift of good and perfect lawes is derived from the father of lights'.[42] Hooker's account of eternal law as the primary analogate balances on the one hand a radically Augustinian hypostatic distinction between God and creation with, on the other hand, Dionysian and Thomist ideas of dispositive hierarchy.[43] The hypostatic distinction

---

unavailable to the human intellect. Indeed, Hooker writes that God wills rationally, that is to say according to the 'counsel of his owne will' even when 'many times no reason [be] knowne to us.' See Ibid., 1:61.19–20, 23; I.2.5. Compare Aquinas, *ST*, I.II.93.4 resp. with Duns Scotus, *Ordinatio*, lib. III, dist. 7, q. 3, § 61 (ediz. Vaticana, 2006, vol. IX, 287, § 61), *Lectura*, lib. III, dist. 7, q. 3, § 77 (ediz. Vaticana, 2003, vol. XX, 214, § 77); and *Lectura*, lib. III, dist. 32, q. unica, § 37 (ediz. Vaticana, 2004, vol. XXI, 262, § 37). Pace the commentary in *FLE*, 6 (1): 482, which argues that Hooker rejects a genealogy of voluntarism from Scotus through to Luther and Calvin, Hooker therefore has Ockham more than Scotus in mind with his critique of unmitigated voluntarism.

[38] Hooker, *Laws*, 1:59.5–6; I.2.2.

[39] I take the phrases 'participated theonomy', 'theonomous' and other similar cognates from Rhonheimer, *Natural Law and Practical Reason*, 234–51. Theonomy contrasts with autonomy and heteronomy since it sees creation and God as distinct but also as related: laws are intrinsic to creatures but causally undergirded by eternal law.

[40] Irish, '"Participation of God Himselfe"', 165.

[41] Hooker, *Laws*, 1:142.9; I.16.8.

[42] Ibid., 1:135.11–13; I.16.1.

[43] See W. J. T. Kirby, 'Law Makes the King: Richard Hooker on Law and Princely Rule', in *A New Companion to English Renaissance Literature and Culture*, ed. Michael Hattaway (Oxford: Blackwell, 2010), 274–88.

secures God's transcendence, increases the distance between eternal law and created laws, and obviates mediation. The dispositive hierarchy in turn lessens the distance by emphasising God's immanent causality within creation, what Kirby calls 'the common participation of the manifold derivative species of law in their one source'.[44]

Eternal law acts as the monistic ground (the 'highest wellspring and fountaine') from which springs variety, the derivation of the many from the one, or created hierarchy from 'the first originall cause' (*archē*). It also frames the dispositive goal of creation (*telos*) for transcendent (re)union.[45] Since 'law' acts as an analogical term, Hooker views eternal law from two very different standpoints: either as a consubstantial quality of God's nature (the *opera Dei ad intra*), or from the perspective of creation as it participates in God (the *opera Dei ad extra*).[46] Hooker's account of eternal law is therefore markedly Dionysian as he remarks upon the apophatic and cataphatic aspects of knowing God. On the one hand, 'dangerous it were for the feeble braine of man to wade farre into the doings of the most High' since 'our soundest knowledge is to know that we know him not as in deed he is, neither can know him: and our safest eloquence concerning him is our silence'.[47] For Hooker, the 'naturall, necessary, and internall operations of God', such as the mystery of Trinitarian relations, are accordingly 'without the compasse of my present intent'. The transcendent simplicity of the divine nature exceeds intellectual comprehension. On the other hand, however, we can apprehend something through rational reflection, experience and divine revelation about God's creation and governance of the world since 'such operations ... have their beginning and being by a voluntarie purpose, wherewith God hath eternally decreed when and how they should be'. As such, Hooker distinguishes between the ultimately apophatic operation of God's nature ad intra and the cataphatic workings of God ad extra within creation. Indeed, 'that little thereof which we darkly apprehend, we admire, the rest with religious ignorance we humbly and meekly adore'.[48]

The twofold perspective of ad intra and ad extra leads Hooker uniquely to depart from scholastic tradition (in which eternal law is undivided) and posit a 'first eternall lawe' and a 'second law eternall'.[49] The first eternal law describes eternal law from God's perspective and secures the radical otherness of God, the hypostatic distinction between God and creation. The internal operations of God contain both the natural or necessary operations of the Trinity and the voluntary operations that have to do

---

[44] W. J. T. Kirby, 'Reason and Law', in *A Companion to Richard Hooker*, ed. W. J. T. Kirby (Leiden: Brill, 2008), 254.
[45] Hooker, *Laws*, 1:111.21–5; I.11.1.
[46] See Richard A. Muller, *Dictionary of Latin and Greek Theological Terms* (Grand Rapids, MI: Baker, 1985), 211–12. The distinction and relation between the internal and external operations of God have a contested history in medieval and Reformed thought. See Muller, *Post-Reformation Reformed Dogmatics*, vol. 3, 44, 78–81, 287–90, 450–75.
[47] Hooker, *Laws*, 1:59.6–19; I.2.2.
[48] Ibid., 1:62.10–11; I.2.5.
[49] Ibid., 1:63.27–9; I.3.1. See Gibbs, 'Book I', in *FLE*, 6 (1): 98 n.30 on the possible roots of the distinction in scholastic thought between God's absolute power (*potentia absoluta*) and ordained power (*potentia ordinata*); Kirby, 'Reason and Law', 252 on the account representing an adaptation of *logos* theology; and Miller, *Vision of God*, 51–3, 58–9 on the possible similarity with Byzantine theology. On the significance of this distinction, see W. J. T. Kirby, ' "Divine Offspring": Richard Hooker's Neoplatonic Account of Law and Causality', *Perichoresis* 13, no. 1 (2015): 3–15.

with 'the law eternall which God himselfe hath made to himselfe, and therby worketh all things wherof he is the cause and author'.[50] While God's necessary and internal actions must be marked by *ratio* since 'God's being is a kinde of law to his working', the divine nature exceeds human comprehension, even in relation to God's voluntary actions in eternal law. God remains *causa sui* and his metaphysical simplicity causes the multiplicity of creation but sharply distinguishes God from it. Thus, Hooker defines the first eternal law in terms of the creative order of God's voluntary decision to share participated being: 'this law therfore we may name eternall, being that order which God before all ages hath set down with himselfe, for himselfe to do all things by'.[51] The emphasis on the radical difference between God and creation, as well as the gratuity of God's voluntary action, reflects what Kirby calls 'a marked Augustinian tendency of [Hooker's] thought, a general theological bent which he shares with other magisterial Reformers'.[52]

Yet, since God creates the cosmos, the latter participates in the first eternal law in some way. Such participation leads Hooker to claim that there is a second eternal law, namely, 'that which [God] ... hath set downe as expedient to be kept by all his creatures'.[53] The second eternal law describes eternal law from the perspective of creation, the pattern of legal actions internal to the created beings subject to participated eternal law. This second eternal law entails a necessary hierarchical subordination between the creature and the Creator. Yet, the second eternal law suspends creation from God and so lessens the distance: the hierarchy of being commonly participates in eternal law, co-identical with God's perfection. As Kirby puts it, 'in effect the second eternal law renders the participation of the manifold forms of law in their eternal source simultaneously both more transcendent and more immanent, thus short-circuiting the gradual, dispositive linkage of derivative creatures with their creative original' typical of earlier scholastic thought.[54] This second eternal law concurs with (and recasts into an Augustinian framework) the Thomistic legal and teleological tradition whereby the rational providence of eternal law of God moves 'all things to their due end', and in which 'all laws insofar as they share in right reason to that extent derive from the eternal law'.[55] While the first eternal law is concerned with 'being' (*esse*, co-identical with and found perfectly in God), the second eternal law revolves around 'becoming' (as creation dynamically receives and seeks its variegated and diminished perfection of *esse* through participation).

Indeed, the legal work of God ad intra and ad extra remain linked through the analogical notion of participated law. The fundamentally unknowable mystery of God's monistic nature immediately generates a Neoplatonic procession of manifold laws that frame and order creation so that it returns to God as the source and site

---

[50] Hooker, *Laws*, 1:62.1–2; I.2.5.
[51] Ibid., 1:63.1–3; I.2.6.
[52] Kirby, '"Divine Offspring"', 9.
[53] Hooker, *Laws*, 1:63.8–9; I.3.1.
[54] Kirby, '"Divine Offspring"', 9.
[55] Aquinas, *ST*, I.II. 93.1 resp. where the 'Divine Wisdom, as moving all things to their due end, bears the character of law'; and *ST*, I.II.93.3 resp. where 'the eternal law is the plan of government in the Chief Governor.' See *Laws*, 1:64 s for Hooker's quotation of Aquinas' following articles 4–6.

of perfection.[56] Hooker explicates the causal link between the ad intra and ad extra, between the primary analogate (God) and participatory analogue (creation), through the medieval transcendentals.[57] The transcendentals have their genesis in Plato (following Parmenides) who considers the co-extensive properties of being-as-such. In turn, Aristotle coins the term 'transcendental' to describe those properties of being that transcend the ten categories, that is to say all the possible things that can be the subject or predicate of a proposition. Of all the medieval thinkers who comment upon the transcendentals, Thomas Aquinas gives them greatest and most influential coverage.[58] Properly speaking, the transcendentals are convertible terms for 'being' (*esse*), which is the ground of possibility for all subsequent perfections. Of particular importance for Hooker are the 'one' (*unum*), the 'good' (*bonum*), the 'beautiful' (*pulchrum*), and the 'true' (*verum*). 'One' adds to 'being' the notion of intelligible unity; 'good' adds to 'being' the notion of plenitude; 'beauty' adds to 'being' the idea of attraction; and 'truth' adds to 'being' the idea of veridical correspondence between a thing and its form. Hooker follows Aquinas and treats the transcendentals as they relate to God's nature, as well as to how they relate to human desires to share in them. As human beings desire perfection, so too do they desire the transcendental qualities found most completely in God.

In order to understand how creation participates in the transcendental properties of eternal law through the mediation of the legal pattern of immanent causality, Hooker looks in the two directions of eternal law. First, he looks at the perfections found in the divine nature. Second, he considers how God's perfection acts as the efficient, exemplary and final cause of all created perfections.[59] This second viewpoint describes the participatory ontology of creation, the suspension of all that exists from God as a participatory analogue. Accordingly, Hooker begins his account of eternal law by explicating in what manner God ad intra is the source and site of all perfections, the primary analogate of participation. Two of the convertible transcendentals in particular – *esse* and *unum* – form God's co-identical, essential perfections As Hooker considers God's nature, he emphasizes that 'Our God is one [unum], or rather verie Onenesse, and mere unitie'.[60] Hooker's account here densely fuses together Christian creedal monotheism with a Neoplatonic emphasis on unity as the goal of creative and intelligible activity.[61] Hooker then emphasizes God's simplicity in ontological terms.

---

[56] See Kirby, 'Neoplatonic Logic', 48–52.
[57] See Patrick D. M. Patterson, 'Hooker's Apprentice: God, Entelechy, Beauty, and Desire in Book One of Richard Hooker's Lawes of Ecclesiastical Politie', *Anglican Theological Review* 84, no. 4 (2002): 961–98.
[58] See J. Aertsen, *Medieval Philosophy and the Transcendentals: The Case of Thomas Aquinas* (Leiden: Brill, 1996).
[59] Hooker here follows Aquinas's attempt to marry Platonic participation with Aristotelian causality. See Loyer, *L'Anglicanisme*, 373–9.
[60] Hooker, *Laws*, 1:59.20–4; I.2.2.
[61] See Proclus, *Elements of Theology*, Proposition 21; in Dodds, 25: 'Every order has its beginning in a monad and proceeds to a manifold co-ordinate therewith; and the manifold in any order may be carried back to a single monad.' Kirby, 'The Neoplatonic Logic', 51 and 61 n.7 lists as further examples the following: Plotinus, *Enneads*, III.8.7, in Mackenna, 240 ('It is certain, also, that as the Firsts exist in vision all other things must be straining towards the same condition; the starting point is, universally, the goal'); Plotinus, *Enneads*, V.4.1 in Mackenna, 387 on the One as origin; and Plotinus, *Enneads*, VI.9.3, in Mackenna, 538 on the One as end; Pseudo-Dionysius, *Celestial*

Recalling Aristotelian-Thomistic arguments, Hooker states that God is essentially self-subsisting being (*esse*) who is completely in act (*purus actus*) and no way in potentiality.[62] Such essentially self-subsisting being constitutes and self-mediates its very own *ratio*, a kind of law to its own working and the unitary source of all created laws.

Hooker therefore identifies the essential ontological plenitude and unity of God as the source and summit of cosmic order. Turning from the nature of God ad intra towards God's creative acts ad extra, Hooker joins the transcendentals with a Neoplatonic structure of *monē-proodos-epistrophē* and Aristotelian physics. Here, God's eternal law acts as an efficient, formal and final cause in creation, that is to say the existential and formal ground of participation in God.[63] Thus, since the simple being of God is co-identical with law, God acts as the unitary First Cause for the genesis of the world through a downward, creative procession of being contained under specific created forms (the efficient and formal cause). God also acts as the final cause to which all things tend through a legal entelechy of desire for the original divine unity and plenitude of being. God's transcendent action operates, then, through mediate, intrinsic causes, honouring the suspended middle of creation. Hooker enumerates two principles behind such participation, both of which follow Aquinas's idea that the cause remains in the thing caused (*causa est in causato*).[64] First, Hooker argues that there is a diminished similitude between effect and cause: 'everie originall cause imparteth it selfe unto those things which come of it.' Second, participation primarily is ontological: 'whatsoever taketh beinge from anie other the same is after a sorte in that which giveth it beinge.' For Hooker, participation therefore describes the causal ordering of the cosmos towards God as creative source and perfective end since 'every effect doth after a sort conteine, at least wise resemble the cause from which it proceedeth.'[65]

Hooker recognizes a consonance between non-Christian and Christian sources that affirm God as efficient and formal cause of participation. In one direction, Hooker points towards 'the wise and learned among the verie Heathens themselves', such as Homer, Mercurius Trismegistus, Anaxagoras, Plato and the Stoics, all of whom recognize 'some First Cause, whereupon originallie the being of all things dependeth.'[66]

Hierarchy, 120B, in *Pseudo-Dionysius: Complete Works*, 145 ('Inspired by the father, each procession of the Light spreads itself generously toward us, and in its power to unify, it stirs us by lifting us up. It returns us back to the oneness and deifying simplicity of the Father who gathers us in'); and Augustine, *Confessiones*, 13.4–5, in *Nicene and Post-Nicene Fathers*, ed. Philip Schaff and Henry Wace, first series, 14 vols (Peabody: Hendrickson, 1994), vol. 1, 191.

[62] Hooker, *Laws*, 1:72.26–30; I.5.1. 'Act' and 'potency' are technical terms derived from Aristotle's distinction, transmitted by Aquinas, between ἐν δυνάμει and ἐν ἐνεργείᾳ. See Aristotle, *Metaphysics*, Book IX.1–8, 1045b-1050a; in *Complete Works*, vol. 2, 1651–60. Compare Aquinas, *ST*, I.3.7 resp.

[63] Aristotle identifies four causes: formal, final, efficient and material. See Aristotle, *Physics*, Book II.1–9, 192a-200b; in *Complete Works*, vol. 1, 329–42. Hooker omits mention of the material cause, but stands within typical scholastic use of Aristotelian causality in the medieval and early modern periods, including that of scholastic theologians within Reformed orthodoxy. See T. Theo J. Pliezier and Maarten Wisse, '"As the Philosopher Says": Aristotle', in *Introduction to Reformed Scholasticism*, ed. Willem J. Van Asselt (Grand Rapids, MI: Reformation Heritage Books, 2011), 26–45, esp. 39–40.

[64] Hooker, *Laws*, 2:234.33–235.3; V.56.1. Compare Aquinas, *ST*, I.44.3. Aquinas argues that God's ideas act as the exemplary, effective and final cause of created things and those creaturely essences participate in the divine mind as an effect participates in its cause.

[65] Ibid., 1:73.7–8; I.5.1. See also *Pride*, III, in *FLE*, 5:341.3–9.

[66] Hooker, *Laws*, 1:59.33–60.14; I.2.3.

In all cases, these pagan authors see the First Cause as a self-mediating, legal and rational principle.[67] Like Aquinas, Hooker then blends in Book Five the Neoplatonic language of self-diffusion and *influentia* with Aristotelian ideas of God as the efficient cause of being: 'God hath his influence into the very essence of all things, without which influence of Deity supporting them their utter annihilation could not choose but follow.'[68] In a Christian vein, Hooker similarly sees in Book One that 'from the Father, by the Sonne, through the Spirit all things are.'[69] In other words, all created forms are said to be from the Father, by the Son and through the Holy Spirit, and thereby analogically participate in the divine being and unity of the Trinity as a diminished similitude.

In terms of final causality, 'the generall end of Gods external working, is the exercise of his most glorious and most abundant vertue: Which abundance doth shew it selfe in varietie.'[70] Hooker again blends non-Christian thought with Christian claims in order to detail how the many share in a unitary source. Following Aristotle, a thing's formal cause determines its end or final cause.[71] As something seeks its formal cause, determined by its nature and mediated through intrinsic laws, it also vicariously participates in the perfect final cause, namely God. As the final cause, God directs creation to its share in the perfection of being through participation in eternal law, co-identical with God's being and unity. It is the sense of God as the final cause that leads Hooker to give a thoroughly Thomistic account of the 'good' (*bonum*), a teleological transcendental at which all forms aim and desire to attain.[72] The 'good' adds to *esse* the notion of perfective fullness such that all perfections 'are conteyned under the generall name of *Goodnesse*'.[73] Since God is *purus actus* and self-subsisting being, then God's nature is also co-identical with the 'good' and 'there can bee no

---

[67] Ibid., 1:60.11–14; I.2.3: 'They all confesse therfore in the working of that first cause, that *counsell* is used, *reason* followed, a *way* observed, that is to say, constant *order* and *law* is kept, whereof it selfe must needs be author unto itself.'

[68] Ibid., 2:236.7–13; V.56.5. The Neoplatonic language of 'influence' and 'causality' can be found in Proclus, *Elements of Theology*, Proposition 35; in Dodds, 37–8, who summarizes the process of emanation and return as follows: 'every effect remains in its cause, proceeds from it, and returns to it.' Compare Aquinas, *ST*, 1.65.3 resp., who follows Proclus in arguing that the causality of higher forms operate through lower forms, even if covertly, such that 'the thing that underlies primarily all things [i.e. Being] belongs properly to the causality of the supreme cause [i.e. God]'.

[69] Hooker, *Laws*, 1:59.28–9; I.2.2.

[70] Ibid., 1:61.6–8; I.2.4.

[71] Ibid., 1:67.y; I.3.4: 'Form in other creatures is a thing proportionable to the soul in living creatures. Sensible it is not, nor otherwise discernable than only by effects. According to the diversity of inward forms, things of the world are distinguished into their kinds.' Forms, or formal causes, are that which give things their being. Accordingly, 'form' corresponds with 'law' in that they both relate to proper ends, the first as formally establishing and the second as directing a creature towards its perfecting telos.

[72] On goodness, see Aquinas, *ST*, I.II.94.2 resp: 'the good has the intelligibility of an end'; *De Ver*, 21.1 'all things found to have the criterion of an end at the same time have the criterion of a good'; and *ST*, I.5.1 resp. 'everything is perfect insofar as it is actual.' For Aquinas, essences are dispositional properties that tend from potency to act insofar as they are realized in or by the substantial subject. Since actuality is perfection, the 'end' is the point at which the dispositional properties of natural substances reach their fulfilment as a likeness to their divine cause. Thus, Aquinas variously describes the end as perfect and as 'good', meaning a diminished similitude of divine ontological plenitude.

[73] Hooker, *Laws*, 1:73.2–3; I.5.1.

goodnesse desired which proceedeth not from God himselfe, as from the supreme cause of all things'.[74] Hooker here affirms the integral goodness of all creation: Hooker parses 'good' in terms of participatory 'being', which all things enjoy to some kind or degree since God is 'the supreme cause of all things'. Transcendental goodness lends to 'being' an ecstatic quality characteristic of participatory metaphysics. As the last chapter showed, participation (*methexis*) means to strive for or be in pursuit of something else, in this case 'being'. For Hooker, a thing's form ecstatically directs it to perfective ends, rendered as 'good' because they qualitatively add to participated being. All things therefore 'covet more or lesse the participation of God himselfe' as the source and site of all goodness.[75] With the outward motion of being emanating from God, beings participate in their efficient cause; in the return to God, things seek their final cause through their formal constitution. Form or law suspends creation from, and ecstatically directs creation back towards, participation in God's goodness.

Hooker establishes, then, the first eternal law as the apophatic fount of the manifold forms of law understood by rational creatures under the aspect of the cataphatic second eternal law. The orders of created laws that participate in eternal law fall under two genera for Hooker: natural (which contains species of physical, celestial and rational law) and revealed. Human laws straddle these two genera, reflecting that they exist under both types. Indeed, Peter Munz perceptively describes how, for Hooker as for Aquinas, human laws represent 'nothing but the rational application to concrete and sometimes varying conditions of the general principles of natural law',[76] and (in Christian societies) such particular determinations must accord with Scripture.[77] Hooker accordingly writes of the architectonic suspension of various laws from eternal law:

> Now that lawe which as it is laid up in the bosome of God, they call *eternall*, recyveth according unto the different kinds of things which are subject unto it different and sundry kinds of names. That part of it which ordereth natural agents, we call usually *natures* law; that which Angels doe clearely behold, and without any swarving observe is a law *coelestiall* and heavenly; the law of *reason* that which bindeth creatures reasonable in this world, and with which by reason they most plainly perceive themselves bound; that which bindeth them, and is not knowen but by speciall revelation from God, *Divine* law; *humane* lawe that which out of the law either of reason or of God, men probablie gathering to be expedient, they make it a law. All things therfore, which are as they ought to be, are conformed unto *this second law eternall*, and even those things which to this eternall law are not conformable, are notwithstanding in some sort ordered by *the first eternall lawe*.[78]

---

[74] Ibid., 1:73.5–7; I.5.2. Hooker stands within a Thomistic tradition again. Aquinas, *ST*, I.6.1 resp. writes: 'All things, by desiring their own perfection, desire God Himself, inasmuch as all things are similitudes of the divine being.'

[75] Hooker, *Laws*, 1:73.10–4; I.5.2.

[76] Munz, *History of Thought*, 54. See Hooker, *Laws*, 1:95.27–110.20; I.10.1–15.

[77] Hooker, *Laws*, 1:237.21–29; III.9.2. For this principle, Hooker cites Aquinas, *ST*, I.II.95.3.

[78] Hooker, *Laws*, 1:63.14–29; I.3.1.

Hooker recognizes the paradox that the eternal law, properly speaking, remains inexplicably 'laid up in the bosome of God', and yet such eternal law 'readeth it selfe to the world' through a pattern of legal causality.[79] The two participatory genera of 'natural law' and 'divine law' are the patterns of such divine action within creation. Although we are 'neither able nor worthy to open and look into' the book of eternal law, God gratuitously self-discloses and shares his nature when he suspends creation from eternal law as a diminished similitude.[80] In both natural and revealed law, then, God accommodates himself to the finite capacity of created forms. As such, the apophatic, transcendent divine nature remains paradoxically 'always before our eyes' since we are capable of discerning immanent divine causality in our own intrinsic forms and in the historical divine self-disclosure.[81] Natural law images the extensive participation of God in creation. Divine law portrays the intensive participation of God in redemption. Unpacking each of these legal genera in turn unveils how Hooker's twin Platonisms continue to form an architecture of participation holding immediacy and mediation in productive tension.

Hooker turns in chapters three through ten of Book One from the primary analogate of participatory metaphysics (eternal law) to the analogue of creation (the natural law tradition). Indeed, Hooker's take on the natural law tradition represents the first way in which eternal law 'reads' or mediates itself into the world, the way in which God adapts his influence to our capacities. Hooker suspends the mediating legal orders of creation from the immediate influence of God as subordinate instrumental causes that participate in their divine efficient cause. As such, the participatory analogue of natural law exhibits a diminished likeness to the order of eternal law as it is causally suspended from (and seeks a unitive return to) the same eternal law. This Dionysian *lex divinitatis* forges all of creation together in a chain of being which participates in God as the highest cause.[82] Hooker considers in turn each of these three legal species (the natural, celestial and rational) contained under the *summa genera* of natural law. The ecstatic quality of participation as a striving towards something sets desire as a watermark stamped through Hooker's account of the two hierarchical extremes of the participated second eternal law, namely, both 'natures law' and the 'law cœlestiall and heavenly'.[83] The former covers laws that govern non-rational and non-voluntary creatures as they intuitively desire natural ends, a kind of precursor to the modern idea of physical science. The latter considers the laws that govern the 'immaterial and

---

[79] Ibid., 1:136.14; I.16.2.
[80] Ibid., 1:62.11; I.2.5.
[81] Ibid., 1:136.4–15; I.16.2.
[82] See Ibid., 3:331.19–332.1; VIII.2.1 where Hooker paraphrases the *lex divinitatis* in the following manner: 'Order is a gradual disposition …. [God] requireth for ever this to be kept as a law, that wheresoever there is a coagmentation of many, the lowest be knit to the highest by that which being interjacent may cause each to cleave unto other, and so all to continue one.' In Hooker's *Autograph Notes*, in FLE, 3:494.2–12, he refers to the Christian Neoplatonism of Pseudo-Dionysius as his source: '*Lex itaque divinitatis est infima per media ad suprema reduci*, inquit B. Dionysius' [And so it is a divine law, says St. Dionysius, for the lowest things to be led back to the highest by those that are intermediate]. See W. J. T. Kirby, 'Creation and Government: Eternal Law as the fountain of laws in Richard Hooker's Ecclesiastical Polity', in *Divine Creation in Ancient, Medieval, and Early Modern Thought*, ed. Willemien Otten, Walter Hannam and Michael Treschow (Leiden: Brill, 2007), 405–23.
[83] Hooker, *Laws*, 1:63.18, 20; I.1.3.

intellectual' angelic orders geared to the supernatural vision of God (*visio dei*) that satiates their cognitive desire.[84] Thus, Hooker moves from the 'footstoole to the throne of God' in order to emphasize both the universality of law and also the saturation of the material and immaterial worlds with a logic of desire that aims at perfection within the bounds of particular forms.[85] Hooker structurally places the human law of reason between these two extremes in order to show that humankind shares non-voluntary and voluntary, material and immaterial, physical and intellectual types of participation in eternal law. As all these species of natural law share a common logic of desire to share in the convertible transcendentals of being (particularly *unum*, *bonum* and *pulchrum*), both the material and immaterial creation are 'sociable partes united into one bodie'.[86] Participation thereby displays a mereological aspect: the varied forms of creation naturally tend towards order, harmony, proportion and goodness pre-eminently caused by and found in God.[87]

Beginning at the 'footstoole', Hooker (like Aquinas) broadly intends 'natures lawe' to 'meane that manner of working which God hath set for each created thing to keep'.[88] More specifically, Hooker means the term to refer to 'naturall agents, which keepe the law of their kind unwittingly, as the heavens and elements of the world, which can do no otherwise then they do'.[89] Such physical, non-cognitive laws of nature participate as a diminished similitude of 'what the eternall lawe of God is concerning things natural'.[90] Participation in eternal law constitutes natural order and stability in the universe. Hooker paraphrases Arnobius of Sicca, suggesting that the whole cosmos would collapse if it were to stray from the order and rule of the law of nature: 'Now if nature should intermit her course, and leave altogether, though it were but for a while, the observation of her own laws ... what would become of man himselfe, whom these things now do all serve?'[91] Indeed, the laws of nature asymmetrically depend upon the perpetual stability and *ratio* of eternal law for both their created content and their perfecting government.[92]

Hooker expresses the government of eternal law over nature within a Neoplatonic structure of procession and reversion (*exitus-reditus* or *monē-proodos-epistrophē*) through which created things naturally desire and pursue the transcendentals of being, unity and goodness. In terms of the production (*exitus*) of the cosmos, Hooker draws an analogy between the participation of the law of nature in eternal law and the production of art. Hooker appeals to the image of God as an 'artist' or 'workman',

---

[84] Hooker, *Laws*, 1:69.25; I.4.1.
[85] Ibid., 1:69.22–3; I.4.1. I take the phrase 'logic of desire' from Nicholas E. Lombardo, *The Logic of Desire: Aquinas on Emotion* (Washington: Catholic University of America Press, 2011).
[86] Hooker, *Laws*, 1:69.11–12; I.3.5.
[87] Again, Hooker has a Thomistic character here with his mereology (i.e. the theory of parthood relations). See Michael Baur, 'Law and Natural Law', in *The Oxford Handbook of Aquinas*, ed. Brian Davies and Eleanore Stump (Oxford: Oxford University Press, 2014), 238–54.
[88] Hooker, *Laws*, 1:64.3–5; I.3.2. Compare Aquinas, *ST*, I.II.91.2 ad 3 where non-rational creatures share in the eternal law by 'inward moving principles', the innate tendencies to certain acts and ends.
[89] Ibid., 1:64.4–8; I.3.2.
[90] Ibid., 1:65.12–13; I.3.2.
[91] Ibid., 1:65.20–66.4; I.3.2. See Lee Gibbs, 'The Source of the Most Famous Quotation from Richard Hooker's Law of Ecclesiastical Polity', *Sixteenth Century Journal* 21, no.1 (1990): 77–86.
[92] Hooker, *Laws*, 1:66.27–67.20; I.3.4.

common in other Neoplatonic and Christian writers, to describe how nature proceeds from the perfect, divine creative source.[93] Hooker writes:

> Notwithstanding with nature it commeth sometimes to passes as with arte ....Those things which nature is said to do, are by divine arte performed, using nature as an instrument.... Nature therefore is nothing else but Gods instrument .... [U]nto us there is one only guide of all agents naturall, and he both the creator and the worker of all in all.[94]

In this passage, Hooker follows Aquinas and distinguishes between the First Cause (God as 'creator-worker') and secondary or 'instrumental' causes (the 'divine arte' of created forms) in order to subsume all activity in creation under the legislative power of the eternal law.[95] Hooker here follows medieval and early modern discussions of Aristotelian causality, including those typically found in Reformed scholasticism. The instrumental cause is a subordinate efficient cause. In this case, describing nature as an instrumental cause guards its integrity: natural forms are not merely passive recipients of God as their efficient First Cause, but enjoy the participatory influence of God's action in their very being. Both the first perfection of *esse* (from God as efficient cause) and the subsequent, secondary perfections (from the instrumental, formal acts of nature) have their source and reference in God. Order, regularity, proportion and the consonance of instrumental causes with the First Cause reveal, for Hooker, that 'nature hath some director of infinite knowledge to guide her in all her ways'.[96] They also show that the space between the creative exit from and redemptive return to God does not evacuate natural agency but honours the suspended middle in its determinate becoming.

Hooker then turns to the perfective return (*reditus*) of nature to its unitive source. The law of nature stems from 'the setled stabilitie of divine understanding....tearmed by the name of Providence'.[97] Hooker rejects the notion that participation consists of creation imitating 'exemplary draughts or patterns....subsisting in the bosome of the highest'.[98] Hooker accordingly embraces Aristotelian entelechy rather than Platonic

---

[93] Ibid., 1:68.25; I.3.4. Hooker refers to God as a 'workman', akin to the Platonic and Stoic name for the Maker of the world (the demiurge of Plato's *Timaeus*). The 'artist' metaphor also recalls Aquinas, *ST*, I.II.93.1 resp. where Aquinas groups art (*ars*), exemplar (*exemplar*), idea (*idea*) and law (*ratio*) together. Here, Aquinas compares the eternal law of God with the exemplar an artist has when he produces a work of art. Pauline Westerman conceptually situates 'exemplar' within medieval theories of art: an exemplar acts as no mere conventional pattern that one copies, but as a criterion to distinguish whether or not a work of art, as a whole, is suitable and proportionate for its purpose, that is to say whether or not it corresponds harmoniously with what the artist intended. See Pauline Westerman, *The Disintegration of Natural Law Theory: Aquinas to Finnis* (New York: Brill 1997), 26–30.

[94] Hooker, *Laws*, 1:66.6–7; 1:68.18–69.5; I.3.3–3.4.

[95] The distinction of causes is Thomist in tone. See Thomas Aquinas, *Compendium Theologiae ad Fratrem Reginaldum*, 17.10. English translation in *Compendium of Theology*, trans. Cyril Vollert (St Louis: Herder, 1947). There, Aquinas argues that 'everything that is moved by another is a sort of instrument of the first mover'.

[96] Hooker, *Laws*, 1:67.15–16; I.3.4.

[97] Ibid., 1:68.6–11; I.3.4. Compare Hooker, *Autograph Notes*, in *FLE*, 3:527.12–8: '*Operatio Dei ad extra est duplex: Creatio. Gubernatio*' [God's external operation is double: creation, government].

[98] Hooker, *Laws*, 1:66.31–67.3; I.3.4.

form. Intrinsic laws act as entelechies and are the means, an 'original draught',[99] through which creatures act purposively but theonomously participate in God, 'some director of infinite knowledge to guide her in all her ways'.[100] Thus, creation is neither autonomous (that is to say, evacuated of divine activity), nor is it heteronomous (that is to say, arbitrarily subject to the divine will). Rather, creation remains theonomous, meaning that created forms instrumentally participate in, and are suspended from, a providentially ordered eternal law.

The internal principles of law direct all things, both non-rational and rational, to particular perfective ends that are participatory similitudes of divine, transcendental perfections. In an account reminiscent of Aquinas, they do so through a natural pattern of desires, a logic that motivates action towards perfection. Here, 'desire' describes what Sarah Coakley defines as 'the physical, emotional, or intellectual longing that is directed towards something or someone wanted'.[101] For Aquinas, natural law participates in eternal law through appetites, that is to say natural inclinations that work as the 'inner principle of motion' directed towards naturally perfective ends.[102] These perfective ends are parsed as 'good' and natural dispositive desires work as a physical (and in the case of rational creatures, psychic) motor to move a creature from inclination to action. Thus, both rational and non-rational creatures orient themselves through natural desire to goodness and 'participate in the divine reason by way of obedience'.[103] Similarly, for Hooker, desire stems from all created things being 'somewhat in possibilitie', which is to say as not yet fully actualized or fulfilled in their potential quality of existence.[104] Desire works as an existential motor driving the ecstatic, formal move from becoming to being through the pursuit of perfective ends.

Like Aquinas, Hooker especially understands this 'becoming' through the medieval transcendental 'goodness', the perfective actuality of 'being'.[105] For Aquinas, goodness evokes appetitive desire: 'the reason that something is good is that it is desirable . . . Goodness and being are the same in actuality, but goodness as such involves the idea of desirability.'[106] Similarly, Hooker notes two 'degrees' of possible 'goodnesse', the 'good' (*bonum*) describing that transcendental which all things desire, namely, the plenitude of being (*esse*) which is co-identical with God's nature. First, all things desire 'the continuance of their being', that is to say, to 'be like unto God in being ever', mainly through survival and propagation. This first desire constitutes participation in being (*esse*), the ground for all other possible perfections, and which is only found absolutely in God as *ipsum esse*. 'The next degree of goodnesse,' Hooker writes, revolves around

---

[99] Ibid., 1:66.31–68.15; I.3.4.
[100] Ibid., 1:67.20–5; I.3.4.
[101] Sarah Coakley, *God, Sexuality, and the Self: An Essay 'On The Trinity'* (Cambridge: Cambridge University Press, 2013), 346.
[102] Aquinas, *ST*, I.II. 93.6 resp; I.II. 94.2 resp. The idea of appetite recurs throughout the *Summa Theologiae*. See *ST*, I.II.8.1: 'Appetite is nothing other than an inclination toward something, something that is both similar and suited to that which desires it.'
[103] Ibid., I.II. 93.5 ad. 2.
[104] Hooker, *Laws*, 1:72.29–30; I.5.1.
[105] Ibid., 1:73.2–74.15; I.5.1–3.
[106] Aquinas, *ST*, I.5.1. See Jan A. Aertsen, 'The Convertibility of Being and Good in St. Thomas Aquinas', *New Scholasticism* 59 (1985): 449–70.

'resemblaunce with God' through 'the constancie and excellencie of those operations which belong unto their kinde', namely, consistency for non-rational agents (to imitate immutability) and excellence in the knowledge of truth and exercise of virtue (for rational agents to imitate God's 'absolute exactness'). This participation in God remains essentially Trinitarian in character such that, as Miller puts it, 'creation is the result of the economic, or outward, life and work of the Trinity'.[107] Just as all things participate in God as effects in their highest cause, so too do all things in some way share in the Father as 'goodness', in the Son as 'wisdom' ordering all things, and in the 'power' of the Spirit as an end.[108] Participation therefore has a mereological aspect: it describes both the derivation of the many from the one, and the parthood relations between created forms that share in, and are united under, desire for the common good derivable from God. He writes that

> lawe directeth them [i.e. natural agents] in the meanes whereby they tende to their owne perfection: So likewise another law there is, which toucheth them as they are sociable partes united into one bodie, a lawe which bindeth them each to serve unto others good, and to preferre the good of the whole before whatsoever their owne particular.[109]

Perfection is the end of the law of nature, and perfection retains an essentially social or relational character, whether horizontally across creation or vertically with God.

Hooker turns from this 'footstoole' to the 'throne of God' in order to discuss the cognitive and rational participation in God as it is found in the immaterial angels. As in his account of nature's law, Hooker's analysis of angelic law combines an entelechy of desire with the wider social character of his legal teleology. The angelic orders are directed by the inherent principles of celestial law to certain desirable ends, namely, the transcendentals of being (*esse*), goodness (*bonum*), and, for the first time, beauty (*pulchrum*). Hooker begins his account of celestial law by noting how God acts as the source and end of desire for transcendental perfections:

> God which mooveth meere naturall agents as an efficient onely, doth otherwise move intellectuall creatures and especially his holy Angels. For beholding the face of God, in admiration of so great excellencie they all adore him; and being rapt with the love of his beautie [*pulchrum*], they cleave inseparably for ever unto him. Desire to resemble him in goodness [*bonum*] maketh them unweariable, and even unsatiable in their longing to doe by all meanes all maner good unto all the creatures of God, but especially unto the children of men .... Angelicall actions may therefore be reduced unto these three generall kindes; first, most delectable love arising from the visible apprehension of the puritie, glory, and beautie of God ... ; second, adoration grounded upon the evidence of the greatnes of God, on whom they see how all things depende; thirdly, imitation bred by the presence of

---

[107] Miller, *Vision of God*, 59.
[108] Hooker, *Laws*, 2:237.10–13; V.56.5.
[109] Ibid., 1:69.9–20; I.3.5.

his exemplary goodnes, who ceaseth not before them daily to fill heaven and earth with the rich treasures of most free and undeserved grace.[110]

Rational agents like angels enjoy a cognitive participation in God: the spiritual sight of God (*visio dei*) properly signals intellectual apprehension of divine perfection, an apprehension which awakens the inherent desire of celestial law to 'adore, love, and imitate' God as the final cause.[111] Angels are moved by God as final cause because they are intellectual agents whose rational capacities and wills are attracted to the perfect and perfecting *ratio* of God's being. Such perfections are, of course, the act of being (*esse*) expressed under the convertible transcendentals of goodness (the fullness of being) and beauty (the attractive, desirable quality of being). Hooker thus suggests that participatory celestial law moves angelic agents to the perfection of their own kind, a limited reflection of divine plenitude, through vision and imitation of God. Indeed, Hooker notes that the book of Job twice calls angels the 'Sonnes of God', a familial term that suggests both generative dependency and mimetic similarity.[112]

As is true for the law of nature, celestial law has a markedly sociable quality. While non-rational agents are 'sociable partes united into one bodie' by non-cognitive, natural participation in eternal law, angels intellectually apprehend God's perfection. As such, angels are deliberately linked 'into a kinde of corporation amongst themselves, and of societie or fellowship with men' through a mutually recognizable, cognitive participation in eternal law. Cognitive participation generates a rational, hierarchical and helpful society between angels and humanity. Hooker accordingly suggests that there are three functions of celestial law.[113] First, celestial law has an intrinsic aspect that calls angels to 'praise' God as the source of all perfection. Second, celestial law has a corporative aspect, establishing a celestial hierarchy of orders, 'an Army, one in order and degree above the other.' Finally, celestial law emphasizes angelic service, the 'ministeriall imployment' with and to humankind, who also reflect the rational participation in eternal law. The obedient angels execute this threefold celestial law with 'joy', an ecstatic expression of a freely embraced law that directs the angels to individual, corporate and cosmic perfection.[114] God is both the source and summit of this celestial law. It is precisely the failure to apprehend God as the perfect good, caused by a faulty estimation of autonomy, which led to the angelic fall from grace. Hooker takes the classical Christian position that 'the fall of Angels therefore was pride', the rejection of God in favour of an 'admiration of their own sublimitie and honor'.[115] The consequence of angelic sin remains profoundly antisocial: the fallen angels 'have by

---

[110] Ibid., 1:70.4–71.3; I.4.1. As Hooker phrases it in *Pride*, II, in *FLE*, 5:333.16-19: 'God hath created nothing simply for it selfe: but ech thing in all things and of everie thing ech part in other hath interest that in the whole world nothing is found whereunto anie thing created can saie, I need thee not.'

[111] Hooker, *Laws*, 1:69.31–2; I.4.1.

[112] Ibid., 1:70 j; I.4.1.

[113] Ibid., 1:71.3–15; I.4.2.

[114] On the link between Pseudo-Dionysius and Hooker, see Feisal G. Mohamed, 'Renaissance Thought on the Celestial Hierarchy: The Decline of a Tradition', *Journal of the History of Ideas* 65, no. 4 (2004): 559–82.

[115] Hooker, *Laws*, 1:72.4–11; I.4.3.

all meanes laboured to effect an universall rebellion against the lawes, and, as far as in them lyeth, utter destruction of the workes of God'.[116]

Finally, within natural law Hooker places the law of reason dialectically between the laws of nature and celestial law, namely, as between the footstool and throne of God. On the one hand, then, human beings exhibit a likeness to the angels: as intellectual analogues of God, both possess reason and will.[117] The final perfection of human nature (just as with the angels) thereby comes from cognitive participation in God:

> If then we be blessed, it is by force of participation and conjunction with him [i.e. God] .... Then we are happie therfor when fully we injoy God, as an object wherein the powers of our soules are satisfied with everlasting delight: so that although we be men, yet by being unto God united we live as it were the life of God.[118]

On the other hand, unlike the angels, human beings 'are at the first without understanding, or knowledge at all' (an Aristotelian tabula rasa), as well as being embodied and mortal.[119] Indeed, human beings are also bound to the physical, non-cognitive world and 'as when we breath, sleepe, move, we set forth the glory of God as naturall agents do'.[120] Hooker remains clear, however, that humanity's vocation remains to 'growe by degrees, till they come at length to be even as the Angels themselves are', that is, to have 'full and complete knowledge in the highest degree that can be imparted [by God] unto them'.[121]

Within creation, this rational capacity reflects a special way, then, of participating in eternal law under the aspect of God's government (*gubernatio*). In *Predestination*, Hooker distinguishes between God's governance over non-cognitive and cognitive types of participation: 'the government of God is: general over all; special over rational creatures'.[122] In the fifth chapter of Book One of the *Laws*, Hooker implicitly expands upon these two kinds of participation in eternal law. He lists the kinds of perfections that humankind seeks by setting out an Aristotelian-Thomistic anthropology that places human beings dialectically between both non-cognitive and cognitive parts of creation.[123] A human being is a substantial form constituted by its soul. According to the powers of the soul, Hooker arranges humankind's natural appetites and gears their desires towards proportionate or connatural ends: vegetative (with a desire

---

[116] Ibid., 1:72.14–17; I.4.3. As with the law of nature, the emphasis on obedience to the hierarchy of laws therefore remains markedly polemical against the perceived disobedience of Elizabethan radical puritans. See Barry Rasmussen, 'The Priority of God's Gracious Action in Richard Hooker's Hermeneutic', in *Richard Hooker and the English Reformation*, ed. W. J. T. Kirby (Dordrecht: Kluwer Academic Publishers, 2003), 3–14.
[117] Hooker, *Laws*, 1:64.9; 1:69.25; 1:77.20–1; 1:113.9; I.3.2; I.4.1; I.7.2; I.11.3.
[118] Ibid., 1:112.17–20; I.11.2.
[119] Ibid., 1:74.20–1; I.6.1.
[120] Ibid., 1:138.23–30; I.16.3.
[121] Ibid., 1:74.17–23; I.6.1.
[122] Hooker, *Predestination*, in *FLE*, 4:86.28–87.12. Hooker echoes the Thomistic distinction that rational creatures participate cognitively in eternal law while irrational creatures only participate 'by way of similitude'. See Aquinas, *ST*, I.II.91.2.
[123] Hooker, *Laws*, 1:75.7–27; I.6.2-3. Compare Aquinas, *ScG*, III.26.8.

for nutrition, growth and reproduction); sensitive (with a desire for sensory input); and rational (with a desire for theoretical and practical speculation). Later, when he turns to divine law (as the next part will detail) Hooker adds a natural desire for an ultimate and disproportionate 'spirituall and divine' perfection, namely, to live in the beatitude of God's presence.[124] On the one hand, therefore, human beings share with all creation in the two types of desirable goodness noted earlier: the natural desire for 'continuance of their being' (*esse*) through all that is required to stay alive and through propagation; and 'resemblaunce with God' through 'the constancie and excellencie of those operations which belong unto their kinde'. On the other hand, however, human beings share with the angels a particular kind of cognitive excellence, namely, the capacity to know truth and exercise virtue, the aspiration to the 'greatest conformity with God'.[125] The order and rectitude of the sentence of reason directs human beings to know 'truth from falshood' and so to direct actions to fulfil the natural and necessary desire for 'the utmost good [*bonum*] and greatest perfection'.[126] Ultimately, since 'no good is infinite but only God', human beings desire God as their end.[127] The natural vocation of humankind is thereby 'union with that it desireth', namely God. As such, God acts directly as the First Cause of the rational human form, but also (through the intrinsic, instrumental acts of those forms) as the final cause that contains all possible perfection.

Hooker accordingly suspends the law of reason from a transcendent source as a kind of theonomous participation. Hooker secures the law of reason as an intrinsic property of human nature since it circumscribes what human beings know by the light of natural understanding and is 'investigable by reason without the helpe of revelation supernaturall and divine'.[128] Yet, reason (like any capacity) cannot 'rightly performe the functions allotted to it, without perpetuall aid and concurrence of that supreme cause of all things'.[129] While the law of reason remains intrinsic to human nature, divine influence undergirds it, giving an essential order that tends towards harmony and the common good. As such, human beings are a microcosm of the cosmic macrocosm that depends upon eternal law for order and harmony.[130] Hooker writes that as long as 'each thing performeth only that worke which is naturall unto it', then all remains preserved. Yet, failure 'would be ruine both to itselfe, and whatsoever dependeth on it'. Similarly, 'man being . . . a very worlde in himselfe' would draw harm to all in 'his transgressing of the law of his nature'. The law of reason, then, constitutes the rational, cognitive participation of human beings in the providential order of the universe. Such

---

[124] Hooker, *Laws*, 1:111.24–112.12; 1:114.8–119.23; I.11.1–2; I.11.4.
[125] Ibid., 1:73.23–74.5; I.5.3.
[126] Ibid., 1:82.1–2; 1:84.7–17; I.8.1; I.8.3.
[127] Ibid., 1:112.11–13; I.11.2.
[128] Ibid., 1:90.2–11; I.10.4.
[129] Ibid., 1:92.25–8; I.8.11. Nigel Voak, *Richard Hooker and Reformed Theology: A Study of Reason, Will, and Grace* (Oxford: Oxford University Press, 2003), 100–12, argues that this passage refers to Calvin's idea of 'common grace' which militates against the deleterious effects of the Fall and allows all humankind to know something of natural law. Nowhere does Hooker use Calvin's term, however. The root rather seems to be Aquinas's ideas of prime causality in *ST*, I.II.109.1: God is the supreme cause of all things, including reason.
[130] Hooker, *Laws*, 1:93.18–29; I.9.1. Hooker seems indebted to Plato's theory of the cosmos as a living creature endowed with a soul and reason, such as found in the 'Timaeus' and in the patristic period.

cognitive participation remains theonomous: just as 'Nature . . . is nothing else but God's instrument', so too is the voice of reason 'but his instrument'.[131] Human beings are 'a law unto themselves'[132] through their rational capacity. Yet, the intrinsic entelechy of law means that human beings are suspended from God as their constitutive cause:

> Laws apparently good are (as it were) things copied out of the very tables of that high and everlasting law even as the book of that law hath said concerning it selfe, *By me Kinges raigne, and* by me *Princes decree justice.* Not as if men did behold that booke, and accordingly frame their lawes, but because it worketh in them.[133]

The law of reason represents the particular 'determination of the wisedome of God', the cognitive participation of the human being in the providential 'rule of divine operations outwards', namely eternal law.

Hooker adds admonitory notes, however, to his account of the law of reason. In the *Notes towards a Fragment on Predestination*, Hooker adds a crucial distinction about divine government: 'There are two forms of government: that which would have been, had free creation not lost its way; that which is now when it has lost its way'.[134] Sin entails that the law of reason proves a curiously difficult thing to realize once humankind 'has lost its way': satanic delusion, the haste of the will to accept apparent goods presented to it, poor habits, laziness and the fact that 'the search of knowledg is a thing painful' all contribute to error and confusion.[135] The counsel of reason is not so certain that there is no room for the will to dissent or turn to another apparent (but perhaps false) good.[136] Furthermore, while unaided human reason can discover of itself certain essential speculative and practical truths, sin frustrates the natural, legal desire for union with goodness, found in the simplicity of God. Hooker warns:

> Of such perfection capable we are not in this life. For while we are in the world, subject we are unto sundry imperfections, griefs of body, defectes of mind, yea the best things we do are painefull, and the exercise of them greevous being continued, without intermission, so as in those very actions, whereby we are especially perfected in this life, wee are not able to persist: forced we are with very wearines and that often to interrupt them: which tediousnes cannot fall into those operations that are in the state of blisse, when our union with God is complete.[137]

---

[131] Ibid., 1:84.1–5; I.8.3.
[132] Ibid., 1:84.8–9; I.8.3.
[133] Ibid., 1:136.8–13; I.16.2.
[134] Hooker, *Predestination*, in *FLE*, 4:87.16–17.
[135] Hooker, *Laws*, 1:80.29–81.23; I.7.7. Compare Hooker, *Dublin Fragments*, 2, in *FLE*, 4:103.11–7. Whether Hooker upholds a Reformed account of the total depravity of nature remains a contested issue. For the argument that he does, see: W. J. T. Kirby, 'The Context of Reformation Thought: the Influence of the Magisterial Reformers on Richard Hooker's Discourse on Natural Law', in *The Theology of Richard Hooker in the Context of the Magisterial Reformation*, ed. W. J. T. Kirby (Princeton, NJ: Princeton Theological Seminary, 2000), 11 and n. 35; E. Grislis, 'The Role of Sin in the Theology of Richard Hooker', *Anglican Theological Review* 84, no. 4 (2002): 881–4; and Voak, *Reformed Theology*, 100–9. For the opposing argument, see: Lake, *Anglicans & Puritans?*, 150; Joyce, *Anglican Moral Theology*, 70–3, 87–8; Miller, *Vision of God*, 72–3, 215–16.
[136] Hooker, *Laws*, 1:79.27–80.6; I.7.6.
[137] Ibid., 1:112.25–113.7; I.11.3.

Hooker thereby exhibits what Rowan Williams calls 'both a positive and a modest valuation of the human': the participatory law of reason describes the excellence of human nature and yet also 'the unbridgeable gap between our finite capacity and the object that satisfies us'.[138] Hooker accordingly distinguishes between the aptness and ability of the will and reason.[139] On the one hand, reason and the will are originally apt (*originaliter apta*) for their purpose. On the other hand, although 'reason can find every necessary good when it is supported by divine aid', human reason remains unable, on account of the sloth of sin, so to do.

Taken as a whole, then, natural law as the first 'reading' of the eternal law into the world describes an overall pattern of inherent behaviours and capacities that flow from divine creativity, unfold within history, and reflect the perfection of God through theonomous participation. Natural law participates in the providential ordering of the cosmos and receives its inner principles as well as its proper ends as a gift from the superabundant, self diffusive and generous character of God, whose very being constitutes the eternal law. As Hooker puts its (quoting Acts 17.28), 'in him wee live, move, and are'.[140] As such, natural law possesses the character of grace, insofar as it represents a participation in God freely and gratuitously gifted by God.[141] In this account, Hooker offers an Augustinian modification of a Dionysian account of law. As Kirby puts it, for Hooker, 'all that is – both the first principle itself and all that derives from it – have their ground concealed within the simplicity of that same first principle or cause, hidden, as it were, like a foundation stone or tree root "in the bosome of the earth"'.[142] Natural law primarily participates in eternal law, then, as the 'weak/extensive/exiting' paradigm of participation, but (in the law of reason) also tends towards the second 'strong/intensive/returning' paradigm where the vocation of humankind rests in immediate union with God. The corrosive nature of sin, however, entails that the natural desire for union will remain frustrated, unless God provides a sure and certain remedy. Hooker readily recognizes this legal lacuna, and hence turns towards the second way in which eternal law 'reads' itself into the world, namely divine law, considered next.

In chapters eleven through fifteen of Book One, Hooker turns towards God's redemptive activity in order to resolve the lacuna between what human beings desire through the entelechy of law and their inability to realize the end of the same law, namely participatory union with God as the source and site of perfection. Since human beings, whatever the nobility of their rational capacities, suffer from 'imbecillitie' due to sin, God provides the divine law recorded through the Holy Scriptures as a remedial aid both to help practical reason and also to provide salvific truths not self-evident to reason, such as the Resurrection.[143] God has indeed 'revealed a way mystical and supernatural, *a way directing unto the same end of life* by a course which groundeth

---

[138] Rowan Williams, *Anglican Identities* (London: Darton, Longman & Todd, 2009), 43.
[139] Hooker, *Autograph Notes*, in *FLE*, 4.18.6-24.
[140] Hooker, *Laws*, 1:67.17; I.3.4.
[141] See Hooker, *Dublin Fragments*, 13, in *FLE*, 4:113.17-20, where he writes of the 'grace of God' that 'wee are by it that wee are, and att the length by it wee shall bee that wee would'.
[142] Kirby, '"Divine Offspring"', 7, quoting Hooker, *Laws*, 1:57.6-20; I.1.2.
[143] Hooker, *Laws*, 1:120.19-121.21; I.12.2.

itself upon the guiltiness of sin, and through sin desert of condemnation and death'.[144] This supernatural law aims to restore human nature to the same end for which the law of reason was originally adequate.[145] Yet, in its gratuity, it also elevates the believer to a new supernatural finality, namely from simply knowing God (and so participating in eternal law through right action) into the eternal contemplation of and union with God's nature through Christ. Scripture delivers how God establishes the supernatural law which is co-identical with Christ, namely redemption 'by the precious death and merit of a mighty Saviour, which hath witnessed of himself, saying, *I am the way, the way that leadeth us from misery into blisse*'.[146] 'The principall intent of scripture', Hooker writes, 'is to deliver the lawes of duties supernaturall', and faith in Christ remains the central duty it details.[147] Indeed, Christ imputes righteousness to sinful people through faith: quoting Jn 6.29, Hooker affirms '*this is the worke of God that ye believe in him whome he hath sent*'.

At the beginning of his account of divine law, Hooker recalls the foundation of law in the Aristotelian principle that the end of all human action is ultimately the highest good (*bonum*).[148] As already noted, Hooker then claims that God is both the first and final cause for human beings, 'desired for it selfe simplie' since 'no good is infinite, but only God'. All natural goods, therefore, are penultimate and should only be pursued instrumentally to aid the return to the original and terminal good. Hooker expresses the attractive force of this terminal good as 'desire' for 'union' by 'force of participation and conjunction' with God.[149] Since 'complete union with him [i.e. God] must be according unto every power and facultie of our mindes', Hooker accordingly argues that union with God must include both understanding and will united in desire for the 'goodness of beautie in it selfe', namely God.[150] Once desire arrives at union, it gives way to satiated 'love' or what Augustine calls the 'sweete affection of them that tast and are replenished'.[151] Thus, goodness (*bonum*) and beauty (*pulchrum*) are convertible names for the divine nature, the perfection of being that evokes desire for (re)union in that human nature which God has created. The gratuitous and superabundant finality for human beings, then, remains supernatural and contemplative: 'the soule . . . perfected by love . . . with these supernaturall passions of joye, peace and delight,' akin to the angels.[152]

Faced with the sinful incapacity of the law of reason, desire remains the constellating category for this second, supernatural way in which eternal law reads itself into the world. The intrusion and obstacle of sin – the rejection of God as the proper end with the concomitant damage to nature – means that union with God remains impossible without divine aid. Appealing to an Aristotelian premise, Hooker argues that God would not create a 'naturall desire' that could be 'frustrate', and so

---

[144] Ibid., 1:118.15–16; I.11.6, emphasis in the original.
[145] See Irish, '"Participation of God Himselfe"', 171–83.
[146] Hooker, *Laws*, 1:118.20–3; I.11.6, emphasis in the original.
[147] Ibid., 1:124.31–2; I.14.1, emphasis in the original.
[148] Ibid., 1:110.24–111.6; I.11.1.
[149] Ibid., 1:112.13–15; I.11.2.
[150] Ibid., 1:113.7–9, 20; I.11.3.
[151] Ibid., 1:113.15–17; I.11.3.
[152] Ibid., 1:113.20–9; I.11.3.

the hierarchy of perfections (the 'sensuall', 'intellectuall' and 'spiritual and divine') that humankind desires remains capable of fulfilment by supernatural means.[153] God acts as the guarantor, then, of desire. While 'the light of nature is never able to finde out any way of obtayning the reward of blisse', God nonetheless recreates the possibility of participatory union through 'a way mysticall and supernaturall .... [which] God in himselfe prepared before all worldes'.[154] The divine law of Scripture points to such a mystical way, especially as it points towards Jesus Christ.

Far from being disjunctive, Hooker's account of divine law therefore presupposes, restores and exceeds natural law, especially the law of reason.[155] Hooker stands within the Augustinian and Thomist tradition that grace does not efface nature but rather perfects it.[156] Indeed, in Book Three of the *Laws*, Hooker parses St Paul's idea that 'nature hath need of grace' as also implying 'that grace hath use of nature'.[157] Accordingly, in chapter fourteen of Book One, Hooker writes 'when we extoll the complete sufficiencie ... of scripture, [it] must ... be understood with this caution, that the benefite of natures lighte be not thought excluded as unnecessary, because the necessitie of a diviner light is magnificent.'[158] Thus, 'when supernaturall duties are necessarily exacted, naturall are not rejected as needlesse.'[159] Indeed, since God instantiates a natural desire for God within the legal entelechy of created forms, God also eternally provides supernatural aid for when such forms suffer corruption:

> We see therefore that our soveraigne good is desired naturally; that God the author of that naturall desire had appointed naturall meanes to fulfill it; that man having utterly disabled his nature unto those meanes hath had other revealed from God, and hath receaved from heaven a lawe to teach him how that which is desired naturally must now supernaturally be attained; finallie we see that because those later exclude not the former quite cleane as unnecessary, therefore together with such supernaturall duties as could not possiblie have beene otherwise knowne to the worlde, the same lawe that teacheth them, teacheth also with them such naturall duties as coulde not by light of nature easilie have bene knowne.[160]

---

[153] Ibid., 1:114.14–25; I.11.4.
[154] Ibid., 1:118.15–23; I.11.6.
[155] See Hooker, *Predestination*, in *FLE*, 4:86.15–16; 87.9–11 where he writes: 'Government presupposes creation .... God does nothing by his government which offends against that which he has framed and ratified by the very act of creation.' See Neelands, 'Scripture, Reason, and Tradition', 80, 85, 88; Gibbs 'Book I', in *FLE*, 6 (1): 97–103; and Irish, '"Participation of God Himselfe"', 183–4.
[156] See Ranall Ingalls, 'Sin and Grace', in *A Companion to Richard Hooker*, ed. W. J. T. Kirby (Leiden: Brill, 2008), 151–84. Ingalls rightly points out that the principle *gratia non tollit naturam sed perficit* is found in Augustine's writings which influenced Aquinas but which are also 'crucially important to the development of Luther and Calvin's thought about sin and grace' (166).
[157] Hooker, *Laws*, 1:223.26–29; III.8.6. In a small departure from Aquinas, Hooker emphasizes again the instrumentality of nature as a subordinate efficient cause in order to preserve God's transcendent causality as the source of perfection.
[158] Ibid., 1:128.30–129.3; I.14.4.
[159] Ibid., 1:119.26–7; I.12.1.
[160] Ibid., 1:121.29–122.5; I.12.3.

While the 'principal intent of scripture is to deliver the lawes of duties supernaturall' that are 'by the light of nature impossible to be attained', scripture is also 'fraught even with the lawes of nature'.[161] As such, divine law supplies the defect of natural law, but also materially presupposes it since there is an inherently rational character to both. Even where divine law remains 'somwhat above capacitie of [human] reason, somewhat divine and heavenly', as law it expresses participation in the providential order of God's ontological *ratio* and so shares an analogical, rational character with natural law.[162] When human beings participate in divine law, it both strengthens what is left of rationality after the Fall and enables union with God through Christ. Such union remains ultimately disproportionate, however, to the ordinary capacities of the human believer: participation in God elevates human beings into Christ's deiform glory.

The unfolding, historical telos of divine law is indeed 'endlesse union' with God for participating believers.[163] In order to describe this union, Hooker translates the three theological virtues of faith, hope and love (taken from 1 Cor. 13:13) into the transcendentals of truth (*verum*), goodness (*bonum*) and beauty (*pulchrum*). Thus, the principal object of faith is truth, the highest object of hope is goodness, and love aims at beauty. Hooker identifies these three transcendentals in turn with the person of Christ:

> Concerning faith the principall object whereof is that eternall veritie which hath discovered the treasures of hidden wisedome in Christ; concerning hope the highest object whereof is that everlasting goodnes which in Christ doth quicken the dead; concerning charitie the finall object whereof is that incomprehensible bewtie which shineth in the countenance of Christ the sonne of the living God.[164]

While such theological virtues respectively begin with 'weake apprehension of things not sene', the 'trembling expectation of thinges far removed', and a 'weake inclination of heart', they end (in a manner akin to the angels) with the 'intuitive vision of God' and union with the eternal Word, namely Christ himself. Unlike natural law, divine law begins as an extrinsic principle but, like natural law, it at the last formally shapes those who participate in it and (through it) Christ.

Hooker's turn to the divine law in Book One begins to translate the 'weak/extensive/exiting' model of creation firmly into the second heuristic paradigm of the architecture of participation, namely the 'strong/intensive/returning' model of deification. Indeed, when Hooker turns to his second metaphysical mini-treatise in Book Five, it is to unpack the meaning of 'that mysticall union whereby the Church is become as neere unto Christ, as any one part of his flesh is unto other', namely how 'God hath deified our nature'.[165] This chapter now turns to that second mini-treatise on participation in Hooker's *Laws*.

---

[161] Ibid., 1:119.29; 1:124.31–2; 1:127.9–10; I.11.6; I.14.1; I.14.3.
[162] Ibid., 1:115.8–9; I.11.4.
[163] Ibid., 1:119.11; I.11.6.
[164] Ibid., 1:118.31–119.3; I.11.6.
[165] Ibid., 1:137.3–4; 2:224.14–15; I.16.3; V.54.5.

'Partakers of him in Christ': Intensive participation in God and deification

Chapters fifty through sixty-eight of Book Five represent Hooker's second explicit account of participation as he describes the dominical sacraments. In these chapters, Hooker details how 'God is in Christ, then how Christ is in us, and how the sacramentes doe serve to make us pertakers of Christ'. With their consistent appeal to participation, these chapters display a metaphysical depth that apparently exceeds the immediate polemical purpose of Book Five, namely the shift from the 'general meditations' of the first four books to the 'particular decisions' of controversy, here the established provisions for public worship and ministry. Hooker's radical puritan opponents argued that the public forms of worship of the Church of England were 'corrupted with popish orders rites and ceremonies banished out of certaine reformed Churches whose example therein we ought to have followed' and that therefore 'there is amongst us much superstition reteined in them'.[166] Yet, while Book Five deals with the particular decisions that occasioned controversy, the central chapters properly form, as did Book One, another treatise within a treatise. As such, Hooker's discussion of participation in Book Five contributes to an architecture of participation that informs the wider concerns of Book Five and also the political thoughts about lay ecclesiastical supremacy in the later 'books of power'. Indeed, Book Five aims to show that the Elizabethan Prayer Book engenders 'true religion' and cultivates the Philonic virtue of 'godliness', with benefits for the here and now in political terms of order, but also preparing believers for their final union with God.[167] As such, godliness remains 'the root of all true virtues and the stay of all well-ordered commonwealths' since it inspires proper behaviour in those who administer justice and 'inflameth everie way men of action with zeale to doe good . . . unto all'.[168] The first forty-nine chapters of Book Five also discuss instruction and prayer, however, as the 'elements, parts or principles' that habitually prepare believers to become 'partakers of him [God] in Christ' through the sacraments. John Booty adroitly recognizes, then, that Book Five 'is a circle whose circumference is the commonwealth and whose centre is the concept of participation'.[169]

Hooker's treatise about sacramental participation in Book Five expands upon the divine law outlined in Book One. Indeed, as Bryan Spinks observes, readers must see Hooker's ideas about sacramental participation in light of his legal ontology: 'the created universe itself, with its laws, allows participation in the divine . . . [E]lection through Christ, justification, and the society of the church allow this participation to be achieved.'[170] Much as in the legal pattern of causality found in Book One, divine law in Book Five is mediated through a series of efficient and instrumental causes: God, Christ, faith and the sacraments.[171] God's self-disclosure in divine law

---

[166] Ibid., 1:271.title; 2:15.title; IV.title; V.title.
[167] Ibid., 2:17.9–11; V.1.2.
[168] Ibid., 2:17.1–18.1; V.1.2.
[169] John Booty, 'Book V', in *FLE*, 6 (1): 193.
[170] Spinks, *Two Faces of Elizabethan Anglican Theology*, 133. See also Irish, '"Participation of God Himselfe"', 166–7.
[171] Irish, '"Participation of God Himselfe"', 171–91.

re-establishes the formal and final causes proper to humankind through a special chain of efficient causes that renew participation in God. Christ's hypostatic union and life efficiently fulfils the law of human nature such that Christ acts as the formal and final cause for participation in God.[172] In Christ, 'God hath deified our nature'. God's immediate, deificatory action in Christ does not preclude the mediation of subordinate causes: namely, faith in Christ (expressed through repentance in Book Six), or that the sacraments act as 'instruments' through which the grace enjoyed by Christ adheres to believers.[173] Just as law has a teleological character, so too do sacraments imply that 'grace is indeed the verie ende for which these heavenlie mysteries [of divine law] were instituted'.[174] Hooker uses a number of reproductive, worldly images to describe how believers are drawn into the life of God through the Church: the Church is the 'verie mother of our new birth', providing the 'seede of regeneration' through the 'generative force' of the sacraments.[175] Hooker thus sees the sacraments as perfecting instruments for the ontological end to which God directs human beings, namely the perfection of 'being' or 'eternall life', 'the union of the soule with God.'[176] Participation in Christ in Book Five renews, perfects and elevates the *exitus-reditus* of the *lex divinitatis* in Book One: in the hypostatic union Christ recreates human nature and, through faithfully sharing in Christ, believers return 'Godward' through him.[177] Christ is thus a mediated immediacy, the means and end of a participated deification for believers.

In Hooker's account of participation in Book Five, he ultimately shifts away, however, from the implicit Platonic language of *methexis* found in Book One towards more biblical idioms. John Booty particularly notes the prevalence of 'communion' or 'inward fellowship' (from κοινωνία, such as found in 1 Cor. 10.16), and 'abiding' (from μένω, such as found in Jn 6.56), each of which can also be translated as 'participation'.[178] Both images retain a sense of analogy that respects close association but also maintains difference. Hooker uses them to explain how Christ's human nature enjoys the grace of union with the divine in a perfect, full sense. Union does not obliterate the difference between Christ's two natures but asymmetrically perfects his human nature. Believers enjoy an analogous (but not univocal) union with God as diminished analogues of Christ through sacramental participation. Believers dwell in Christ as their cause, and Christ abides in them as a cause resides in its effects. Participation yields a mutual communion that maintains difference but intimately links cause and effect together as a transformative dynamic. More importantly, in this account of participation in Christ, Hooker also appeals to two other biblical idioms symptomatic of deification: union

---

[172] Hooker, *Laws*, 2:232.23–233.5; V.55.8.
[173] Ibid., 2:207–9; 2:254–62; 3:54.7–28; V.50; V.60; VI.5.2–3.
[174] Ibid., 2:208.9–11; V.50.3.
[175] Ibid., 2:207.13–19; V.50.1.
[176] Ibid., 2:208.21–2; V.50.3.
[177] Ibid., 2:290.28–31; V.63.1. See Paul Dominiak, '"From the Footstool to the Throne of God": *Methexis, Metaxu*, and *Eros* in Richard Hooker's *Of the Lawes of Ecclesiastical Polity*', *Perichoresis* 12, no. 1 (2014): 57–76.
[178] Booty, 'Book V', in *FLE*, 6 (1): 197–9. κοινωνία has the sense of fellowship, close relationship, participation or gift, while the noun κοινωνός means companion, partner, or sharer. μένω means to remain, abide, live or dwell. See Warren C. Trenchard, *Complete Vocabulary Guide to the Greek New Testament* (Grand Rapids, MI: Zondervan, 1998), 58, 69.

and adoption. Hooker's second use of participation in the *Laws* represents, then, the firm turn from the first paradigm of the architecture of participation towards the second, intensive, deificatory use. In order to show this shift, this part will follow in turn Hooker's threefold moments of participation: God in Christ; Christ in us; and sacramental participation in Christ. This *explicatio textus* will show how, just as it does it Book One, Augustinian immediacy works through Dionysian mediation, namely the participatory union with, and supernatural fulfilment of the natural desire for, God through a pattern of transformative causality.

As shown earlier, Hooker's account of the first and second eternal laws in Book One balances hypostatic distinction with dispositive hierarchy (and so Augustinian immediacy with Dionysian mediation). Similarly, his account of how 'God is in Christ' in Book Five balances the claims of transcendence and immanence when he discusses Christ's hypostatic union of divine and human natures. In chapters fifty-one through fifty-four, Hooker condenses the history of doctrinal development over the doctrine of God and Christ's Incarnation into 8,000 words, producing what Rowan Williams calls 'a beautifully lucid summary of patristic Christological teaching'.[179] As he did with eternal law, Hooker first considers the nature of God in chapter fifty-one, emphasizing again the inexpressible unity of the divine nature: 'The Lord our God is but one God'.[180] The persons of the Trinity are distinguished by a double procession in a manner which recalls Aquinas and which quotes John of Damascus.[181] Thus, 'wee adore the father as beinge altogether of him selfe, wee glorifie that consubstantiall worde which is the Sonne, wee blesse and magnifie that coessentiall Spirit eternallie proceeding from both which is the holie Ghost'.[182] From this brief doctrine of the Trinity ad intra, Hooker turns to God's economy ad extra in the Incarnation, the participable order of salvation. In a Thomistic manner, for Hooker the Incarnation is fitting or 'convenient' (*convenientia*) for the purpose of salvation.[183] For Aquinas, the Incarnation is the 'convenient' way to restore participation in God after the Fall since it alone forms the ground of possibility for renewed communion and has an aesthetic fittingness to strengthen and transform the believer.[184] Similarly for Hooker, in the postlapsarian sphere 'the worldes salvation was without the Incarnation of the Sonne of God a thing impossible' and so 'there is cause sufficient why divine nature should assume humane, that so God might be in Christ reconciling to him selfe the world'.[185] Hooker quotes Augustine's variation of the exchange formula to explain the aesthetic convenience of the Incarnation in terms of participation: '*In illo Divinitas est unigeniti facta particpeps mortalitatis nostrae, ut es*

---

[179] Williams, *Anglican Identities*, 27.
[180] Hooker, *Laws*, 2:209.8; V.51.1.
[181] Ibid., 2:209.12–24 and m; V.51.1. Compare Aquinas, *ST*, I.27–43, especially 33, 34 and 36. See W. David Neelands, 'Christology and the Sacraments', in *A Companion to Richard Hooker*, ed. W. J. T. Kirby (Leiden: Brill, 2008), 369–73.
[182] Hooker, *Laws*, 2:209.9–12; V.51.1.
[183] Ibid., 2:210.21; V.51.3. On *convenientia*, see Gilbert Narcisse, *Les Raisons de Dieu: Argument de convenance et esthétique théologique selon saint Thomas d'Aquin et Hans Urs von Balthasar* (Fribourg: Editions universitaires, 1997), esp. 184–92.
[184] Aquinas, *ST*, III.2 resp.
[185] Hooker, *Laws*, 2:210.25–211.10; V.51.3.

nos participes ejus immortalitatis essemus.[186] Hooker appeals to the Pauline language of adoption and filiation to image such participation: 'could wee which are born the children of wrath be adopted the sonnes of God through grace, any other then the naturall sonne of God beinge mediator betwene God and us?'[187]

Hooker acknowledges the metaphysical tension between God's transcendence ad intra and the cataphatic workings ad extra through Christ's union of human and divine natures. Indeed, the outward working of God's transcendence in Christ's hypostatic union is a 'divine mysterie . . . more true then plaine'.[188] In the next five chapters, then, Hooker adumbrates the various Christological controversies of the past 1,500 years in order to show how Christ's human nature asymmetrically participates his divine nature, as well as how the hypostatic union forms the efficient cause of salvific participation in God without violating either nature. In chapter fifty-two, Hooker notes how the Church had to contend with controversies over what the two natures united in Christ's person meant. For Hooker, Nestorius in particular violated the unity of Christ's natures with his description of a moral union ('two persons linked in amity') rather than 'two natures human and divine conjoined in one and the same person'. Against Nestorius, Hooker instead commends the Alexandrian account of the hypostatic union, derived from Cyril of Alexandria, adopted at the Councils of Ephesus and Chalcedon, and enhanced by Aquinas with the language of subsistence (*subsistens*).[189] Hooker writes:

> If the Sonne of God had taken to him selfe a man now made and already perfected, it would of necessitie follow that there are in Christ two persons, the one assuming and the other assumed, whereas the Sonne of God did not assume a mans person unto his own, but a mans nature to his owne person, and therefore tooke *semen* the seed of Abraham, the verie first original element of our nature before it was come to have anie personall humaine subsistence. The flesh and conjunction of the flesh with God began at one instant, his takinge to him selfe our flesh was but one act. So that in Christ there is no personal subsistence but one, and that from everlastinge. By taking only the nature of man he still continueth one person, and changeth but the maner of his subsisting, which was before in the mere glorie of the Sonne of God, as is now in the habit also of our flesh....Christ is a person both divine and humaine, howbeit not therefore two persons in one, neither both these in one sense, but a person divine because he is *personallie* the Sonne of God, humane because *he hath* reallie *the nature* of the children of men.[190]

While Christ is divine, Christ has a fully human nature united to his subsistent person.

---

[186] Ibid., 2:210.q. 'By our head we are reconciled to God, for in Him the Godhead of the Only Begotten is made partaker of our mortality in order that we also might be partakers of His immortality.'
[187] Ibid., 2:211.4–6; V.51.3.
[188] Ibid., 2:211.29–30; V.52.1.
[189] See Aquinas, *ST*, III.2–6. See also Neelands, 'Christology and the Sacraments', 370–2. Neelands notes the common dependency on Alexandrian Christology in Aquinas, Luther, Calvin and Hooker, although the language of subsistence is more markedly Thomist.
[190] Hooker, *Laws*, 2:213.24–214.31; V.52.3.

The question remains, however, about how these apparently incommensurable natures can inhere within one person. In chapter fifty-three, then, Hooker turns to the asymmetrical participation of Christ's human and divine natures such that 'there groweth neither gaine nor losse of essential properties to either'. Here, Hooker denies what he takes to be an implicit suggestion by Gregory of Nyssa that the hypostatic union entails a *tertium quid* such that '*the nature which Christ tooke weake and feeble from us by beinge mingled with deitie became the same which deitie is*'.[191] Hooker quotes Cyril of Alexandria in order to describe how Christ's two natures 'have knit themselves' without obliterating difference.[192] Thus, 'lett us therefore sett it downe for a rule or principle . . . that of both natures there is a *cooperation* often, an *association* always, but never any mutuall *participation* whereby the properties of the one are infused into the other.' Instead, again like Aquinas, Hooker accordingly employs a reduplicative strategy, listing what can properly be said of Christ's divinity and humanity.[193] Here, Christ's two natures 'are as causes and originall groundes of all things which Christ hath done'. Hooker lists the 'operations of [Christ's] deitie': Christ is the highest cause, the wellspring of immortality, has no beginning or end, is omnipresent, and remains impassible.[194] Hooker then quotes Irenaeus to show the 'operations of [Christ's] manhood': Jesus shows hunger, thirst, fear and grief.[195] Yet, through a *communicatio idiomatum* ('crosse and circulatory speeches'), one can loosely predicate across the two natures since they are united in a Thomistic *suppositum*, or what Hooker calls the 'whole person' of Christ.[196] While they remain distinct, Christ's two natures 'concurre unto one effect'.[197] Christ's human nature acts as an instrument of divine, efficient action aiming at salvation, just as nature is a subordinate instrument of eternal law or the sacraments are subordinate instruments of efficient grace.

It would be 'too cold an interpretation', however, to see Christ's Incarnation merely as a formal sharing in human nature.[198] Indeed, the Incarnation absolutely associates God's transcendence with the frailty of humanity such that the former enfolds the latter as a cause encompasses its effects. While the Incarnation involves kenotic 'loss and detriment' for Christ, it also remains the salvific ground upon which believers may too stand and experience the effect of divine action without losing their humanity.[199] Thus, in chapter fifty-five, Hooker has to deny the Lutheran idea that the glorified

---

[191] Ibid., 2:217.22–23; V.53.2, emphasis in the original. See Williams, *Anglican Identities*, 27. While most modern commentators certainly agree with Hooker's condemnation of Gregory of Nyssa in relation to the language of 'mixture' or 'mingling' (μίξις, κρᾶσις and similar cognates), Coakley provides a cogent defence. See Sarah Coakley, '"Mingling" in Gregory of Nyssa's Christology: A Reconsideration', in *Who Is Jesus Christ for Us Today? Pathways to Contemporary Christology*, ed. Andreas Schuele and Gunter Thomas (Louisville, KY: Westminster John Knox, 2009), 72–84.
[192] Hooker, *Laws*, 2:218.12–219.3; V.53.2.
[193] Compare Aquinas, *ST*, III.16.4, emphasis in the original.
[194] Hooker, *Laws*, 2:217.1–7; V.53.1.
[195] Ibid., 2:217.7–14; V.53.1. See Irenaeus, *Adversus omnes haereses*, 3.22. English translation in *Ante-Nicene Fathers*, ed. Alexander Roberts and James Donaldson, 10 vols (Peabody: Hendrickson, 2004), vol. 1, 309–567 (454–5).
[196] Hooker, *Laws*, 2:219.3–18; V.53.4. See Aquinas, *ST*, III.2.3 resp. The communication of idioms is not merely verbal since the natures are hypostatically united.
[197] Hooker, *Laws*, 2:218.26; V.53.3.
[198] Ibid., 2:239.13; V.56.7.
[199] Ibid., 2:223.13; V.54.4.

humanity of Christ is ubiquitous: having taken an actual human nature, Christ remains forever united to a specific, limited, material body bound by a particular history, the 'skarres and markes of former mortalitie' as Hooker phrases it.[200] Yet, by virtue of union with divinity, Christ's humanity remains present (and so effective) 'by waie of conjunction' such that the 'soule of Christ is present with all thinges which the deitie of Christ worketh' and so has an infinite 'presence of force and efficacie throughout all generations of men'.[201] The union of natures in Christ remains the mysterious ground through which the whole person of Christ remains present to believers, even in apparent absence, and through which 'wee are made partakers of Christ both otherwise and in the sacramentes them selves'.[202] The Incarnation acts as the cause through which believers share in a transfigured humanity and through which the divine cause itself dwells in them as an effect and acts through the quotidian realities of temporal existence.

This model of participatory union in effect and act shapes the gifts that Christ's human nature receives in the hypostatic union and, by extension, how and what believers receive in the sacraments. In chapter fifty-four Hooker considers 'what Christ hath obtained according to the flesh, by the union of his flesh with deitie'. Hooker details the three 'gifts' Christ receives: by the gift of eternal generation, Christ receives deity; by the gift of union, his flesh is made one with God, a union which bestows supernatural gifts on his human nature; and by the gift of unction, his human nature receives power and perfection beyond its nature, namely universal (but not infinite) knowledge and material incorruptibility.[203] The gift of union represents the deification of Christ's human nature 'for by vertue of this grace man is reallie made God' and (echoing Johannine language) 'God hath deified our nature . . . by makinge it his owne inseparable habitation'.[204] Hooker distinguishes, however, between such deified human nature and the divine nature: 'which union doth ad perfection to the weaker, to the nobler no alteration at all'.[205] Such asymmetry maintains that the hypostatic union transforms human nature in erotic terms while maintaining its creatureliness:

> The verie cause of his [i.e. Christ] taking upon him our nature was to change it, to better the qualities and to advance the condition thereof, although in no sorte to abolish the substance which he tooke, nor to infuse into it the naturall forces and properties of his deitie. As therefore wee have showed how the Sonne of God by his incarnation hath changed the maner of that personal subsistence which before was solitarie and is now in the association of flesh, so alteration thereby accruing to the nature of God; so neither are the *properties of mans nature* in the person of Christ by force and vertue of the same conjunction so such altered, as not to staie within those limites which our substance is bordered withal; nor the *state and*

---

[200] Ibid., 2:226.5–7; V.54.8.
[201] Ibid., 2:232.7–8; 2:234.2–13; V.55.7; V.55.8–9.
[202] Ibid., 2:227.25–33; V.55.1.
[203] Ibid., 2:220–7; V.54.1.
[204] Ibid., 2:222.21; 2:224.14–15 ; V.54.3; V.54.5.
[205] Ibid., 2:223.6–7; V.54.4.

qualitie of our substance so unaltered, but that there are in it many glorious effectes proceeding from so neere copulation with deitie.[206]

The effect and act of God also works the grace of unction. Christ's humanity receives 'by the influence of Deitie' all perfections that human nature is apt to obtain as well as supernatural perfection.

Having established the grammar in which Christ's human nature participates his divine nature, Hooker next turns towards the second moment, namely 'Christ in us', again holding in productive tension the two Platonisms of Dionysian mediation and Augustinian immediacy. The manner in which God is in Christ forms the efficient cause of renewed, salvific participation. Thus, 'God in Christ is generally the medicine which doth cure the world, and Christ in us is that receipt of the same medicine whereby wee are everie one particularlie cured'.[207] If God in Christ acts as the efficient cause of salvation, then Christ is 'in us' as an effect, a participable presence which transfuses grace. Just as God's effect transforms and deifies Christ's human nature, Christ's effect in us (his 'person and presence') likewise renews our capacity to fulfil our theonomous nature and return to God as a deified analogue. Hooker's erotic definition of participation in Christ strongly recalls the earlier use of Aristotelian causality, Neoplatonic *influentia* and analogy in the legal ontology of Book One. Of particular note is Hooker's repetition from his account of natural law that the cause resides in the thing caused (*causa est causato*) and that an effect analogically resembles its cause. Hooker writes:

> Participation is that mutuall inward hold which Christ hath of us and wee of him, in such sort that ech possessth other by waie of special interest propertie and inherent copulation. For plainer explication whereof we may from that which hath bene before sufficientlie proved assume to our purpose two principles, that *everie original cause imparteth it selfe unto those things which come of it*, and *Whatsoever taketh beinge from anie other the same is after a sorte in that which giveth it beinge* .... God hath his influence into the verie essence of all things .... So that all things which God hath made are in that respect the ofspringe of God, they are *in him* as effectes in their highest cause, he likewise actuallie is *in them*, thassistance and influence of his deitie is *theire life*. Let hereunto *saving efficacie* be added and it bringeth forth a special ofspringe amongst men conteininge them to whome God hath him selfe given the gratious and amiable name of sonnes.[208]

Christ fulfils the legal ontology of Book One, the natural desire for perfective goodness. Participation in Christ renews the manner in which creatures participate in God as efficient, formal and final cause. Just as law suspends all of creation from God as an analogue of the eternal law, so too does participation in Christ suspend the believer

---

[206] Ibid., 2:223.16–29; V.54.5, emphasis in the original.
[207] Ibid., 2:227.25–8; V.55.1.
[208] Ibid., 2:234.28–235.3; 2:236.22–3; 2:237.22–8; V.56.1–6, emphasis in the original.

from Christ as the primary analogate, the source and site of perfection.²⁰⁹ On the one hand, as with law, Hooker emphasizes transcendence and that believers are in Christ eternally. The Trinity concur in goodness, wisdom and power within both creation and redemption, Christ's saving work 'inwrapped within the bowells of divine mercie, written in the booke of eternall wisdom, and held in the handes of omnipotent power, the first foundations of the world beinge as yet unlaide'.²¹⁰ On the other hand, as with law again, Hooker turns to the immanent unfurling of transcendent causality. As Christ is in them, believers become like Christ analogically or 'after a sort'. Hooker describes how believers participate in Christ's saving work through an erotic metaphor, as an 'inherent copulation'. The Latin root of 'copulation' (*copulare*) means to bind, tie, unite or couple, typically in a sexual sense. R. C. Schwarz illustrates how Hooker uses similar language to describe participation and marriage: copulation, affection, fellowship, bodily unity, faithfulness, knowledge and love, and joining are characteristics of both in Book Five of the *Laws*.²¹¹ Hooker indeed continues the reproductive image as he describes how all things 'which God hath made are in that respect ofspringe of God' and the saved are a 'special ofspringe' or 'sonnes'. Participation conceptually images erotic creation, unity and transformation while maintaining difference between Creator and creature.

In Book One, Hooker images God as the Platonic and Stoic artificer of the law of nature, the formal cause of the intrinsic principles which make up creation. In Book Five, Hooker casts the participation of believers in God's eternal purpose within the same image. Through adoption into God's predestining purpose, 'the artificer is in the worke which his hand doth presentlie frame'.²¹² Just as a cause resides in its effects, Christ resides immanently in believers making them analogously like him 'after a sort'. Thus, natural and supernatural forms of participation alike draw creatures into the life of the Trinity. Hooker calls this draw 'the participation of divine nature', a paraphrase of 2 Pet. 1.4 ('participants [κοινωνοὶ] of divine nature'), a favourite soteriological text for mystical theologies of deification.²¹³ Such deification does not mean divinity subsumes believers. Rather, as Hooker develops it, deification means the 'realisation of human potential in relationship with the creator' (as Edmund Newey phrases it) through participation in Christ.²¹⁴

The manner in which believers participate Christ revolves around the Pauline language of adoption and union, a semantic field typically found in patristic accounts of deification. Hooker offers an Adamic Christology in which Christ recapitulates Adam.²¹⁵ The first Adam works as 'an original cause of our nature and of that corruption of nature which causeth death'. Christ, as the second Adam, works as 'the cause original of restauration to life'. Thus, 'as therefore wee are reallie partakers of the bodie of

---

²⁰⁹ See Egil Grislis, 'Richard Hooker and Mysticism', *Anglican Theological Review* 87, no. 2 (2005): 253–71.
²¹⁰ Ibid., 2:237.18–22; V.56.5.
²¹¹ See Schwarz, 'Dignified and Commodious', 16–30.
²¹² Hooker, *Laws*, 2:238.9–12; V.56.6–7.
²¹³ See Pheme Perkins, *First and Second Peter, James, and Jude* (Louisville, KY: Westminster John Knox, 1995), 168–9. See also Boquet and Nagy, *Medieval Sensibilities*, 15–6.
²¹⁴ Newey, 'The Form of Reason', 2.
²¹⁵ Hooker, *Laws*, 2:237–40; V.56.6–8.

synne and death received from Adam', the hypostatic union instead make us 'trulie partakers of Christ'. Indeed, 'wee are therefore adopted sonnes of God to eternall life by participation of the onlie begotten Sonne of God, whose life is the wellspring and cause of ours.' Participation in Christ implies the mediating role of secondary causes that concur with and figure Christ's immediate presence. Hooker writes that 'but in God wee actuallie are no longer then onlie from the time of our actuall adoption into the bodie of his [Christ's] true Church'. Hooker appeals to a list of biblical images about union to describe the Pauline metaphor that the Church is the body of Christ: we are in Christ 'even as partes of him selfe' (Jn 15.9); just as 'God made Eve of the ribbe of Adam ... his Church he frameth out of the verie flesh ... of the Sonne of man' (Gen. 2.22–3); the crucifixion makes the Church 'such as him selfe is of whome wee com' (1 Cor. 15.48); and through 'the union of his deitie with our nature' we participate as 'branches in that roote out of which they growe' (Jn 15.5). The way believers participate Christ's deifying hypostatic union is therefore 'only seen in image, analogy, and metaphor' and not 'one-to-one correspondence'.[216]

Hooker develops how Christ acts as an efficient cause in several ways.[217] First, 'it must be confest that of Christ, workinge as a creator, and a governor of the world by providence, all are partakers.' Christ is the *ratio* of God's creative and providential activity. Second, 'as he dwelleth not by grace in all, so neither doth he equallie worke in all them in whom he dwelleth.' Participation in Christ admits of degrees, that is to say, it takes into account the ordinary need for growth even in the extraordinary vocation of union with God. Thus,

> the participation of Christ importeth, besides the presence of Christes person, and besides the mysticall copulation thereof with the partes and members of his whole Church, a true actuall influence of grace whereby the life which wee live accordinge to godlines is his, and from him we receave those perfections wherein our eternall happines consisteth. Thus wee participate Christ partelie by imputation, as when those things which he did and suffered for us are imputed unto us for righteousness; partlie by habituall and reall infusion, as when grace is inwardlie bestowed while wee are on earth and afterwards more fullie both our soules and bodies made like unto his in glorie.[218]

Hooker holds together immediacy and mediation: believers participate in Christ through extrinsic imputation (justification) and by the intrinsic infusion of grace (sanctification) within the Church as an extension of Christ's body. While the former is immediate and complete, and as Grislis points out, 'in agreement with traditional Augustinian-Calvinist views, in sanctification Hooker expected a continued progress and intensity of participation in Christ and consequently a growth in goodness'.[219]

---

[216] Schwarz, 'Dignified and Commodious', 25.
[217] Hooker, *Laws*, 2:242.11–26; V.56.10.
[218] Ibid., 2:242.28–243.9; V.56.10–11. Hooker, *Justification*, 21, in *FLE*, 5:129.7-16 remains clear that God is the cause of both kinds of righteousness, as the efficient cause of imputed grace and as the cause dwelling in the effects of infused grace.
[219] Grislis, 'Mysticism', 268.

The paradigm of how Christ's two natures relate becomes also the paradigm for how the Church participates in Christ. On the one hand, Hooker again rejects Gregory of Nyssa's language of mixture (μίξις, κρᾱσις) which would seem to abolish the distinction between Christ and the believer: 'as for anie mixture of the substance of his fleshe with oures, the participation which wee have of Christ includeth no such kinde of grosse surmise'.[220] Yet, on the other hand, participation yields a transformative link between the two. The imputation of Christ's righteousness restores communion (κοινωνία, participation) with God. Such extrinsic, immediate divine action does not preclude humanity: believers are made anew and spiritually grow through the intrinsic 'participation of Christes infused grace'.[221] Thus, over time and through the Church, 'by steppes and degrees they receave the complete measure of all such divine grace' such that they become in their 'finall exaltation' participatory, deified analogues of Christ in glory.[222] Once again, Hooker images such participation in erotic terms as a 'mysticall copulation'. Although believers retain the essential characteristics of humanity, they also receive the transformative benefits of divine life as they are drawn into the Trinity through Christ's hypostatic union. These benefits include immediate 'newnes of life' and the 'future restoration of our bodies' in the resurrection.[223] Using Russell's fourfold typology of deification laid out in the last chapter, Hooker's account of deification is therefore analogical but also realistic, imaging the ontological and ethical transformation of the believer.

Indeed, the temporal, embodied growth of grace sets the stage for the final moment of Hooker's account: 'how the sacramentes doe serve to make us pertakers of Christ'. Given that God through Christ works as the efficient cause of salvation and renews human nature such that it can formally participate in God as the final cause, Hooker turns in chapter fifty-seven of Book Five to how the dominical sacraments instrumentally draw believers into participation of Christ's person and effects. Here, Christ acts as a new *exitus-reditus*: his hypostatic union immediately recreates human nature (justification or imputed grace) and also acts as the dispositive ground through which believers returns 'Godwards' (sanctification or infused grace). As Irish puts it, Hooker 'was simply too committed a Reformer to countenance the placement of any cause of participation between Christ and the soul'.[224]

As such, Hooker's account of 'participation of Christ' therefore remains closely linked to his account of law in Book One. While the first eternal law has an apophatic, unknowable and transcendent quality, the second eternal law reads God's nature into the world through an immanent pattern of causality. Similarly, while Christ in glory remains transcendent, the sacraments read him into believers through an intrinsic pattern of secondary causality. Sacraments take part as God's ordering of the Church, rooted in the legal structure of the universe which aims at God's goodness; mediatory causes are suspended from and tend towards God as First Cause. Sacraments are the ordinary means or instruments announcing imputed grace and delivering infused

---

[220] Hooker, *Laws*, 2:244.23–5; V.56.13.
[221] Ibid., 2:244.4–5; V.56.12.
[222] Ibid., 2:244.19–23; V.56.13.
[223] Ibid., 2:242.1–2; V.56.10.
[224] Irish, '"Participation of God Himselfe"', 182.

grace. Just as Christ's human and divine natures 'concurre unto *one effect*', the mediatory, material signs of the dominical sacraments concur with and manifest the effect of God's transcendent grace in the lives of believers.[225] As such, sacraments are 'causes instrumentall', the 'instruments of God' or 'morall instrumentes', just as nature is an instrument of eternal law in Book One. Natural laws tend towards God's goodness as entelechies but also depend upon God for their existence. In a consonant vein, the sacraments have as their end grace, the plenitude of God. God guarantees that this end accompanies the physical signs of the sacraments, making them necessary for eternal life. Primarily, the sacraments mark the moment when God imparts the grace of participation. Christ and his effects 'give notice of the times when they use to make their access'.[226] Yet, while Christ's atoning power remains immediately sufficient as a cure for sin, God causally mediates it through the sacraments, 'the use whereof is in our handes the effect in his'.[227]

The two dominical sacraments 'both signifye and cause grace', instrumentally unfurling the two kinds of participation in Christ: namely, imputation (justification) and infusion (sanctification). In baptism 'wee receive Christ Jesus and from him that saving grace which is proper unto baptisme'.[228] Yet, the end of baptism also involves an intrinsic transformation as well as an extrinsic righteousness imputed to the believer. Hooker writes that

> baptism is a sacrament which God hath instituted in his Church to the ende that they which receave the same might be incorporated into Christ and so through his most pretious merit obteine as well that savinge grace of imputation which taketh away all former guiltines, as also that infused divine vertue of the holie Ghost which giveth to the powers of the soule theire first disposition towards newnes of life.[229]

Baptism therefore is a 'seale perhapes to the grace of election before received, but to our sanctification here a step that hath not anie before it'. Baptism represents the outward sign of the recreation and return of believers to God through Christ, a renewed *exitus-reditus*. In other words, baptism imprints the supernatural finality of human beings to participate immediately in the divine nature. It also incorporates believers, however, into the visible church, the body of Christ on earth.[230] As such, union with Christ is experienced in an ecclesial, mediated, corporate, but mystical context: 'Christ is whole with the whole Church, and whole with everie parte of the Church', and the church is a

---

[225] See Hooker, *Laws*, 3:85.6–27; VI.6.1. In response to the charge that sacraments are only 'naked, empty and uneffectual signs', Hooker responds that just as certain things can be predicated of Christ's human nature by itself and more exalted things in virtue of its union with the divine nature, so too are sacraments only 'outward signs' in themselves and yet are 'assisted always with the power of the Holy Ghost'.
[226] Ibid., 2:246.15–18; V.57.3.
[227] Ibid., 2:247.9–10; V.57.5.
[228] Ibid., 2:248.6–7; V.57.6.
[229] Ibid., 2:255.6–13; V.60.2.
[230] Ibid., 1:196.3–7; III.1.3.

'body mysticall, because the mysterie of their conjunction is removed altogether from sense'.[231]

If baptism is the 'inchoation of those graces', then the Eucharist works their 'consummation . . . often as beinge by continewall degrees the finisher of our life'.[232] The Eucharist involves the move from becoming to being, from potentiality to final, eschatological actuality. In chapter sixty-seven, Hooker turns in detail to Eucharistic participation. While baptism instrumentally imputes grace and begins sanctification, Hooker recognizes that the quotidian travails of sin mean that 'wee are both subject to diminution and capable of augmentation in grace'.[233] The Eucharist helps believers grow by steps and degrees into grace and union with God: 'such as will live the life of god must eate the fleshe and drinke the blood of the Sonne of man.'[234] Hooker therefore surveys the Eucharistic controversies of his day in order to find out a 'generall agreement, concerning that which alone is material, Namelye the *reall participation* of Christe and of his life in his bodie and bloode *by meanes of this sacrament*'.[235] Hooker finds no sentence of scripture that definitively necessitates either Lutheran consubstantiation or Catholic transubstantiation as the only way to understand what 'real participation' means.[236] Instead, Hooker parses Eucharistic reception in terms of a reciprocal participation: the believer participates in Christ (as a thing participates in its cause); and Christ participates in the believer (as a cause imparts itself into its effects). Thus, 'noe side deniethe but that the *soule of man* is the receptacle of Christes presence'.[237]

In an extended passage, Hooker therefore reprises the definition of participation as 'that mutuall inward hold which Christ hath of us and wee of him' in order to describe the twofold participation in Christ. The biblical idiom of participation as 'communion' here becomes crucial. The Geneva Bible translates κοινωνία, such as found in 1 Cor. 10.16, as 'communion', but Hooker rightly sees it could also be translated as 'participation'. Like *methexis*, for Hooker 'communion' denotes a cause-and-effect relationship between Christ and believers typical of participatory metaphysics.[238] When he turns to an exegesis of Christ's words of institution found in Mk 14.22–24, he therefore conflates communion and participation to describe this pattern of causality:

---

[231] Ibid., 1:195.2–3; 2:242.26–7; III.1.2; V.56.10.
[232] Ibid., 2:248.4–6; V.57.6.
[233] Ibid., 2:330.25; V.67.1.
[234] Ibid., 2:331.2–5; V.67.1.
[235] Ibid., 2:331.22–4; V.67.2, emphasis in the original.
[236] Ibid., 2:334–41; V.67.5-12.
[237] Ibid., 2:331.28–9; V.67.2, emphasis in the original.
[238] The biblical notion of κοινωνία does not necessarily entail any metaphysical claim in itself: both it and the noun κοινωνός (companion, partner or sharer) can simply denote being or taking part of a whole, as in Lk. 5.10 ('who were partners [κοινωνοί] with Simon') or 1 Cor 10.16 ('The bread that we break, is it not a sharing [κοινωνία] in the body of Christ?'). Yet, κοινωνία and κοινωνός do hint at the participatory relationship between the many and the one where the one constitutes and contains the many, such as in 1 Cor. 10.17, which does use μετέχω (to participate): 'because there is one bread, we who are many [πολλοί] are one body, for we all partake [μετέχομεν] of one bread'. Hooker grafts κοινωνία onto the metaphysical tradition of *methexis* with some justification.

My body, 'the communion [κοινωνία] *of my bodie', My blood, 'the communion' of my blood* .... The bread and cup are his bodie and blood because they are causes instrumentall upon the receipt whereof the *participation* of his boodie and bloode ensueth. For that which produceth any certaine effect is not vainlie nor improperlie said to be that verie effect whereunto it tendeth. Everie cause is in the effect which groweth from it. Our soules and boodies quickned to eternall life are effectes the cause whereof is the person of Christ, his bodie and bloode are the true wellspringe out of which this life floweth. So that his boodie and blood are in that verie subject whereunto they minister life not onlie by effect or operation even as the influence of the heavens is in plantes, beastes, men, and in everie thinge which they quicken, but also by a farre more divine and mytsicall kind of union which maketh us one with him even as he and the father are one . .. [T]hese holie mysteries received in due manner doe instrumentallie both make us pertakers of the grace of that bodie and blood which were given for the life of the world, and besides also imparte unto us even in true and reall though mysticall maner the verie person of our Lord him selfe whole perfect and intire .... [T]hey are thereby made such instrumentes as mysticallie yeat trulie, invisiblie yeat reallie worke our communion or fellowship [κοινωνία] with the person of Jesus Christ as well in that he is man as God, our participation also in the fruit grace and efficacie of his bodie and blood, whereupon there ensueth a kind of transubstantiation in us, a true change of soule and bodie, an alteration from death to life.[239]

Through the instrumental causality of the Eucharistic species, believers participate the transcendent Christ in a pattern of mutual communion: they are in Christ as the First Cause, who re-creates them (imputed grace), and Christ is in them as a cause in its effects (infused grace). The latter aspect transforms or 'transubstantiates' believers such that they become diminished but real analogues of Christ and receive eternal life, that is to say they are mystically united with Christ and thereby with God. Hooker's use of 'transubstantiation' is a provocative reworking of Catholic accounts of the Eucharist. Hooker turns Christ's presence away from the Eucharistic species and towards the recipients: while believers maintain the same outward appearance, Christ (and so God) constitutes their formal reality through the Eucharistic act and consumption. This double participation intimates the Christification of believers, a form of analogous and implicit deification. Indeed, grace orders believers to share an end proper to the divine nature, that is to say the divine life itself. As Robert Slocum phrases it, 'our participation involves us in a co-operative mutuality of unequals as we accept God's saving offer of a divine life.'[240]

---

[239] Hooker, *Laws*, 2:334.13–30; 2:336.24–9; 2:339.3–340.1; V.67.5–11, emphasis in the original. See Neelands, 'Christology and the Sacraments', 383 n.69, placing Hooker as a 'receptionist'. Compare Spinks, *Two Faces of Elizabethan Anglican Theology*, ch.7, which argues that Hooker's 'sacramental theology . . . places him firmly within the Reformed tradition' (158). See also T. C. Holtzen, 'Sacramental Causality in Hooker's Eucharistic Theology', *Journal of Theological Studies* 62, no. 2 (2011): 607–48, which places Hooker within medieval debates about sacramental causation.

[240] Slocum, 'An Answering Heart', 1015.

The sacraments and faith therefore work together as subordinate instrumental causes of participation in Christ which forms us for divine union: 'it is a branch of beliefe that sacramentes are in theire place no less required then beliefe it selfe.'[241] Hooker commends faith as an intellectual gift and habit.[242] Yet, faith remains a supernatural grace and virtue since 'the mysteries of our religion are above the reach of our understanding . . . thaffection of faith is above hir reache, hir love to Godward above the comprehension which she hath of God'.[243] As such, 'the true reason wherefore Christ doth love believers is because theire beliefe is the gift of God.'[244] Hooker develops how God is the efficient cause of faith in Book Six when he turns to repentance. God's grace works repentance in believers as 'the highest cause from which man's penitency doth proceede'.[245] Grace links the theological virtues of faith, hope and love in a chain such that they orient the sinner towards righteousness. Through faith, the Holy Spirit illuminates the mind and inclines the will to its proper good, namely God.[246] Faith gives rise to hope when it conceives 'both the possibilitie, and the meanes to avert evill'.[247] Hope then yields to love, the end of union with God: 'What is love toward God, but a desire for union with God? And shall we imagine a sinner converting himself to God, in whom there is no desire for union with God presupposed?'[248] While God (through Christ) is the efficient cause of justification and sanctification, faith constitutes the subordinate efficient cause of imputed grace and the formal cause of infused grace.[249] In turn, the sacraments are instrumental causes that announce and deliver these graces.

Hooker balances, then, the immediacy of Christ's saving relationship to the soul with the mediation of such immediacy through a series of secondary causes, namely faith and the sacraments. Just as it did in his legal ontology, participation images both the transcendence of the primary cause (God) as well as the dispositive, mediatory immanence of divine causality within material creation. Immediacy and mediation form the enlivening tension of participatory metaphysics. Together they describe the natural vocation for union with God through creation and the elevation of believers into deification through redemptive participation in Christ. A. M. Allchin defines deification as teaching 'not only that God has come down to be where we are, in our human mess, but that he has lifted us up to where he is in his divine splendour'.[250] Hooker typically uses the philosophical and scriptural languages of

---

[241] Hooker, *Laws*, 2:257.7–8; V.60.4.
[242] Ibid., 2:291.21; V.63.2.
[243] Ibid., 2:290.24–31; V.63.1.
[244] Ibid., 2:291.6–7; V.63.1.
[245] Ibid., 3:13.11–16; VI.3.6.
[246] Ibid., 3:8.4–6; VI.3.3.
[247] Ibid., 3:9.6–7; VI.3.3.
[248] Ibid., 3:9.21–3; VI.3.3.
[249] See Hooker, *Autograph Notes*, in *FLE*, 4:21.33–4. Here, Hooker chastises the authors for claiming that faith is the formal cause of justification. In his works, Hooker follows Aristotle's idea in *Metaphysics*, 5.2 that the formal cause is that which makes it what it is. For Hooker, the formal cause of justification is Christ and his righteousness imputed to us. God efficiently causes faith, which then works as a subordinate cause of justification because through it the believer participates in Christ. As an inherent gift, faith does work, however, as the formal cause of infused grace, that which essentially forms the believer into the image of Christ through sanctification. See Hooker, *Justification*, 21, 31, in *FLE*, 5:129.7–16; 5:153.4–15.
[250] Allchin, *Participation in God*, 2–3.

participation rather than explicit references to *theōsis*, but even John Booty (who remains sceptical that Hooker advocates deification) writes Hooker would 'accept Allchin's definition'.[251]

'Bugs wordes': The two Platonisms and participation in Christ

As shown earlier, participation informs Hooker's metaphysical claims about creation and salvation, forming a Neoplatonic architecture of *exitus-reditus*. Participation accordingly holds together God's utter transcendence with his immanent causality in creation. As a result, Augustinian immediacy and Dionysian mediation stand in productive tension. In Book One, God's utter transcendence immediately generates creation. The Dionysian idea of a *lex divinitatis* structures creation, however, as a hierarchy that mediates divinity and drives creation to return to God through its connatural operations. Legal participation therefore describes the ontological move from becoming to being. As such, Book One describes the first heuristic paradigm of participation: all that exists as a divine gift and similitude, a proportionate sharing in God's 'most glorious and most abundant vertue.' Yet, sin frustrates such reversion and creates the problem of mediation: it reopens an infinite gulf between creation and the perfect Creator. Divine law accordingly opens up a new mode of participation, namely a return to Augustinian immediacy. As it points to Christ, divine law acts as a remedy for the imbecility of human faculties occasioned by sin. Yet, divine law also images a disproportionate, direct and supernatural union with Christ and God through grace. In Book Five Christ's hypostatic union forms the immediate ground for this new mode of participatory union. Participation in Book Five images the second heuristic paradigm: an intensive (re)union with God which analogously deifies the believer through participation in Christ. Here, Christ alone fulfils human nature and restores the return to God. Christ's hypostatic union alone also elevates human nature from the connatural participation in God to an intensive, supernatural union with God. Just as the transcendent eternal law 'reads itself' into the world through a pattern of immanent divine influence and legal causality in Book One, so too in Book Five does the transcendent Christ read himself into the world through a causal pattern of participation in the dominical sacraments administered by the Church. Participation in Christ has the character of law in that it again describes the move from becoming to being. Immediacy again grounds mediation, just as in law. While Hooker details on the one hand a divinely mediated cosmos ('order is a graduall disposition'), participation also allows him to assert the soul's immediate relationship to God, a supernatural elevation to participated *theōsis*. In deification, nature and grace coincide in an analogous fashion to the union of Christ's human and divine natures. Indeed, as Newey points out, 'revealingly, it is by use of the prime biblical reference to *theōsis* at 2 Peter 1.4 ["the participation of divine nature"] that Hooker finds the resolution of all

---

[251] Booty, 'The Spirituality of Participation', 16.

these threads, of God and humanity, of transcendent and immanent, of ecclesial and personal, of grace and nature.'[252]

For Hooker, the tension between Dionysian mediation and Augustinian immediacy reflects the core feature of an architecture of participation. Participation separates the transcendent analogate (God or Christ) and the created analogue (creation or believers) as cause and effect. Yet, participation also makes every separation a link: God's gratuitous action in creation and salvation yokes together natural, finite, created forms to a unitive and transcendent source and goal who utterly transcends them. As already noted, these two Christian Platonisms seem difficult to reconcile, however, as a coherent whole. The immediacy of salvation in Christ (grace) seems to preclude mediation (hierarchy) as the latter threatens to undermine the integrity of the former and its gratuity. Indeed, the anonymous authors of *A Christian Letter* accuse Hooker of heterodoxy in how he treats nature and grace. In relation to Book One, *A Christian Letter* complains that, while Article Six of the Thirty Nine Articles states 'Holy Scripture contayneth all things which are necesarie to salvation', Hooker writes 'it sufficeth that nature and scripture doe serve in such full sorte, that they both jointlie and not severallie eyther of them be so complete, that unto everlasting felicitie we need not the knowledge of anie thing more than these two'.[253] For the authors of *A Christian Letter*, the total depravity of human nature makes nature redundant and grace absolutely necessary: only Christ's immediacy (*solus Christus*), and not natural mediation, can effect salvation, a Reformed tenet they believe Hooker violates. In relation to Book Five, *A Christian Letter* further complains that, in Hooker's treatment of the sacraments, he threatens to 'overturne the fayth of our church' by insisting 'the grace of God is tyed to anie time, as namelie the time of the Sacraments'. They also accuse that he makes for the 'additatment of workes unto fayth' when he insists the sacraments are conditional means to salvation.[254] In his *Autograph Notes* on *A Christian Letter*, Hooker responds to such allegations, writing that,

> There are certaine woordes such as Nature, Reason, Will and such like which wheresoever you find them named . . . you suspect them presently as bugs wordes, because what they mean you doe not in deed as you ought apprehend. You have heard that mans Nature is corrupt his reason blind his will perverse. Wherupon under coulor of condemning corrupt nature you condemn nature and so in the rest.[255]

In order, then, to defend the coherency of Hooker's participatory metaphysics, this final part will first examine the 'bugs wordes' which set up an apparent incoherency, namely nature and grace. It will show how Hooker ultimately elides too strict a distinction between nature and grace as both analogically represent God's gratuitous action. Indeed, creation is an act of gratuitous donation, while salvation is an act of

---

[252] Newey, 'The Form of Reason', 9.
[253] *A Christian Letter*, 3, in *FLE*, 4:11.10–20, quoting *Laws*, 1:129.10–13; I.14.5.
[254] *A Christian Letter*, 14, in *FLE*, 4:40.26–33.
[255] Hooker, *Autograph Notes*, in *FLE*, 4:17.23–9.

gratuitous return and elevation. Both creation and salvation exist on a participatory continuum: the first is an extensive, connatural participation in God as Creator, and the second an intensive, supernatural (re)union with God through Christ, a deifying elevation into the life of God that assumes union with God as the natural human vocation. 'Grace' mediates, then, between nature and glory. This part will also show how Christ acts as the key to unlock and defuse the tension between Dionysian mediation and Augustinian immediacy. For Hooker, Christ represents the personal, sapiential principle behind both the *lex divinitatis* and also the salvific reversion and elevation of believers through the hypostatic union.

Hooker seems at first glance to distinguish clearly between the way of nature (Dionysian mediation) and the way of grace (Augustinian immediacy). As we have seen, in the *Laws* Hooker makes clear the necessity of grace for salvation and that nature has no other recourse to cure sin.[256] Indeed, Hooker's distinction between (corrupted) 'nature' and 'grace' in *A Learned Sermon of the Nature of Pride* seems to shape the structure of Book One of the *Laws*:

> Wee are not dust and ashes but wourse .... By which reason all being wrapped up in sinne and made thereby the children of death . . . shall wee think that god hath endued them with so many excellencies moe not only then any but then all the creatures in the world besides to leave them all in such estate that they had bene happier if they had never been? Heere cometh necessarily in a nue waie unto salvation so that they which were in the other perverse maie in this be found straight and righteous. This the waie of nature, this the waie of grace.[257]

The first ten chapters of Book One in the *Laws* chart 'the waie of nature' and the eleventh chapter onwards the 'waie of grace' occasioned by sin. The way of grace does not supplant nature but it has its origins only in the Incarnation since 'the guift whereby God hath made Christ a fountaine of life is that conjunction of the nature of God with the nature of man in the person of Christ'.[258] Yet, the divine law contained in Scripture guides Christian believers into this way of grace in the person of Christ. As such, Hooker seems to stand clearly within the Reformed emphases on *sola scriptura*, *solus christus* and *sola gratia*. As Hooker phrases it in *Notes Toward a Fragment on Predestination*, 'Christ alone <could earn> was able to remove and has removed the hindrance to our salvation; . . . he alone has procured all the means to salvation, and this for all men. Salvation never comes to any man without Christ.'[259]

Yet, both 'nature' and 'grace' are highly ambivalent terms for Hooker because of his participatory metaphysics. He notes that 'the want of exact distinguishing between these two waies . . . hath bene the cause of the greatest part of that confusion whereof

---

[256] See also Hooker, *Dublin Fragments*, 7, in *FLE*, 4:106.15–17: 'To finde our supernaturall lawes, there is noe natural way, because they have not their foundation or ground in the course of nature.'
[257] Hooker, *Pride*, I, in *FLE*, 5:312.24–313.7.
[258] Hooker, *Laws*, 2:222.14–16; V.54.3.
[259] Hooker, *Predestination*, in *FLE*, 4:95.7–16: 'Christus solus <mereri potuit> salutis nostrae impedimentum tollere potuit et sustulit; . . . solus media ad saultem omnia obtinuit idque pro omnibus.'

christianity at this daie laboureth'.²⁶⁰ On one hand, 'nature' and the 'law of nature' are multivalent concepts for Hooker that need careful handling. Hooker inherits the Hellenistic and scriptural matrix of ideas about 'nature'. The English word derives from the Latin *natura*, itself inheriting presuppositions from the Greek word *physis*. Both Latin and Greek words denote a literal meaning (being born or growing) as well as philosophical undertones (as the essence of a thing).²⁶¹ These meanings are also present in the Greek books of the Septuagint where 'contrast and competition' between nature and grace often frames the usage, although in the New Testament there is largely 'no detectable contrast of natural and supernatural' and most texts 'do not presuppose any particular Christian or Jewish belief'.²⁶² In turn, 'natural law' (*lex naturalis*) refers to the observable laws of the phenomenal world, including human nature, by which people can know and fulfil moral obligations, even prescinding from divine revelation.

Hooker understands 'nature' and 'natural law' through this same matrix of meanings, but sets them within an architecture of participation where nature never prescinds from some form of grace. Although, as Muller points out, 'the Protestant orthodox include virtually no natural theology in their systems',²⁶³ Hooker's architecture of participation allows him to do so without threatening the priority of grace. Hooker develops three different senses of what 'the lawe . . . of nature' means. First, it can refer to a manner of working under the eternal law, which sets the laws for each created thing to keep. Second, it can refer specifically to the laws that govern non-rational, non-voluntary agents. Third, it can refer to the law of reason guiding rational, voluntary agents. When he later uses the term 'nature', Hooker means the first sense here, encompassing physical nature, celestial law and the law of reason as they participate in eternal law. Since all these possible meanings of 'nature' refer to participation in eternal law, the term hardly lends itself to modern notions of nature's atomistic autonomy and mere materiality. As such, 'nature' remains a theonomous term for Hooker, describing (as it does) the multiplicity of created forms (material, non-material, rational, non-rational) participating in the unitary *ratio* of God's own generous, self-diffusive being. Nature therefore remains gratuitous: it is God's act of self-donation in creation, the diffusion of being. Participation freights nature with divinity; it describes how God's immanent causality saturates creation. When Hooker handles the concept of 'nature', therefore, he follows what Muller describes as the 'three primary meanings in scholastic theology and in Protestant orthodox usage'.²⁶⁴ Nature therefore denotes an essence, the kind of thing something formally is, and the hierarchical whole of creation *coram Deo*. It can also refer, of course, to sinful nature, set in opposition to God's purposes.²⁶⁵ In the positive senses, however, 'nature' represents the gift of the Creator; and in all cases,

---

[260] Hooker, *Pride*, I, in *FLE*, 5:313.19–28.
[261] See Raymond Williams, *Keywords: A Vocabulary of Culture and Society*, rev. edn (London: Fontana, 1976), 219–24.
[262] Bernard Mulcahy, *Aquinas's Notion of Pure Nature and the Christian Integralism of Henri de Lubac* (New York: Peter Lang, 2011), 23–4.
[263] Muller, *Dictionary*, 302.
[264] Ibid., 199.
[265] See Egil Grislis, 'The Role of Sin', 881–96.

'nature' infers some relationship with grace through the completion or frustration of the legal architecture of participation.

On the other hand, then, 'grace' similarly remains fraught with interpretive difficulty. For Aquinas, the definition of grace (from the Latin *gratis*, freely given) excludes 'the notion of something being due', either on the basis of nature or as a reward for personal merit.[266] As such, creation itself represents an analogous act of grace because it is God's free and gratuitous donation. In Book One of the *Laws*, Hooker similarly uses 'grace' to cover a number of different ideas about God's causality within creation. First, 'grace' can refer to the end of God's external works, namely the variety of creation participating in God. Hooker quotes from Wisdom literature to underscore the grace-filled nature of creation: "*The Lord hath made all things for his owne sake* [Prov. 16.4]. Not that any thing is made to be beneficiall unto him, but all things for him to shew beneficence and grace in them."[267] Later, 'grace' expresses again the goodness of God's operation within creation which the angels strive to imitate since God 'ceaseth not before them daily to fill heaven and earth with the rich treasures of most free and undeserved grace'.[268] Similarly, human reason cannot 'rightly performe the functions allotted to it, without perpetuall aid and concurrence of that supreme cause of all things'.[269] In a comparable vein, Hooker again notes in the *Dublin Fragments* that 'in grace there is nothing of soe great difficultie as to define after what manner and measure it worketh'.[270] Hooker offers there a triple distinction:

> Thus of the three kinds of Grace: the Grace whereby God doth incline towards man, the grace of outward instruction, and the grace of inward sanctification, which twoe worke mans inclination towards God, as the first is the well spring of all good, and the second the instrument thereof to our good, soe that which giveth effect to both in us . . . is the gratious and blessed guift of his Holy Spirit.[271]

While Hooker here gives causal priority to God's action of grace, he also links such action to the (super) natural 'effect . . . in us'. Indeed, Hooker appeals to Pseudo-Dionysius in order to stress that 'grace' describes the care of God to preserve 'the nature of each individual' since it is 'not worthy of Providence to violate nature'.[272] Hooker then nods in the two directions of grace, first towards creation and then towards the telos of participated perfection: 'Wee are by it [i.e. grace] that wee are, and att length by it wee shall bee that wee would'.[273] While Hooker seems to distinguish between the ways of nature and grace, in practice such distinctions become blurred since all of creation expresses, in its createdness, an aspect of divine grace or gratuity. Indeed,

---

[266] Aquinas, *ST*, I.II.111.1 ad. 2.
[267] Hooker, *Laws*, 1:61.9–12; I.2.4.
[268] Ibid., 1:70.24–71.3; I.4.1.
[269] Ibid., 1:92.25–8; I.8.11.
[270] Hooker, *Dublin Fragments*, 12, in *FLE*, 4:111.32–3.
[271] Ibid., 13, in *FLE*, 4:112.1–8.
[272] Ibid., 13, in *FLE*, 4:113.10–17. See Pseudo-Dionysius, *The Divine Names*, 4.33. English translation found in the textual notes of *FLE*, 4:246–7.
[273] Hooker, *Dublin Fragments*, 13, in *FLE*, 4:113.18–20.

'grace' circumscribes a non-competitive double donation, both the undeserved gift of being and the economy of salvation directed towards sharing God's goodness.

Since the line between 'grace' and 'nature' is blurred, their relationship becomes a matter of degrees within a non-competitive continuum of divine self-giving. As Kirby points out, 'Hooker's position is dialectically complex' and his account of grace and nature exhibits 'simultaneously disjunction and conjunction'.[274] Within Hooker's concept of creation-as-gifted, the supernatural gifts of grace in divine law work within as well as beyond the first grace of creation. As a superadded quality, supernatural grace both aids human nature and also exceeds it 'so that in morall actions, divine lawe helpeth exceedingly the law of reason to guide mans life, but in supernaturall it alone guideth'.[275] In the *Dublin Fragments*, Hooker explores the relationship between nature and grace through an unspecified commentator's note on one of Aquinas's articles in the *Summa Theologiae* about 'whether man can wish or do any good without grace'.[276] In the article itself, Aquinas argues that

> in the state of perfect nature man needs a gratuitous strength superadded to natural strength for one reason, viz., in order to do and wish supernatural good; but for two reasons, in the state of corrupt nature, viz., in order to be healed, and furthermore in order to carry out the works of supernatural virtue, which are meritorious. Beyond this, in both states, man needs the Divine Help, that he may be moved to act well.

Nature here carries the freight of grace in different senses for Aquinas, both prelapsarian and postlapsarian. Hooker uses the commentator's gloss that Aquinas means to indicate how 'a special supernatural aid is necessary to elicit an act meritorious and worthy of bliss'. Such actions are effective through Christ alone, but nonetheless 'since there are in us two sources of action, God's grace and our nature, even our best acts savour of both sources'. Like Christ's two natures, nature and grace co-operate and unite even though they remain distinct. In all of these instances, Hooker shows little concern rigidly to contrast nature and grace. Since desire for participation in God is 'natural' in some sense, 'grace' analogously describes both the created status of the cosmos and the supernatural act of redemption. While the grace of creation inclines created forms towards proportional perfections through participation in God, supernatural grace restores and elevates rational creatures into an intense, contemplative union with God through Christ.

There are good reasons to argue, then, that while Hooker shows great care in places to distinguish between 'nature' and 'grace', ultimately he elides strict distinctions. As such, the dialectic proves useful only so far as one takes note of such elisions. Indeed, for Hooker (as for Aquinas) 'grace' works as a mediating term, somewhere between nature and glory. Like Aquinas, Hooker seems to talk of three kinds of participation: through nature, through grace and through glory, where glory is the fulfilment of nature

---

[274] Kirby, 'Reason and Law', 269–70.
[275] Hooker, *Laws*, 1:139.8–10; I.16.5.
[276] Hooker, *Dublin Fragments*, 10, in *FLE*, 4:109.g. Hooker refers to Aquinas, *ST*, I.II.109.2.

drenched in and elevated by God's grace.[277] Grace draws a participatory dynamic, then, between the transcendence of God's causality and the immanent reception of such causality such that believers are elevated to glory. Indeed, in *A Learned Discourse of Justification*, Hooker distinguishes three types of righteousness:

> There is a glorifyinge righteousness of men in the Worlde to comme, and there is a justefying and a sanctefyinge righteousness here. *The righteousnes wherewith we shalbe clothed* in the world to comme, is both perfect and inherente: that whereby here we are justified is perfecte but not inherente, that wereby we are sanctified, inherent but not perfecte.[278]

Justification thus comes from Christ and is imputed as actual righteousness by grace to the believer.[279] Sanctification is the habitual righteousness grafted by the Holy Spirit within believers. For Hooker, while justification remains logically prior, both it and sanctification are united *in tempore* through the instrumental causality of the sacraments. Participation in Christ through the sacraments therefore yields a simultaneity. On the one hand, sacraments declare the believer to be righteous extrinsically through participation in Christ, the 'inward hold' they have 'of Christ'. On the other hand the sacraments augment the progressive, incremental, intrinsic increase in virtue as Christ mutually takes inward hold of believers, 'the effectes thereof are suche accions, as the apostle doth calls *the fruites the workes the operacions* of the spirit.'[280] The growth of the believer through sanctifying grace reconciles this simultaneity in glory: 'by the one we are interested in the righte of inheriting, by the other we are brought to the actuall possessinge of eternall blisse, and so thend of both is everlasting life.'[281] The perfect, inherent righteousness of Christ becomes formally (not extrinsically) that of the believer in the beatitude of glory. Until such glory, believers exist simultaneously in eternity and in time through participation in Christ. The natural and supernatural ultimately become one in bliss as the order of laws that mediate divinity returns to the immediacy of (re)union with God.

For Hooker, Christ is the key who unlocks and unites the Platonic tension between transcendence (the immediacy of grace) and immanence (the mediating hierarchy of nature).[282] Christ represents the personal, divine dynamic who suspends creation and the believer in the unfolding moments of creation and redemption. In Christ, then, Dionysian mediation and Augustinian immediacy meet. Hooker accordingly calls Christ the 'woord or Wisdom of God'.[283] As a logocentric and sapiential figure,

---

[277] See Rziha, *Perfecting Human Actions*, 80 n.175 on these modes of participation in Aquinas.
[278] Hooker, *Justification*, 3, in *FLE*, 5:109.6–11.
[279] Hooker here denies Aquinas's idea in *ST*, I.II.110 2 resp. that 'gratia justificans' is a 'habit' of the soul since this confuses, for Hooker, the modes of grace. See Hooker, *Justification*, 5, in *FLE*, 5:110.11–111.7.
[280] Hooker, *Justification*, 21, in *FLE*, 5:129.15–16, emphasis in the original.
[281] Ibid., 6, in *FLE*, 5:114.2–4.
[282] William H. Harrison, 'The Church', in *A Companion to Richard Hooker*, ed. W. J. T. Kirby (Leiden: Brill, 2008), 315 asserts the same point in relation to ecclesiology, but concludes this 'does not resolve the larger question of the relationship between the two Platonisms in law and soteriology'.
[283] Hooker, *Laws*, 2:213.13–23; V.52.3.

Christ forms both the immediate first principle of all created, hierarchical order, and also the only *via* of return to God in redemption through his hypostatic union of natures.[284]

In describing Jesus as the 'woord or Wisdom of God', Hooker aligns himself with the scriptural, patristic and medieval exegesis that equates the Johannine language of Christ as the eternal Word (λογος) with the personified figure of Wisdom (σοφία) from wisdom literature. Both λογος and σοφία express the rational, creative and loving aspect under which creation relates to the divine. In the Hebrew Scriptures, divine Wisdom appears as a female personification, especially in Job Proverbs, Sirach and the Wisdom of Solomon. Roland Murphy lists the following as examples: Job 28; Prov. 1, 8, 9; Sir. 1.9-10, 4.11-19, 6.18-31, 14.20-15.8, 51.13-21; Baruch 3.9-4.4; and Wisdom 6.12-11.1.[285] In these texts, her primary role is relational: she radiates from God as an image, remains an intimate friend, and lovingly connects and communicates between human beings and God. Sophia represents God's presence to the universe of God's continuing creativity. In turn, New Testament texts regularly identify Jesus as divine Wisdom.[286] For example, Wisdom themes regularly appears within the liturgical hymns found in Phil. 2.6-11, Col. 1.15-20, Eph. 2.14-16, 1 Tim. 3.16, 1 Pet. 3.18-22 and Heb. 1.3. Paul further writes of Christ as Wisdom in 1 Cor. 1.22-4, 30-1. Christ as Wisdom also becomes identified as Christ the Word largely on account of the striking similarity between the images in terms of the loving suspension of creation from them as divine principles. As a prime example, John's Prologue (Jn 1.18) casts Jesus as the Word (λογος). The λογος has a complex Greek and Jewish history.[287] It became a crucial plank in evolving Christian thought about the Trinity through the conflation of selective scriptural texts with philosophical and religious ideas of the ancient Hellenistic milieu. In Stoic philosophy, for example, the λογος was the active reason penetrating the whole universe. Alternatively, in Jewish thought, for Philo the λογος is the immaterial Word of God, a subordinate and intermediary being who provides the exemplar for creation. Yet, in the Prologue to his Gospel, John describes the λογος in language reminiscent of Wisdom: the Word is united to the divine, active in creation, reflects God's glory, delights to be with human beings, and immanently dwells among them as an act of redemption.[288] Like John, patristic and medieval exegetes regularly unite σοφία and λογος in order to explore how Christ acts as the eternal, divine reason (*ratio*) or paradigm (*παράδειγμα*) lovingly active in creation and redemption. λογος and σοφία theology can be found in the Christological thought of Justin Martyr, Clement of Alexandria, Origen, Ambrose, Jerome, Eusebius of Caesarea, Gregory of Nyssa, Cyril of Alexandria and

---

[284] Hooker again follows Aquinas. See W. J. Hankey, *God in Himself: Aquinas' Doctrine of God as Expounded in the Summa Theologiae* (Oxford: Oxford University Press, 1987) who argues that Christ alone is the *via* of return in Aquinas's thought.

[285] Roland Murphy, *The Tree of Life: An Exploration of Biblical Wisdom Literature* (Grand Rapids, MI: Eerdmans, 2002), 146.

[286] See James D. G. Dunn, *Christology in the Making: A New Testament Inquiry into the Origins of the Doctrine of the Incarnation* (Grand Rapids, MI: Eerdmans, 1996), 163–212.

[287] See Marian Hillar, *From Logos to Trinity: The Evolution of Religious Beliefs from Pythagoras to Tertullian* (Cambridge: Cambridge University Press, 2012).

[288] Raymond Brown, *The Gospel and Epistles of John* (Collegeville: Liturgical Press, 1992), 21–2.

Augustine, as well as in the medieval thought of Richard of St Victor and Bonaventure. The mutuality of λογος and σοφία continues into the later medieval period, especially through the influence of Aquinas.[289]

Indeed, Hooker's favourite Wisdom text (Wis. 8.1) also regularly features in Aquinas's thought, as W. David Neelands has shown.[290] Wis. 8.1 describes how 'Wisdom reacheth from one end to another mightily, and sweetly [χρηστῶς] doth she order all things'. Hooker appeals to this text (as well as Wis. 11.17) in Book One when he discusses how the various orders of creation are a diminished and participatory similitude of an original, unlimited divine perfection. Diminishment in creation, however, does not imply imperfection. Hooker writes:

> If therfore it be demanded, why God having power and habilitie infinite, th'effects of that power are all so limited as we see they are: the reason hereof is the end which he hath proposed, and the lawe whereby his wisedome hath stinted th'effects of his power in such sort, that it doth not worke infinitely but correspondently unto that end for which it worketh, even al things χρηστῶς, in most decent and comely sort, *all things in measure, number, and waight*.[291]

As caused, creation variously participates in God's perfection through analogical laws that direct created things to appropriate perfective ends. Finitude does not constitute imperfection, but rather frames the creaturely conditions for variegated perfection.[292] Participation in God reflects a wise and amiable [χρηστῶς] ordering of the various ways that creation shares in God's 'most glorious and abundant vertue'.

Hooker implicitly identifies Christ as this amiable *Sophia* and *λογος* within the act of creation in Book One of the *Laws*. The coda of Book One casts law in terms very close to the Wisdom of the sapiential books of Hebrew Scripture: 'her seate is the bosome of God, her voice the harmony of the world.'[293] That Christ is the Wisdom who orders creation remains the background to this coda and explains Hooker's high estimation of nature. Indeed, in Book Five, Hooker describes how all of creation participates in Christ as an efficient cause: 'it must be confest that of Christ, working as a creator, and a governor of the world by providence, all are partakers.'[294] Christ forms the wise, rational, free and loving divine donation of being, the paradigm for the first heuristic paradigm of participation. When Hooker appeals to Wisdom theology (especially Prov. 8.23) in his discussion of how eternal law generates creation, Hooker tacitly implies, then, that this involves natural participation in Christ as Wisdom:

---

[289] Kirby, 'Reason and Law', 251; and Kirby, 'Neoplatonic Logic', 54.
[290] W. David Neelands, 'Predestination', in *A Companion to Richard Hooker*, ed. W. J. T. Kirby (Leiden: Brill, 2008), 185–220 (209–10).
[291] Hooker, *Laws*, 1:60.28–61.6; I.2.3. Compare ibid., 2:227.34–228.8; V.55.2. Hooker draws a strict distinction between the finitude of created beings and the infinity of God. Yet, being finite does not signal imperfection: limitedness rather signals 'both the perfection and preservation' of the variety of creation, as well as suggesting a measure by which things are directed to some particular end.
[292] Ibid., 1:61.12–17; I.2.4.
[293] Ibid., 1:142.8–9; I.16.8.
[294] Ibid., 2:242.11–13; V.56.10.

That law eternall which God himself hath made to himselfe, and thereby worketh all things whereof he is the cause and author, that law in the admirable frame whereof shineth with most perfect bewtie the countenance of that wisedome which hath testified concerning her self, *The Lord possessed me in the beginning of his way, even before his works of old, I was set up etc.*[295]

The *Folger Library Edition* commentary denies that Hooker equates here the creative *Sophia* with the divine λογος since God voluntarily chooses to self-impose eternal law.[296] Yet, pace this commentary, Hooker's discussion of law as it relates to God makes it clear that λογος and *Sophia* are co-identical in this text as one might expect from the exegetical tradition. Indeed, the gloss in the Geneva Bible of 1560 on Proverbs comments that, 'he [Solomon] declareth hereby the divinitie and eternitie of this wisedome . . . meaning thereby the eternall Sonne of God Jesus Christ our Saviour, whome St. John calleth the worde that was in the beginning, John 1, 1.' In Book One, Hooker works through how λογος and *Sophia* relate. While the λογος or *ratio* of law remains necessary ad intra (God simply is law), God voluntarily chooses to act ad extra upon the creative archetype of the divine *Sophia* in order to create the cosmos. Indeed, for Hooker, eternal law represents 'that *order* [λογος] which God before all ages hath set down with himself, for himselfe to all things by', while Wisdom (*Sophia*) is the 'patterne [παράδειγμα] to *make*, and is the card to *guide the worlde by*'.[297] Thus, in one direction, law (circumscribed by λογος or *ratio*) is eternal, immutable, unchangeable and perfect, co-identical with the being of God and constituting a book 'we are neither able nor worthie to open and looke into'.[298] In the direction of creation, however, eternal law expresses the free, loving and generous diffusion of being from God into all created things through *Sophia*, the rational παράδειγμα. Hooker's statement in Book Five that all creation participates in Christ as creator shows that Hooker therefore implicitly sees Christ as both λογος and *Sophia* in Book One. There, Christ is a 'necessary' and 'internall' member of the Trinity and also acts as the creative archetype voluntarily embraced in the divine donation of being.[299] Indeed, when he turns to the creation of the world in Gen. 1, Hooker makes it clear that the divine *fiat* reflects not an arbitrary will but rather rational 'speech' [λογος] which institutes the 'law naturall to be observed by creatures'.[300] In the Word or Wisdom, God knows all the different ways in which creation can participate in the essential goodness of divine nature. Creation becomes a diminished image, then, of the second person of the Trinity through the descending imitation of law.

In Book One, then, Christ implicitly acts as the transcendent sapiential principle (the 'woord or Wisdom') co-identical with the work of eternal law in which the

---

[295] Ibid., 1:61.28–62.6; I.2.5, emphasis in the original.
[296] Ibid., 1:62.29–63.1; I.2.6: 'Nor is the freedom of the wil of God any whit abated, let or hindered by meanes of this, because the imposition of this law upon himself is his own free and voluntary act.' For the commentary notes, see *FLE*, 6 (1): 482.
[297] Hooker, *Laws*, 1:62.6–7; 1:63.1–3; I.2.5–6 (my emphasis).
[298] Ibid., 1:62.10–11; I.2.5.
[299] Ibid., 1:59.6–12; I.2.2.
[300] Ibid., 1:64.18–65.7; I.3.2.

whole system of created laws participates. Hooker returns again to the sweet and amiable [χρηστῶς] character of Wisdom in Wis. 8.1 when he discusses how creation participates in divine Wisdom. Hooker's definition of law as 'a directive rule unto the goodness of operation' revolves around analogical participation in God's Wisdom and the co-identical transcendental perfections of goodness and beauty. Hooker therefore expands the definition in the following manner:

> The rule of divine operations outward, is the definitive appointment of Gods owne wisedome set down within himself. The rule of naturall agents that work by simple necessity, is the determination of the wisedome of God .... The rule of ghostly or immateriall natures, as spirits and Angels, is their intuitive intellectual judgement concerning the amiable [χρηστῶς] beautie and high goodnes of that object, which with unspeakable joy and delight, doth set them on worke ... The rule of voluntary agents on earth is the sentence that reason giveth concerning the goodness of those things which they are to do.[301]

In this passage, Hooker develops briefly how law operates analogously: God's wisdom simply is law; animals keep the law of nature unwittingly through their natural actions; and both angels and human beings operate rationally, respectively 'concerning the amiable [χρηστῶς] beautie and high goodness of that object [i.e. God]' as well as 'concerning those things which they are to do'. While such laws operate as interior principles, they theonomously participate in the providential wisdom of God, namely Christ himself, an amiable order of λογος and *Sophia*. At the end of Book One, Hooker appeals to the figure of Wisdom in Prov. 8.15 again to portray a descending imitation of eternal law throughout creation: 'lawes apparently good, are (as it were) things copied out of the very tables of that high everlasting law, even as the booke of that law hath sayd concerning itself, *By me Kinges raigne, and* by me *Princes decree justice*.'[302] Yet, here such imitation is not simply that of an external principle, for there is a strict difference between the infinity of God and finitude of creation. Imitation is rather an intrinsic principle ('it worketh in them'), a theonomous participation, an analogical similarity between the *ratio* of Wisdom (Christ) and the *ratio* of created forms. Christ as Wisdom 'reads' himself into the world through such immanent causality. Indeed, when Hooker later describes how God influences human beings, he casts God's causality as a 'sweet [χρηστῶς] compulsion', an orderly and fitting correspondence or *convenientia*.[303]

In the *Dublin Fragments*, Hooker therefore indexes both nature and grace to the sweet amiability [χρηστῶς] of Wisdom in which transcendent causality unfolds immanently. Hooker writes:

> The axiome of the providence of God in general, whereby he is said to governe all thinges amiablie according to the severall condition and qualitie of their natures, must needs especiallie take place, in ordering the principall actions whereunto

---

[301] Ibid., 1:84.16–85.4; I.8.4.
[302] Ibid., 1:136.8–15; I.16.2, emphasis in the original.
[303] Ibid., 2:356.1–8; V.60.3.

the hand of his grace directeth the soules of men .... God hath ordeyned grace . . . that thereby wee which cannot moove ourselves, may be drawne, but amiablie drawne.[304]

Nature and grace share the amiable character of Wisdom. The whole life of grace concurs with the *ratio* of nature and reflects that God 'ordereth, but yet with gentleness; mightily, but yet in an amiable manner'.[305] As with nature, so with redemption since God 'leadeth still to eternall life by an amiable course, framed even according to the verie state wherein wee now are'.[306] Indeed, in the *Laws* the redemptive return to God through Christ turns on eternal Wisdom just as creation does: 'behold how the wisedome of God hath revealed a way mysticall and supernaturall .... The supernaturall way hath God in himselfe prepared before all worldes'.[307] In Book Five, Hooker equates the 'woord' (λογος) with the 'Wisdom' (*Sophia*) of God in the Incarnation. Parsing Jn 1.14, Hooker writes that 'wisdom to the ende that she might save manie made not *this or that man* hir habitation but *dwelt in us*'.[308] Hooker rejects the Arian idea that there are two 'wisdoms' in God, one uncreated, the other (Jesus) created.[309] Jesus, the eternal λογος, is also eternal *Sophia*. Since Christ is amiable Wisdom, Christ immediately orders creation and redemption, the exit from and return to God. Such immediacy does not remove nature but condescends to work through the mediation of immanent natural causes, the Incarnation, and sacramental instrumentality. The 'woord or Wisdom of God' theonomously suspends creation from God as an act of gentle love, working for its redemption. Immediacy and mediation meet in Christ as Word and Wisdom. Christ the key distinguishes only in order to unite both nature and grace, unlocking their relationship.

In Book Five of the *Laws*, Hooker expands upon the metaphysical role of participation for the salvific union between Christ and believers. Hooker's language elevates the weak sense of participation in Christ as Creator into the strong sense of reunion with God and deification. For Hooker, the Incarnation entails that by 'personal union', Christ's 'deitie' is 'inseparablie joined' to the body and soul of his humanity.[310] Thus, Hooker generates the double sense in which Christ is the foundation of all participation in God: as the eternal Word or Wisdom of God creating and directing the cosmos, and also as the wise Word who perfects those who believe in His Incarnation, death and Resurrection. Thus, all things participate in God because 'his influence [is] in the verie essence of all thinges'.[311] This general participation is also Trinitarian, being in the Father as 'goodness', in the Son as 'wisdom' ordering all things, and in the power of the Spirit as an 'power'.[312] Yet, in addition to this general participation is a unique filiation by the saving grace of Christ so that believers are 'given the gratious

---

[304] Hooker, *Dublin Fragments*, 2, in *FLE*, 4:102.9–13, 103.21–8. Compare Aquinas, *ST*, I.II.110.2.
[305] Hooker, *Dublin Fragments*, 27, in *FLE*, 4:134.23–4.
[306] Ibid., 31, in *FLE*, 4:140.31–141.1.
[307] Hooker, *Laws*, 1:118.14–23; I.11.6.
[308] Ibid., 2:213.13–23; V.52.3, emphasis in the original.
[309] Ibid., 2:215.17–21; V.52.4.
[310] Ibid., 2:216.4–18; V.52.4.
[311] Ibid., 2:236.22–3; V.56.5.
[312] Ibid., 2:237.10–13; V.56.5.

and amiable name of sonnes [1 Jn 3.1]'.[313] Such gratuitous filiation ultimately works towards participation in glory since we 'are therefore in God through Christ eternallie' and are 'adopted sonnes of God to eternall life by participation of the only begotten Sonne of God.'[314] Since 'God hath deified our nature' in Christ's Incarnation, adoption analogously deifies believers. The 'woord or Wisdom' of God draws believers into the life of God, and ultimately into the eternal union of the natural with the divine. The 'woord or Wisdom of God' immediately works eternal salvation, then, but also doubly condescends into the patterns of natural causality, first in the Incarnation and then in the sacraments in order to unfold transcendence within concrete historical communities.

The sacraments indeed establish the transcendental participation in Christ as an immanent pattern of causality whereby 'Christ is in us' just as believers dwell in him. The Eucharist in particular conforms the recipient unto Christ as Wisdom. In his account of Eucharistic reception in Book Five of the *Laws*, Hooker emphasizes taste. The Eucharistic mysteries 'doe as nailes fasten us to his verie crosse' and 'in the woundes of our redeemer wee there dip our tongues' such that 'our hunger is satisfied . . . our thirst for ever quenched'.[315] The logic of desire which ultimately aims at participation in the divine nature is here pictured as hunger and thirst. Such desire finds non-discursive satiation in Christ, imaged as gustatory delight. The Latin root of taste (*sapere*) figuratively relates to wisdom (*sapientia*), identified by Hooker as Christ's creative and saving influence, and now united with the Eucharistic consumer. Mediation yields to immediate union, the gratuitous reversion of created forms to the Wisdom of God from whom they originally came as a gratuitous gift, a prolepsis of heavenly deification.

C. S. Lewis accordingly points out that Hooker's universe is 'drenched with Deity'.[316] In both extensive and intensive modes of participation, Hooker sees Christ as the key who unlocks the tension between Dionysian hierarchy and Augustinian immediacy or nature and grace. As Word and Wisdom, Christ forms the sapiential principle of creation as well as the loving gratuity of salvation. Christ alone is the exit from and return to God, whether natural or supernatural. As a result, extensive and intensive forms of participation (and the corollaries of hierarchy and grace) always imply one another, either disjunctively (in light of sin) or conjunctively (as non-competitive intensities of divine gift). The metaphysical tension between immediacy and mediation meets in Christ and disappears when seen as aspects of a single divine knowing, loving and making.

---

[313] Ibid., 2:237.28; V.56.6.
[314] Ibid., 2:238.18–19; 2:239.10–12; V.56.7.
[315] Ibid., 2:343.7–31; V.67.12.
[316] C. S. Lewis, *English Literature in the Sixteenth Century, Excluding Drama* (Oxford: Clarendon Press, 1954), 462.

3

'A drop of that unemptiable fountain of wisdom': Cognitive participation in God

Introduction

This chapter unveils how Hooker's architecture of participation establishes a certain homology between his ontology and epistemology. The previous chapter argued that Hooker's architecture of participation unites both extensive and intensive forms of metaphysical participation. Accordingly, it describes three aspects, namely, the existential, formal and henological relationship between creation and God. In that architecture, Christ as 'woord or Wisdom' forms the key who unlocks the distinct but related textures of nature and grace. In Book One, Christ acts as the rational, divine pattern ($παράδειγμα$) who freely, wisely and lovingly makes creatures as extensive, diminished, hierarchical and formal analogues of divine being. In Book Five, Christ's Incarnation immediately forms the wise *ratio* which restores the integrity of nature and through which believers enjoy an intensive (re)union with God, imaged as an analogous form of deification.

When he turns to epistemological questions about how we know what is right in matters of Church discipline and practice in Books Two through Five, Hooker upholds this richly textured architecture of participation. He does so against his radical puritan opponents who 'hold that only one law, the Scripture must be the rule to direct, in all things', including in church polity and what constitutes the proper liturgical means for edification.[1] Accordingly, Andrea Russell argues that participation as well as persuasion is key to understanding Hooker's epistemology: 'he seems to have a greater vision that goes beyond the certainty offered by right answers and looks to nothing less than the possibility of sharing in God's life and wisdom'.[2] As Hooker responds to his puritan interlocutors, reason and desire emerge from the architecture of participation to become the constellating categories for a mixed cognitive ecology that circumscribes both extensive (natural) and intensive (supernatural) forms of cognitive participation in God, moments which Christ as 'woord or Wisdom' again unites. First, in Books One through Three, Hooker explores how God extensively authors the light and word

---

[1] Hooker, *Laws*, 1:145.12–13; II.1.2.
[2] Russell, *Beyond Certainty*, 88–92, 105.

of reason as well as that of Scripture. Divine influence renders reason and Scripture as complementary participants in the *ratio* of God's 'unemptiable fountaine of wisdom', necessary epistemic elements which manuduct (literally, 'guide by the hand') humanity to the intensive 'participation of God himselfe'. Here, 'as her waies are of sundry kinds', divine wisdom 'inspireth', 'leadeth and trayneth' human understanding in natural as well as supernatural cognitive participation in God.[3] Second, in Books Four and Five, Hooker addresses how the 'elements, parts or principles' of instruction and prayer in worship reform and edify physical, emotional and intellectual desires such that they become 'holie'. Such 'holie desires' also serve 'as a hand to lead, and a way to direct' believers towards an intensive cognitive participation in God, issuing in love.[4] Together, reason and desire thereby reveal a fourth and final participatory turn: as godlike images, human beings are essentially both created and creative sharers in the sapiential unfolding of divine influence within human communities.

Yet, the architectural role of participation in Hooker's epistemology has gone largely unnoticed despite Hooker's intention to relate 'general' principles to 'particular' points of controversy. As a result, modern scholars typically miss the homology between Hooker's ontology and epistemology, creating an exegetical Scylla and Charybdis. A. S. McGrade therefore wryly observes that Hooker 'has the unusual distinction of being severely criticised for both *hypo-* and *hyper-rationalism*', meaning that Hooker allegedly either undermines the integrity of human reason with the gratuity of grace, or extols the autonomy of reason at the expense of revelation.[5] In both cases, readings typically disparage the emotions as inherently irrational and corrupt. As a heuristic device to explain the difficulties that a participatory reading of Hooker's epistemology faces, it remains useful to develop briefly the exegetical Scylla and Charybdis.

Hypo-rationalist readings typically argue that Hooker subsumes reason under the contrastive, heteronomous and irrational activity of grace.[6] As such, Hooker's early emphasis in Books One through Four on a modern hermeneutic of public reason, historical pragmatism and account of linguistic change gives way to an affective inwardness of faith and liturgical mysticism in Book Five. This latter turn involves the same irrational appeal to the emotions that Hooker has denounced in his puritan opponents in the preface. First, Hooker emphasizes the capacity of human reason in the early books of the *Laws* as a polemical strategy against the radical puritans in order to undermine what he alleges is an emotional delusion behind their claims to interior divine inspiration. Hooker thereby disallows 'an experiential participation

---

[3] Hooker, *Laws*, 1:147.23–148.6; II.1.4.
[4] Ibid., 1:275.21–4; IV.1.3.
[5] McGrade, 'The Coherence of Hooker's Polity', 166 (my italics).
[6] A number of studies together make up the above heuristic model of hypo-rationalist readings of Hooker, although only some draw critical conclusions. See the following examples: Robert V. Kavanagh, 'Reason and Nature in Hooker's Polity' (Unpublished PhD thesis, University of Wisconsin, 1944; Gunnar Hillerdal, *Reason and Revelation in Richard Hooker*; Egil Grislis, 'Richard Hooker's Image of Man', *Renaissance Papers: The Southeastern Renaissance Conference* (1964): 73–84; Robert Faulkner, 'Reason and Revelation in Hooker's Ethics', *The American Political Science Review* 59 (1965): 680–90; Debora Shuger, *Habits of Thought in the English Renaissance* (Toronto: University of Toronto Press, 1997); Corneliu Simut, *The Doctrine of Salvation in the Sermons of Richard Hooker* (Berlin: Walter de Gruyter, 2005); and Voak, *Reformed Theology*, esp. 241–51.

of the Spirit by interposing the interpretive act [of reason] between object [i.e. God, revelation, Scripture] and subjectivity'.[7] Yet, grace accordingly becomes problematic and the Spirit's activity, irrational. Hooker cannot explain how non-Christians have knowledge of God without grace, and 'vagueness stamps the whole argument' when he writes of a specifically Christian kind of ratiocination, since he cannot account for how sanctification transforms mental faculties.[8] At the same time, Hooker lets slip back in an alternative and discontinuous participatory epistemology in Book Five. Whereas the intellect remains concerned with rational evidence, religious faith revolves around the certainty of adherence based on illogical desire. Hooker's emotional encomium of Eucharistic participation as a mystical, deifying activity represents an incoherent departure from a polemical concern with reasonableness, 'an astonishing turn to a kind of irrationalism' which implies 'that the Christian can move to a point over and above logical discourse and that all questions then will be answered by the grace of God'.[9]

In contrast, *hyper-rationalist* readings of Hooker argue that he grants to dispassionate human reason an unabashed, self-sufficient autonomy in Books One through Three, even in relation to revelation.[10] Of course, the earliest critics who cast Hooker as a hyper-rationalist are the anonymous authors of *A Christian Letter* from 1599. Those conforming puritan authors accuse him of extolling natural law, reason and pagan thought over the perfect sufficiency of Scripture: they decry that, in Hooker's thought, 'reason is highlie sett up against holie Scripture'.[11] The authors accordingly demand that Hooker 'shew us therefore howe your positions agree with our church and the scriptures'.[12] Later hyper-rationalist exegetes similarly argue that, in Books One through Three, Hooker exaggerates the superiority of an autonomous rationality upon which the content and authority of Scripture has a 'pervasive dependence'.[13] Indeed, Scripture presupposes 'the powers and autonomous action of human reason to decode its message', meaning that 'the possession and use of reason was a *sine qua non* for conversion'.[14] More importantly, Hooker thereby 'evolved in the end a conception of a truly omnipotent reason' and 'established the complete autonomy of

---

[7] Shuger, *Habits of Thought*, 37.
[8] Hillerdal, *Reason and Revelation*, 135–7.
[9] Ibid., 126, 135.
[10] A number of studies make up this heuristic model of hyper-rationalist readings of Hooker, although only some draw critical conclusions. See the following examples: L. S. Thornton, *Richard Hooker: A Study of his Theology* (London: SPCK, 1924); Peter Munz, *The Place of Hooker in the History of Thought*; Dewey Wallace, *Puritans and Predestination: Grace in English Protestant Theology, 1552–1695* (Chapel Hill: University of North Carolina Press, 1982); Brian Vickers, 'Public and Private Rhetoric in Hooker's Lawes', *Richard Hooker and the Construction of Christian Community*, ed. A. S. McGrade (Tempe: Medieval and Renaissance Texts and Studies, 1997), 95–145; Joan Lockwood O' Donovan, *Theology of Law and Authority in the English Reformation* (Atlanta: Scholars Press, 2000); and Esther Reed, 'Richard Hooker, Eternal Law, and the Human Exercise of Authority', *Journal of Anglican Studies* 4, no. 2 (2006): 219–38.
[11] *A Christian Letter*, 20, in *FLE*, 4:67.1. See H. C. Porter, 'Hooker, the Tudor Constitution, and the Via Media', in *Studies in Richard Hooker*, ed. W. Speed Hill (Cleveland: The Press of Case Western Reserve University, 1972), 77–116, agreeing that Hooker's critics were right: 'the whole of Hooker's work... was a celebration of "our natural faculty of reason"' (103).
[12] *A Christian Letter*, 3, 5, 20, in *FLE*, 4:11.10–24; 19.1–2; 65.16–68.19.
[13] O'Donovan, *Theology of Law*, 137, 142, 145.
[14] Lake, *Anglicans &Puritans?*, 152, emphasis in the original.

human reason over the whole of life'.[15] Hooker's work constitutes 'before all else a great appeal to reason in matters of religion', itself a rhetorical move of 'calm and reasoned discussion' against the 'uninformed enthusiasm' of his puritan critics.[16] The emotions are therefore banished to the private realm. Only reason has a public place since it alone produces a 'coherent structure of argument'. In contrast, the emotions have a limited, private aim in the Eucharistic encomium of Book Five, namely, 'the singling out of the precious elements of Christian belief [which] invites the reader to share in the writer's celebration'.[17] The autonomy of human reason ultimately entails, then, a specious naturalism that denudes public life of the supposedly subrational emotions, evacuates creation of God's immanent causality, and so separates ethics and politics from metaphysics.

This chapter considers in turn the constellating categories of Hooker's cognitive ecology, namely reason and desire, and shows how the architecture of participation cuts through the Gordian knot of hypo- and hyper-rationalism, rescuing the emotions as rationally constitutive of human flourishing *coram Deo*. First, this chapter considers Hooker's account of reason, a power that enjoys natural and supernatural forms of cognitive participation in God. As Egil Grislis points out, Hooker often equivocates in whether he takes the 'light of reason' to refer to natural reason unaided by special grace, a capacity blighted by sin, or a power redeemed by (sanctifying) grace.[18] Untangling this equivocation will illumine how Hooker's account navigates between hypo- and hyper-rationalism: divine influence works within and through intrinsic, natural capacities, underwriting and restoring their integrity. This chapter then turns to the liturgical re-creation of divinely instantiated desire. Here, far from being inherently irrational, for Hooker emotions exhibit a logical, intentional structure and even a kind of perceptive cognition that drives human beings not only to know but also to enjoy loving union with God. Finally, this chapter will return to Christ as the key who unlocks the tensions between nature and grace in human cognition. Here, Christ acts as the principium or form of reason, Scripture and desire, circumscribing for Hooker the extensive and intensive ways in which human beings cognitively participate in God through their creation and redemption.

'The light of reason': Natural cognitive participation in God

In the legal ontology of Book One, Hooker discusses natural intellectual faculties at some length and sets reason as the first constellating category of a cognitive ecology which leads human beings to the 'participation of God himselfe'. Nigel Voak adroitly claims that 'Hooker's philosophy of mind was thoroughly scholastic in its orientation'.[19]

---

[15] Munz, *The Place of Hooker*, 61–2.
[16] Thornton, *Richard Hooker*, 24.
[17] Vickers, 'Public and Private Rhetoric', 145.
[18] Egil Grislis, 'Scriptural Hermeneutics', in *A Companion to Richard Hooker*, ed. W. J. T. Kirby (Leiden: Brill, 2008), 297–301. See also Robert Hoopes, *Right Reason in the English Renaissance* (Cambridge: Harvard University Press, 1962), 123–4.
[19] Voak, *Reformed Theology*, 25.

In order to extrapolate Hooker's 'philosophy of mind', Voak traces the similarity between Hooker's account of reason, appetite and imagination with that of Aquinas, as well as the supposed consonance between Hooker's account of the will and that of Duns Scotus.[20] Broadly speaking, within this scholastic, faculty-based anthropology, 'the object of wil is that good which reason doth leade us to seek'.[21] Here, reason (or the 'shew of reason') 'prescribeth the thing desired [i.e. the good]' to the will which, as an intellectual desire, chooses it and moves to act. In turn, the 'inferiour naturall desire' called 'appetite' has as its object 'whatever sensible good may be wished for' and accordingly solicits the will. Reason mediates such solicitation, however, as it presents to the will the intelligibility of the appetite's desires, 'now pursuit and refusal in the will do follow, the one the affirmation, the other negation of goodnes, which the understanding apprehendeth, grounding it selfe upon sense.'[22] In *Pride*, Hooker succinctly paraphrases what the 'orderly disposition of the mind of man should be' in such a faculty-based anthropology, namely that 'perturbations and sensuall appetites [are] all kept in aw by a moderate and sober will; will in all things framed by reason; reason directed by the law of god and nature.'[23]

Yet, Voak crucially omits the central importance of participation for Hooker and Aquinas, who both refuse to see human capacities in merely autonomous, secular terms, or the work of grace as heteronomous to natural integrity. Instead, they commonly understand natural reason as a cognitive participation in the eternal *ratio* of God. Hooker, following Aquinas, gives a theological account of reason as an intrinsic power nevertheless suspended from God's causality as a gift.[24] The central chapters (eight through ten) of Book One of the *Laws* are concerned with 'the naturall way of finding out laws by reason to guide the will unto that which is good', 'the benefit of keeping that law which reason teacheth', and 'how reason doth leade men unto the making of humane lawes'. While Hooker considers the integrity of natural reason in these texts, the 'participation of God himselfe' entirely frames the natural epistemic pursuit of 'that which is good' such that, for human beings, there is a natural cognitive participation in God, a participated theonomy. Generated out of the architecture of participation, natural cognitive participation in God thereby involves formal, existential and henological aspects: it describes the intelligibility, facticity and purpose of reason in relation to God as rational source and end. It also involves, however, a creative turn: the causation of some transcendent source does not empty out human agency; rather, human reason displays a participated creativity in which its own contingent historical

---

[20] Ibid., 28–67.
[21] Hooker, *Laws*, 1:78.15–26; I.7.3.
[22] Ibid., 1:80.6–11; I.7.6. For a negative appraisal of Hooker's allegedly Suárezian account of reason and the will, see Westberg, 'Thomistic Law', 209–12. Compare a later sanguine reading in Daniel Westberg, *Renewing Moral Theology* (Downers Grove: IVP Academic, 2015), 27, 146–7.
[23] Hooker, *Pride*, I, in *FLE*, 5:314.16–20.
[24] Voak, *Reformed Theology*, 27 demurs on this point and only uses Aquinas as a comparison 'with some reluctance' as an accessible cipher for the 'very basic common features' of scholastic theories of the mind. In contrast, Joyce, *Anglican Moral Theology*, 69, 86–7 argues that Hooker's thought 'coheres' with Aquinas and so Hooker owes 'much to Aristotelian-Thomist tradition in his theological anthropology'. Also, see Peter Sedgwick, *The Origins of Anglican Moral Theology* (Leiden: Brill, 2019), 236–9.

activities instrumentally mediate the *ratio* of divine artisanship. This part unpacks how Hooker places natural reason as an analogy of divine rationality and positions divine causality within natural reason. It concludes with the manner in which natural cognitive participation in God forms an important prelude to supernatural cognitive participation.

Hooker's metaphysical dependence on Aquinas's account of law, analogy and participation in Book One matches a comparable vestige around the natural cognitive participation of the human intellect in God through the law of reason. An analogical account of participation remains crucial to understanding how Hooker comprehends the human intellect as imaging the divine intellect 'after a sort', and accordingly the created 'light of reason' as a natural cognitive participation in God. Here, cognitive participation undercuts notions of autonomy and heteronomy, namely hyper- and hypo-rationalism: the form of reason is theonomously suspended from its transcendental origin as a created and creative similitude. Here, analogy holds together the four aspects of the architecture of participation. The ideality, existence and unitive purpose of reason derive from its causal relationship with divine reason. In turn, since reason helps constitute human nature as being made in the image of God, it also sets humanity as a fabricating animal: the creative capacity of human reason to make meaning echoes, in a limited fashion, the nature of God as the rational creator. The principle of analogy implied in participatory metaphysics therefore holds together the integrity of the intellectual form with its causal dependence upon a higher principle. It remains helpful, therefore, initially to revisit Aquinas's account of analogy, and sketch out his ideas about natural cognitive participation in God, as that which informs Hooker's epistemology.[25]

For Aquinas, analogy involves three elements. First, a source that possesses some perfection in total and unrestricted fashion (the analogate). Second, a subject that possesses the same perfection, but in a limited and restricted way (the analogue). Third, that the subject depends on the donating source of the perfection to receive that perfection, as an effect from a cause (the suspension of the analogue from the analogate). For Aquinas, analogy images how the human intellect is causally suspended as an analogue from God. As pure act (*purus actus*), God is understanding essentially (*per essentiam*), the primary analogate of reason.[26] Human beings, as they move from potency to act, understand through participating God's act of understanding (*per participationem*) and represent the analogue of reason.[27] The participation of the human intellect in the divine intellect accordingly displays a double aspect: first, God causes the intellectual power in human beings as well as the intelligible forms by which they understand;[28] and second, the power of human reason, in its own secondary, intrinsic operations, participates as an effect in such divine influence.[29] Thus, the 'natural light' of the human intellect depends upon God's 'enlightenment' in two ways: 'inasmuch as

---

[25] For Aquinas's account of natural and supernatural cognitive participation, see Rziha, *Perfecting Human Actions*, 184–256.
[26] Aquinas, *ST*, I.14.1–2.
[27] Ibid., I.79.4.
[28] Ibid., I.105.3.
[29] Ibid., I.14.8.3; I.84.5.

it is from Him that it has the form whereby it acts; secondly, inasmuch as it is moved by Him to act.'[30] Thus, for Aquinas the intrinsic 'light' of human reason participates in the light of divine reason as an analogous effect from a transcendent cause, but the same cause remains as a constituting influence within it.[31]

Hooker, like Aquinas, sets the natural power of reason as an analogous participant in the *ratio* of its uncreated source, namely God. God's intellectual nature forms the primary analogate of rationality for Hooker.[32] 'Law' expresses the rule (*ratio*) and measure of action: the essence of law is accordingly something rational (*aliquid rationis*). As pure act, God exists simply as law (*per essentiam*), the perfect, primary analogate of rational order. 'Law' images, then, the perfect *ratio* of the divine nature itself and identifies God as pure reason or intellect. Hooker here shares a similarity with patristic writers who, though they rarely define mind (*mens*) or intellect (*nous*), assume it as a divine characteristic and so set the relationship between divine rationality and the human rational capacity as the ground for seeing humanity as being made in the *imago dei*.[33] For Hooker, the rational character of God remains publically accessible without the need for special revelation. As evidence, Hooker references pagan authors who see the First Cause of creation as a self-mediating, legal and rational principle. Hooker lists Homer, Mercurius Trismegistus, Anaxagoras, Plato and the Stoics as examples, concluding that 'they all confesse therfore in the working of that first cause, that *counsell* is used, *reason* followed, a *way* observed, that is to say, constant *order* and *law* is kept, whereof it selfe must needs be author unto itself'.[34] In turn, Hooker identifies the divine rationality exhibited within eternal law as the scriptural figure of divine Wisdom, eternal and beyond human understanding.[35]

Since the law of reason participates in the *ratio* of eternal law, Hooker sees reason as the highest intrinsic power within human nature, 'that divine power of the soule.'[36] As such, wise human beings are diminished analogues of divine rationality, 'though not Gods, yet as gods, high, admirable, and divine.'[37] Diminishment does not infer a pejorative intellectual status. The power of 'naturall reason' elevates humankind above other creatures incapable of ratiocination and makes human beings 'capable of a more divine perfection', namely, the ability for self-direction, creativity and 'reaching higher then unto sensible things'.[38] Hooker defines the law of reason twice, and each definition

---

[30] Ibid., II.I.109.1. See David L. Whidden III, *Christ the Light: The Theology of Light and Illumination in Thomas Aquinas* (Minneapolis, MN: Fortress, 2014), 135–72.
[31] Aquinas, *ST*, I.12.11 ad. 3; I.89.1. Indeed, Aquinas, *ST*, I.12, 2 resp. sees human rationality, whether in its natural operations or as enlivened by special grace, as a *participatio divini luminis*.
[32] The essential rationality of God can be seen elsewhere in Hooker's writings. For example, see Hooker, *Predestination*, in *FLE*, 4:84.9–19 where he employs the scholastic distinction of *scientia simplicis intelligentiae* and *scientia visionis* in order to describe God's knowledge (*scientia Dei*) as it relates to the divine will. For an extended discussion of the categories as used by Hooker, see Nigel Voak, 'English Molinism in the Late 1590s: Richard Hooker on Free Will, Predestination, and Divine Foreknowledge', *Journal of Theological Studies* 60, no. 1 (2009): 130–77. See also Muller, *Dictionary*, 274–6.
[33] See Anna N. Williams, *The Divine Sense: The Intellect in Patristic Theology* (Cambridge: Cambridge University Press, 2007), 5–7.
[34] Hooker, *Laws*, 1:59.33–60.14; I.2.3, emphasis in the original.
[35] Ibid., 1:61.23–62.11; I.2.5.
[36] Ibid., 1:77.8; I.7.1.
[37] Ibid., 1:74.5–10; I.5.3.
[38] Ibid., 1:75.7–20; I.6.2-3.

emphasizes that reason is an intrinsic power to discern appropriate courses of action 'without the helpe of revelation supernaturall and divine'.[39] First, 'the lawe of reason or humaine nature is that which men by discourse of naturall reason have rightly found out themselves to be all for ever bound unto in their actions.' Second, 'lawe rationall therefore . . . comprehendeth all those thinges which men by the light of their naturall understanding evidently know . . . good or evill for them to doe.'[40] Since 'the laws of well doing are the dictates of right reason', the law of reason practically guides the human agent to right action.[41] Right reason (*recta ratio*) is, of course, a scholastic term with Stoic roots, where it reflects living in conformity with a rationally perceived universal law. Thus, although the law of reason describes an intrinsic power, Hooker casts it as a participated theonomy. Indeed, human nature represents an analogue of the divine artisan: 'Man in perfection of nature being made according to the likenes of his maker [*imago dei*] resembleth him also in the maner of working'; thus, 'capable we are of God [*capaces dei*] both by understanding and will.'[42] In the *Dublin Fragments*, Hooker reiterates the analogical character of human reason when he describes 'reasonable creatures' such as the angels and humankind as the 'liveliest representations of [God's] owne perfection and glorie'.[43] In the *Laws*, human beings particularly bear a logocentric similarity to divine rationality as linguistic animals. God's 'speech' [λογος] imparts the 'law naturall to be observed by creatures', that is to say, the divine *ratio* of participable order.[44] Since human nature reflects this divine influence in a special way through its rational capacity, 'the chiefest instrument of humaine communion therefore is speech [λογος], because thereby we impart mutuallie one to another the conceiptes of our reasonable understanding.'[45] Indeed, as he explores the analogical similarity between human and divine reason, Hooker twice translates the Neoplatonist Mercurius Trismegistus to the effect that, through their rational capacity, 'man ascends even to heaven, and measures it' and accordingly 'frame themselves according to the PATERNE of the father of spirits'.[46]

Finally, Hooker suspends the natural 'light of reason' from God, 'the father of lights', through a pattern of causality: natural reason exists as an intrinsic power nevertheless derived from and tending back towards God's enlightenment as the rational source and end. This pattern of causality explains the formal, existential, henological and creative aspects of reason's participatory constitution. Accordingly, like Aquinas again, Hooker imbeds a 'vertical' causality within 'horizontal' causality, suspending creation and created powers from God.[47] Vertically, Hooker sets God as the efficient and formal cause of all created things that participate in God: 'God hath his influence into the

---

[39] Ibid., 1:90.5–6; I.8.9.
[40] Ibid., 1:89.28–31; 1:90.19–22; I.8.8–9. Compare *Pride*, I, in *FLE* 5:312.8–9 where law is 'an exact rule whereby human actions are measured'.
[41] Hooker, *Laws*, 1:79.11–12; I.7.4.
[42] Ibid., 1:77.20–1; 1:113.9; I.7.2; I.11.3.
[43] Hooker, *Dublin Fragments*, 28, in *FLE*, 4:135.25–7.
[44] Hooker, *Laws*, 1:64.18–65.7; I.3.2.
[45] Ibid., 1:107.6–9; I.10.12.
[46] Ibid., 1:74.13–14 ; 1:74.t; 1:75.v; I.5.3; I.6.3.
[47] On 'vertical' and 'horizontal' causation, see F. C. Bauerschmidt, *Thomas Aquinas: Faith, Reason, and Following Christ* (Oxford: Oxford University Press, 2013), 49–50.

very essence of all things.'[48] In order to explain how participation suspends created forms from their divine source, Hooker reformulates the Thomistic principle that the cause remains in the thing caused (*causa est in causato*): 'every effect doth after a sort conteine, at least wise resemble the cause from which it proceedeth.'[49] As effects from the First Cause, all created forms therefore bear a participatory similitude to God and (as they move from potency to act) participate in divine perfections.[50] In other words, the horizontal, secondary, intrinsic acts of creatures remain dynamically suspended from their original, vertical, divine cause. For Hooker (as for Aquinas) God therefore illumines the 'light of reason' in two ways. First, God vertically causes the form of reason: Hooker explains that St Paul intends the phrase in Rom. 2.14 ('they are a law unto themselves') to mean 'the light of reason, wherwith God illuminateth every one which commeth into the world'.[51] Second, God moves reason to act: reason (like any capacity) cannot 'rightly performe the functions allotted to it, without perpetuall aid and concurrence of that supreme cause of all things'.[52] In its ordinary, horizontal, intrinsic operations then, human reason reveals vertical divine influence. The 'light of reason' already possesses God's enlightenment, at least in this limited sense: gratuitous divine donation and activity are required even for natural knowing, and the purposive activity of reason tends towards (re)union with God as source and end.

As Hooker further considers the ordinary, horizontal operations of natural reason, he balances its intrinsic integrity with the pivotal role of gratuitous, vertical divine causality. Once again, Aquinas's account of the human intellect forms the background to understand these disparate comments about the process of natural reasoning in Book One of the *Laws*. Aquinas distinguishes between two aspects of the intellect in his account of the intellectual powers, traces of which are evident in Hooker's own thought: namely, the passive (or receptive) and the active (or agent) intellect.[53] The former describes the natural, horizontal, intrinsic operations of the intellect, while the latter sees what Hooker labels as the 'principall cause' of the intellect as something vertically beyond itself, that is to say, in God as the First Cause of natural intellectual illumination. Again, Hooker's notion of participated theonomy deflates any charge of hypo- or hyper-rationalism since it renders rational acts as a series of participatory mediations between the intrinsic, rational human form and the *ratio* of the immediately causative 'father of lights' which underpins all of creation. Here, Hooker holds together human agency and the transcendental perfection coextensive with divine nature: the latter does not defer or evacuate the former; rather, the latter immediately constitutes the integrity of the former and, in doing so, also directs it to stand in its own co-creative relation to the world through moral and political action. A comparison between Aquinas and Hooker in relation to the passive and active aspects of the intellect will illustrate the balance struck between human and divine agency in natural cognitive participation.

[48] Hooker, *Laws*, 2:236.7–13; V.56.5.
[49] Ibid., 1:73.7–8; I.5.2. See also *Pride*, III, in *FLE*, 5:341.3–9.
[50] Hooker, *Laws*, 2:234.33–235.3; V.56.1.
[51] Ibid., 1:84.7–12; I.8.3. Compare ibid., 1:238.31–239.4; III.9.3. See also *Pride*, I, in *FLE*, 5:312.12–18.
[52] Hooker, *Laws*, 1:92.25–8; I.8.11.
[53] Aquinas, *ST*, I.79.2–5.

Aquinas argues that the passive aspect of the intellect (the *intellectus possibilis*) receives and retains the intelligible species abstracted from sensory experience.[54] The passive intellect essentially describes how human beings come to know and understand. Hooker never uses the term 'passive intellect', but a number of features in his account of reason clearly places scholastic thought as the background to his epistemology, as Nigel Voak points out.[55] Both Aquinas and Hooker agree that, while God's intellect is pure act (*purus actus*), the created intellect of the human being has to pass from potency to act.[56] Aquinas and Hooker therefore both stand within an Aristotelian tradition of the tabula rasa: the human intellect starts like 'a clean tablet upon which nothing is written'; all knowledge accordingly begins in the senses, and human understanding grows 'by degrees'.[57] For Aquinas, the passive aspect of the intellect has two operations, traces of which are evident in Hooker as well.[58] First, the passive intellect infallibly apprehends simple ideas as true (*intelligentia indivisibilium*). Such simple ideas are general concepts derived from experience of individual things. Second, it also makes more complex but fallible affirmative and negative judgements about particular propositions (*compositio et divisio*). Without this technical language, Hooker similarly notes that the mark of the human soul reaching 'higher then unto sensible things' will be an ability to comprehend 'differences of time, affirmations, negations, and contradictions in speech'.[59]

For Aquinas, the passive intellect also has certain habits (*habitus*) of thought which enable it to reason, namely the non-derivable, general first principles of speculative and practical reasoning, simply apprehended as true by the intellect much like simple ideas and from which the intellect creatively derives more specific principles for particular circumstances. The first principle of speculative reason is noncontradiction, and the first principle of practical reason is to pursue the good and avoid evil.[60] These speculative and practical intellects are not, however, distinct powers since they are both concerned with truth, the former for its own sake, the latter for some further end. Indeed, 'the speculative intellect through extension becomes practical' and thus ratiocination becomes 'causative' of particular actions.[61] As such, natural reason takes on a moral character indexed against participable divine perfection: truth remains convertible with goodness, and all rational actions aim at (and are measured against the *ratio* of) the good as a perfective quality found pre-eminently in the divine nature.

In a similar vein, Hooker uses 'right reason' to describe the intrinsic character of natural reason as a moral instrument where 'goodnesse is seene with the eye of the understanding. And the light of that eye is reason.'[62] Accordingly, 'the lawes of well

---

[54] Ibid., I.79.2.
[55] See Voak, *Reformed Theology*, 30–1.
[56] Hooker, *Laws*, 1:72.26–30; 1:74.21–3; I.5.1; I.6.1.
[57] Aquinas, *ST*, I.79.2 resp. quoting Aristotle's *De Anima* 3.4. Compare Hooker, *Laws*, 1:74.20–8; I.6.1: 'the soule of man being therefore at the first as a booke, wherein nothing is, and yet all thinges may be imprinted.'
[58] Aquinas, *ST*, I.79.8; I.85.6.
[59] Hooker, *Laws*, 1:75.24–8; I.6.3.
[60] Aquinas, *ST*, I.II.94.2 resp.
[61] Ibid., I.70.11 sc; I.II.64.3; and II.II.4.2 ad.3.
[62] Hooker, *Laws*, 1:78.3–4; I.7.2.

doing are the dictates of right reason.'[63] As the intellect moves from potency to act, 'the right helps of true art and learning' aid it to know truth and so goodness. Indeed, such 'education and instruction' enable natural reason 'the sooner able to judge rightly betweene truth and error, good and evill'.[64] Echoing Aquinas, Hooker identifies two ways in which the intellect discerns goodness: knowledge of first 'causes' or 'principles'; or 'signs and tokens' such as the 'generall and perpetuall voice of men', evident in good 'customs' which take on the character of 'the sentence of God him selfe'.[65] While the former has the greatest certainty as intrinsically true, the second gains its apparent force either by 'strong and invincible demonstration' or as the 'way greatest probability leadeth'.[66] The 'sentence which reason giveth concerning the goodnes of those things which they are to do' derives from self-evident, universally applicable and binding 'maine principles of reason' immediately recognized by the intellect as true.[67]

Given that Hooker remains concerned with law, and law aims at right action, it is unsurprising that he focuses on practical principles, even if he also notes that human beings are inherently speculative.[68] Hooker's main principle closely resembles Aquinas's first principle of practical reason. Hooker reworks Aquinas's first practical principle as *'that the greater good is to be chosen before the lesse'*, a principle which embeds the law of reason 'upon an infallible rule of comparison'.[69] In addition, there are also 'axiomes

---

[63] Ibid., 1:79.11–12; I.7.4.
[64] Ibid., 1:75.28; 1:76.20–3; I.6.3; I.6.5. On the moral quality of reason, see Hoopes, *Right Reason*, 123–31; and Voak, *Reformed Theology*, 31–2. By 'right helps', Hooker identifies himself with an Aristotelian scholasticism against the 'Ramystry' popular across Europe and especially at Cambridge, the intellectual centre of English nonconformity and puritanism. See the textual commentary in *FLE*, 6:493–4; and Lee W. Gibbs, 'Theology, Logic, and Rhetoric in the Temple Controversy between Richard Hooker and Walter Travers', *Anglican Theological Review* 55 (1983): 177–88.
[65] Hooker, *Laws*, 1:82.27–83.4; 1:83.17–19; I.8.2–3. Compare Aquinas, *ST*, I.II.93.2. As Loyer, *L'Anglicanisme*, 142 notes, for Hooker customs become filtered over the course of time and take on a character close to natural law as it participates in eternal law, an example of vox populi, vox dei. On the link between 'signs' and common law, see Charles Watterson Davies, '"For conformities sake": How Richard Hooker Used Fuzzy Logic and Legal Rhetoric against Political Extremes', in *Richard Hooker and the Construction of Christian Community*, ed. A. S. McGrade (Tempe: Medieval and Renaissance Texts and Studies, 1997), 332–49. Hooker also acknowledges, however, in *Laws*, 1:91.25–92.22; I.8.11 that customs can contrarily be 'lewde and wicked' and so 'smother the light of naturall understanding'.
[66] Hooker, *Laws*, 1:179.8–18; II.7.5.
[67] Ibid., 1:85.6–7; I.8.5. On the universally applicable and binding nature of these main principles, see *Laws*, 1:89.25–31; 1:90.26–91.7; 1:91.21–5; 1:130.15; I.8.8; I.8.10; I.15.1.
[68] Ibid., 1:86.11–21; I.8.5. For a refutal that Hooker's thought exhibits a Thomistic emphasis on prudence, see Daniel Westberg, *Right Practical Reason: Aristotle, Action, and Prudence in Aquinas* (Oxford: Oxford University Press, 1994), 210. Other studies emphasize the various presence of prudence, practical wisdom, and equity in Hooker's thought. See: William H. Harrison, 'Prudence and Custom: Revisiting Hooker on Authority', *Anglican Theological Review* 84, no. 4 (2003): 897–913; Damian Grace, 'Natural Law in Hooker's *Of the Lawes of Ecclesiasticall Polity*', *Journal of Religious History* 21, no. 1 (1997): 10–22; Joyce, *Anglican Moral Theology*, 197–214; John Stafford, 'Practical Divinity', in *A Companion to Richard Hooker*, ed. W. J. T. Kirby (Leiden: Brill, 2008), 131–47; and Sedgwick, *Origins*, 254–62.
[69] Hooker, *Laws*, 1:85.10–25; I.8.5, emphasis in the original. Joyce, *Anglican Moral Theology*, 172–4 suggests that Hooker differs from Aquinas in order to gain polemical advantage over the puritans who advocate a 'lesser' good than the established order. See also Linwood Urban, 'A Revolution in English Moral Theology', *Anglican Theological Review* 53, no. 1 (1971): 5–20; and Rudolph P. Almasy, 'Language and Exclusion in the First Book of Hooker's *Politie*', in *Richard Hooker and the English Reformation*, ed. W. J. T. Kirby (Dordrecht: Kluwer Academic Publishers, 2003), 227–42.

lesse general, yet so manifest that they need no further profe', which are 'first found out by discourse, and drawne from out of the very bowels of heaven and earth'.[70] Like Aquinas, Hooker appeals to examples from the Mosaic Decalogue to illustrate these lesser axioms.[71] Hooker then grounds even the 'great mandates' of Christ in Mt. 22.38 that his disciples ought to love God and to love their neighbours as consonant with 'the sentence of reason' which is 'the naturall measure wherby to judge our doings'.[72] Hooker describes how the 'sentence of reason' which measures human actions may be either mandatory ('shewing what must be done'), permissive ('declaring what may bee done') or admonitory ('opening what is the most convenient for us to doe').[73] In turn, human laws are rational, creative, probabilistic and expedient applications of the general sentence of reason or divine law to more particular, contingent affairs.[74] Here, Hooker distinguishes between the 'mixedly' and the 'meerly' human laws.[75] The former contains laws which 'plain or necessarie reason bindeth men unto', which is to say they ratify the law of reason in the public square, such as in the prohibition of incest or polygamy.[76] The latter deal with matters in which reason 'doth but probablie teach to be fit and convenient', such as inheritance laws, which may reasonably take a number of different forms.[77] As such, all these complex distinctions around the 'sentence of reason' entail that, while the main principles of reason are self-evident and universally valid, some human laws derived from them are open to change according to evolving circumstances, although they must remain consonant with reason and Scripture.[78] As a participatory analogue, human reason explores and makes meaning, acting as a kind of word which creatively shares in and applies the *ratio* of eternal law within historical contingencies.

While the passive intellect describes how human beings come to know and understand, for Aquinas the active intellect (*intellectus agens*) explains how they can know or understand at all. The active intellect vertically suspends the horizontal integrity of the human intellect from its illuminating, causative first principle, namely God. For Aquinas, the active intellect abstracts the quiddity of an individual object in order to arrive at the intelligible species that will be impressed upon and retained in the passive intellect. Aquinas inherits from Augustine the tradition of explaining the power of such intellectual understanding in terms of divine illumination: 'the human soul derives its intellectual light' from God.[79] Indeed, quoting psalm 4, Aquinas notes

---

[70] Hooker, *Laws*, 1:86.10–11; I.8.5.
[71] Ibid., 1:86.4–7; I.8.6. Compare Aquinas, *ST*, I.II.100.1 and 3.
[72] Hooker, *Laws*, 1:87.9–89.2; I.8.6–8. W. David Neelands, 'Hooker on Scripture, Reason, and "Tradition"', 75–94 regards Hooker as particularly 'daring' in this regard since it means' reason has a genuine value in the natural discovery of what is also given in revelation' (76–7).
[73] Hooker, *Laws*, 1:89.2–5; I.8.9. On the permissive natural law tradition and Hooker, see Brian Tierney, *Liberty & Law. The Idea of Permissive Natural Law, 1100–1800* (Washington: Catholic University of America Press, 2014), 172–90.
[74] Hooker, *Laws*, 1:63.24–6; 1:95.27–110.20; 1:237.27–9; I.3.1; I.10; III.9.2. Compare Aquinas, *ST*, I.II.91.3; I.II.99.3.
[75] Hooker, *Laws*, 1:105.6–14; I.10.10.
[76] Ibid., 1:105.14–106.1; I.10.10.
[77] Ibid., 1:106.6–20; I.10.10.
[78] Ibid., 1:237.21–9; III.9.2 which references Aquinas, *ST*, I.II.95.3. See also *ST*, I.II.95.2.
[79] Aquinas, *ST*, I.79.5 resp.

'the light of your countenance, O Lord, is signed upon us'. Aquinas here treads a fine line between the integrity of the human intellectual power and the gratuity of divine action. The active intellect exists as a power of each individual soul and the act of understanding belongs properly to each individual human being. Yet, God remains the first mover in the universe and, as such, illumines each individual as the beginning of a chain of per se causation.[80] Thus, the created active intellect participates in the uncreated divine light and this participation works through each individual soul.[81] Participation yields similitude between cause and effect: 'the intellectual light in us is nothing other than a certain participated likeness of the uncreated light' of God's knowledge.[82]

While Nigel Voak claims that Hooker has 'no equivalent of Aquinas' agent intellect', Hooker's images of illumination and divine causation suggest that he does.[83] As already discussed, Hooker writes of the 'light of reason' within the context of the vast array of participatory laws derived from God as the 'father of lights.' Hooker sets up a causal relationship between the 'light of reason' and the 'father of lights'. Indeed, God individuates intellectual light (the power to know) in all human souls such that they can be 'inabled to know truth from falsehood, and good from evil'.[84] That the natural light of reason can illumine even 'our dutie towardes God or towardes man' presupposes 'that knowne relation which God hath unto us as unto children . . . whereof himselfe is the principall cause'.[85] God sits at the beginning of a chain of per se causation that vertically illuminates natural reason but does not violate the horizontal intrinsic integrity of each reasoning individual. The law of reason does not require any additional 'helpe of revelation supernaturall and divine' for its intrinsic operations.[86] Yet, the natural power of thought participates as an effect in the uncreated, intelligible and causative 'father of lights'. It also naturally tends towards God as the final cause of beauty and goodness, the transcendental perfections pre-eminently found in God and which express the attractive and plenitudinous character of participated being. As Hooker considers 'the naturall way of finding out laws by reason to guide the will unto that which is good', he cites the Aristotelian idea of the καλοκα'γαφία (*kalokagathia*), the perfectly good and beautiful person who does things well and orderly.[87] The rectitude of moral goodness thereby allows human beings 'divinely' to be called 'good' and 'beautiful', that is to say, to be diminished images of God's ontological perfection, the 'goodness of beautie in it self'.[88] For Hooker, following his Thomist sympathies,

---

[80] Ibid., I.II.109.1.
[81] Ibid., I.76.2.
[82] Ibid., I.84.5. Also, see *De Ver*, 10.6 ad.6, pars 2 in which Aquinas sees the inborn and self-evident first principles available to the human intellect as 'a kind of reflected likeness in us of the uncreated truth'.
[83] Voak, *Reformed Theology*, 30 n.16.
[84] Hooker, *Laws*, 1:84.9–12; I.8.3. See also ibid., 1:238.25–239.4; III.9.3.
[85] Ibid., 1:87.12–21; I.8.7.
[86] Ibid., 1:90.6–7; I.8.9.
[87] Ibid., 1:82.4–27; I.8.1. The commentary in *FLE*, 6 (1): 497 on this passage notes the occurrence of the word in Aristotle's *Magna moralia*, 2.9 and *Politics*, 4.6.2. The word itself is a substantive elision of the adjectives 'beautiful' (*kalos*) and 'good' (*agathos*). See Miller, *Vision of God*, 202–3.
[88] Hooker, *Laws*, 1:113.18–20; I.11.2.

natural illumination therefore establishes a participatory likeness to God.[89] It provides the ground for sanctifying grace to establish the soul's direct, supernatural communion with God,[90] and explains why the beatific vision primarily involves an act of intellect as the proper end of human nature, the will resting in love following this activity as an affective perfection that depends upon it.[91] Neither hypo- nor hyper-rationalism adequately captures the intricacy of Hooker's account of natural cognitive participation in God. The integrity of rational human agency remains undergirded by gratuitous divine causality. In turn, the transcendental perfections do not empty human agency, but rather fulfil it as the participant stands *coram Deo*.

The natural cognitive participation of the 'light of reason' in the 'father of lights' accordingly generates three significant structural features of supernatural cognitive participation in Books Two and Three of the *Laws*. First, Hooker posits divine illumination as even the natural means by which human beings come to know the truth. Human rationality (as a created analogue of divine reason) represents an extensive gift of cognitive participation in God, the presupposed cognitive capacity for an intensive (re)union wrought by grace. As such, Hooker places natural cognitive participation in God far beyond anything that could count as hypo- or hyper-rationalist. Pace Debora Shuger, natural reason is not simply an empirical faculty 'bounded by sense perception and therefore intrinsically secular'.[92] Rather, natural reason reveals divine action and presence within and through its own integrity. Accordingly, Hooker recognizes the capacity of non-Christians to know and understand both natural and certain spiritual truths. Indeed, he obviates what John Marenbon has called the 'problem of paganism', namely how to account for pagan knowledge and virtue.[93] As McGrade points out, in Hooker's *Laws* 'the most obvious feature of his nomological cosmology is the preponderance of classical references', with 16 per cent of Hooker's textual references in total (and 25 per cent in Book One) coming from classical sources.[94] As well as using pagan authorities such as Hesiod and Sophocles to support the idea that law structures the universe and makes it universally intelligible, Hooker also often notes the natural spiritual knowledge of pagan authors.[95] Even 'meere naturall men', writes Hooker, 'have attained to knowe, not onely that there is a God, but also what power, force, wisedome, and other properties that God hath, and how all things depende on him'.[96] Conversely, Hooker regularly quotes from scriptural texts in order to illustrate his metaphysical arguments, and maintains that Scripture 'is fraught even with lawes of nature'.[97] Hooker's positive valuation of the natural light of reason explains

---

[89] Ibid., 1:77.20–1; I.7.2. Compare Aquinas, *ST*, I.12.2 resp.
[90] Hooker, *Laws*, 1:128.30–129.3; I.14.4.
[91] Ibid., 1:113.7–29; 1:118.31–119.15; I.11.3; I.11.6. Compare Aquinas, *ScG*, III.c.26.
[92] Shuger, *Habits of Thought*, 43.
[93] John Marenbon, *Pagans and Philosophers: The Problem of Paganism from Augustine to Leibniz* (Princeton, NJ: Princeton University Press, 2015), esp. 1–15.
[94] A. S. McGrade, 'Classical, Patristic, and Medieval Sources', in *A Companion to Richard Hooker*, ed. W. J. T. Kirby (Leiden: Brill, 2008), 51–88 (esp. 58, 87).
[95] For example, see Hooker, *Laws*, 1:59.33–60.4; 1:70.16–22; 1:73.32–74.6; 1:86.21–3; 1:90.6–11; I.2.3; I.4.1; I.5.3; I.8.5; I.8.9.
[96] Ibid., 1:87.13–17; I.8.7.
[97] Ibid., 1:119.29; I.12.1. See Neelands, 'Scripture, Reason, and Tradition', 78–81.

why in Book Two he insists that the law of reason remains 'an infallible knowledge imprinted in the mindes of all the children of men'. Such innate knowledge allows 'meere natural men' to derive particular choices for 'the daylie affaires of this life' from 'generall principles for directing humaine actions', meaning from the 'maine principles of reason' which Hooker has discussed in Book One.[98] It also explains why, in Book Three, Hooker casts moral virtues as human rather than exclusively Christian.[99] Accordingly, Hooker reserves some of his strongest language in Book Three to decry how his puritan opponents allegedly 'thinke they cannot admire as they ought the power and authoritie of the word of God, as in things divine they should attribute any force to mans reason'.[100] For Hooker, that both Christ and the Apostles exhibit the form of reason ultimately means that 'the light therefore, which the starre of natural reason and wisdom casteth, is too bright to be obscured by the mist of a word or two uttered to diminish that opinion'.[101] Against the biblical singularity of his opponents, Hooker's architecture of participation opens up space in Books Two and Three for the multivocal character of manifold laws, including the law of reason, as they participate in, and are suspended from, eternal law.

Second, reason exhibits an instrumental and public character as it cognitively participates in God. The intrinsic goodness of natural reason entails that 'grace hath use of nature' in Books Two and Three, just as Book One insists that 'righteous life presupposeth life'.[102] Just as 'Nature . . . is nothing else but God's instrument', so too is the voice of reason 'but his instrument' and 'all good lawes are the voyces of right reason, which is the instrument wherewith God will have the world guided'.[103] In Books Two and Three, Hooker continues to give a crucial role to the instrumentality of reason in its relationship to Scripture and theological science. That natural reason constitutes a participated theonomy also renders it as a power indexed against cosmic order and which therefore especially has a public or corporate charisma.[104] Indeed, when Hooker considers 'the benefit of keeping that law which reason teacheth', he images human nature as a 'very world in himselfe' in which natural operations 'preserve' the goodness of the created order, while 'transgressing' the law of reason draws 'harme after it', even 'ruine'.[105] The public character of reason explains why Hooker intends to open up the laws of the Church to 'the general trial and judgement of the whole world' and to ask his opponents to discern if their 'opinions' carry the 'force of reason'.[106] It also explains why Hooker highly values the voices of the wise and the *consensus gentium* ('agreement of the people') which have stood the test of time, coming close to being

---

[98] Hooker, *Laws*, 1:190.12–16; II.8.6.
[99] Ibid., 1:198.1–4; III.1.7.
[100] Ibid., 1:221.17–27; II.8.4.
[101] Ibid., 1:234.2–31; III.8.17.
[102] Ibid., 1:97.17; I.10.2.
[103] Ibid., 1:68.18–69.5; 1:84.1–5; 2:45.2–4; I.3.4; I.8.3; V.9.3.
[104] See A. S. McGrade, 'Reason', in *The Study of Anglicanism*, ed. Stephen Sykes, John Booty and Jonathan Knight (London: SPCK, 1998), 115–30. See also W. Bouwsma, 'Hooker in the Context of European Cultural History', 41–58.
[105] Hooker, *Laws*, 1:93.18–29; I.9.1. Hooker's image shares a strong similarity with Plato's theory of the cosmos as a living creature endowed with soul and reason in the 'Timaeus', 30B.
[106] Hooker, *Laws*, 1:51.24–31; 1:58.5–10; Pref.9.1; I.3.

principles of natural law. In turn, the public nature of reason explains why Hooker remains suspicious of claims to truth that contradict received wisdom and cause public disturbance. Hooker illustrates this danger in Book Two when he considers how the 'vulgar sort', swayed by dubious puritan arguments, 'blusheth not in any doubt concerning matter of scripture to thinke his own bare *Yea*, as good as the *Nay* of all the wise, grace, and learned judgements that are in the world.'[107] Instead, Hooker insists that only wise men have the requisite rational capacity to make binding public laws, but that even 'companies of learned men be they never so great and reverend, are to yeeld unto reason'.[108]

Third, Hooker retains a sanguine but humble appraisal of the natural 'light of reason' because he takes the epistemological limits of sin seriously. When Hooker, considers, for example, in chapter ten of Book One 'how reason doth leade men unto the making of humane lawes whereby politique societies are governed', he distinguishes between 'sincere' and 'depraved' nature.[109] Hooker details three separate categories of law which pertain to the topic of the chapter: first, the law that governs 'men as men' (by which he means the 'law of reason'); second, the positive laws that govern 'men linked with others in some forme of politique societie'; and third, the 'law of nations' which stand between natural and positive law.[110] In each of these cases, Hooker then distinguishes between 'primarie' and 'secondarie' laws, 'the one grounded upon sincere, the other built upon depraved nature.'[111] Hooker provides an example from the law of nations: 'sincere nature' entails primary laws about diplomacy, hospitality to foreign visitors, and 'commodious trafique'.[112] Such sincere nature reflects an Aristotelian 'naturall inclination, wherby all men desire sociable life and fellowship'.[113] In contrast, 'depraved nature' necessitates secondary laws to regulate an 'unquiet world', such as military laws. Such depraved nature reflects an Augustinian awareness that 'the will of man' remains 'inwardly obstinate, rebellious, and averse from all obedience unto the sacred lawes of his nature', 'little better then a wild beast.'[114] Hooker remains clear that, whatever the intrinsic value of reason, human beings often prefer their own good, are capable of self-deception, resist moral rebuke, reject the teachings of the wise and require political regiment in order to restrain their violent tendencies.[115] Hooker consistently rejects that 'meere naturall men' can, through their own power, discern 'things divine above nature', namely salvific truths required for supernatural cognitive participation.[116] Hooker's other extant works go even further and emphasize the calamitous impact of sin on human capacities: the 'minds of all men' are 'darkned'

---

[107] Ibid., 1:183.16–17; II.7.6.
[108] Ibid., 1:102.3–8; 1:181.14–16; 2:43.1–30; I.10.7; II.7.6; V.9.2. This caveat about the public character of reason deflates the criticism that Hooker simply restricts *phronesis* to intellectual elites, such as found in Westberg, *Right Practical Reason*, 210.
[109] See Joyce, *Anglican Moral Theology*, 88–97.
[110] Hooker, *Laws*, 1:106.30–107.2; I.10.12.
[111] Ibid., 1:108.14–17; I.10.13.
[112] Ibid., 1:108.17–19; I.10.13.
[113] Ibid., 1:96.17–19; I.10.1.
[114] Ibid., 1:96.24–32; I.10.1.
[115] Ibid., 1:57.2–24; 1:100.11–15; 1:101.12–14; 1:102.9–13; 1:121.2–4; 2:26.18–21; 3:256.19–24; I.1.2; I.10.4; I.10.5; I.10.7; I.12.2; V.2.4; VII.18.5.
[116] Ibid., 1:178.20–179.1; 1:223.20–6; II.7.4; III.8.6.

with the 'foggie damp of original corruption' and are unable to gain salvific knowledge unaided; and through sin 'our nature hath taken that disease and weakenes, whereby of itselfe it inclineth only unto evill'.[117] As Rowan Williams puts it, Hooker calls his readers to recognize that they are 'never in a state of pure rationality' but rather are contingent, historical beings who participate in the living wisdom of God as it unfurls in broken communities.[118]

Yet, Hooker also remains committed to the idea that remedial grace works against the 'imbecillitie' of sin and activates natural powers and faculties such that they can know and assent to the saving knowledge of Scripture.[119] In the *Dublin Fragments*, Hooker distinguishes between aptitude and ability in his account of the Fall: 'had aptnes beene also lost [as well as ableness], it is not grace that could worke in us more then it doeth in brute creatures.'[120] Accordingly, much like Aquinas, Hooker links reason, as part of what makes human beings as capable of God (*capaces dei*), to a passive aptitude (*aptitudo passiva*) which the 'aid and assistance of God's most blessed Spirit' can activate and illumine, restoring human nature as the rational image of God (*imago dei*).[121] In short, then, Hooker extracts the intrinsic nature of the 'light of reason' from the experience of human corruption in order to show the aptness which healing and elevating grace presupposes as necessary for supernatural cognitive participation in God. The precise way, however, in which grace and nature cohere together within this participatory dynamic forms the hub of the epistemological issues of Books Two and Three, to which the next part turns.

'Supernaturall endowmentes': Supernatural cognitive participation in God

Nigel Voak correctly describes the human reception of supernatural grace as being at the 'polemical heart of the *Lawes*'.[122] In Books Two and Three, Hooker considers various 'proofs' designed to defend two general assertions advanced by those 'who urge reformation in the Church of England': 'That Scripture is the only rule of all things which in this life may be done by men' and also, as a consequence, 'that in Scripture there must be of necessity contained a form of Church-polity the laws whereof may in no wise be altered.' At ultimate stake in these assertions is the integrity of human nature as well as the gratuity of grace. Hooker thinks his puritan opponents render the former otiose with the singularity of biblical law ('the name of the light of nature is made hatefull with men'). In turn, they accuse him of denying the latter ('you infer that the light of nature teacheth some knowledge naturall whiche is necessary to salvation').[123] Against the singularity of biblical law, Hooker continues the commitment of Book One

---

[117] Hooker, *Certaintie*, in *FLE*, 5:71.16–22; *Dublin Fragments*, 2, in *FLE*, 4:103.11–17.
[118] Williams, *Anglican Identities*, 47.
[119] See Hooker, *Dublin Fragments*, 2, in *FLE*, 4:103.17–24; *Laws*, 1:120.15–122.5; I.12.2–3.
[120] Hooker, *Dublin Fragments*, 1, in *FLE*, 4:101.30–1.
[121] Hooker, *Laws*, 1:234.31–235.2; III.8.18. See Newey, 'The Form of Reason', 7–8.
[122] Voak, *Reformed Theology*, 168.
[123] Hooker, *Laws*, 1:221.17; III.8.4; *A Christian Letter*, 3, in *FLE*, 4:11.22–24.

that, as they commonly participate in eternal law, the law of reason and divine law are analogically 'in the substance of law all one'.[124] The unity of purpose between nature and grace – namely, the 'participation of God himselfe' – transforms natural reason as sanctifying grace aids it supernaturally to participate in God's saving knowledge. While Hooker still often refers in Books Two and Three to the 'light of nature' or 'starre of reason', he continues to equivocate between the natural and supernatural. As Hooker has turned from the 'waie of nature' to the 'waie of grace', he more precisely takes reason to mean a natural power sanctified by grace through the infused habit of faith.[125] Here, faith is to reason as grace is to nature: as grace 'hath use of nature', so too does faith use reason. Accordingly, supernatural cognitive participation in God anticipates the Chalcedonian logic of Book Five: just as Christ's hypostatic union perfects but does not abolish his human nature, reason retains its integrity even as grace enlivens it through faith. In both existential and epistemological terms, then, while 'supernatural endowmentes are an advancement, they are no extinguishment of that nature whereunto they are given'.[126]

This part unpacks, therefore, how Hooker establishes Scripture as a *principium cognoscendi theologiae* and reason as a natural and supernatural instrument of understanding. Hooker again obviates accusations of hypo-rationalism: sanctifying grace influences the power of reason through its own natural integrity. This part then turns to Hooker's account of the role reason plays in the authentication of Scripture as sacred. While many modern exegetes argue that Hooker exaggerates the priority of reason over revelation in establishing the sacred nature of Scripture, Hooker's account remains far more subtle: the Holy Spirit demonstrates its influence within and through the integrity of reason as a public instrument of persuasion. As such, supernatural cognitive participation in God variously establishes and draws out the extensive gift of reason into an intensive *via* of return to God.

As the intellect is the principle of natural knowledge for Hooker, so faith is the intellectual principle of saving knowledge. Natural cognitive participation revolves around the analogical suspension of human reason from its divine source. Similarly, supernatural cognitive participation revolves around the gratuitous suspension of rational faith from God's knowledge. Just as the architecture of participation allows Hooker to retain the integrity of natural reason alongside the foundational role of divine influence, so too does it allow him to account for how sanctifying grace transforms and relates to natural rational capacities. As Hooker considers supernatural cognitive participation in God, the scholastic idea of subalternation emerges as an almost hidden buttress to structure how grace and nature, or faith and reason, relate in human understanding.[127] Broadly speaking, in certain streams of scholastic thought shaped by Aristotle's *Posterior Analytics*, a science (*scientia*, 'way of knowledge') is subalternate to another when it depends upon (*subalternatio*, literally 'hangs down from') another science, such as music to mathematics or optics to geometry. Unlike sciences which

---

[124] Hooker, *Laws*, 1:237.13; III.9.2.
[125] Ibid., 1:129.3–8; I.14.5.
[126] Ibid., 2:230.28–9; V.55.6. Compare *Dublin Fragments*, 13, in *FLE*, 4:113.12–13: 'for to destroy nature is not the part of Providence.'
[127] See D. H. Marot, 'Aux origines de la Théologie anglicaine', *Irénikon* 33 (1960): 321–43 (333).

contain their own self-evident principles (*principia per se nota*), a subaltern science instead depends upon a higher science for its first principles. As such, subalternation describes a binary, asymmetrical relationship between a pair of sciences in which one superior science suspends the other subordinate science from itself as participated source of self-evident principles. Bonaventure seems to be the first person to apply subalternation to theology, and Aquinas developed the case.[128] In Aquinas's thought, *sacra doctrina* (sacred doctrine) has the character of a subaltern *scientia* because it shares in, proceeds from, and has a likeness to premises or first principles proven by 'the light of a higher science', namely the *scientia* of God shared with the blessed in heaven.[129] Aquinas's account forms the most likely source structuring Hooker's thought about supernatural cognitive participation in God. As such, it is therefore worthwhile first to unpack Aquinas's account as a prolegomenon to Hooker.

Aquinas concatenates subalternation, theology (*theologia*), sacred doctrine (*sacra doctrina*), sacred scripture (*sacra scriptura*), faith and reason when he considers supernatural cognitive participation in God. Although Aquinas accepts Aristotle's notion of *theologia* as a synonym for first philosophy or metaphysics that proceeds from the power of reason alone, the *theologia* of sacred doctrine rather proceeds from divine revelation.[130] Sacred doctrine therefore has as its formal object God as first truth, and God and all things as they relate to God as its material object.[131] It primarily involves the principal truths necessary for salvation contained in sacred scripture but unavailable to unaided natural reason.[132] Accordingly, sacred doctrine is a subaltern science that takes its first principles from *sacra scriptura*, which has no higher science.[133] Sacred doctrine accordingly subordinates the human knower to the pedagogic activity of God, which in its wisdom extrinsically orders all knowledge to God as the highest cause.[134] Aquinas understands *scientia*, then, in terms of analogy: *scientia* in God is 'pure substance and act' while the perfection of *scientia* imperfectly belongs to creatures in diminished form as they participate in the perfect actuality of God.[135]

The *theologia* of *sacra doctrina* does not render natural reason redundant. Rather, it involves the notion of scientific reasoning in which the philosophical sciences inculcate

---

[128] Other theologians like Duns Scotus and William of Ockham were uncertain about the application. See John Marenbon, *Later Medieval Philosophy* (London: Routledge, 1991), 81–2.

[129] Aquinas, *ST*, I.1.2. Aquinas does not here use the language of subalternation, but he does in *Super Sent*, Lib.1 pr.a. 3 qc.2; *Super De Trinitate*, q.2 a.2 *ad* 5 and 7; *De ver*, q.14 a.9 *ad* 3; and *Lectura Romana*, pr.q. 1 a.1 *ad* 1. On these texts, see Denis J. Bradley, *Aquinas on the Twofold Human Good: Reason and Human Happiness in Aquinas's Moral Science* (Washington: Catholic University of America Press, 1999), 65–78.

[130] See Brian Davies, 'Is Sacra Doctrina Theology?', *New Blackfriars* 71 (1990): 141–7; and James Weisheipl, 'The Meaning of Sacra Doctrina in Summa Theologiae I, q.1', *Thomist* 38 (1974): 49–80.

[131] Aquinas, *ST*, I.1.7.

[132] Ibid., I.1.1, 3, 5, and 9. Aquinas understands *sacra scriptura* to encompass the scriptural canon as well as authoritative documents or teachings within the history of the Church. The subalternation of sacred doctrine to sacred scripture means that Aquinas even conflates their identity in *ST*, I.1.2 ad 2: '*scriptura seu sacra doctrina*'. See W. G. B. M. Valkenberg, *Words of the Living God: Place and Function of Holy Scripture in the Theology of St. Thomas Aquinas* (Leiden: Peeters, 2003), 9–11.

[133] Aquinas, *ST*, I.1.8 sc.

[134] Ibid., I.1.6.

[135] Ibid., I.1.14.1 ad.1. See John Jenkins, *Knowledge and Faith in Thomas Aquinas* (Cambridge: Cambridge University Press, 1997), 51–77.

understanding 'as handmaidens'.¹³⁶ For Aquinas, then, while 'faith rests on infallible truth', grace perfects nature and 'natural reason should minister to faith as the natural bent of the will ministers to charity'.¹³⁷ However, Aquinas ultimately takes reason to mean an intellectual power enlivened and perfected by the infused theological virtue of faith, 'a habit of the intellect, by which eternal life is begun in us, which makes the intellect assent to things which are unseen'.¹³⁸ Such faith 'is said to surpass reason, not because there is no act of reason in faith, but because reasoning about faith cannot lead to the sight of those things which are matters of faith'.¹³⁹ Rational assent to the principles of *sacra doctrina* involves the influence of grace upon natural cognitive powers such that they can immediately apprehend these principles as divinely revealed and as true. This supernatural cognitive participation in divine knowledge assumes some natural capacity and participated likeness, 'an intelligible light . . . derived from the first light, whether this be understood of the natural power, or of some perfection superadded of grace or of glory'.¹⁴⁰ Supernatural cognitive participation perfects both the speculative and the practical aspects of reason through an intellectual light beyond nature.¹⁴¹ Ultimately, this divine illumination yields the glory of beatitude.¹⁴² Here, the intellect sees the divine essence itself through a participation in divine understanding, which 'establishes in the intellect a kind of deiformity', making it 'like to God'.¹⁴³ In glory, the intellect finally knows and follows the eternal law as perfectly as its form permits.¹⁴⁴ As such, faith enlivens reason, and reason ministers to faith as God teaches and draws humanity actively to participate in, contemplate and enjoy (re)union with the divine nature.¹⁴⁵

Hooker curiously only explicitly mentions the scholastic idea of subalternation in his account of marriage in Book Five of the *Laws*, but that remains enough to indicate his familiarity with the concept.¹⁴⁶ Indeed, like Aquinas, Hooker concatenates theology, science, faith and reason through an implicit structure of subalternation. In Book One, along with all other forms of law, Hooker analogously suspends the divine law contained in Scripture from eternal law. Unlike other laws, however, which are intrinsic principles of action, divine law is God's extrinsic declaration of supernatural truths drawing broken humanity back to God. Hooker thereby acknowledges the premodern notion of science as a 'way of knowledge' in his pedagogical account of Scripture: it exists to draw and enlighten humanity into a saving relationship with God as final cause and end. Given the frustration of the natural desire for 'union which that it desireth', namely God as the metaphysically simple and ultimate good (*ultimum*

---

¹³⁶ Aquinas, *ST*, I.1.2; I.1.3; I.1.5 ad.2; and I.1.8
¹³⁷ Ibid., I.1.8 ad.2.
¹³⁸ Ibid., II.II.4.1.
¹³⁹ Aquinas, *De Ver*, q.14 a.2 ad 9. Compare Aquinas, *ST*, II.II.4.1–2.
¹⁴⁰ Aquinas, *ST*, I.12.2 resp.
¹⁴¹ Ibid., II.II.2.3; compare I.88.3.1 and II.II.8.3.
¹⁴² Ibid., I.12.5.
¹⁴³ Ibid., I.12.5–6.
¹⁴⁴ Ibid., I.II.93.2.
¹⁴⁵ See Anna N. Williams, 'Mystical Theology Redux: The Pattern of Aquinas' *Summa Theologiae*', *Modern Theology* 13, no. 1 (1997): 53–74.
¹⁴⁶ Hooker, *Laws*, 2:402.6–19; V.73.2.

bonum simpliciter), 'there resteth therefore eyther no way unto salvation, or if any, then surely a way which is supernaturall.'[147] The 'mysterie or secret way of salvation' God has 'in himselfe prepared before all worldes', incarnated in Christ, and published in Scripture.[148] Accordingly, Scripture as 'the rule of divine law . . . should herein help our imbecillitie, that we might the more infallible understand what is good and what evill', both in natural and supernatural ends.[149] Hooker accepts that Scripture contains principles of revealed truth which unaided human reason alone cannot attain, such as in the case of Festus in Acts 25.19, 'a meere naturall man' who rejected the resurrection as 'idle superstitious fancies not worth the hearing'.[150] Scripture forms, then, the *principium cognoscendi theologiae* in matters of faith and doctrine. In Book Five he describes these principles as 'infallible axioms and precepts of sacred truth', which flow from 'the credit of divine testimonie'.[151] Scripture takes on the 'nature of a doctrinall instrument', the divine means to make people 'wise unto salvation' through the 'vertue which it hath to *convert*, to *edifie*, [and] to *save* soules', that is to say to enjoy the intensive participation of (and union with) God.[152]

Again, like Aquinas, Hooker understands Scripture as the pedagogical source of theological science with a series of rhetorical questions: 'The whole drift of the scripture of God what is it but only to teach *Theologie*? *Theologie* what is it but the science of thinges divine?'[153] As with all subaltern sciences, theology 'leadeth men into knowledge' by presupposing first principles derived from another higher science, in this case the *scientia* of God in which the angels and beatified participate. As for Aquinas, *scientia* represents an analogical term. Indeed, since Hooker casts human beings as creatures who participate in God between the 'footstoole' and the 'throne of God', theology takes on a metaxological character: unlike the intrinsic certainty of divine *scientia*, it unfolds *scientia* within believers who move from becoming to being. As creatures, human beings are composites of material and intellectual principles, and naturally move from potency to act as they participate in the perfect actuality of God. Human knowledge therefore 'growes by degrees' from 'utter vacuitie' until (through faith) they supernaturally share with the angels the intuitive vision of God in beatitude, 'the full and complete knowledge in the highest degree that can be imparted unto them.'[154] Standing in this Aristotelian-Thomist tradition, Hooker argues that all sciences take their first principles as given, 'either as plaine and manifest in them selves' or, as in the case of theology, 'as proved and graunted already, some former knowledge having made them evident.'[155] For theological *scientia*, 'Scripture teacheth al supernaturally revealed truth.' God reveals this supernatural truth 'by immediate divine inspiration' to the prophets and apostles such that we 'have no word of God but the Scripture'.[156] Since

---

[147] Ibid., 1:116.4–8; I.11.5.
[148] Ibid., 1:118.22–30; 1:122.7–16; I.11.6; I.13.1.
[149] Ibid., 1:119.24–124.26; I.12–13.
[150] Ibid., 1:118.11–119.23; 1:188.2–7; 1:223.20–4; I.11.5–6; II.8.3; III.8.6.
[151] Ibid., 2:89.13–91.28; V.22.2–5.
[152] Ibid., 2:83.22–88.10; V.21–22.1.
[153] Ibid., 1:229.33–231.15; III.8.11.
[154] Ibid., 1:74.17–25; I.6.1.
[155] Ibid., 1:230.32–231.2; III.8.13.
[156] Ibid., 2:84.5–18; V.21.2. Compare *Jude*, First sermon, 3–4, in *FLE*, 5:15.17–17.9.

God's knowledge remains intrinsically true and certain, Scripture provides infallible first theological principles to theological science sufficient for salvation.[157] Indeed, Hooker reiterates in Book Five how the first principles of Christian doctrine, like the first principles of any scientific endeavour, 'require no proofe in any kind of science, because it sufficeth if either theire certaintie be evident in it iselfe, or evident by the light of some higher knowledge, and it selfe such as no man knowledge is ever able to overthrow.'[158] As such, the way that theologians pursue their science differs in no way from how philosophers pursue natural truths from natural first principles.

The *scientia* of 'thinges divine' bears the similarity and dissimilarity of analogy, then, from merely human sciences. While natural first principles are self-evident through particular natural intellectual habits, the principles of faith are only assented to as true by someone who accepts the revealed knowledge of Scripture through the supernatural intellectual 'habit of faith'.[159] Hooker understands the habit of faith in thoroughly Thomistic terms. Faith begins as an extrinsic divine gift gratuitously given to the believer and forms the principal duty of Christians to believe in Christ. Faith is also an infused 'intellectual habit of the mind' with her 'seate in the understandinge' gifted at baptism and which intrinsically transforms the cognitive capacity of believers through sanctifying grace to participate supernaturally in God and enjoy salvific (re)union.[160] Once Scripture has left an '*apprehension* of thinges divine in our understandinge, and in the mind an *assent* thereunto', it can furnish infallible and intrinsically certain supernatural first principles which work, like first principles within natural reasoning, 'to procure our assent unto such conclusions as the industrie of right discourse doth gather from them'.[161] Pace Gunnar Hillerdal, Hooker obviates hypo-rationalism and clearly accounts for how sanctifying grace transforms cognitive capacities without recourse to an intractable form of irrationalism.

Hooker, following Aquinas and in tune with his own contemporary Reformed scholastics, gives sanctified reason in particular an instrumental role in theological discourse.[162] Hooker sees reason as an instrumental cause of understanding, a subordinate efficient cause enlightened by and dependent upon the efficient causality of God. Hooker writes of theology: 'What science can be attained unto without the help of natural discourse and reason?'[163] In his *Answer to the Supplication*, Hooker makes clearer what he means by reason: 'I alleged therefore that which mighte under no pretence in the worlde be dissalowed namely a reson not meaning thereby *myne owne reason* as now it is reported, but true sounde divyne reason . . ., reson proper to that science whereby the thinges of god are knowne, theologicall reason.'[164] In

---

[157] Hooker, *Laws*, 1:189.2–11; compare 1:127.27–128.3; 1:167.29–168.1; 2:84.23–33.
[158] Ibid., 2:290.9–13; V.63.1.
[159] Ibid., 2:290.20–4; V.63.1.
[160] Ibid., 2:291.20–1; V.63.2. Hooker talks of inward graces and virtues infused through sanctifying grace in a number of passages without going into much detail about what they are. See ibid., 1:206.9–11; 2:224.23–225.4; 2:241.18–244.25; 2:255.1–13; III.1.14; V.54.6;.V.56.10; V.60.2.
[161] Ibid., 2:84.31–85.24; V.21.3, emphasis in the original. See Voak, *Reformed Theology*, 197–9 for a criticism of Hooker's alleged imprecision in this passage compared with his scholastic sources.
[162] On instrumental causality, see. Pliezier and Wisse, '"As the Philosopher Says": Aristotle', 40.
[163] Hooker, *Laws*, 1:230.2–3; III.8.11.
[164] Hooker, *Answer*, 24, in *FLE*, 5:255.4–16, emphasis in the original.

Book One of the *Laws*, Hooker gives examples where theological discourse rationally deduces 'by collection' from scriptural propositions necessary beliefs 'no where to be found by expresse literall mention', such as the Trinity, the coeternity of the Son, the double procession of the Holy Spirit and the duty of infant baptism.[165] The use of reason does not here constitute a 'supplement of any maime or defect' in Scripture, which is 'perfect, exact, and absolute in it selfe'. Rather, reason works as an elicitive tool, a 'necessary instrument, without which we could not reape by the scriptures perfection, that fruite and benefite which it yieldeth'.[166]

The instrumentality of reason also allows Hooker to blur, however, the boundary between natural and supernatural cognitive participation in God. Against the biblical singularity of his opponents, Hooker opens up space for the creative capacity of natural reason to make meaning by qualifying what Charles Miller, following Olivier Loyer, calls a 'triad of characteristics', namely, the sufficiency, perfection and clarity of Scripture.[167]

On one side, Hooker clearly affirms the sufficiency, perfection and clarity of Scripture in recognizably Reformed terms. Hooker links sufficiency and perfection together in terms of Scripture as a scientific *principium cognoscendi theologiae*. 'The absolute perfection of scripture', writes Hooker in the final chapter of Book Two, 'is seene by relation unto that end wherto it tendeth', namely 'a full instruction in all things unto salvation necessary'.[168] The nuance carries polemical weight: it allows Hooker to avoid two dangerous extremities 'repugnant unto truth' about the sufficiency of Scripture, one from the puritans and the other from Tridentine Catholicism.[169] For Hooker, the radical puritans enlarge 'the necessarie use of the word of God', 'racking and stretching it further than by [God] was ment', making Scripture 'a snare and torment to weake consciences, filling them with infinite perplexities, scrupulosities, doubts insoluble, and extreme despaires'.[170] Hooker also rejects the puritan assumption that scriptural silence in any issue implies disapproval, a form of negative argument that might threaten many established ecclesial and political practices.[171] While 'in some cases a negative argument taken from scripture is strong', this principle cannot universally hold as true because the context of the negative argument may well limit its historical force.[172] At the opposite extreme, Hooker argues that Tridentine Roman Catholicism teaches the insufficiency of Scripture without additional unwritten traditions, a notion which he also firmly rejects.[173] In Book Five, Hooker also emphasizes the clarity of Scripture, casting the saving 'word of life' as 'alwaies a treasure, though precious, yeat

---

[165] Hooker, *Laws*, 1:126.18–24; I.14.2.
[166] Ibid., 1:227.2–6; III.8.10.
[167] Miller, *Vision of God*, 89–91.
[168] Hooker, *Laws*, 1:189.9–16; II.8.5.
[169] Ibid., 1:191.14–27; II.8.7.
[170] Ibid., 1:145.7–8; 1:189.25–190.19; II.1.2; II.8.5–6. See Cargill Thompson, 'The Philosopher of the "Politic Society"', 24 who points out that Hooker consistently exaggerates the extent of puritan Biblicism for polemical effect. Similarly, Hooker may be guilty of exaggerating the Tridentine teachings about tradition too. See Joseph Cardinal Ratzinger, *God's Word: Scripture, Tradition, Office* (San Francisco: Ignatius Press, 2008), 41–90.
[171] Hooker, *Laws*, 1:157.30–174.20; II.5–6.
[172] Ibid., 1:173.28–30; II.6.4.
[173] Ibid., 1:189.23–5; II.8.5.

easie, as well to attaine, as to finde'.[174] He argues that the public reading of Scripture can 'furnish the verie simplest and rudest sorte with such infallible axioms and preceptes of sacred truth' that will allow them to judge ecclesial doctrine and instructions.[175] Indeed, in Book Three Hooker lauds Christ for choosing twelve 'simple and unlearned men, that the greater their lack of naturall wisdom was, the more admirable that might appeare, which God supernaturally indued them with from heaven'.[176]

Yet, Hooker makes room for natural reason in relation to Scripture as an already divinely enlightened instrument of understanding, developing a complex method of scriptural interpretation hardly open to the 'verie simplest and rudest sorte'.[177] First, the limits of Hooker's teleological definition of Scripture as perfectly sufficient for the end of salvation opens up space for the wisdom of other participatory laws, especially the law of reason, in other spheres of life. Scriptural sufficiency does not relate to natural or rational laws, which it simply republishes to 'helpe our imbecillitie'. Neither does scriptural sufficiency entail that all of Scripture has the direct character of supernatural law. Scripture contains other natural sciences and 'doth take out of all kinds of truth' as much as the particular purpose requires, either for the exigency of the historical occasion, or to make it 'more playne, apparent, and easye' to know necessary supernatural truths.[178] Grace presupposes nature in this regard, which is not a defect in Scripture but a recognition of how grace works in nature such that they 'joyntly and not severallye eyther of them be so complete' that they may not together serve to lead people into the knowledge required for 'everlasting felicitie'.[179] Furthermore, positive laws found in Scripture may well be mutable since they are context bound and relate to particular historical ends.[180] Indeed, the mutability of certain kinds of scriptural laws forms the capstone of Hooker's final two chapters of Book Three in which he rejects the thesis that Scripture contains a necessary form of church polity commanded by God as the 'author of laws'. Rather, the 'carefull discretion of the Church' discerns convenient and fit laws for its government *coram Deo*, creatively drawing 'from the lawes of nature and God, by discourse of reason, aided with the influence of divine grace'.[181]

Hooker also displays markedly elitist exegetical notions of who can interpret Scripture properly, all of which privilege the role of natural reason. Indeed, as Hooker points out in the preface, in the 'more obscure, more intricate and hard [matters] to be judged of', the majority require the guidance of those few who have dedicated themselves to 'the studie of things divine'.[182] Historical and philological methods of

---

[174] Ibid., 2:84.28–31; V.21.3.
[175] Ibid., 2:89.12–17; V.22.2.
[176] Ibid., 1:227.8–15; III.8.10.
[177] Debora Shuger, 'Society Supernaturall: The Imagined Community of Hooker's *Lawes*', in *Richard Hooker and the Construction of Christian Community*, ed. A. S. McGrade (Tempe: Medieval and Renaissance Texts and Studies, 1997), 309–29 similarly notes how Hooker seems to offer 'two seemingly antithetical versions of community', namely the populist and elitist. The former is especially concerned with the universal availability of law and the affective quality of worship. The latter is especially concerned with humanist erudition and Thomistic rationalism.
[178] Hooker, *Laws*, 1:125.2–6; 1:127.21–7; I.14.1; I.14.3.
[179] Ibid., 1:128.28–129.16; I.14.4–5.
[180] Ibid., 1:130.5–134.18; 1:261.9–11; I.15; III.11.13.
[181] Ibid., 1:235.12–16; 1:236.3–8; III.8.16; III.9.1.
[182] Ibid., 1:13.14–18; Pref.3.2.

humanist scholarship inform such judgement, which again open up space for the activity of natural reason, even if only among those with the right training.[183] Hooker's account of scriptural exegesis recalls the idea of reason's innate but developed capacity to make complex but fallible affirmative and negative judgements about particular propositions, namely Aquinas's *compositio et divisio* or what Hooker calls an ability to comprehend 'differences of time, affirmations, negations, and contradictions in speech'. In Book Five, with an emphatically humanist bias, Hooker holds 'for a most infallible rule in expositions of sacred scripture' that the literal sense of the text ought to be preferred.[184] The 'literal sense' includes the exegete taking into account literary type, metaphor, cultural context and authorial intent of a particular text.[185] Therefore, as Paul Forte emphasizes, Hooker here largely 'eschews the excesses of patristic and scholastic exegesis, with its theory of *multiplex intelligentia*, multiple senses'.[186] Instead, Hooker demands that an exegete have a strong humanistic grasp of linguistic change, as well as what William Haugaard calls 'a gift of the Renaissance: historical contextualization'.[187] The exegete must attend, then, to 'the difference of times, places, persons, and other the like circumstances' in order to understand Scripture and its laws.[188] Together with historical sense, Hooker further expects exegetes to understand something akin to juridical science as it had developed in sixteenth-century English common law.[189] Hooker explicates how general common laws that 'continewallie and universallie' are found should equitably be applied and adjusted to particular circumstances 'according to theire right meaninge'.[190] Similarly, in Book Three, as he considers the divine law of Scripture, Hooker explains how even scriptural laws with permanent ends may require equitable 'alteration, if there bee anye unfitness in the meanes which they prescribe unto that end'.[191] There is, of course, a polemical advantage in such a hermeneutic. Philological and historical analysis allow Hooker to dismiss, for example, what Debora Shuger calls the naïve 'putative isomorphism of past and present' employed by his radical puritan opponents, namely, their normative use of typological arguments about proper church and political order drawn from scriptural texts.[192] Instead, Hooker's notions about mutability, historical context and teleology

---

[183] See Shuger, *Habits of Thought*, 26–37; Haugaard, 'Books II, III, & IV', in *FLE*, 6 (1): 154–61; and R. J. Schoeck, 'From Erasmus to Hooker: An Overview', in *Richard Hooker and the Construction of Christian Community*, ed. A. S. McGrade (Tempe: Medieval and Renaissance Texts and Studies, 1997), 59–73. On Hooker's historicism, see John K. Luoma, 'Who Owns the Fathers? Hooker and Cartwright on the Authority of the Primitive Church', *Sixteenth Century Journal* 8, no. 3 (1977): 45–59.

[184] Hooker, *Laws*, 2:252.5–7; V.59.2.

[185] See Marshall, *Hooker and the Anglican Tradition*, 46–7.

[186] Paul Forte, 'Hooker as Preacher', in *The Folger Library Edition of the Works of Richard Hooker*, ed. W. Speed Hill, 7 vols (vols. 1–5, Cambridge: Belknap Press, 1977–90; vol. 6, Binghamton: Belknap Press, 1993; vol. 7, Tempe: Medieval and Renaissance Texts and Studies, 1998), 5:668.

[187] Haugaard, 'Books II, III, & IV', in *FLE*, 6 (1): 125–82 (157). See also Williams, *Anglican Identities*, 26 who writes that, in effect, Hooker is 'perhaps the first major European theologian to assume that history, corporate and individual, matters for theology'.

[188] Hooker, *Laws*, 1:261.10–11; I.11.13.

[189] See Loyer, *L'Anglicanisme de Richard Hooker*, 167–75; Miller, *Vision of God*, 94–5.

[190] Hooker, *Laws*, 2:44.17–24; V.9.3.

[191] Ibid., 1:242.13–16; III.10.3.

[192] Shuger, *Habits of Thought*, 30–5.

allow him to see positive laws (such as those that order lay ecclesiastical supremacy) as contingently mutable. At the same time, when rationally ordered, they participate in divine wisdom: 'which shineth in the bewtifull varietie of all thinges, but most in the manifold and yet harmonious dissimilitude of those ways, whereby his Church upon earth is guided from age to age.'[193]

Hooker erects no strict barrier, therefore, between natural and supernatural cognitive participation: the former 'hath need of' the latter, but the latter 'hath use of' the former. Natural cognitive participation sets reason as an extensive gift that dynamically images, and draws humanity back towards, the creative divine nature. Supernatural cognitive participation unfolds sanctifying grace within the power of reason in order to bring about an intensive (re)union with God as rational end. As a 'supernaturall endowment', supernatural cognitive participation does not obliterate the natural operations of reason, however, but perfects and elevates them. In both forms of cognitive participation, Hooker affords priority to grace, that is to say, to God's gratuitous and causative donation. Hooker therefore unites both natural and supernatural forms of cognitive participation in what Daniel Hardy (appealing to Coleridge) labels as 'abduction', the capacity of reason to be drawn by an inner light which belongs to, but does not originate or end within, itself.[194] Grace coheres rather than conflicts with nature because nature is gratuitous in the first place. Yet, the divine abduction of human reason does not empty it of agency: as human knowers participate in God's *scientia*, it becomes their own and the inner light of reason calls them to stand as co-creators of meaning. To be a creative participant in God reveals the gift and responsibility of reason: 'That which by right exposition buildeth up Christian faith, being misconstrued breedeth error: betweene true and false construction, the difference reason must shew.'[195]

Hyper-rationalist exegetes of Hooker argue, however, that the balanced coherence he sets up between natural and supernatural cognitive participation in God breaks down when he considers the meta-principle of how human beings come to know that the scriptures are sacred. Such critics contend that Hooker rejects the Reformed idea that Scripture self-authenticates its identity, known technically as *Logos autopistos* (λογος αὐτόπιστος). Instead, Hooker allegedly claims that natural demonstrative reasoning establishes the meta-principle of scriptural authenticity, thus stepping outside of what might count as Reformed orthodoxy.[196] As such, hyper-rationalist

---

[193] Hooker, *Laws*, 1:253.15–20; III.11.8.
[194] Daniel W. Hardy, *Wording a Radiance: Parting Conversations about God and the Church* (London: SCM Press, 2010), 49–50.
[195] Hooker, *Laws*, 1:233.18–20; III.8.16.
[196] See, for example, Lake, *Anglicans & Puritans?*, 153–5; Shuger, *Habits of Thought*, 28, 41–2; Joyce, *Anglican Moral Theology*, 114–18; Voak, *Reformed Theology*, 253–4; Nigel Voak, 'Richard Hooker and the Principle of *Sola Scriptura*', *Journal of Theological Studies* 59, no. 1 (2008): 96–139; O'Donovan, *Theology of Law*, 143–5; Mohamed, 'Renaissance Thought on the Celestial Hierarchy', 559–82. The textual commentary in *FLE*, 6:516 similarly insists that Hooker 'is challenging the Calvinistic principle of the self-authenticating authority of Scripture'. Mark LeTourneau, 'Richard Hooker and the Sufficiency of Scripture', *Journal of Anglican Studies* 14, no. 2 (2016): 134–55 argues that Hooker 'departs' from Reformed orthodoxy by denying the 'autopisticity of Scripture', but that this disavowal is part of his polemics against the assertion of biblical omnicompetence. On the contrary, Nigel Atkinson, *Richard Hooker and the Authority of Scripture, Tradition and Reason* (Carlisle: Paternoster Press, 1997), 93, 108 argues that Hooker's account does remain

exegetes essentially concur with the anonymous authors of *A Christian Letter* who claim that Hooker infers 'that the light of nature teacheth some knowledge naturall which is necessarie to salvation, and that the Scripture is a supplement and making perfect of that knowledge'.[197] The conclusion of this part instead demonstrates how Hooker's account of reason's role in authenticating the scriptures as sacred offers a subtle interpretation of *autopistos* in which 'the special grace of the holy ghost' informs the rational 'inlightning of our minds' such that we can participate in the intrinsic truth of divine *scientia*.

As a prolegomenon, it remains useful to understand the claims involved in the idea of *Logos autopistos*. Reformed orthodox theologians commonly state that Scripture exhibits its own sure authority (*autopistos*) and that the Holy Spirit testifies within believers (*testimonium Spiritus sancti internum*) such that they can recognize Scripture as sacred. This idea originates as a novel *theologoumenon* in Reformed orthodoxy directly out of Calvin's works, although H. Bullinger may well in turn have influenced him.[198] Calvin only uses the term *autopistos* eleven times as an adjective for *scriptura* across his works, and only once in the 1559 *Institutes*, but it soon became a key confessional term for Reformed theologians. *Autopistos* seems to have roots in Greek logic and geometry, as well as medieval scholasticism.[199] In Greek thought, the term is connected with the word 'axiom' (ἀξίωμα), that is to say propositions accepted as true, self-convincing and trustworthy without the need for proof. Various scholastic notions also influence Calvin's idea of *Logos autopistos*. The medieval idea that Scripture acts as a primary scientific *principium* of Christian knowledge with its own self-evident principles (*principia per se nota*) presages Calvin's idea that Scripture has ultimate and independent autopistic authority. Aquinas's distinction between things that are evident by themselves (*secundum se*) and those that are evident for us (*quoad nos*) also stands behind Calvin's account of the Spirit's testimony as it establishes scriptural authority for us (*apud nos*).[200] That Calvin prefers the Greek adjective *autopistos* to these Latinate medieval philosophical terms does not suggest, then, that he arrives at the concept in a vacuum; rather, in using the Greek term, he emphasizes the theological elements of faith and trust involved in the autopistic character of Scripture. Indeed, in terms of etymology, while the prefix *auto* simply means 'by itself', *pistos* recalls the theological

consonant with the Reformed idea of *Logos autopistos*. See also W. J. T. Kirby, 'The "sundrie waies of Wisdom": Richard Hooker on the Authority of Scripture and Reason', in *Richard Hooker. His Life, Work, and Legacy*, ed. Daniel Graves and Scott Kindred-Barnes (Bradford: St Osmund Press, 2013), 145–60; John K. Stafford, 'Richard Hooker's Pneumatologia', *Perichoresis* 11, no. 2 (2013): 161–86; and Andrew Fulford, '"A Truth Infallible": Richard Hooker and Reformed Orthodoxy on Autopistos', in *Richard Hooker and Reformed Orthodoxy*, ed. Scott Kindred-Barnes and W. Bradford Littlejohn (Göttingen, Bristol: Vandenhoeck & Ruprecht, 2017), 203–20.

[197] *A Christian Letter*, 3, in *FLE*, 4:11.10–32. The quotation from Hooker is *Laws*, 1:129.10–16; I.14.5.
[198] H. Bullinger, *Ad Ioannis Cochlei d Canonicare Scripturae . . . authoritate labellum responsio* (Tiguri [Zurich]: Froschouer, 1544) writes that the books of Scripture are 'canonical and authentic, just like someone calls those things αὐτόπιστοι, that gain faith by themselves also without arguments and have their truth and authority completely from themselves and not from elsewhere'. Translated and quoted in Henk van den Belt, *The Authority of Scripture in Reformed Theology: Truth and Trust* (Leiden: Brill, 2008), 92.
[199] The following account of the sources behind *autopistos* is gleaned from van den Belt, *The Authority of Scripture*, 71–115.
[200] Aquinas, *ST*, I.2.1.

idea of faith, itself containing notions of trust and confidence (from the Greek πίστις, *pistis*; translated in Latin as *fides*, also from the same root as *fiducia*).²⁰¹ Rather than simply meaning 'self-evident' as it might in philosophical terms, the theological meaning of *autopistos* therefore rather indicates 'self-convincingly leading to faith', as Henk van den Belt translates it.²⁰²

Calvin discusses *autopistos* in the first book of the 1559 *Institutes* entitled *De Cognitione Dei Creatoris* ('The Knowledge of God the Creator'). In context, *autopistos* works as a confessional rather than philosophical statement: it does not refer to self-evident axioms as such but instead places the authoritative trustworthiness of Scripture in itself; the Spirit sanctions (*sancire*) and confirms (*constare*) Scripture rather than the judgement (*iudicium*) of the (Roman) Church.²⁰³ At the end of chapter seven, Calvin explicitly uses *autopistos* and links it directly to the dynamic, internal and non-inferential witness of the Spirit:

> Let this point therefore stand: that those whom the Holy Spirit has inwardly taught truly rest upon Scripture, and that Scripture indeed is self-authenticated [αὐτόπιστον]; hence it is not right to subject it to proof and reasoning. And the certainty it deserves with us [*apud nos*], it attains by the testimony [*testimonium*] of the Spirit. For even if it wins reverence for itself by its own majesty, it seriously affects us only when it is sealed upon our hearts through the Spirit.²⁰⁴

Here, Calvin adapts the medieval idea that Scripture is a scientific *principium* of theology: Scripture gains reverence for itself by its own majesty and 'exhibits fully as clear evidence of its own truth as white and black things do of their colour, or sweet and bitter things do of their taste.'²⁰⁵ The Spirit mediates the trustworthiness of scriptural self-evidence within the believer; the *principia* of Scripture would only be an analogy, then, of the self-evident *principia* of natural sciences. Calvin accordingly baptizes the Aristotelian notion of *scientia* in order to emphasize the elements of faith, trust and pneumatic illumination. *Logos autopistos* does not depend on 'proof and reasoning' since the Spirit inspires Scripture and is more excellent than any rational proof.²⁰⁶ Yet, it nevertheless cannot be isolated in existential terms of assurance from the subjective, internal *testimonium* of the Spirit which makes it certain with us (*apud nos*) and through which we find rest (*acquiescere*). The testimony of God in Scripture and the testimony of the Spirit within believers are not identical, then, but they are inseparable in the existential act of human knowing: 'The same Spirit . . . who has spoken through the mouths of the prophets must penetrate into our hearts to persuade us that they faithfully proclaimed what had been divinely commanded.'²⁰⁷

---

[201] H. G. Liddell, R. Scott and H. S. Jones, *A Greek-English Lexicon* (Oxford: Clarendon Press, 1968), 281. Muller, *Dictionary*, 54–5 points out that Protestant scholastic theologians often pair αὐτόπιστος with ἀξιόπιστος ('trustworthy').
[202] Van den Belt, *The Authority of Scripture*, 4.
[203] Jean Calvin, *Institutes of the Christian Religion*, trans. F. Battles, 2 vols (Louisville, KY: Westminster John Knox Press, 2006), I.vii.1; 1.74–75.
[204] Ibid., I.vii.5; 1.80.
[205] Ibid., I.vii.2; 1.75–6; I.viii.1; 1.81–2
[206] Ibid., I.vii.4; 1.78–9.
[207] Ibid., I.vii.4; 1.79.

In the eighth chapter, however, Calvin immediately introduces a caveat about *autopistos* and the *testimonium* of the Spirit. He considers how human reason [*humana ratio*] can provide 'sufficiently firm proofs [*probationes*]' to 'establish the credibility of Scripture'.[208] While Calvin elsewhere pejoratively contrasts *humana ratio* to faith, here he links it to *probationes* that are strong enough to confirm the authority of Scripture.[209] The *probationes* exist independently of internal pneumatic testimony. As 'secondary aids' they demonstrate (*demonstrare*), prove (*evincere*) or offer proof (*demonstratio*), and make clear the trustworthiness of Scripture, establishing them as indubitable to human reason. While the *probationes* confirm (*stabilire*) the trustworthiness of Scripture, they do not share in, however, the absolute existential certainty of the Spirit's testimony. Consequently, reason plays a subordinate role in the ratiocinative analysis of the marks of Scripture, namely, the objective evidence that can confirm and defend beliefs for us (*apud nos*). The *probationes* do not render the *testimonium* as superfluous: Calvin distinguishes, for example, between a general opinion (*opinio*) about the plausibility of scriptural majesty for which the *probationes* serve as an apologetic aid, and the full persuasion of 'firm faith' through the testimony of the Spirit which allows believers to rest (*acquiescere*) in the intrinsic certainty of Scripture without proof.[210] Yet, the *ratio* of the Word examines the private testimony of the Spirit: the 'Word and Spirit belong inseparably together' such that 'the Holy Spirit is recognised in his agreement with Scripture' and is, in fact, present in Scripture itself.[211] Calvin's account of *autopistos* represents, then, what Richard Muller calls a balancing act between the 'subjective and inward certainty resting on the Spirit and on faith alone' and 'an external objective certainty resting on evidence' which allows the subjective aspect 'to be grounded in reality' and rationality.[212]

There are admittedly grounds for the hyper-rationalist exegetical claim that Hooker rejects Calvin's Reformed account of *autopistos* and the *internum testimonium*. Hooker certainly rejects that scriptural marks can indefeasibly assure people that the scriptures are sacred. He also uses the Anabaptists in the preface to the *Laws* as an example of the dangers of special claims to pneumatic illumination: 'when they and their Bibles were alone together, what strange phantasticall opinion soever at any time entred into their heads, their use was to thinke the Spirit taught it them.'[213] Hooker implicitly places his puritan opponents in the troubling shadows of the Anabaptists. He thinks that the 'common' people are not convinced of the puritan case from first principles but are rather 'credulous' and induced that 'it is the speciall illumination of the holy Ghost, whereby they discerne those things in the word, which others reading yet discerne them not'.[214] Hooker opposes non-demonstrable claims to internal pneumatic certainty

---

[208] Ibid., I.viii.1–13; 1.81–92.
[209] Ibid., I.xiv.2; II.ii.18; 1.161–2; 1.277–8.
[210] Ibid., I.vii.5, I.viii.1, I.ix.13; 1.80–2, 1.92.
[211] Ibid., I.ix.2–3; 1.94–6.
[212] Richard Muller, *Post-Reformation Reformed Dogmatics*, vol. 2, 259.
[213] Hooker, *Laws*, 1:44.10–26; Pref.8.7. Compare ibid., 2:46.7–47.11; V.10 where Hooker considers how 'the rule of mens private spirits [are] not safe in these cases to be followed', namely in relation to 'where the worde of God leaveth the Church to make choice of hir own ordinances'.
[214] Ibid., 1:17.10–18.8; Pref.3.10. See Cargill Thompson, 'The Philosopher of the "Politic Society"', 15 who sees Hooker's discussion about the Anabaptists as a final smear tactic against the puritans since they too, by implication, illustrate the dangers of unrestrained private judgements. Also, see

because they seem to imply that reason remains of little to no value in faith. In Book Three, Hooker summarizes this incredulous position: 'If I believe the Gospell, there needeth no reasoning about it to perswade me: If I doe not believe, it must be the spirit of God and not the reason of man that shall convert my hart unto him.'[215] Instead, Hooker allegedly exaggerates the priority of reason and subalternates the authenticity of scripture to it, especially as he writes that we know 'by reason that the scripture is the word of God'.[216] Here, Hooker apparently denies both the autopisticity of Scripture and the internal testimony of the Spirit as the source of assurance.[217]

Yet, a close reading, provided in the following paragraphs, of the three texts in which Hooker considers the meta-principle of scriptural authenticity obviates accusations of hyper-rationalism by revealing a parallel between his account of supernatural cognitive participation and the relationship between the Spirit and the form of reason in scriptural authentication.[218] Just as God's *scientia* suspends theological science and divine influence abducts the light of reason, the 'power of the holy goste' sits at the beginning of a chain of per se causation in the authentication process through which the believer receives assurance of, and reason apprehends and assents to, the autopistic quality of Scripture.[219] In turn, the participatory mediation of reason publically unveils the presence of the Spirit.

The problem of why anyone should accept the authenticity of Scripture first briefly rears its head in the fourteenth chapter of Book One on the 'sufficiency of scripture unto the end for which it was instituted'.[220] Hooker acknowledges that Duns Scotus has 'affirmatively concluded' in his commentary on the *Sentences* that only Scripture contains the necessary knowledge for its appointed end of salvation. In this manner, Hooker clearly affirms the substance of *autopistos*, namely the veridical nature of Scripture. Yet Scripture (like any 'Arte or Science') has 'certaine boundes and limits' and presupposes 'many necessarye things learned in other sciences and knowne beforehand'. Hooker acknowledges, then, that the necessary saving knowledge of Scripture presupposes 'knowledge concerning certaine principles whereof it receaveth us already persuaded'. One of these principles is the sacred authority of Scripture. Hooker does not take this as self-evident to us, even if scriptural science contains necessary salvific knowledge. The meta-principle of which books are holy is 'confest impossible for the scripture it selfe to teach', although Hooker does not develop here why that might be the case. Hooker argues that scriptural authenticity presupposes 'being therefore persuaded by other meanes that these scriptures are the oracles of God'. Only then can Scripture 'teach us the rest, and laye before us all the duties which God requireth at our hands as necessary unto salvation'.

Voak, *Reformed Theology*, 224–39 discussing the idea of *autopistos* in Cartwright, Calvin, and the Anabaptists.
[215] Hooker, *Laws*, 1:222.22–8; III.8.4.
[216] Ibid., 1:230.9–10; III.8.12.
[217] See LeTourneau, "Richard Hooker and the Sufficiency of Scripture", 137.
[218] Hooker, *Laws*, 1:124.29–126.13; 1:153.13–25; 1:229.13–233.9; I.14.1; II.4.2; III.8.11–15.
[219] See David Neelands, 'The Use and Abuse of John Calvin in Richard Hooker's Defence of the English Church', *Perichoresis* 10, no. 1 (2012): 3–22.
[220] Hooker, *Laws*, 1:124.29–126.13; I.14.1.

In the second and third texts, Hooker gives a stronger account of the sense in which the scriptures cannot self-authenticate and the consequential role of reason. In the fourth chapter of Book Two Hooker repeats a classic Roman Catholic argument against the principle of *sola scriptura* that criticizes what it sees as an indissoluble problem of infinite regress:

> Finally we all beleeve that the Scriptures of God are sacred, and that they have proceeded from God; our selves we assure that wee doe right well in believing. We have for this point a demonstration sound and infallible. But it is not the worde of God which doth or possiblie can assure us, that wee doe well to thinke it his worde. For if any one booke of Scripture did give testimonie to all; yet still that Scripture which giveth credite to the rest, would require another Scripture to give credite unto it: neither could we ever come unto any pause whereon to rest our assurance this way, so that unlesse besides scripture there were some thing which might assure us that we do well, we could not thinke we do well, no not in being assured that scripture is a sacred and holie rule of well doing.[221]

In the eighth chapter of Book Three, Hooker repeats the same argument.[222] Hooker develops how the meta-principle of scriptural authenticity is not self-evident in the way that the proposition '*every whole is more then any parte of that whole*' is a *per se nota* principle. Instead, 'there must be therefore some former knowledge presupposed which doth herein assure the hartes of all believers. Scripture . . . presumeth us taught otherwise that it selfe is divine and sacred'. Scriptural authenticity remains in this regard comparable to all scientific knowledge: 'no science doth make knowne the first principles whereon it buildeth, but they are alwaies either taken as plaine and manifest in them selves, or as proved and graunted already, some former knowledge having made them evident'. In this third passage, Hooker explicitly mentions the vital role of reason in theological *scientia*: 'Scripture indeed teacheth things above nature, things which our reason by it selfe could not reach unto. Yet those things also we believe, knowing by reason that the scripture is the word of God.'

Nigel Voak offers the most extensive, naturalistic interpretation of these three texts as examples of Hooker's hyper-rationalism. For Voak, in the first passage, 'Hooker is taking the immensely significant step of rejecting the view that Scripture is self-authenticating' in relation to its sacred status, which implies that 'knowledge of this principle must come from a higher science'.[223] As such, Voak implicitly suggests that, in relation to the meta-principle of scriptural authenticity, Scripture becomes a subaltern *scientia* in relation to reason.[224] Voak then argues in relation to the first two passages that the 'other meanes' and 'demonstration sound and infallible' that Scripture presupposes are 'basic truths of natural law and natural theology'. That is to say, natural reason shows the authenticity of Scripture through infallible demonstrative rational

---

[221] Ibid., 1:153.13–25; II.4.2.
[222] Ibid., 1:229.13–233.9; III.8.11–15, emphasis in the original.
[223] Voak, 'Richard Hooker and the Principle of *Sola Scriptura*', 129.
[224] Compare Atkinson, *Authority of Scripture, Reason, and Tradition*, 93.

arguments which involve 'natural principles such as the existence and qualities of God, taught by human reason' and available to all.[225] Accordingly, in the final passage from Book Three, Hooker makes natural reason the inferential arbiter for knowing that Scripture is divine. Thus, Hooker rejects 'the Reformed view that Scripture can be infallibly authenticated non-inferentially on the basis of the internal witness of the Holy Spirit'.[226] He furthermore 'implicitly makes demonstrative reasoning a second *principium cognoscendi theologiae* in matters of Christian doctrine', the sine qua non for conversion, as Peter Lake has it.[227] For Voak, the exaggerated advantage of reason over Scripture places Hooker 'decisively outside the Reformed tradition over the issue of religious authority'. As O'Donovan argues, in Hooker's thought,

> the authority of Scriptural revelation is everywhere bounded by reason's own assured authority; reason disposes of divinely revealed truth according to its invariable principles and operations, without itself apparently being at the disposal of faith's immediate and certain knowledge, without itself being demonstrably directed and empowered in its work by the Holy Spirit.[228]

Indeed, for Voak, Hooker thereby opposes 'characteristically Reformed doctrine under the cover of an attack on puritanism and presbyterianism'.[229]

There are, however, two significant problems with such naturalistic readings of these three texts. First, Hooker never directly uses or abuses the term *autopistos* (and there are no contemporary criticisms of him doing so).[230] Neither does he reject the Spirit's testimony per se. He rather casts Scripture in the scholastic terms of *scientia*, *per se nota* and *subalternatio*, terms which are not simply equivalent to *autopistos*. As such, the question Hooker poses does not revolve around the intrinsic, autopistic nature of Scripture as objectively self-convincing per se, but rather turns on the existential question of assurance, namely, how human beings subjectively come to know and accept the sacred identity of Scripture. The emphasis on existential assurance in all three texts, rather than the intrinsic identity of Scripture, makes Hooker's claims less controversial. Since theology represents a subalternate science, the first principles are of course only self-evident (*per se nota*) within the higher *scientia dei*. The supernaturally infused habit of faith allows the human intellect to apprehend and assent to these first principles as self-evident to us. Aquinas's scholastic distinction between principles evident by themselves (*secundum se*) and to us (*quoad nos*) therefore forms the correct interpretive paradigm for the passages from the *Laws* about scriptural authenticity. Indeed, Hooker's example in the third passage of a self-evident proposition ('every whole is more then any parte of that whole') echoes Aquinas's thought as he explores whether God's existence is self-evident.[231] There, the proposition about 'whole and

---

[225] Voak, 'Richard Hooker and the Principle of *Sola Scriptura*', 129–31.
[226] Ibid., 135
[227] Ibid., 137.
[228] O'Donovan, *Theology of Law*, 145.
[229] Voak, *Reformed Theology*, 225.
[230] LeTourneau, 'Richard Hooker and the Sufficiency of Scripture', 149–50.
[231] Aquinas, *ST*, I.2.1.

part' is self-evident (*per se nota*) in itself (*secundum se*) and to us (*quoad nos*) as we understand the terms of the predicate and subject. In contrast, God's existence is self-evident 'for the predicate is the same as the subject', but not self-evident to us 'because we do not know the essence of God'. In the texts at hand, Hooker's similar concern is to distinguish between the intrinsic credibility of Scripture as the Word of God and its subjective credibility for us. 'Things are made credible', Hooker writes, 'eyther by the knowne condition and qualitie of the utterer, or by the manifest likelihood of the truth which they have in themselves.'[232] For Hooker and Calvin, Scripture remains more intrinsically credible and veridical than rational demonstration or even sense data because it reveals what God himself sees. Thus, Scripture contains 'the strongest proofe of all, and the most necessaryly assented unto by us'.[233] Yet, such credibility floats above the existential question of why or how we should 'thus receive the scripture'. Hooker considers that, while 'reason' and 'sense' (much like Calvin's *probationes*) can demonstrate 'a certaine beliefe evidentially grounded upon other assurance then Scripture', some kind of existential motor is required to mediate the intrinsic credibility of Scripture as a subjective reality.[234] Just as Calvin places the *testimonium internum* as this existential motor, Hooker suggestively lists the 'secret inspiration of the holy Ghost' along with 'revelation from heaven' and 'instruction upon earth' as the 'means' by which rational believers can know, for example, theological principles such as that God exists and rewards the faithful.[235]

Second, Hooker does not develop what might constitute 'other meanes' or a 'demonstration sound and infallible' in the way that Voak envisages. That scriptural authenticity presupposes 'other meanes' neither necessarily subalternates Scripture to reason nor denies a role for the Holy Spirit. Indeed, Hooker's example in Book One of the 'other meanes' which one science presupposes does not involve an act of subordination. Hooker argues that the art of oratory presupposes the precepts of grammar; and yet in the premodern period both rhetoric and grammar were both commonly seen as subalternate to logic, just as both the law of reason and divine law are suspended from eternal law.[236] Similarly, Aquinas gives a clear sense in which utility can suggest a particular kind of dependence without involving subalternation.[237] Aquinas writes that *sacra doctrina* 'can in a sense depend upon the philosophical sciences, not as though it stood in need of them, but only in order to make its teaching clearer'. As such, sacred doctrine 'does not depend upon other sciences as upon the higher, but makes use of them as of the lesser, and as handmaidens'. Hooker most probably has a comparable, non-subaltern notion of 'other meanes', especially reason, in relation to the authenticity of Scripture. Furthermore, Hooker never offers an example of a 'demonstration sound and infallible' for scriptural authenticity, and he does not link such demonstrations to the full existential assurance of firm faith. Voak's

---

[232] Hooker, *Laws*, 1:151.27–152.1; II.4.1.
[233] Ibid., 1:179.18–25; II.7.5. Compare Calvin, *Institutes*, I.vii.5; 1.80
[234] Hooker, *Laws*, 1:152.9–15; II.4.1.
[235] Ibid., 1:229.27–9; III.8.11.
[236] See Theresa Enos (ed.), *Encyclopedia of Rhetoric and Composition: Communication from Ancient Times to the Information Age* (Abingdon: Routledge, 2010), 401–2.
[237] Aquinas, *ST*, I.1.5 ad.2.

argument that Hooker refers to natural demonstrative reasoning in these passages ignores Hooker's qualification that while 'the force of naturall reason is great . . . the force whereof unto those effects is nothing without grace'.[238] While demonstrations can certainly take a logical or deductive form as Voak argues, they can also take the form of signs or manifestations that exhibit that something is true. Indeed, Hooker makes clear in Book One that the demonstration of goodness (and so truth) comes either from direct knowledge of some infallible first principle, or from 'signs and tokens' which, as they mount up in human experience, also take on the infallible character of 'the sentence of God him selfe'.[239] Neither of these kinds of demonstrations precludes the causal activity of the Holy Spirit in some regard, especially given the causative role given to divine influence in the architecture of participation.

In order to understand properly the ancillary role that Hooker affords to reason in relation to the meta-principle of scriptural authenticity, it is necessary to consider in more detail the third of these passages. In the eighth chapter of Book Three, Hooker examines by 'what meanes we are taught' that the Scriptures are sacred.[240] First, 'the first outward motive leading men so to esteeme of the scripture is the authority of Gods Church.' Here, Hooker accepts (as did Calvin) the Augustinian dictum, 'I should not believe the gospel except as moved by the Catholic church'. Hooker's interpretation of the dictum seems to differ, however, from that of Calvin.[241] The latter reformer interprets Augustine's dictum as referring to unbelievers, making the consensus of the Church important since (as Calvin puts it) 'those who have not yet been illumined by the Spirit of God are rendered teachable by reverence for the church' and so 'prepared for faith in the gospel'.[242] Hooker instead more traditionally interprets the dictum as referring to believers 'bredde and brought up in the Church'. It is clear, then, that such believers already have some kind of faith, but that the first move towards evidential certainty begins with an appeal to ecclesial authority which cannot be questioned 'without cause' and which itself is persuasive, although not indefeasibly. As such, Hooker recognizes human authority as 'the key which openeth the dore of entrance into the knowledge of the scripture' because such authority 'may enforce assent'.[243] Second, after having accepted the testimony of the Church, the individual discovers that the ratiocinative analysis of the marks of Scripture 'doth answer our received opinion concerning it', resulting in a firmer sense of evidential certainty. The *ratio* of the scriptures as 'we bestow our labor in reading or hearing the misteries thereof' corresponds, then, with the witness of the Church. Such ratiocinative analysis recalls, of course, Calvin's *probationes* that confirm the identity of Scripture to human reason.[244] Indeed, like Calvin's *probationes*, such 'infallible' rational 'arguments' and

---

[238] Hooker, *Laws*, 1:229.15–16; III.8.11.
[239] Ibid., 1:82.27–84.4; I.8.2–3.
[240] Ibid., 1:231.18–232.16; III.8.14.
[241] Augustine, *Contra epistulam Manichaei quam vocant fundamenti*, 5(6), in *Nicene and Post-Nicene Fathers*, first series, vol. 4, 131. (Peabody: Hendrickson, 1994). Compare Calvin, *Institutes*, I.vii.3; 1.76–78.
[242] Calvin, *Institutes*, I.vii.3; 1.77.
[243] Hooker, *Laws*, 1:177.27–34; II.7.3.
[244] Fulford, 'Reformed Orthodoxy on Autopistos', 207–11 persuasively points out inconsistencies in Calvin's thought on the role of proofs and the interpretive variety across early Reformed orthodoxy on the matter.

'proofes' have an apologetic use against 'Infidels or Atheists' who question the church's testimony or personal persuasion about the authenticity of the scriptures. Since they conform to human reason (Calvin's *humana ratio*), they are open to all and cannot be denied without 'denying some apparent principle such as al men acknowledge to be true'. Like Calvin's *probationes*, for Hooker the rational analysis of the marks of scripture also 'confirmeth . . . beleefe the more' in the believer and, as they show how the witness of the Church corresponds to the *ratio* of Scripture, may 'somwhat help' to convert and persuade unbelievers.

Immediately following this passage, however, Hooker makes it clear that, while the witness of the Church and ratiocinative analysis of scriptural texts provide objective evidence, they cannot produce subjective assurance or faith in the principle that the scriptures are sacred. Like Calvin, Hooker places pneumatic illumination as the posterior and interior source of faith and existential assurance about this meta-principle:

> Neither can I thinke that when grave and learned men do sometime hold, that of this principle there is no proofe but by the testimony of the spirit, which assureth our harts therin, it is their meaning to exclude utterly all force which any kind of reason may have in that behalfe; but I rather incline to interpret such their speeches, as if they had more expresly set downe, that other motives and inducements, be they never so strong and consonant unto reason, are notwithstanding uneffectual of them selves to worke faith concerning this principle, if the special grace of the holy ghost concur not to the inlightning of our minds.[245]

Voak alleges that if Hooker takes 'grave and learned men' to refer to Calvin and other major Reformed theologians, 'then his interpretation is very free, if not disingenuous.'[246] Yet, Hooker's interpretation, as has been shown, shares a great deal of similarity with Calvin's. For the latter, the witness of the Holy Spirit confirms the intrinsic *autopistos* of Scripture within the believer, giving a full assurance and firm faith not possible through the witness of the Church or the *probationes* alone. Similarly, for Hooker, 'if the special grace of the holy ghost concur not to the inlightning of our minds', then all other 'motives and inducements' remain ineffectual to work faith.

Behind these passages, Hooker offers a quiet and subtle account of the Holy Spirit that he nevertheless believes remains consonant with Reformed orthodoxy. Polemics rather than heterodox theological commitments drive his subtlety. As W. Speed Hill argues, Hooker reduces his appeals to grace and the Spirit in order to shift his puritan adversaries away from indemonstrable appeals to interior illumination and towards public rational argument.[247] Hooker's architecture of participation goes deeper than this, however, and he interprets pneumatic illumination as, what David Neelands calls,

---

[245] Hooker, *Laws*, 1:232.16–25; III.8.15.
[246] Voak, *Reformed Theology*, 228. Compare Neelands, 'The Use and Abuse of John Calvin', 10–13, who shows how Hooker uses the phrase 'grave and learned man' as a 'code phrase for John Calvin (and those who agree with him)'. See Hooker, *Laws*, 1:5.23–4; Pref.2.3 as an example.
[247] W. Speed Hill, 'The Doctrinal Background of Richard Hooker's Laws of Ecclesiastical Polity' (PhD thesis, Cambridge: Harvard University, 1964), 199–201.

'the engracing of human reason itself, not an interruption of it'.[248] As such, the causal activity of the Holy Spirit displays continuity with reason and the voice of the Church. Hooker emphasizes that the Holy Spirit demonstrates its influence within and through reason as a public instrument of persuasion. Thus, 'the spirit leadeth men into all truth' either through an extraordinary 'speciall divine excellency' (such as in the direct 'Revelation' given to biblical prophets) or through the manuduction of 'Reason . . . the hande which the Spirit hath led'.[249] That puritan 'men, women and children' would cast themselves as isomorphic 'Prophets' constitutes an absurdly egoistic proposition for Hooker. He caustically observes of his opponents: '*It is not therefore the fervent earnestness of their perswaion, but the soundes of those reasons whereupon the same is built, which must declare their opinions in these things to have been wrought by the holie Ghost, and not by the* fraud *of that evill Spirit which is even in his illusions strong*'.[250] Claims to inner illumination require public scrutiny to avoid demonic delusion. Hooker commends public reason as an arbiter for the discernment of true pneumatic illumination:

> [E]ven to our own it needeth caution and explication how the testimony of the spirit may be discerned, by what means it may be knowen, lest men thinke that the spirit of god doth testifie those things which the spirit of error suggesteth. The operations of the spirit, especially these ordinary which be common unto all true Christian men, are as we know, things secret and undiscernible even to the very soule where they are, because their nature is of another and an higher kind then they can be perceived in this life. Wherefore albeit the spirit lead us into all truth and direct us in all goodnes, yet bicause these workings of the spirit in us are so privy and secret, we therfore stand on a plainer ground, when we gather from the qualitie of things beleeved or done, that the spirit of God hath directed us in both; then if we settle our selves to beleeve or to do any certaine particular thing, as being moved thereto by the spirit.[251]

Within this public scrutiny, reason and the Spirit conform to one another, just as the Word and Spirit conform for Calvin: the light of reason works as the ordinary 'effectuall instrument' of the Spirit which illumines it, and as the legal 'instrument wherewith God will have the world guided'.[252] In turn, the true presence of the Spirit remains discernible when there is 'soundnes' of reason displayed in public discourse.[253] Indeed, in Book Five Hooker further writes against the 'rule of mens private spirits' which wreaks 'utter confusion . . . under pretense of beinge taught, led, and guided by [the Holy] spirit'. The insufficiency of their arguments makes 'against them a stronge

---

[248] Neelands, 'The Use and Abuse of John Calvin', 18.
[249] Hooker, *Laws*, 1:17.15–27; Pref.3.10. See Russell, *Beyond Certainty*, 92–106, using Candler, *Theology, Rehtoric, Manuduction*, esp. 3–30 and the idea of the 'grammar of participation' in which certain theological texts imitate the pedagogic activity of God by in a process of manuduction ('leading by the hand).
[250] Hooker, *Laws*, 1:18.4–8; Pref.3.10, emphasis in the original.
[251] Ibid., 1:232.30–233.9; III.8.15.
[252] Ibid., 2:45.2–3; V.9.3.
[253] Ibid., 1:18. 4–6; Pref.3.10.

presumption, that God hath not moved theire hartes to thinke such thinges, as he hath not inabled them to prove'.[254] The instrumentality of reason does not preclude, therefore, the illuminatory role of the Holy Spirit; it rather safeguards a proper means of public discernment through which the Spirit unveils itself. Revelation must have a rational character in order to be intelligible. Likewise, rationality, in its very constitution, has a revelatory character.

Hooker's notion of reason as an 'effectual instrument' of the Spirit broadly sits within Reformed orthodoxy, a set of polychromatic traditions displaying remarkable breadth and plasticity.[255] As both this chapter and the previous one have argued, Reformed scholastics within Reformed orthodoxy regularly use the causal theory of Aristotle as mediated through medieval scholasticism, just as Hooker does. Reformed theologians often speak of the instrumental cause (*causa instrumentalis*) as a subordinate efficient cause (*causa efficiens*). Here, while God is the primary efficient cause of all that exists and takes place in reality, God also involves humanity as an instrumental cause. Rather than being merely passive recipients of God's efficient activity, the human form (and all of its actions) reciprocally participates in God as a subordinate efficient (or instrumental) cause. Reformed thought commonly holds the integrity of creation and the gratuity of grace in productive tension. As such, Hooker's account of reason as an 'instrument which God doth use' stands within such a Reformed scholastic context.[256] God or the Holy Spirit sit at the beginning of a chain of per se causation. As such, God remains the primary efficient cause of knowledge; this establishes the integrity of reason as a subordinate efficient cause, and casts that integrity as a form of revelation in itself. While Hooker creatively interprets Calvin's account of the internal witness of the Holy Spirit in order to emphasize the instrumentality of reason, this does not put him outside of Reformed orthodoxy as such. As with Calvin, for Hooker as well it was 'the secret and mystical operations of the Holy Spirit that created and transformed objectivity into lived experience by which divine grace could be understood and received, joining us to Christ, and incorporating believers in mystical union'.[257]

Indeed, Hooker's account of how faith and human reason relate prefigures, for example, the later Reformed orthodox thought of Gisbertus Voetius in the seventeenth century.[258] In Voetius's first disputation of the *Disputationes theologicae selectae* (1648–1669), he argues that while human reason is the receiving subject of faith (*subjectum fidei recipiens*), it is also the instrumental or elicitive principle (*principium elicitivum*) of faith because it draws out rational conclusions from the inner illumination of faith.[259] Like Hooker, then, Voetius argues that Scripture acts as the source of faith, the Spirit's

---

[254] Ibid., 2:46.7–47.9; V.10.1.
[255] Fulford, 'Reformed Orthodoxy on Autopistos', 215–18 argues, for example, that Francis Turretin 'holds the same position as Hooker' on *autopistos*. On the 'discovery of diverse trajectories' in Reformed orthodoxy, see Willem J. van Asselt, 'Reformed Orthodoxy: A Short History of Research', in *A Companion to Reformed Orthodoxy*, ed. Herman J. Selderhuis (Leiden: Brill, 2013), 22–4.
[256] Hooker, *Laws*, 1:232.13–14; III.8.14.
[257] Stafford, 'Richard Hooker's Pneumatologia', 161.
[258] See van den Belt, *The Authority of Scripture*, 167–9.
[259] G. Voetius, *Disputationes Selectae*, vols 1–3 (Utrecht: J. Waesberge, 1648–59), I.i.2. The phrase *principium elicitivum* is a scholastic term drawn from Aquinas, *Scriptum super Sententiis*, I, d.3, q.5, a.1, ad 5.

illumination efficiently causes faith, and reason is the ordinary receptive psychological faculty in which faith finds its proper place. For both Hooker and Voetius, the light of reason enjoys a vital, but ancillary and instrumental status as a secondary *principium* of faith, but Scripture alone is the primary *principium*.[260] As Voetius puts it, reason is an elicitive *principium quod* of faith, a scholastic term meaning a passive principle that is acted upon, rather than the *principium quo* which is the basis for an event or effect. The priority Hooker gives to divine action in both natural and supernatural cognitive participation suggests that he similarly sees reason as an instrumental (and therefore subordinate efficient) cause of faith, but not as its ground, a preserve kept for the illumination of God or the Holy Spirit. Indeed, in Book Five Hooker gives a hierarchical list of religious authorities in which reason remains secondary to Holy Scripture: 'what scripture doth plainelie deliver, to that the first place both of credit and obedience is due; the next whereunto is whatsoever anie man can necessarily conclude by force of reason; after these the voice of the Church succeedeth.'[261] Having a broader sense of what constitutes 'Reformed orthodoxy' means that Hooker does not need to be cast irrevocably outside of the Reformed pale as Voak and others insist. Rather, he constitutes one part of its rich, varied and complex historical and theological tapestry.

Within his cognitive ecology, Hooker's architecture of participation therefore navigates between hypo- and hyper-rationalism, intimately connecting divine influence with the form of reason. Just as natural cognitive participation involves a similitude to God as first mover, so too does supernatural cognitive participation involve the action of the Holy Spirit within and through the integral operation of reason. Indeed, Hooker describes Scripture's role as a doctrinal instrument in terms of the believer's participation or reciprocal indwelling of Christ, with the Holy Spirit sitting at the beginning of a chain of *per se* causation in rational cognition:

> The cawse of life spirituall in us is christ, not carnally nor corporally inhabitinge but dwelling in the soule of man as a thinge, which when the minde apprehendeth it is said to inhabitt and posses the mynde. The mind conceyveth Christe by hering the doctryne of christianitye ... [O]ur life is Christe by the hearing of the gospell apprehended as a saviour and assented unto through the power of the holy goste.[262]

Christ is the formal cause of spiritual life, and the Spirit acts as the primary efficient cause of doctrinal knowledge within the ordinary rational process of apprehension and assent. Pace Shuger and Voak, who variously argue that Hooker sets up reason as 'an interpretive act',[263] or 'a kind of barrier, or filter, between the Spirit and the believer',[264] the form of reason, whether natural or supernatural, presupposes divine activity, rendering reason as a divine instrument even within its own integrity. Hooker therefore ends the eighth chapter of Book Three by making the necessity of the Spirit's activity within cognition abundantly clear. 'The force and use of mans

---

[260] Voetius, *Disputationes Selectae*, III.lxvii.4.
[261] Hooker, *Laws*, 2:39.8–11; V.8.2.
[262] Hooker, *Justification*, 26, in *FLE*, 5:137.27–138.9.
[263] Shuger, *Habits of Thought*, 37.
[264] Voak, *Reformed Theology*, 238.

reason in thinges divine' ultimately depends upon the 'aide and assistance of Gods most blessed spirite'. Human laws, even as they draw from the laws of nature and God through rational discourse, are 'aided with the influence of divine grace' and the '*instinct of the holy Ghost*'.[265]

'Union with that it desireth': Desire and cognitive participation in God

Although scholars most commonly depict that Hooker composes his epistemology in a rationalist key, desire forms the second constellating category of his cognitive ecology and sets the emotions as constitutive of human happiness *coram Deo*.[266] If reason directs people to know God's truth, then desire moves them to love God's goodness. As such, W. J. Bouwsma perceptively notes two anthropological models in Hooker's thought: the scholastic structure of discrete faculties all subject to the rational rule of the mind; and the biblical and humanist image of the heart where the passions are a source for good.[267] If the former model dominates Hooker's account of cognitive participation in God in Books Two and Three of the *Laws*, then the latter model re-emerges in Books Four and Five as the cognitive motor of such participation. In the latter two books, Hooker tackles the claims of his puritan opponents that 'our forme of Church-politie is corrupted with popish orders rites and ceremonies' and that 'there is amongst us much superstition' retained in the Book of Common Prayer. At heart, the debate revolves around what constitutes the proper means of liturgical edification. Just as divine influence manuducts reason to participate cognitively in God, Hooker argues that the established liturgy affords 'mutuall conference and as it were commerce to be had betwene God and us', creatively crafting appropriate 'holie desires' which lead believers both to know and also to love God in sacramental union with Christ.[268] For Hooker, worship therefore creates 'emotional communities' (i.e. social groups whose members express and evaluate emotions together) through an 'emotional regime' (meaning a shared affective set of cultural, embodied, creative and symbolic practices).[269] Like reason, desire stands within the rational architecture of participation and exhibits both an extensive as well as an intensive aspect and logic. Just as the divinely suspended 'light of reason' enlightens truth for the human participant, desires are created existential motors which drive the ecstatic, formal move from becoming to being through the pursuit of perfective ends parsed as 'good'. Ultimately, since 'no good is infinite but only God', human beings naturally desire an intensive 'union with

---

[265] Hooker, *Laws*, 1:234.31–235.18; III.8.18.
[266] For an excellent rebuttal of accounts that cast Hooker as 'the champion of [secular] reason', see Russell, *Beyond Certainty*, 107–80. Compare Newey, 'The Form of Reason', 1–4. While Russell sees that Hooker places reason and emotion together, she fails to develop satisfactorily how a shared logic of participation binds them, instead arguing that the importance of desire emerges in the 'vista beyond reason, beyond certainty' (180).
[267] Bouwsma, 'Hooker in the Context of European Cultural History', 41–58.
[268] Hooker, *Laws*, 2:65.7–8; V.18.1.
[269] See Ole Riis and Linda Woodhead, *A Sociology of Religious Emotion* (Oxford: Oxford University Press, 2010), 1–19.

that it desireth', namely (re)union with God as their first and final cause, resting in the affective perfection of joyful love.[270]

This part explores Hooker's essential logic of extensive desire in Book One. It then considers the cognitive role of desire in faith as that which effects an intensive participation in God. Finally, it shows how the established liturgy for Hooker displays the fourth, creative aspect of participation: the work of worship unites heaven and earth, recreating desire as the existential motor driving an intensive return to God.

As Charles Miller puts it, desire, goodness and perfection run 'through the whole of Book I and beyond like a silver thread'.[271] As created desires move an actor to pursue cognized goodness as a perfective quality, they also drive the actor 'to covet more or lesse the participation of God himselfe' as the source and end of all participable perfection. Yet, modern exegetes often claim that the silver thread of desire represents an illogical interruption of an otherwise strongly rationalist epistemology. For example, A. J. Joyce claims that Hooker, unlike Aquinas, 'is in general inclined to be . . . disparaging of the role played by emotion, . . . [implying] a fundamental conflict between emotion and reason'.[272] Like Bouwsma, Debora Shuger notes 'two epistemologies or discourses' in Hooker's thought, but sets them in conflict: a 'rational consciousness' and a 'participatory consciousness' form contrary 'habits of thought, that is, the culturally based ways the mind categorizes and structures the world'.[273] The 'rational consciousness' empties 'cosmos, state, and history of . . . numinosity' since it involves an objective and secular 'hermeneutic based on reason and historical evidence'. In turn, the 'participatory consciousness . . . assumes the primacy of desire in the act of knowing' and subjectively enchants material things such that they 'reflect the supernatural order and symbolize transcendence'. As such, Hooker's rational emphasis in the early books of the *Laws* gives way to 'a traditional mystic epistemology' by Book Five, where 'Hooker's spiritual psychology consistently makes desire rather than reason the epistemic ground'. Yet, the desire that characterizes religious belief remains 'illogical' because it exceeds and even contradicts rational evidence. However, the architecture of participation debunks Shuger's claim that reason is intrinsically secular for Hooker, as the previous portions of this chapter have shown. The architecture of participation similarly challenges the idea that desire and the emotions tout court are inherently irrational. Hooker distinguishes in the *Laws* between a corrupted experience of desire and its essentially logical structure. Like reason, the essential logic of desire remains bound up with a Neoplatonic participatory metaphysic of exit and return: as created desires perceptively move towards the *ratio* of goodness, they ultimately drive human beings to love God's nature, coextensive with transcendental goodness, and so enjoy an intensive cognitive (re)union with their transcendent origin.

Hooker's logic of desire in Book One of the *Laws* represents the confluence of medieval theories of the emotions. 'Emotion' remains, of course, an anachronistic term for Hooker's Elizabethan period since it only came into regular use from the

---

[270] Hooker, *Laws*, 1:112.11–13; I.11.2.
[271] Miller, *Vision of God*, 201.
[272] Joyce, *Anglican Moral Theology*, 163.
[273] Shuger, *Habits of Thought*, 43–6.

mid-seventeenth century and in subsequent centuries became a flattened, secular denuding of theological notions of the passions and affections.[274] Instead, premodern categories used by Hooker (e.g. passions, affections, habits, virtues and vices) exhibit significant overlap with the modern category of emotion. While no single theory of the emotions dominated the medieval period, Augustine and Aquinas proved the most influential thinkers, with the latter building upon the former in light of the 'Aristotelian revolution' of the thirteenth century.[275] Augustine principally addresses the emotions in *De civitate Dei* in Book 9.4–5 and Book 14, while Aquinas particularly considers them at length in his 'treatise on the passions' in the *Summa Theologiae* I.II.22–48.[276] In both cases, Augustine and Aquinas develop a syncretistic account of the emotions, adopting and transforming elements from Stoic, Platonic and Aristotelian thought into a Christian vision, where created desires relate emotions (as perceptive forms of cognition which move an agent) to love sourced in God. Neither Augustine nor Aquinas cast the emotions in merely secular terms but variously index them against divinity. As the background to Hooker's account, then, it remains useful first to draw out the relevant aspects of Augustine and Aquinas's thoughts on the emotions and desire.

Augustine and Aquinas distinguish between two kinds of emotional phenomena, namely the passions (*passiones*) and the affections (*affectiones*). The passions are involuntary movements of the lower appetitive or sensitive soul towards sensible goods; they affect both the body as well as the rational soul, and (for Aquinas) are somatic. The affections are voluntary movements of the higher appetitive soul (the intellective self) towards intelligible goods; Thomas Dixon accordingly calls the affections 'the emotions of the rational mind'.[277] Augustine adopts the Stoic fourfold classification of the 'emotions' paired into binaries according to the type and presence or absence of good and evil objects: delight (*laetitia*) and desire (*libido/cupiditas/appetitus*) for present and future goods; or distress (*aegritudo/dolor*) and fear (*metus*) for present and future evils.[278] Aquinas gives a more complex taxonomy but similarly argues that all emotions are objectual in that they offer an intentional form of perception coloured by cognitive evaluation of perfective goods.[279] Like Augustine, Aquinas's taxonomy puts desire for

---

[274] On the history of emotion and its relationship to early modern categories, see the following: Susan James, *Passion and Action: The Emotions in Seventeenth-Century Philosophy* (Oxford: Oxford University Press, 1997); Thomas Dixon, *From Passions to Emotions: the Creation of a Secular Psychological Category* (Cambridge: Cambridge University Press, 2003); Simo Knuutila, *Emotions in Ancient and Medieval Philosophy* (Oxford: Oxford University Press, 2004); and Gail Kern Paster, Katherine Rowe, and Mary Floyd-Wilson (eds), *Reading the Early Modern Passions: Essays in the Cultural History of Emotion* (Philadelphia: University of Pennsylvania Press, 2004).

[275] See Peter King, 'Emotions in Medieval Thought', in *The Oxford Handbook of Philosophy of Emotion*, ed. Peter Goldie (Oxford: Oxford University Press, 2012), 167–88.

[276] Aquinas also gives extended treatments of emotion in *Scriptum super libros Sententiarum*, 3 d.15 q.2, d.26 q.1 and d.27 q.1, in *On Love and Charity: Readings from the Commentary on the Sentences of Peter Lombard. Thomas Aquinas in Translation*, trans. Peter A. Kwasniewski, Thomas Bolin and Joseph Bolin (Washington: Catholic University of America Press, 2008). See also Aquinas, *De ver*, qq. 25–6.

[277] Dixon, *From Passions to Emotions*, 54–5.

[278] Augustine, *De civitate Dei*, 14.5–6, in *Nicene and Post-Nicene Fathers*, first series, vol. 2, 265–6.

[279] See Peter King, 'Emotions', in *The Oxford Handbook of Aquinas*, ed. Brian Davies and Eleanore Stump (Oxford: Oxford University Press, 2012), 209–26.

the good as the central principle of motion. Concupiscible passions include the first-order desires (*concupiscentia*) and aversions/repulsions (*fuga/abominatio*) for absent sensible goods or evils, as well as the pleasures (*delectatio*) and sorrows/pains (*tristitia/dolor*) of present sensible goods or evils. The irascible passions (hope, *spes*; despair, *desperatio*; daring, *audacia*; fear, *timor*; and anger, *ira*) are second-order emotional phenomena which presuppose and defend the concupiscible passions, 'rising against whatever gets in the way of what is agreeable, which is whatever the concupiscible power desires.'[280] The intellectual affections reside in and move the intellectual appetite rather than the sensitive, but follow the structure of the concupiscible passions while aiming at intelligible goods.

While Augustine and Aquinas offer different emotional taxonomies, they give logical priority to love in the intentional cognition of the good. The principle of love unites all emotions, which relate in some way, then, to created desires that orient and propel an actor towards a desirable object through attraction to the cognized good. Here, desire takes on a central perceptive and motivational role in cognition: it engages the world directly and exhibits a certain kind of logic that moves the basic inclination to love towards final rest in, and joyful union with, the beloved. For Augustine, as love tends toward its end, it signifies desire for the good; and as love reaches its end, it rests in the delight of union.[281] All love involves attraction, then. Love orders (according to the *ratio* of the good) the desire of the lover to enjoy union with the beloved. Similarly, for Aquinas, love is the first of the passions and affections since they both 'presuppose love of some kind'.[282] Love is the first inclination towards the possession of a sensible good, and desire moves the lover towards possession of, and union with, that cognized sensible good.[283] Love also forms the 'first movement of the will' and so orients the affections to seek union with the intellectual good.[284] The intellectual affection of desire (*desiderium*) springs as a principle of motion from the intellectual appetite towards the cognized good when it is absent, and joy (*gaudium*) occurs as a species of pleasure (*delectatio*) when the loved intellectual good becomes present.[285]

Augustine and Aquinas offer an ambivalent but ultimately holistic view of emotional phenomena, relating them to cognitive participation in God as source and end of love. As such, both extract an essential logic of desire from an inherently corrupted experience. Like the Stoics, Augustine at times pejoratively labels emotional phenomena as 'disturbances' or 'upheavals' (*perturbationes*), and both Augustine and Aquinas argue that the passions need to be subject to reason or they can lead to irrational sins of passion.[286] At other times, however, Augustine refers to passions in a

---

[280] Aquinas, *ST*, I.81.2.
[281] Augustine, *De civitate Dei*, 14.7, in *Nicene and Post-Nicene Fathers*, first series, vol. 2, 266–7.
[282] Aquinas, *ST*, I.II.27.4.
[283] Ibid., I.II.36.2.
[284] Ibid., I.20.1.
[285] Ibid., I.II.31.3.
[286] Augustine, *De civitate Dei*, 8.17, 9.4, 9.6, 14.15, in *Nicene and Post-Nicene Fathers*, first series, vol. 2, 155–6, 167–8, 274–5. Aquinas, *ST*, I.95.2; I.II.77. Aquinas, *ST*, I.II.24.2 rejects Cicero's idea that the passions are *perturbationes* since insofar as emotion is controlled by reason, 'it is part of the virtuous life.' See Thomas Dixon, 'Revolting Passions', in *Faith, Rationality, and the Passions*, ed. Sarah Coakley (Chichester: Wiley-Blackwell, 2012), 181–96.

morally neutral sense, and consistently praises the affections, linking them to the 'rule of reason' and virtue.[287] In a stronger vein, for Aquinas, while the passions 'sometimes oppose reason', it remains 'natural' for the passions to 'obey reason' and human passions are accordingly 'rational by participation' when they enjoy the political rule of reason.[288] Virtuous habits produce ordinate passions that produce, insofar as they are consonant with 'reason's command', an affective knowledge of the good, rendering the passions as essential for human flourishing.[289] Like Augustine, for Aquinas the inferior passions do not exhaust the affective capacity of the soul since godly affections produce imperturbable love which binds humankind with the desire of the angels and the love of God.[290] For both Augustine and Aquinas, then, while created desires are existential motors intrinsic to human beings, right desires also reveal a transcendental charisma, namely, the drive towards an intensive return to, or reunion with, God. For Augustine, proper love is caritas, 'that affection of the mind which aims at the enjoyment of God for His own sake, and the enjoyment of one's self and of one's neighbour in subordination to God.'[291] Such human caritas only becomes possible through participation in the divine nature, which is coextensive with goodness and love; human caritas refers love for the world to the ultimate love of God.[292] Right desire orders an actor to pursue union with God as the cognized source of love and goodness, the ground of beatific happiness, and the eternal beloved.[293] Hence, Augustine prays about desire at the beginning of the *Confessiones*, using the 'heart' to signify both rational and affective forms of cognition: 'man . . . desires to praise Thee . . . for Thou hast formed us for Thyself, and our hearts are restless till they find rest in Thee.'[294] Similarly, for Aquinas the will's basic inclination is towards the unrestricted goodness only found in God's nature, knowledge of which elicits a natural desire (*desiderium naturale*) to 'see' God. The theological virtue of charity presupposes rational cognition of God and orients the will towards God as supreme good through an affective habitual disposition of benevolence.[295] Aquinas therefore defines 'charity' as 'friendship' (*amictia*) with God, a reciprocal relationship of love tending towards 'a union of affection'.[296] Accordingly, Aquinas links the intellectual appetite and affection of desire to the final happiness of beatitude where, as they cognitively participate in God, believers experience loving union with the divine beloved, the joy of rest following as an affective consequence.[297]

---

[287] Augustine, *De civitate Dei*, 14.9, in *Nicene and Post-Nicene Fathers*, first series, vol. 2, 268–9.
[288] Aquinas, *ST*, I.81.3 ad.2; I.II.24.2 ad.3; I.II. 56.4 ad.1 and 3; I.II.56.6 ad.2; I.II.60.1
[289] Ibid., 59.2 ad.3.
[290] Ibid., I.82.5 ad.1.
[291] Augustine, *De doctrina christiana*, 3.10.16, in *Nicene and Post-Nicene Fathers*, first series, vol. 2, 561. Augustine opposes *caritas* with *cupiditas*, 'that affection of the mind which aims at enjoying one's self and one's neighbour, and other corporeal things, without reference to God.'
[292] See A. P. Scrutton, *Thinking Through Feeling: God, Emotion, and Passibility* (New York: Bloomsbury, 2011), 39–42.
[293] Augustine, *De civitate Dei*, 9.23, in *Nicene and Post-Nicene Fathers*, first series, vol. 2, 279–80.
[294] Augustine, *Confessiones*, 1.1, in *Nicene and Post-Nicene Fathers*, first series, vol. 1, 45. See Eric Jager, *The Book of the Heart* (Chicago: University of Chicago Press, 2001), 27–43.
[295] Aquinas, *ST*, I.II.27.4 ad.2.
[296] Ibid., II.II, 23.1, 27.2.
[297] Ibid., I.19.3, 59.1; I.II.2.7–8, 3.8, 5.8

The scattered account of the emotions in the *Laws* shows three crucial points of contact with Augustine and Aquinas. First, like the two medieval theologians, Hooker links the sensitive appetite to the 'inferiour naturall desire' for sensible goods and describes the will as an intellectual appetite or desire, which takes as its object 'that good which reason doth leade us to seeke'.[298] Accordingly, he also broadly speaks of 'passions' and 'affections' as phenomena which move appetitive inclinations from potency to act, relating them to the emotional life of human beings and Christ,[299] as well as to affective states in the immaterial angels[300] and God, whose perfectly loving 'harte' abducts creation through 'that naturall desire which his goodness hath to shew and impart himself'[301] and whose loving 'desire is to have all men saved'.[302] Hooker regularly recognizes, then, the central epistemic and motivational role of emotional phenomena such as delight, desire, distress, fear, joy, love, pleasure, hope, despair, grief and anger, even if he does not arrange them into an Augustinian or Thomistic taxonomy. Second, like Augustine and Aquinas, Hooker remains ambivalent about such emotional phenomena and at times certainly suggests a conflict between them and reason. In the preface to the *Laws*, for example, Hooker remains scathing of those whose 'affections doe frame their opinions'.[303] He opposes the 'mist of passionate affection' and 'vehemencie of affection' found in his puritan opponents with 'the light of sound and sincere judgement' and the 'force of reason'.[304] Hooker later suggests that, since emotions spring out of appetitive powers, 'it is not altogether in our [rational] power, whether we will be stirred with affections or no'.[305] Alongside the puritans, Hooker regularly points to heretics from the patristic era as another class of people in whom inordinate 'corrupted affections' led to malign or irrational behaviour,[306] as well as in the fallen angels,[307] Anabaptists,[308] atheists,[309] and even Calvin and his followers.[310] More broadly, Hooker argues in his *Sermon on Pride* that a sinful person suffers from 'immoderate swelling', an Augustinian perturbation in which the will tyrannizes 'over reason, and brutish sensuality over will'.[311] Yet, at the same time Hooker criticizes any appearance of 'couldnes in affection' in the unyielding legalism of his opponents,

---

[298] Hooker, *Laws*, 1:78.10–16; I.7.3.
[299] Ibid., 2:196.19–199.23; V.48.9–11.
[300] Ibid., 1:70.6–16; I.4.1.
[301] Ibid., 2:202.24; V.49.1.
[302] Hooker, *Dublin Fragments*, 32–3, in *FLE*, 4:143.5–24 distinguishes between God's general loving inclination that 'would have all men saved' and a secondary kind of will which takes into account how sin frustrates God's general inclination. Here, Hooker echoes Aquinas, *ST*, I.19.6 ad.1 who parses desire in God as a wishful inclination (*velleitas*) that may go unfulfilled even as it expresses the excessive love of God. Compare Hooker, *Laws*, 2:204.25–32; V.49.3.
[303] Hooker, *Laws*, 1:17.29–18.8; Pref.3.10.
[304] Ibid., 1:34.21–3; 1:51.29–31; Pref.7.1; Pref.9.1.
[305] Ibid., 1:78.16–22; I.7.3. Compare 2:3.25–4.1; V.Ded.5.
[306] Ibid., 1:225.24–8; III.8.8. See also Ibid., 1:164.3–165.8; 2:123.22–6; 2:166.7–20; 3:76.8–15; 3:199.9–12; II.5.7; V.29.2; V.42.2; VI.6.6; VII.9.1. See Voak, *Reformed Theology*, 83–91 on sins of passion.
[307] Hooker, *Laws*, 1:71.16–72.24; I.4.3. Barry Rasmussen, 'The Priority of God's Gracious Action in Richard Hooker's Hermeneutic', 3–14 persuasively argues that the inordinate self-love of the angels mirrors for Hooker the inordinate sense of self-righteousness he finds displayed by the puritans.
[308] Hooker, *Laws*, 1:48.10–13; Pref.8.11.
[309] Ibid., 2:23.6–19; V.2.1.
[310] Ibid., 1:10.12–13; 1:26.9–27.1; Pref.2.7; Pref.4.8.
[311] Hooker, *Pride*, I, in *FLE*, 5:314.22–8.

and, as will be shown, puts desire as the second constellating category of his cognitive ecology.[312] Third, then, despite such ambivalence over the moral value of emotional phenomena, Hooker (following Augustine and Aquinas) unifies them under the priority of love and the concomitant emotions of desire and pleasure, all of which are finally indexed to participation in God as site of transcendental goodness and beatitude. Far from opposing reason and emotion, Hooker sees desire as a kind of cognitive state or intelligent appraisal of the world that remains vital for the participation of God. Like Augustine and Aquinas, then, the pressing epistemological question for Hooker does not revolve around how to extract a dispassionate secular rationality from irrational desire, but rather around how to extract desire's essential transcendental logic from an inherently corrupt experience. Accordingly, Hooker's two accounts of desire in Book One of the *Laws* respectively draw upon Aquinas and Augustine in order to pull the 'silver thread' that logically suspends desire, goodness and perfection from the architecture of participation of God, placing the emotions as essential for human intellectual growth.

Hooker first considers created human desires in the fifth chapter of Book One entitled 'the law wherby man is in his actions directed to the imitation of God'. Hooker immediately appeals to three Aristotelian-Thomistic principles to explore how desire moves and informs extensive and intensive forms of participation in God, rooting the law of reason within notions of movement, appetite and goodness. First, God is *purus actus* and in contrast all created forms are 'somewhat in possibilitie', that is capable of being moved from potency to act.[313] Second, there is therefore 'in all things an appetite or desire, whereby they [i.e. creatures] incline to something which they may be'. Aquinas similarly understands appetites to be passive inclinations towards what is perfective or completing, and natural inclinations in fact constitute natural law.[314] Third, as creatures move from potency to act through desire, Hooker thereby writes that 'they shall be perfecter then nowe they are', with perfections 'conteyned under the generall name of *Goodnesse*', ultimately identified with God. For Hooker, as for Aquinas, creation here displays a dynamic quality: desire affectively drives a creature towards 'the participation of God himselfe' as 'supreme cause' and exemplary pure act. Appetites direct human beings towards partial happiness in this life and beatific union with God in the next.[315] In the fifth and sixth chapters of Book One, then, Hooker essentially rehearses an Aristotelian-Thomistic anthropology in order to describe the perfective goods desired by human beings as they imitate God's perfection.[316] Hooker arranges humankind's natural appetites into an ascending hierarchy, gearing their desires towards proportionately perfective terminal goods: vegetative (with a desire for nutrition, growth and reproduction); sensitive (with a desire to experience the world); and rational (with a desire for theoretical and practical speculation). As people grow in knowledge and virtue, they participate in God's actuality conditioned to their

---

[312] Hooker, *Laws*, 2:421.22–32; V.76.8.
[313] Compare Aquinas, *ST*, I.3.1 resp. On Aquinas's appropriation of Aristotle's distinction between ἐν δυνάμει (potentiality) and ἐν ἐνέργεια (actuality), see James, *Passion and Action*, 48–64.
[314] Aquinas, *ST*, I.II.8.1; II.II.133.1.
[315] Compare ibid., I.II.1–5.
[316] Hooker, *Laws*, 1:73.10–23; 1:75.7–27; I.5.2; I.6.2–3. Compare Aquinas, *ScG*, III.26.8

rational form; the logic of desire drives this appetitive movement towards the *ratio* of perfection and so sets the emotions as a source for good.

Hooker gives a second account of desire in the eleventh chapter of Book One that combines elements from Aquinas and Augustine, linking appetitive desire to love and participation in God. For Hooker, the rational appetite in human beings moves cognitive participation in God through its orientation towards the 'sovereign *good* or *blessedness*'.[317] Desire springs from this rational appetite, moving the capacity to know and love the world and ultimately God as 'that wherin the highest degree of al our perfection consisteth'.[318] Hooker here navigates an Augustinian course between worldly and divine love. Augustine distinguishes between love as use (*uti*) and love as enjoyment (*frui*).[319] 'Use' is the correct love for creation as a means through which human beings can come into fellowship with God. 'Enjoyment' is the right love for God as 'an end in Himself' and site of terminal happiness. Hooker implicitly employs this Augustinian distinction when he describes the triple perfection sought by human beings, arranged into an ascending Aristotelian hierarchy of desire: the 'sensuall', the 'intellectual' (meaning the 'law of morall and civil perfection) and the 'spirituall and divine'.[320] The former two properly involve desires 'linked and as it were chained one to another' as people pursue 'convenient' sensible and intellectual goods 'with reference to a further end', namely 'some thing . . . desired for it selfe simplie and for no other'.[321] While use of worldly goods remains proper, for Hooker such love is not the ultimate goal and must be referred to some transcendental origin and end. The 'spiritual and divine' perfection orients an actor, therefore, to desire the infinite good of God such that, 'by force of participation and conjunction with him', he or she enjoys intellectual union with the beloved divine 'soveraigne truth' and 'sea of goodness'.[322] Although the intellectual appetite of the will 'doth now worke upon that object by desire, which is as it were a motion towards the end as yet unobtained', in beatitude desire yields to love and rests in 'the sweete affection' of 'those supernaturall passions of joye peace and delight'.[323] Desire produces a double dilation, then, allowing human beings to engage with the horizontal goodness of creation but ultimately referring humanity vertically to the love of God, who ought to be desired and loved for Himself.

The essential logic of desire, abstracted from an inherently corrupt experience, therefore remains vital for human flourishing and constitutes the essential motive force in both natural and supernatural cognitive participation in God. Rather than constituting an obstacle to the telos of humanity, the emotions are indispensable to its attainment. The logic of desire allows Hooker to remain critical of his puritan adversaries because their egoism has distorted the emotions and deluded the 'common multitude'. Pace Shuger and Joyce, then, Hooker does not see the emotions per se

---

[317] Hooker, *Laws*, 1:111.2; I.11.1. Compare Aquinas, *ST*, I.59.1; I.93.3, 6, and 7.
[318] Hooker, *Laws*, 1:110.24–111.6; 1:112.11–2; I.11.1–2.
[319] Augustine, *De doctrina christiana*, 1.22.20, in *Nicene and Post-Nicene Fathers*, first series, vol. 2, 527.
[320] Hooker, *Laws*, 1:114.18–25; I.11.4. Compare Aristotle, *Nichomachean Ethics*, 1.5, in *Complete Works*, vol. 2, 1731–2.
[321] Hooker, *Laws*, 1:111.6–25; I.11.1.
[322] Ibid., 1:112.11–113.12; I.11.2–3.
[323] Ibid., 1:113.13–24; I.11.3.

as fundamentally irrational; they are rational by participation insofar as they order human beings both to know and to love the transcendental *ratio* of the true and the good. Indeed, as the second constellating category of Hooker's cognitive ecology, desire extensively moves human beings to participate in, and enjoy intensive union with, God as the eminently desirable good. As such, the re-emergence of desire in Books Four and Five does not interrupt Hooker's rationalist epistemology. Instead, the logic of desire plays a key epistemic role in faith, creating an emotional regime geared towards adhering to God through shared liturgical practices that are affective as well as intellectual.

Before turning to the liturgical recreation of desire, we must first consider how the logic of desire relates to faith. Debora Shuger diagnoses that desire, as the second constellating category of Hooker's cognitive ecology, interrupts his 'incipient rationalism and historicism'.[324] Shuger perceptively notes that, while Hooker affirms in the *Laws* that 'we have necessary reason' for holding that the scriptures are sacred, he never says what that necessity might be; indeed, Shuger suggests that Augustine and Aquinas claim that only probable reasons can ever be evidenced. Accordingly, Shuger writes that 'if, therefore, assent should be proportioned to evidence, Christianity dwindles to a hypothesis'.[325] Shuger looks to Hooker's first extant sermon, *Of the Certaintie and Perpetuity of Faith in the Elect*, in order to explore how Hooker might address this dilemma, turning to the role of desire in his account of faith. In that sermon, it is desire (rather than reason) that orients and directs the believer to 'cleave to God' since 'faith grasps its object by love, not evidence'.[326] Yet, for Shuger such 'self-warranting desire' remains 'illogical' because the faith it produces believes 'against all reason' and 'one can feel very strongly and still be very wrong'.[327] A closer analysis of *Certaintie* suggests, however, an alternative to Shuger's reading: the logic of desire promises, as it orients the whole person to the *ratio* of divine goodness, to overcome the doubts of human reason in order to fulfil the capacity of believers to enjoy supernatural cognitive participation in God. As Russell puts it, 'the goodness of God experienced by Christians ... results in love and trust ... [namely] an inner participation in God wrought through the tasting of God's life'.[328] Desire here constitutes the key emotional phenomena that can allay existential doubt and inculcate intellectual assurance in which the knower conforms to the intrinsic *ratio* of God's nature and love.

In *Certaintie*, Hooker uses Hab. 1.4 to address the problem of doubt and anxiety even within the elect assured of salvation, a common pastoral issue within Reformed orthodoxy. As Shuger points out, Hooker unusually reframes the pastoral problem within the Aristotelian dilemma of knowability: for Aristotle, there are two kinds of knowability, either the experience of particulars or the inherent truth of universals; yet, the latter remains harder to know, even if it is most excellent.[329] In short, there is an inverse

---

[324] Shuger, *Habits of Thought*, 41.
[325] Ibid., 42.
[326] Debora Shuger, *Sacred Rhetoric: The Christian Grand Style in the English Renaissance* (Princeton, NJ: Princeton University Press, 1988), 197.
[327] Shuger, *Habits of Thought*, 43–4.
[328] Russell, *Beyond Certainty*, 171, 180.
[329] Compare Aristotle, *Posterior Analytics*, 1.2; 71b35-72a6, in *Complete Works*, vol. 1, 115–16.

relationship between the excellence of an object and its knowability, what Wesley Trimpi calls the 'ancient dilemma of knowledge and representation' common to all premodern epistemologies.[330] So it is that God, as most excellent and true, is also most unknowable to the human intellect. As Shuger phrases it, 'the ancient dilemma entails . . . that the subjective certainty of faith always exceeds the objective evidence'.[331] The gap between subjective certainty and objective evidence produces anxiety in believers. Yet, in *Certaintie*, Hooker argues that believers can navigate doubt and enjoy the assurance of faith if they cultivate desire for God, leading to an affective experience and knowledge of divine love.

Using a scholastic distinction derived from Aquinas, Hooker therefore develops two kinds of certainty, that of evidence and that of adherence, in order to explain doubt but also offer its remedy.[332] Hooker begins with the certainty of evidence:

> Certainty of evidence wee call that, when the mind doth assent unto this or that; not because it is true in it selfe, but because the truth therof is cleere, because it is manifest unto us. Of things in them selves most certain, except they be also most evident, our persuasion is not so assured as it is of things more evident although they in themselves be lesse certain.[333]

Nigel Voak argues that Hooker describes three descending 'subtypes' of evidential certainty in the *Laws*: 'plaine aspect and intuitive beholding' (i.e. empirical experience or speculative first principles); 'strong and invincible demonstration' (meaning demonstrative reasoning); and 'greatest possibility'.[334] Hooker also mentions the intrinsic certainty of things in themselves. While Voak places intrinsic certainty alongside evidential certainty, Hooker rather takes it to 'float above' (as Russell puts it) the actual experience of an object, making it 'not a category of knowing but rather a given'.[335] In the *Laws*, for example, while Scripture reveals what God sees, having an intrinsic and 'infallible certaintie' as 'the strongest proofe of all', that does not explain how people actually experience that the scriptures are sacred.[336] As Hooker considers in *Certaintie* how faith relates to evidential certainty, then, he preaches that faith often seems weak apart from in the angels, who immediately see God 'by the light of glorie'.[337] While God remains the most certain object in intrinsic terms, the divine nature nonetheless remains unavailable to the senses and beyond propositional demonstration for human beings. Faced with uncertain objective evidence, the faith of believers experiences a subjective motion of doubt. Pace Voak, this does not mean that faith remains doomed to assent always 'in an imperfect, and at times a weak and faltering manner', with only rational reflection able to bring believers to know 'with

---

[330] Wesley Trimpi, *Muses of One Mind: The Literary Analysis of Experience and Its Continuity* (Princeton, NJ: Princeton University Press, 1983), 87–129.
[331] Debora Shuger, 'Faith and Assurance', in *A Companion to Richard Hooker*, ed. W. J. T. Kirby (Leiden: Brill, 2008), 221–50 (250).
[332] See Aquinas, *ST*, II.II.4.8.
[333] Hooker, *Certaintie*, in *FLE*, 5:70.1–71.2.
[334] Hooker, *Laws*, 1:179.8–18; II.7.5. See Voak, *Reformed Theology*, 71–5.
[335] Russell, *Beyond Certainty*, 149.
[336] Hooker, *Laws*, 1:167.27–168.1; II.6.1.
[337] Hooker, *Certaintie*, in *FLE*, 5:70.14–16.

demonstrative certainty'.³³⁸ Rather, Hooker simply recognizes the pastoral consequence of the Aristotelian dilemma of representation, namely, the unavoidable gap between intrinsic certainty and the type of subjective assurance which objective evidence can render in relation to matters of faith.

Hooker then turns to the certainty of adherence that, in contrast to evidential certainty, represents goodness apprehended and desired, offering an affective logic in which faith subjectively reassures the believer. In the second kind of certainty, faith trumps any other science because it directs both the intellect to truth and the will to goodness, both of which are co-identical with the intrinsic certainty of God:

> The other which wee call the certaintie of adherence is when the hart doth cleave and stick unto that which it doth beleeve. This certaintie is greater in us then the other. The reason is this: the fayth of a Christian man doth apprehend the wordes of the law, the promises of god, not only as true but also as good, and therefore even then when the evidence which he hath of the trueth is so small that it greaveth him to feele his weaknes in assenting thereunto, yeat there is in him such a sure adherence unto that which he doth but faintly and fearfully beleeve that his spirit *having once truly tasted the heavenly sweetnes* thereof all the worlde is not able quite and cleane to remove him from it but he striveth with him selfe to hope even against hope to beleeve even against all reason of believing, being settled with Job upon this unmoveable resolution, *thought god shall kill me I will not geve over trusting in him*. For why? this lesson remayneth for ever imprinted in his hart, *it is good for me to cleave unto God*.³³⁹

Faith fixes the believer upon God by reason of desire's draw to cognized goodness under the habit of love even where the certitude of material evidence seems slim. For Hooker the visceral, loving experience of God's 'heavenly sweetnes' induces belief, then, rather than rational calculation. Voak changes 'heart' to 'will' and 'apprehend' to 'assent' in order to recast this passage simply as a confused and inchoate scholastic treatment of a rational phenomenon.³⁴⁰ Shuger and Russell more appropriately insist that, unlike Aquinas in this regard, Hooker lends an emotional and sensuous dimension to adherence beyond merely rational movement.³⁴¹ Indeed, for Hooker 'desire' writes in what Eric Jager calls the medieval tradition of the 'book of the heart.'³⁴² Here, the 'heart' connotes the 'supreme symbol of the self' rooted in scriptural images where the heart (Hebrew: *lev, levav*; Greek: *kardia*) refers moral beings to God as law and Christ as love, signifying the interior centre of a person as rational, emotional, volitional and embodied. In short, for Hooker the 'heart' means the whole person. Pace Shuger,

---

³³⁸ Voak, *Reformed Theology*, 245, 265.
³³⁹ Hooker, *Certaintie*, in *FLE*, 5:70.31–71.15, emphasis in the original.
³⁴⁰ Voak, *Reformed Theology*, 70, 197–9, 244.
³⁴¹ Shuger, *Habits of Thought*, 43; Russell, *Beyond Certainty*, 162–7.
³⁴² Jager, *Book of the Heart*, xv, 44. Hooker certainly at points identifies the 'heart' with the 'mind' (e.g., *Laws*, 1:34.20–3; Pref.7.1) but even here the organization of the human person according to what is central rather than what it highest suggests holistic rather than hierarchical categorization.

however, the desires of the heart are not illogical. The logic of desire, as it aims at goodness, allows believers to cleave to God not simply against reason per se but against particular reasons which threaten belief, such as the pastorally vexing experiences of Habbukuk, Job, and (it can be assumed) the hearers of the sermon.[343] Desire, springing from love received from God and returned, offers a visceral perception of (and motivation towards) God's experienced goodness and grace, even amidst the sense of desolation or evidential doubt, and even as a consequence of it. As such, the emotions offer a form of knowledge and understanding not available as a purely rational exercise. The affective certainty of adherence ought to be cultivated, then, in order to secure and build up the faith that promises union with God.

The central role Hooker affords to desire in faith finds its corollary in the *Laws* as he considers the theological habits that shape Christian life under love. Hooker's account of faith, hope and love recalls that of Aquinas. For Aquinas, the initial moment of justification sees all three theological virtues infused as habits such that they sanctify the intellectual faculties to be able to enjoy supernatural cognitive participation in God.[344] Whereas faith is primarily a habit of the intellect that illuminates the principles of theology, love and hope are habits of the will: the former causes the will also to seek friendship with God and desire the divine good; the latter causes the will to see participation in God as attainable. Like Aquinas,[345] then, Hooker unites the theological virtues of faith and love in order also to speak of 'thaffection of faith', noting 'hir love to Godward [is] above the comprehension which she hath of God'.[346] Faith here takes on the affective logic of desire alongside its intellectual habit of illumination. Again like Aquinas, Hooker argues that 'the whole traine of vertues, which are implied in the name of Grace, [are] infused att one instant', namely, in the initial moment of justification leading to sanctification, logically beginning with faith.[347] As with Aquinas, for Hooker the theological virtues (like all virtues) are habits that incline human beings towards perfection, in this case the supernatural cognitive 'participation of God himselfe'.[348] For Hooker, just as faith moves the intellect to assent to the 'promises of god' as true,

---

[343] See Russell, *Beyond Certainty*, 164–5.

[344] Aquinas, *ST*, I.II.62.4 resp. On sanctification and sacred doctrine, see Fáinche Ryan, *Formation in Holiness: Thomas Aquinas on "Sacra Doctrina"* (Leuven: Peeters, 2007).

[345] Aquinas, *ST*, II.II.4.3–4; II.II.5.2–3. Aquinas distinguishes between unformed and formed faith. Only the latter is faith shaped by love (*fides formata caitate*) and so moves the person to will as well as know the good and true. Aquinas contrasts this formed faith with unformed faith such as that held by the demons who know but do not love God. For a comparable example in Hooker, see *Justification*, 26, in *FLE*, 5:136.30–137.3 in which 'devills know the same thinges which wee beleeve' but do not apprehend the knowledge of faith as good.

[346] Hooker, *Laws*, 2:290.28–31; V.63.1. Hooker does not mention the theological virtue of hope in any of these passages about faith and cognition in the *Laws*, but earlier describes it as a 'trembling expectation' of that which will end 'with reall and actuall fruition of that which no tongue can expresse' (1:119.6-9; I.11.6).

[347] Ibid., 3:7.29–31; VI.3.1–2.

[348] Hooker, *Justification*, 21, in *FLE*, 5:129.2–21 clearly thinks of faith, hope, and love as habits since he links them to the formal cause of '*habituall*' sanctification, and in *Laws*, 1:118.31–119.15; I.11.6 sets them as the habitual grounds for salvation which drive believers from potency to act or perfect union with God 'by force of participation and conjunction with him.' Compare Aquinas, *ST*, I.II.62.1 where he speaks of the need for theological virtues in order that human beings can attain eternal happiness, 'a kind of participation of the Godhead about which is written (2 Pet. i.4) that by Christ we are made *partakers of the Divine nature*.'

the theological virtue of love forms faith to direct human desire 'Godward' as it moves the will to the perfect good through intellectual apprehension of that good.³⁴⁹ This represents Hooker's formulation of the Thomistic idea of faith formed by love (*fides formata caitate*). Indeed, the end of love is 'endlesse union with God', which is to say that believers are made partakers of God, a perfection which Hooker (like Aquinas) primarily casts in intellectual terms as the endless vision of God, with love following this activity as an affective perfection which depends upon it.³⁵⁰ Far from opposing reason and desire, or (as Russell does) seeing desire as taking over where reason ends,³⁵¹ Hooker sees the two constellating categories of his cognitive ecology as commonly and coextensively directing human beings to an intensive and supernatural cognitive participation in God. Reason directs humankind to the *ratio* of the true, and desire to the *ratio* of the good, both convertible with the divine nature. Desire is rational by participation in divine love, just as 'the light of reason' is rational insofar as the light of eternal law illumines it.

Hooker's *Laws* contains, of course, a pastoral parallel with *Certaintie*, namely the problem of doubt. The importance of cultivating desire for God re-emerges in Books Four and Five of the *Laws* because Hooker seeks to redress how the puritans' insistence on the singularity and omnicompetency of biblical law fills weak consciences 'with infinite perplexities, scrupulosities, doubts insoluble, and extreme despaires'.³⁵² In Books Four and Five, the way the puritans assert that the established forms of worship do not constitute a properly Reformed means of liturgical edification gives an example of how tender souls may be left vexed within the Elizabethan Religious Settlement. Hooker returns to desire in order to craft the sense in which the liturgical practices of the Elizabethan Book of Common Prayer are indeed fit and convenient to edify and produce holiness. Just as a vast array of participatory laws shape life together under eternal law, the established form of worship for Hooker creatively unites the earthly with the heavenly as an emotional community in order to manuduct 'holie desires' towards God through a regime of shared material, affective and intellectual practices shaped by participation in God's love. This final part expands how, then, Hooker envisages the liturgical recreation of the essential logic of desire, reclaiming the emotions as central to Christian life and participation in God.

Hooker responds in the *Laws* to the critics of established worship by offering a robust apology for 'the publique duties of Christian religion'.³⁵³ In Book Four, Hooker refuses to capitulate to the puritans' demand that ceremonies displaying Catholic liturgical sensibilities simply be abandoned wholesale: what edifies should remain in use. He then turns in Book Five to the varied practices of the Book of Common Prayer in order to show their edifying potential. The central concern therefore of Books Four and Five, easily concealed by the vast panoply of liturgical issues surveyed, turns on what constitutes the proper means of liturgical edification.³⁵⁴ Hooker aims to counter

---

[349] See Hooker, *Certaintie*, in *FLE*, 5:71.2–4. Compare Hooker, *Justification*, 26, in *FLE*, 5:137.3–7.
[350] Hooker, *Laws*, 1:119.3–11; I.11.6.
[351] Russell, *Beyond Certainty*, 180.
[352] Hooker, *Laws*, 1:189.25–190.19; II.8.5.
[353] Ibid., 2:15; V.title.
[354] See W. Bradford Littlejohn, 'The Edification of the Church: Richard Hooker's Theology of Worship and the Protestant Inward/Outward Disjunction', *Perichoresis* 12, no. 1 (2014): 3–18.

the biblical singularity and perfectionism of his puritan opponents who insist that the Word alone edifies the inner self and that Scripture ought to sanction directly all forms of outer worship. As an alternative vision, he turns to how a participatory tapestry of natural, social, rational and emotional threads rehabilitates the logic of desire in worship, linking our physical, emotional, intellectual, social and spiritual practices and selves with the knowledge and love of God. If Book One extracts an essential logic of desire extensively suspended from divine goodness, then Books Four and Five unpack how the 'elements, parts or principles' of worship manuduct or lead 'holie desires' by the hand in response to God's 'heavenly inspiration', creating an intensive, participative and affective journey of return towards (re)union with the Creator. As with his metaphysical architecture of participation, Hooker here holds together two Christian Platonisms, namely Augustinian immediacy and Dionysian mediation. Along with Reformed traditions, Hooker holds that the incarnate Christ immediately establishes the union between the soul and God by grace alone in forensic justification. As such, descending 'heavenly inspirations' emphasize the pedagogical character of God who immediately reforms the inner cognitive life and desires of the believer through the doctrinal gift of divine, saving knowledge, cleaved to as true and good within the believer through faith. Yet, sanctification unfurls by steps and degrees as an intrinsic reality in the life of the believer through a series of participatory mediations which yield ascending 'holie desires', the 'habituall and reall infusion' of grace.[355] As a psychic motor for natural and supernatural cognitive participation in God, communal, liturgical and sacramental activities draw out and reform intrinsic desires. Worship binds the hierarchies of angelic and ecclesiastical orders with the divine *ratio* convertible with the true, the good and the beautiful, the last of which transcendental qualities expresses the attraction of love towards God's perfect and perfecting being.[356] Hooker's account of edification holds together these Augustinian and Dionysian moments in a Chalcedonian paradigm: the inner life of the heart and the outer form of worship are united through a 'communication of attributes' but never simply conflated.[357]

At the beginning of Book Four, Hooker gives an account of edification that shapes all of his subsequent claims. There, he argues that the purpose of religious ceremonies is to edify the Church through inculcating appropriate intellectual and affective forms of cognition:

> Now men are edified, when either their understanding is taught somewhat whereof in such actions it behoveth all men to consider, or when their harts are moved with suitable affection therunto, when their minds are in any sorte stirred up unto that reverence, devotion, attention and due regard, which in those cases seemeth requisite. Because therfore unto this purpose not only speech but sundry sensible meanes besids have alwaies bene thought necessary, and especially those meanes

---

[355] Hooker, *Laws*, 2:243.4–9; V.56.11.
[356] See W. J. T. Kirby, 'Angels Descending and Ascending: Hooker's Discourse on the Double Motion of Common Prayer', in *Richard Hooker and the English Reformation*, ed. W. J. T. Kirby (Dordrecht: Kluwer Academic Publishers, 2003), 111–30.
[357] See Kirby, *Doctrine of the Royal Supremacy*, 51–8.

which being object to the eye, the liveliest and the most apprehensive sense of all other, have in respect seemed the fittest to make a deepe and strong impression.[358]

For Hooker, outward religious acts can stir the inner intellectual and emotional life of the mind and heart through a series of ritualized correspondences that inculcate sanctifying habits. Hooker casts this capacity in thoroughly Dionysian terms whereby symbol and ritual bring the believer towards deified union with God. For Pseudo-Dionysius 'in the realm of intellect . . . it is love of God which first moves us towards the divine' and 'divinization'.[359] Hooker therefore recapitulates a Dionysian theology of sign and edification in Book Five: the 'sensible excellence' of ceremonies creates 'celestial impressions in the mindes of men' and conforms 'our wills and desires' to God's excellence through shared practices which build up faith and love.[360] 'That which inwardlie each man should be,' Hooker writes, 'the Church outwardlie ought to testify.' Similarly, in the passage at hand from Book Four, ceremonies respond to the Aristotelian dilemma of representation addressed in *Certaintie*: 'sensible meanes' in worship vividly represent the otherwise ineffable greatest object in order to move the affections to a form of knowing and loving that same object, namely God. Hooker therefore quotes Pseudo-Dionysius in order to explain how the material practices of worship mediate the supernatural cognitive participation of God: 'the sensible things which Religion hath hallowed, are resemblances framed according to things spiritually understood, whereunto they serve as a hand to lead and a way to direct.'[361] As Shuger points out, Hooker here also stands in the Renaissance grand style, where the imagination arouses the emotions in order to allow the self to respond to God's love, in this case through worship.[362] Peter Lake puts Hooker's account in stronger terms: 'this was little short of the reclamation of the whole realm of symbolic action and ritual practice from the status of popish superstition to that of a necessary, indeed essential, means of communication and edification.'[363] In worship, then, reason and emotions alike are reformed and moved such that the believer may share in the 'eternall affection of love' found in the Trinity.[364] As such, Hooker sees both as essential for human cognitive flourishing *coram Deo*, and as logically united under the aspect of participating in God. Indeed, as worship rehabilitates the logic of desire through an emotional regime of shared intellectual and affective practices, it forms a remedial gift that, like grace, helps our 'imbecillitie and weakness' by referring the 'affection of harte' to God.[365]

---

[358] Hooker, *Laws*, 1:273.30–274.8; IV.1.3.
[359] Pseudo-Dionysius, *The Ecclesiastical Hierarchy*, 2.1, in *Pseudo-Dionysius: Complete Works*, 200–1.
[360] Hooker, *Laws*, 2:33.23–34.20; 2:205.16–17; V.6.1–2; V.49.4.
[361] Ibid., 1:275.21–4; IV.1.3. Compare Pseudo-Dionysius, *The Ecclesiastical Hierarchy*, 2.3.2, in *Pseudo-Dionysius: Complete Works*, 204–5.
[362] Shuger, *Sacred Rhetoric*, 199.
[363] Lake, *Anglicans & Puritans?*, 165. See also James Turrell, 'Uniformity and Common Prayer', in *A Companion to Richard Hooker*, ed. W. J. T. Kirby (Leiden: Brill, 2008), 337–67, esp. 352–60.
[364] Hooker, *Laws*, 2:236.7; V.56.3.
[365] Ibid., 2:113.19–26; V.25.1. On the rational formation of emotions in the Book of Common Prayer, see David Bagchi, '"The Scripture moveth us in sundry places": Framing Biblical Emotions in the Book of Common Prayer', in *The Renaissance of Emotion: Understanding Affect in Shakespeare and*

As the site of Dionysian mediation, the Church becomes a creative repository of spiritual illumination and a training school for the virtuous habits of 'holie desires' recreated by divine influence. Hooker casts the Church as a both a 'visible mysticall bodie' and as a 'societie supernaturall'.[366] Shuger labels the latter as an 'imagined community'[367] populated by 'God, Angels, and holie men',[368] suspending the horizontal, visible Church from a vertical, heavenly communion. Outward worship binds natural and supernatural communities together and refers them to God through what Anna Wierzbicka calls an 'emotional script', meaning the verbal and non-verbal expressions that shape how and what to feel as well as know about the self, others and (in Hooker's case) God.[369] In earlier parts of the *Laws*, Hooker notes a Dionysian resemblance between celestial orders, angelic desires and the heavenly vision of God with the solemn outward worship of the Church. In Book One the angelic vision of God has a markedly affective character, which sets the tone of earthly worship and renders participation in God as a supernaturally social phenomenon. Through imitation of God's goodness, the angels form a generous 'societie or fellowship with men', acting as a 'paterne and a spurre' to human desires bonded with theirs as a community of cognitive participants in God.[370] In Book Five, public liturgy therefore extends angelic ministration and reflects heavenly devotion characterized by the common desire to share in God's truth and goodness. Accordingly, Hooker images doctrine and prayer as an exchange between humanity and God mediated, at least in similitude, by angels:

> Betwene the throne of God in heaven and his Church upon earth here militant if it be so that Angels have theire continuall intercourse, where should we finde the same more verified then in these two ghostlie exercises, the one 'Doctrine', and other 'Prayer'? For what is thassemblie of the Church to learne, but the receiving of Angels descended from above? What to pray, but the sendinge of Angels upward? His heavenly inspirations and our holie desires are as so many Angels of entercorse and comerce betwene God and us. As teaching bringeth us to know that God is our supreme truth; so prayer testifieth that we acknowledge him our soveraigne good.[371]

The double angelic motion of doctrine and prayer orients the believer to God as the transcendental source of 'supreme truth' and 'soveraigne good', and so abducts the believer to God as the transcendent end of both rational intellect and affective

---

His Contemporaries, ed. Richard Meek and Erin Sullivan (Manchester: Manchester University Press, 2015), 45–64.

[366] Ibid., 1:130.31–2; 2:111.26; I.15.2; V.24.1.
[367] Debora Shuger, 'Society Supernatural: The Imagined Community of Hooker's *Laws*', in *Religion and Culture in Renaissance England*, ed. Claire McEachern and Debora Shuger (Cambridge: Cambridge University Press, 1997), 116–41.
[368] Hooker, *Laws*, 1:131.6–10; I.15.2.
[369] Anna Wierzbicka *Emotions across Languages and Cultures: Diversity and Universals* (Cambridge: Cambridge University Press, 1999), 240–1.
[370] Hooker, *Laws*, 1:71.6–7; 1:137.18–138.2; I.4.2; I.16.4.
[371] Ibid., 2:110.7–16; V.23.1.

desire. Reason and emotion accordingly form part of the same script ordering all understanding to cognitive participation in God.

Hooker turns to the seductive quality of beauty in order to link the true with the good in the theurgic re-creation of the logic of desire, reclaiming the emotions as central to knowing and loving God. Here, the inventive capacity of the liturgy as a form of work uniting heaven and earth places the Church as an emotional community which co-creatively shapes desire alongside God. The public duties of religion are best ordered when 'the militant Church doth resemble by sensible meanes . . . that hidden dignitie and glorie wherewith the church triumphant in heaven is bewtified'.[372] Churches should visibly evoke a sense of God's attractive beauty, a 'sensible help to stirre up devotion' and reflect 'cherefull affection' for God.[373] They form a space which allows for 'mutuall conference and as it were commerce to be had betwene God and us'.[374] Worship becomes a sensorium in which the human body and mind becomes oriented to God through the double angelic motion of doctrine and prayer. Sermons become 'keyes to the kingdom of heaven, as winges to the soule, as spurres to the good affections of man, unto the sound and healthie as food, as phisicke unto diseased minds'.[375] In turn, prayers represent 'most gracious and sweet odors; those rich presentes and guiftes which being carryed up into heaven doe best testifie our dutifull affection'.[376] Prayer for earthly things engages with 'hartie affection and zeale' the natural love for immediately desirable objects, an affective motion 'more easily raysed higher' to supernatural love for God as most desirable.[377] In public prayer, 'the alacrity and fervour of others' serves as a spur to zeal in everyone else.[378] Likewise, the fervour of the minister remains vital to inspire the faithful or how otherwise could they experience anything but 'frosen couldnes, when his affections seeme benummed from whom theires should take fire?'[379] Visible signs deliver a 'strong impression' of eternal truths, while music expresses 'the turns and varieties of all passions' and can move and moderate the affections and delight the mind.[380] Mimetic manual acts such as making the sign of the cross or kneeling shape appropriate physical passions and engender, as silent teachers, right affections.[381] Festivals produce a joyful concurrence of earthly cycles with celestial motions, inspiring hearty praise, charitable bounty and physical rest in light of God's goodness.[382] Although worship is not meritorious in a salvific sense, outwards acts of public rituals have a real relationship with the inward sanctification of the heart and so are of significant benefit to believers. Sensible

---

[372] Ibid., 2:34.3–6; V.6.2.
[373] Ibid., 2:58.13–20; 2:61.7–8; V.15.3; V.16.2.
[374] Ibid., 2:65.7–8; V.18.1.
[375] Ibid., 2:87.20–4; V.22.1.
[376] Ibid., 2:110.27–31; V.23.1.
[377] Ibid., 2:144.34–145.16; V.35.2.
[378] Ibid., 2:112.19–21; V.24.2.
[379] Ibid., 2:115.20–4; V.25.3.
[380] Ibid., 2:151.14–152.13; V.38.1. On early modern attitudes towards the affective influence of music, see Jonathan Willis, 'Protestant Worship and the Discourse of Music in Reformation England', in *Worship and the Parish Church in Early Modern Britain*, ed. Natalie Mears and Alec Ryrie (Farnham: Ashgate, 2013), 131–50.
[381] Hooker, *Laws*, 2:305.13–308.3; 2:346.23–8; V.65.6; V.68.3.
[382] Ibid., 2:363.2–364.14; V.70.1–3.

ceremonies 'testify' to the truth, 'signify' spiritual realities, 'betoken' the exemplary goodness of God, 'set forward godliness', and abduct the believer 'Godward'. In all of these cases, the emotions further rather than hinder the edification of the believer: an imaginative correspondence between the outer habits of worship and the inner habit of faith binds together higher and lower faculties in worship as the 'bewtie of holines' seduces them.[383]

The relation that inheres between desire and beauty in the attraction of love also places Hooker's thought, then, within Renaissance philosophical retrievals of Platonic theories. There, love as a desire for the beautiful moves the mind to a state of self-transcendence in which the knower also becomes the lover of wisdom and love leads to a union of the mind with the beloved object.[384] For Hooker, being a lover entails a form of cognitive participation in God, entailing an erotic union with Christ as beloved source and end through the motion of desire under the attraction of beauty. The double motion of doctrine and prayer forms 'the act correlative to God's disclosure of the truth' in Christ's Incarnation.[385] As such, the Dionysian mediation of desire through sensible means both prepares for and assumes the Augustinian immediacy of Christ received in the sacraments. The logic of desire, rehabilitated through the 'elements partes or principles' of outward worship, prepares the believer to experience as well as know 'the union of the soul with God' directly through Christ. Participation in Christ is erotic and reciprocal, a 'mysticall copulation' between the believer and Christ. Eucharistic reception sees sensible means dissolve into the immediacy of erotic union. Desire yields to joy in a consummated motion of love or charity: through the Eucharistic species, believers imaginatively share in the physical passion of Christ through touch, taste and sight, affectively resting not in pain but in the enflamed joy of union, cleaving to 'that incomprehensible bewtie which shineth in the countenance of Christ'.[386] Yet, the logic of desire depends upon Christ not only to elicit the movement towards loving union with the 'bewtie of holiness' but also to undergird its own integrity: public worship 'deals with the whole of that humanity assumed by Christ', as Rowan Williams phrases it, which naturally includes the passions, affections, will, imagination and reason.[387] Public worship recreates the logic of desire, then, because it takes it (alongside reason) already to be a divine gift, part and parcel of that which Christ and grace assumes in order to transform human nature and erotically unite it with God as beloved.

As the two constellating categories in Hooker's cognitive ecology, then, reason and desire cut through both hypo- and hyper-rationalist readings as well as the supposed dichotomy between rationality and the emotions. Hooker's account of natural and supernatural cognitive participation in God challenges what Charles Taylor calls 'two

---

[383] Ibid., 2:61.13; V.16.2.
[384] See Sabrina Ebbersmeyer, 'The Philosopher as a Lover: Renaissance Debates on Platonic *Eros*', in *Emotion & Cognitive Life in Medieval & Early Modern Philosophy*, ed. Martin Pickavé and Lisa Shapiro (Oxford: Oxford University Press, 2012), 133–55.
[385] Francis Paget, *Introduction to the Fifth Book of Hooker's Ecclesiastical Polity* (Oxford: Oxford University Press, 1899), 138.
[386] Hooker, *Laws*, 1:119.1–3; I.11.6. Russell, *Beyond Certainty*, 178 draws a link between Hooker's accounts of certainty and the Eucharist.
[387] Williams, *Anglican Identities*, 31.

connected illusions' in the modern 'myth' of 'disengaged' scientific reason.[388] First, for Hooker there is no created reserve of autonomy, even in the operations of reason. All of creation remains suspended from the eternal law in which it theonomously participates. Even in its own integrity, reason exists as a kind of divine revelation that God's remedial revelation in the Word does not disturb but rather restores and elevates. Second, for Hooker reason cannot be disengaged from culturally embedded practices and affective forms of making meaning. Rather, it has rational continuity with them in the pursuit of truth, goodness and beauty, found in exemplary fashion in God. As James Turrell puts it, while the words of worship act as '"rational instruments," they also worked on the emotions and brought the individual in contact with the transcendent'.[389] In both constellating categories, cognitive participation in God does not evacuate the natural actions of reason and desire of any substance; it is not simply heteronomous. Rather, it abducts human nature to become co-creative analogues of God's own creativity, makers of meaning in rational discourse and theurgy. This final part considers how once again Christ forms the key who unlocks this participatory relationship between nature and grace (or mediation and immediacy) in cognition.

'Her waies are of sundry kinds': Christ as the key to participated wisdom

The previous chapter showed how Christ as 'woord or Wisdom' unlocks the textures of nature and grace in Hooker's ontology. The idea of participation in Christ as 'woord or Wisdom' continues in Books Two through Five of the *Laws* as the 'general' architectural principle which informs the shape of Hooker's polemical response over more 'particular' epistemological points of controversy. Christ immediately unites and unlocks reason and desire as participatory mediations of cognitive participation in God, whether natural or supernatural. As he begins his polemical defence in Book Two of the *Laws*, Hooker crucially returns to the scriptural figure of divine Wisdom in order to address the origin and manner of human knowing. Hooker uses Thomas Cartwright's 'pretended proofe' from Prov. 2.9 for biblical omnicompetency to show, on the contrary, the 'sundry' divine influences on human understanding. Hooker therefore corrects the 'basic epistemological error'[390] of the puritans, emphasizing instead how participation in God animates and unites natural and supernatural ways of knowing:

> To teach men therfore wisedome professeth, and to teach them every good way: but not every good way by one way of teaching. Whatsoever either men

---

[388] Charles Taylor, 'Reason, Faith, and Meaning', in *Faith, Rationality, and the Passions*, ed. Sarah Coakley (Chichester: Wiley-Blackwell, 2012), 13–28.

[389] Turrell, 'Uniformity and Common Prayer', 363. See Bagchi, '"The Scripture moveth us in sundry places"', 58–9.

[390] Peter Lake, 'The "Anglican Moment"? Richard Hooker and the Ideological Watershed of the 1590s', in *Anglicanism and the Western Christian Tradition*, ed. Stephen Platten (Norwich: Canterbury Press, 2003), 90–121 (99).

on earth, or the Angels of heaven do know, it is as a drop of that unemptiable fountaine of wisdom, which wisdom hath diversly imparted her treasures unto the world. As her waies are of sundry kinds, so her maner of teaching is not meerely one and the same. Some things she openeth by the sacred books of Scripture; some things by the glorious works of nature: with some things she inspireth them from above by spirituall influence, in some thinges she leadeth and trayneth them onely by worldly experience and practise. We may not so in any one special kind admire her that we disgrace her in any other, but let all her ways be according unto their place and degree adored.[391]

As a direct consequence of Hooker's participatory ontology, the transformative patterns of divine influence set both natural capacities (the 'glorious works of nature') and revealed theology ('the sacred books of Scripture') as discrete but consonant epistemic participations commonly united in the *ratio* of eternal Wisdom. Indeed, alongside 'the sacred books of Scripture', human nature inherently discloses the 'sundry' causal influences of divine Wisdom. Together, Scripture and reason lead human beings to the extensive and intensive 'participation of God himselfe'. For Hooker, then, Christ (as 'woord or Wisdom') acts as the principium who informs reason, Scripture and desire alike as first and final cause.

Hooker identifies Christ with the form and end of reason. In Book Three, Hooker returns to the Neoplatonic and biblical image of the 'fountain' in order to cast the manifold variety of human wisdom evident in Moses, Daniel, Solomon and Paul as participatory mediations of God's 'principall truth'. This *Logos*, 'being that light which none can approach unto, hath sent out these lights whereof we are are capable, even as so many sparkls resembling the bright fountain from which they rise.'[392] Since the law of reason and divine law are suspended from eternal law, God extensively authors both the light and word of scripture and that of reason. This authorship renders both as complementary participants in the eternal light of Christ, namely the Word from John's Prologue: 'He is the author of all that we thinke or doe by vertue of that light, which him selfe hath given.'[393] In supernatural cognitive participation, faith as an intellectual habit has as its final object the 'eternal veritie which hath discovered the treasures of hidden wisedome in Christ'.[394] As Edmund Newey puts it, 'human reason shares in the divine wisdom or logos, through the mediation of Christ . . . [who] is both the form of reason, and the only means of its true realisation in us through the Spirit.'[395]

Egil Grislis further points out that Hooker gives a Christocentric shape to Scripture and scriptural exegesis.[396] While the Old and New Testaments both make believers 'wise unto salvation', they do so in a different regard: 'the difference betwene them

---

[391] Hooker, *Laws*, 1:147.23–148.6; II.1.4. Miller, *Vision of God*, 85, and Sedgwick, *Origins*, 269–70 see the influence of Augustine's *De Doctrina Christiana* on this passage.
[392] Hooker, *Laws*, 1:226.11–14 ; 1:127.21–7; III.8.9–10. See John Booty, *Reflections on the Theology of Richard Hooker* (Sewanee: University of the South Press, 1998), 5–24.
[393] Hooker, *Laws*, 1:238.30–1; III. 9.3. Hooker footnotes John 1.5 immediately before this quotation.
[394] Hooker, *Laws*, 1:118.31–2; I.11.6.
[395] Newey, 'Form of Reason', 1, 4.
[396] Egil Grislis, 'The Hermeneutical Problem in Hooker', in *Studies in Richard Hooker*, ed. W. Speed Hill (Cleveland and London: Case Western Reserve University Press, 1972), 159–206 (191–2).

consisting in this, that the old did make wise by teaching salvation through Christ that should come, the newe by teaching that Christ our Saviour is come.'³⁹⁷ Hooker therefore distinguishes between central and peripheral ideas in Scripture, rather than give all texts an equal weighting, but still see them as united in their relation to Christ as the saving 'woord or Wisdom'. He can also give an instrumental role to natural and supernaturally endowed reason in reading the scriptures since, as already shown, Christ exists as a constituting influence within the form of reason itself. The word of reason and the word of Scripture examine and conform to one another through the eternal Word who yokes them together as mirrors of divine love. Indeed, Scripture abducts all kinds of wisdom into its Christocentric message: 'everie booke of holie scripture doth take out of all kinds of truth, naturall, historicall, forreine, supernaturall, so much as the matter handled requireth.'³⁹⁸ For Hooker, therefore, the puritans 'restraine the manifold ways which wisdom hath to teach men by, unto one only way of teaching, which is by scripture'.³⁹⁹ Hooker has an alternative, generous vision: 'the boundes of wisedome are large' and the 'school of nature' mediates divine wisdom within created forms just as Scripture publishes the way of salvation; but both are immediately united in Christ as the font of wisdom.

Finally, Christ exemplifies human affectivity in relation to divine love, as well as being the transcendental draw for reason and desire to participate cognitively in God. In Book Five, Hooker considers Christ's prayer in the garden of Gethsamene before his passion and distinguishes between two voluntary desires, 'the one avoyding, and the other accepting death'.⁴⁰⁰ The former desire was a natural (and so not sinful) 'effect' of the wish to avoid death, even when God has ordained it: 'the presence of dolorous and dreadfull objects even in mindes most perfect, may as cloudes overcast all sensible joy'. The latter desire was an 'affection' drawn to God's will: 'mercie worketh in Christ all willingness of minde' to share in and act upon God's goodness in order 'to procure the salvation of the world'. As Barry Rasmussen insightfully writes, as Hooker considers human prayer and desire in relation to Christ's prayer and suffering, 'the determining factor is not a simple alignment of the human will with the divine but is an examination of the context of human desire and will set by the gracious action of God in Christ.'⁴⁰¹ As such, Christ models the reformed logic of desire: God's love gives birth to an affection that orients human identity to cleave to God's goodness, even amidst 'present conflicts'. More broadly, then, while the theurgic manuduction of desire in worship takes the form of mediatory sensible acts, Christ immediately sits behind such mediation in order to transform believers, leading and training them as the 'woord or Wisdom of God' through intermediate 'worldly experience and practise'. Indeed, the logic of desire shaped within worship draws liturgical communities to the participation of Christ in

---

³⁹⁷ Hooker, *Laws*, 1:128.3–21; I.14.4.
³⁹⁸ Ibid., 1:127.24–7; I.14.3.
³⁹⁹ Ibid., 1:147.3–11; II.1.4.
⁴⁰⁰ Ibid., 2:197.9–199.23; V.48.10–11. Compare Aquinas, *ST*, III.18.2–5 who distinguishes three types of willing in Christ: the will of sensuality, the will-as-nature, and the will-as-reason. For Aquinas, in Gethsamene Christ's will of sensuality 'naturally shrinks from sensible pains' and the will-as-nature 'turns from what is against nature' such as death. The will-as-reason, however, 'may choose to will these things' for particular ends, in this case for what God has willed.
⁴⁰¹ Rasmussen, 'The Priority of God's Gracious Action', 9.

the sacraments, inviting them to share in the life of the Trinity. 'The bewtie of holines' seduces desire so that believers may share in the Father as 'goodness', in the Son as 'wisdom' ordering all things, and in the power of the Spirit as an end.[402]

In conclusion, Hooker's participatory metaphysics and epistemology display a certain systematic homology in which Christ unites and unlocks the relationship between natural capacities and divine influence. The systematic quality of Hooker's epistemology stems from the assumption, equally present in patristic and medieval thought, that all which exists only exists insofar as it participates in divine wisdom (and so in God).[403] While in modern thought the ideal subject is an isolated unit who interacts with the world through an autonomous and dispassionate rationality, Hooker's premodern subject is ecstatic, that is to say is someone whom divine love forms from the outside and draws back to itself through Christ, whether in the enlightening of reason or in the abduction of desire.[404] Unlike the later Enlightenment, Hooker's sanguine appraisal of reason and the emotions celebrates not human autonomy but rather the beauty of divine wisdom ordering creation as a diminished image of God. Indeed, the end of both reason and desire is (re)union with beloved wisdom, namely God. Here, the architecture of participation undercuts notions of autonomy and heteronomy, both of which assume radical contrast between God and creation. Instead, creation is theonomously and noncontrastively suspended from God. Accordingly, 'reason' has a multivalent texture: it is an intellectual power natural to the human form, but also comes as a divine gift that participates in God's rational nature as a diminished similitude. Sin corrupts the ability, but not the aptness, of this intellectual gift. Grace supplies the want and need of natural reason as a further, remedial, complementary gift. Similarly, the 'emotions' (or rather Hooker's premodern analogues of passions and affections) are also multivalent: they are part of the formal giftedness of human nature and are essential for human flourishing; but, the disorder wrought by sin requires remedial grace, which (through the habitual, embodied practices of worship) reorders and trains the emotions towards participation of God's nature. The logic of desire circumscribes both the intellect and the emotions, placing them together on a rational continuum of holy desires oriented to participate in, and enjoy union with, God. Hooker holds reason and the emotions together within what Béata Tóth calls a 'traditional logic of Christian affectivity' where 'affectivity and reason, love and *logos* coincide and, without losing their distinctive identities, interact in multiple mediations'.[405] Divine rationality drenches, then, both the material and immaterial aspects and powers of created forms such that desire variously draws them in non-cognitive and cognitive ways alike towards goodness. Far from the model of an incorporeal autonomy or evacuated heteronomy, cognitive participation becomes theonomous, suspended from God, warm, hearty, affective and embodied within the legal, participatory order of desire.

---

[402] Hooker, *Laws*, 2:237.10–3; V.56.5.
[403] See Williams, *The Divine Sense*, 3–4.
[404] See Julia Kristerva, *Tales of Love* (New York: Colombia University Press, 1987), 137–88.
[405] Béata Tóth, *The Heart Has Its Reasons: Towards a Theological Anthropology of the Heart* (Eugene: Cascade, 2016), xi.

4

'Politique societie': The politics of participation

Introduction

In the last three so-called 'books of power' in the *Laws*, Hooker finally defends episcopal orders and lay ecclesiastical supremacy against their radical puritan detractors, a closing movement from the 'general meditations' of earlier books to the disputed 'particular decisions' of the Tudor polity. Here, Hooker generates a celestial fusion of politics with metaphysics and epistemology: just as the 'statelinesse of houses' and the 'goodliness of trees' depend upon a hidden 'foundation' or 'root', his defence of the established Church and Commonwealth springs from the architecture of participation.[1] Indeed, the architecture of participation developed in his metaphysics and epistemology yields the substructure upon which Hooker constructs his political ecclesiology. While W. J. T. Kirby and Charles Miller designate Hooker's tendency to ground authority in theological foundations as a form of 'political theology',[2] the proper label might rather be 'politicized metaphysics' since the architecture of participation centrally engenders, limits and exceeds political discourse, making it provisional in relation to the divine source of power.[3] Four features from Hooker's architecture of participation generate a kind of 'grammar of participation' that proves crucially important in this endeavour, uniting Aristotelian-Thomistic ideas with tenets of Reformed orthodoxy that distinguished between the invisible and visible regiments, or the inner and external fora.[4] This 'grammar of participation' textually leads the reader 'by the hand' to see the Elizabethan Religious Settlement as a provisional but authentic way to participate in God. First, as Kirby argues, Hooker uses the twin Platonisms of Augustinian immediacy and Dionysian mediation from his participatory metaphysics in order to distinguish

---

[1] Hooker, *Laws*, 1:57.6–16; I.1.2.
[2] Kirby, *Doctrine of the Royal Supremacy*, 1–4. See also Miller, *Vision of God*, 251–3.
[3] Compare Stephen Collins, *From Divine Cosmos to Sovereign State: An Intellectual History of Consciousness and the Idea of Order in Renaissance England* (Oxford: Oxford University Press, 1989) who similarly writes that 'though polemical in structure, Hooker's *Lawes* extended beyond the boundaries of political order and described the historical and psychological premises upon which cultural meaning resides' (103).
[4] I take the phrase 'grammar of participation' from Candler, *Theology, Rhetoric, Manuduction*, 21–51, where the idea of participation in God as a form of deification 'is embodied in a grammar, in the way that texts are organized as structures for the manuduction . . . of readers along an itinerary of exit and return from creation to eschatological beatitude' (4).

between (but also causally connect) divine and temporal authority. Ultimate power remains the immediate hypostatic preserve of invisible divinity, but the twin hierarchs of bishops (as 'angels among men' and 'Image of God') and the monarch (as 'God's lievtenant' and 'highest uncommanded Commander') dispositively mediate power as diminished, public, participatory analogues of God's *ratio*.[5] Second, as Kirby notes elsewhere, Hooker uses the Chalcedonian logic of Christ's hypostatic union in order to distinguish between but also connect the unseen 'mystical' and 'visible Church', as well as the Church and Commonwealth as a 'politique societie'.[6] Third, adding to Kirby's insights, the architecture of participation also contains a scholastic account of causality typical of Reformed orthodoxy in which every separation nevertheless remains a link. Here, secondary causes (whether human acts in general, the 'light of reason' or political acts) receive divine approval insofar as God as the First Cause undergirds them. Thus, episcopal orders and lay ecclesiastical supremacy contingently emerge from the way that Scripture under-determines political matters. Nevertheless, as they emerge from the space left open for human reason (the 'divine power of the soule' undergirded by God), their demonstrable rationality reflects a participation in God's providential order. Fourth, from Hooker's logic of desire, the twin hierarchs of bishop and monarch guide right political desires since 'true religion is the roote of all true virtues and the stay of all well ordered common-wealthes'.[7] This chapter accordingly explores how these four grammatical aspects of Hooker's architecture of participation structure and govern what he has to say about ecclesial and political order.

Yet, Hooker's books of power face numerous challenges over their coherency. Some scholars accuse Hooker of abandoning an earlier rational outlook in favour of an irrational voluntarism in the later books of power where lay ecclesiastical supremacy receives authority *de jure divino*. Indeed, writers like Peter Munz and H. F. Kearney see Hooker as incoherently abandoning his earlier Thomistic, rational conception of law in favour of a Marsilian, voluntaristic and positivistic justification of the civil magistrate's authority.[8] The argument takes the following heuristic shape. First, Hooker erects a Thomistic edifice in Book One whereby all laws dispositively participate in eternal law. Laws inherently govern creation and share in the providential *ratio* of God's own self-diffusive being. Participation in eternal law includes the positive human laws that establish the Tudor lay ecclesiastical supremacy through Parliament and Convocation. The Dionysian *lex divinitatis* remains a corollary of these Thomistic first principles, however, and this law of divine power typically subordinates temporal powers to the spiritual, much like grace supervenes over nature. Therefore, when Hooker explicitly turns in the final books towards an *apologia* for the Erastian Tudor constitution, his Thomistic foundations crumble and a ramshackle Marsilian edifice emerges from

---

[5] Kirby, '"Law Makes the King"', 274–88. See also W. J. T. Kirby, 'From "General Mediations" to "Particular Decisions": The Augustinian Coherence of Richard Hooker's Political Theology', in *Sovereignty and Law in the Middle Ages and Renaissance*, ed. R. Sturges (Turnhout: Brepols, 2011), 41–63.
[6] Kirby, *Doctrine of the Royal Supremacy*, 51–2, 74–9. See also Kirby, *Reformer and Platonist*, 79–96.
[7] Hooker, *Laws*, 2:16.1–2; V.1.1.
[8] See Munz, *The Place of Hooker*, 49–57; and Kearney, 'Richard Hooker: A Reconstruction', 300–11. For a helpful analysis, see W. Bradford Littlejohn, *The Peril and Promise of Christian Liberty. Richard Hooker, the Puritans, and Protestant Political Authority* (Grand Rapids, MI: Eerdmans, 2017), 179–90.

the rubble. Indeed, for Munz, Hooker has to buttress the historical contingencies of the Tudor Reformation that his speculative Thomist foundations cannot bear with 'diametrically opposed' ideas from Marsilius of Padua.[9] In the books of power, the will of the Crown becomes law and the monarch properly controls the governance of the national church by 'divine right' in lay ecclesiastical supremacy. Thomistic rationalism gives way to what Munz labels 'Tudor Averroism', a political modality in which politics functions as an autonomous secular realm.[10]

Other scholars like Rory Fox argue that 'Hooker's ecclesiastical polity is muddled, incomplete, and quite simply incoherent'.[11] This claim of incoherency in relation to episcopacy takes the following heuristic shape. In Book Three, Hooker argues against any prescriptive and unalterable order of church governance that is derivable from Scripture and therefore possessing divine warrant. Thus, while 'the necessitie of politie and regiment in all Churches may be helde ... sundrie [forms] may equally be consonant unto the general axioms of the Scripture'.[12] In Book Seven, however, he claims that bishops are apostolic and thus divinely ordained, a strong (if not irreconcilable) contrast with the earlier position.[13] Indeed, the office of bishops is 'truely derived from God, and approved of him', and the bishop, like the king, acts as a hierarchic analogue of divinity, 'the Image of God and of Christ.'[14] Even a sanguine defender of Hooker like W. Speed Hill admits that, faced with the historical emergence of *jure divino* accounts of the episcopacy in the thought of Richard Bancroft, Thomas Bilson and Hadrian Saravia, Hooker simply gives ground and struggles to make it cohere with his earlier moderate position.[15] Furthermore, Hooker's allegedly *jure divino* defence of episcopacy poses an insurmountable and unacceptable constraint upon the authority of the civil magistrate in royal supremacy: if episcopal orders are indeed permanently binding and divine, the monarch would not have untrammelled powers over church governance after all. Similarly, if Hooker calls upon puritan dissenters to obey the superior authority of the English bishops as those who protect peace and unity, then

---

[9] Munz, *The Place of Hooker*, 101.
[10] Compare W. D. J. Cargill Thompson, '"The Philosopher of the "Politic Society"', 139–40 who argues that, while Hooker at 'no point comes close to suggesting that the State is a purely secular institution', he cannot 'be acquitted of the charge of subordinating his political ideas to the immediate needs of the controversy'. Also compare Robert Eccleshall, 'Richard Hooker and the Peculiarities of the English', *History of Political Thought* 2, no. 1 (1981): 63–117 who writes that scholarship often claims that Hooker only provides 'window dressing for the command structure of Elizabethan society' (63).
[11] Fox, 'Richard Hooker and the Incoherence of the *Ecclesiastical Polity*', 57. There has been exegetical disagreement over the authenticity of the books of power given their sometimes incomplete state, posthumous publication, and later aspersions over the corruption of Hooker's manuscripts. This work concurs with the judgement of A. S. McGrade and P. G. Stanwood that textual reasons for the authenticity of the books of power remain compelling. See McGrade, 'The Coherence of Hooker's Polity', 164–5; and P. G. Stanwood, 'Works and Editions I', in *A Companion to Richard Hooker*, ed. W. J. T. Kirby (Leiden: Brill, 2008), 27–39.
[12] Hooker, *Laws*, 1:207.8–10; 1:208.7–8; III.2.1.
[13] For example, see F. J. Shirley, *Richard Hooker and Contemporary Political Ideas* (London: SPCK, 1949), 109.
[14] Hooker, *Laws*, 3:210.4–211.16; 3:4.25–5.7; VII.11.9–10; VI.2.2.
[15] W. Speed Hill, 'Hooker's Polity. The Problem of the "last three books"', *Huntingdon Library Quarterly* 24, no. 4 (1971): 317–36. Compare M. R. Sommerville, 'Richard Hooker and His Contemporaries on Episcopacy. An Elizabethan Consensus', *Journal of Ecclesiastical History* 35, no. 2 (1984): 177–87 who argues against the exegetical 'orthodoxy' that Hooker's claims about episcopacy are incoherent.

so too (logically) should the English Church assent to the universal authority of the Catholic Church and the Pope as they sit in Council, again undercutting the claims for lay ecclesiastical supremacy.

Both sets of accusations betray, however, the marked tendency from the twentieth century onwards to read Hooker's political vision without due attention to the systematic role of the architecture of participation and in isolation from much else other than the preface, Book One and small sections of Book Three.[16] Indeed, as A. S. McGrade points out, scholars should rather attempt to see each part of the *Laws* as 'presenting different parts of a total position, not as re-iterating (or failing to re-iterate) a position presented in its full essentials elsewhere in the work'.[17] Accordingly, Kirby notes that, excluding his own work, 'no thorough, critical study of [the] theological dimension of the Royal Supremacy has been undertaken by a modern scholar.'[18] The majority of modern studies of Hooker's political thought instead eschew the theological framework which surrounds the royal supremacy and so elide or misread the systematic role of participation.

This chapter therefore builds upon Kirby's seminal work in showing how the architecture of participation informs the character of episcopacy and lay ecclesiastical supremacy. The fourfold 'grammar of participation' gestures towards coherency and system across the *Laws*. Hooker's coherency derives from his systematic application of the grammar of participation to specific ecclesiological and political ends. The first part details how the grammar of Hooker's architecture of participation allow him to parse the episcopal character of the Church as contingent and yet binding, undercutting the puritans' insistence on the omnicompetency of Scripture as well as their denuding of the created participatory order. The next part similarly explicates how the grammar of participation shapes Hooker's account of lay ecclesiastical supremacy in the same ambivalent terms. The final part shows how Hooker's participatory account of the ecclesiastical polity ultimately sees him return to the twin Platonisms seen in Book One, namely Augustinian immediacy and Dionysian mediation. Here, Hooker unites the sacred and the secular not in the Pope or the Church as a self-subsisting authority, but rather in the monarch. For Hooker, the monarch visibly mediates the immediate dominion of Christ over Church and Commonwealth in a diminished, derivative and subordinate manner. Unveiling how the grammar of Hooker's architecture of participation holds together his politics with his metaphysics and epistemology shows how, as well as being made in the *imago dei*, the human political agent is a homo faber, a fabricating animal. The public laws and figures of the Elizabethan Religious Settlement are divinely undergirded 'instruments to work by', catching the English Church up in the providential work of God but also rendering it as dependent upon and penultimate to God as its ultimate cause and eschatological fulfilment.[19]

---

[16] See Kirby, *Doctrine of the Royal Supremacy*, 11–15.
[17] McGrade, 'The Coherence of Hooker's Polity', 164.
[18] Kirby, *Doctrine of the Royal Supremacy*, 9.
[19] See A. Paddison and N. Messer (eds), *The Bible. Culture, Community, Society* (London: Bloomsbury T & T Clark, 2013), 219–22.

'A societie and a societie supernaturall': The grammar of the Church

In Books Three and Seven Hooker defends the ecclesiology of the established Church of England, as well as the office of bishops within its life. In Book Three, Hooker addresses the radical puritans' assertion that Scripture determines a normative and unalterable form of presbyterian polity. For Hooker, the claim of scriptural omnicompetency also contains a latent political threat: if only the Bible mandates the proper ecclesiastical polity, then the legal basis of the English Reformation, enacted through Parliament and Convocation, becomes heterodox. Indeed, the 'implications of their logic would lead to the overthrow of the English legal and political system, in favour of a form of government and law based directly on the Bible'.[20] In response, for Hooker the claim that the Scriptures are omnicompetent disturbs a peaceable kingdom. Such biblicism deflates the whole participatory order in which rational human communities are free to determine their ecclesial polity within the bounds of the legal orders that participate in eternal law. Hooker's ecclesiology therefore gestures back to the epistemology of Book Two, which in turn develops the metaphysical architecture of participation established in Book One. Indeed, his ecclesiology is the practical outworking of the theological commitment that the manifold legal, rational and political acts of human communities, as they participate in eternal law, read divine wisdom into the world alongside divine law. The following unpacks how the architecture of participation shapes Hooker's ecclesiology and account of episcopacy, as well as how its grammar deflates the modern accusations of incoherency.

Participation serves practical, theological and polemical purposes in Hooker's ecclesiology. As William Harrison points out, Hooker's primary practical concern in the *Laws* is with the outward, visible Church as the site for sanctification.[21] In this context, Hooker's architecture of participation and its attendant grammar shapes the complex nature and telos of the Church, as well as its liturgical practices, in such a way as to mitigate against the radical puritan critique of the Elizabethan Religious Settlement. Participation also points beyond the immediate controversy to a greater vision of sharing in the life of God. For Hooker, the end of the Church is participation in and union with Christ as its constitutive head. The Pauline image Hooker unsurprisingly adopts to describe the Church is the 'Body of Christ', and he parses that body in the dual terms of 'visible' and 'mysticall'. While many scholars argue that Hooker intends to 'conflate' these two aspects so that 'the invisible mystical church essentially becomes one with the visible', the contrary reading remains more accurate.[22] In his ecclesiology,

---

[20] See Rosenthal, *Crown under Law*, 15–16.
[21] See William H. Harrison, 'Powers of Nature and Influences of Grace', in *Richard Hooker and the English Reformation*, ed. W. J. T. Kirby (Dordrecht: Kluwer Academic Publishers, 2003), 15–18; and Harrison, 'The Church', 305–36.
[22] See Lake, *Anglicans & Puritans?*, 180; Harrison, 'The Church', 306–12; and W. David Neelands, 'Richard Hooker on the Identity of the Visible and Invisible Church', in *Richard Hooker and the English Reformation*, ed. W. J. T. Kirby (Dordrecht: Kluwer Academic Publishers, 2003), 99–110. For an excellent analysis, see W. Bradford Littlejohn, *Richard Hooker: A Companion to His Life and Work* (Eugene: Cascade, 2015), 147–62.

Hooker upholds Calvin's twofold distinction[23] between the *forum conscientiae* (the inner forum of conscience) and the *forum externum* (the external forum of politics), as well as Luther's idea of two regiments[24] (the *geistliches* and *weltliches Reich*, or the spiritual and the temporal). Hooker parses the dual aspect of the Church through the grammar of the architecture of participation in order to maintain a separation, but also a real relation between the visible and the mystical, the outer and the inner fora. As such, he takes his place among Protestant or Reformed scholastics of the period, who carefully distinguished between inner and outer fora as well as emphasizing their final unity in the life of the faithful.[25] He also undercuts the call of his puritan opponents for 'further reformation' along disciplinarian lines: for Hooker, 'conformity was completely in tune with the substance of reformed doctrine.'[26]

Hooker parses the dual nature of the Church through the first grammatical feature of the architecture of participation. At its core, for Hooker the dual aspect of the Church expresses the two Platonisms (Dionysian mediation and Augustinian immediacy) originally found in the legal distinction between the first and second eternal law. On the one hand, the Church mediates participation in Christ through the contingent, dispositive practices of the 'visible' political body of the institutional Church as it administers the dominical sacraments, reveals Christ's saving work, and habituates sanctification. The contingent external practices and constitution of the Church, as they participate in God, unfurl the second eternal law into the world. On the other hand, the Church also represents the invisible 'mysticall' body 'removed altogether from sense' and known only to God, being constituted by Christ's salvific action alone and the saving grace he immediately imputes to the inner soul of the believer.[27] The first eternal law hypostatically contains this 'mysticall' body, hidden and unknowable. Hooker relates the 'visible' and 'mysticall' bodies through another grammatical aspect of the architecture of participatory: namely, the logic of Chalcedonian Christology, through which Hooker analogously describes how the two natures of the Church are not to be conflated or confused, but relate in that the visible shares in, and ultimately enjoys union with, the mystical. As such, Hooker nestles ecclesiology within his soteriology, where imputed justification unites with imparted sanctification in final glory. Within such soteriological confines, the visible Church exists as an intermingled body of saints and sinners, or wheat and tares, until 'the final consummation of the world'.[28] Hooker therefore sacralizes the temporality of the visible Church through its liturgical participation in Christ, but desacralizes it as penultimate to and dependent upon the mystical Church. As Kirby notes, this constitutes a 'humanizing' of the visible Church, 'with the consequence that there is

---

[23] Calvin, *Institutes*, III.19.15; 1.847–9. See Bernard Bourdin, *The Theological-Political Origins of the Modern State* (Washington: Catholic University of America Press, 2011), 30–4.

[24] Martin Luther, *Temporal Authority: To What Extent It Should Be Obeyed*, in *Selected Writings of Martin Luther*, ed. G. Tappert, trans. J. J. Schindel, 4 vols. (Minneapolis, MN: Fortress, 2007), 2.281. For the consonance between Calvin and Luther, see Kirby, *Doctrine of the Royal Supremacy*, 30–58. See also W. Bradford Littlejohn, 'The Edification of the Church', 3–18.

[25] See Littlejohn, *Peril and Promise*, 143–52.

[26] Kirby, *Doctrine of the Royal Supremacy*, 67.

[27] Hooker, *Laws*, 1:195.3; III.1.2.

[28] Ibid., 1:199.4; III.1.8.

no longer a theological or metaphysical necessity for an essential distinction to be drawn between ecclesiastical and civil power.'[29] Through the grammar of participation, Hooker here doubly undercuts his puritan opponents. On one hand, lay ecclesiastical supremacy over the visible Church remains legitimately possible without violating Christ's final headship of the Church. On the other hand, the radical puritans confuse and conflate the visible and mystical aspects of the Church when they insist that Scripture determines a normative visible form of ecclesiastical polity, thereby sinking the invisible (inner, spiritual) into the visible (outer, temporal) sphere.[30] Instead, Hooker refuses to transplant the perfection of the mystical Church onto the visible, but still retains a sense that the visible performance and polity of the established Church remains suspended as a participatory body from God's gracious influence, striving towards mystical fulfilment.

Hooker first turns to the nature of the Church in Book One and notes its dual aspect as both a visible political society and also an invisible supernatural society uniting heaven and earth, or what Deborah Shuger calls an 'imagined community'.[31] Using Aristotle's doctrine, mediated through Aquinas, that human beings are political creatures by nature, Hooker writes:

> The Church being a supernaturall societie, doth differ from naturall societies in this, that the persons unto whom we associate our selves, in the one are men simplye considered as men, but they to whome wee be joyned in the other, are God, Angels, and holie men. Againe the Church being both a societie and a societie supernaturall, although as it is a societie it have the selfe same original grounds from which other politique societies have, namely, the naturall inclination which all men have unto sociable life, and consent to some certaine bond of association, which bond is the lawe that appointeth what kinde of order they shall be associated in: yet unto the Church as it is a societie supernaturall this is peculiar, that part of the bond of their association which belong unto the Church of God, must be a lawe supernaturall, which God himself hath revealed concerning that kind of worship which his people shall do unto him.[32]

The Church retains both natural and supernatural aspects nevertheless united in eternal law. The Church as a visible, natural society exists as a political body in time and history through the human positive laws it promulgates. Such laws are mutable participations in eternal law. Yet, the Church as a supernatural society suspends believers from a participatory communion with God, angels and saints through supernatural law, also suspended from eternal law. The Church dynamically exists, then, under both earthly and heavenly aspects, between the footstool and throne of God, as an ecstatic participatory movement from becoming to being, from visible polity to invisible communion and union with God. As Kirby points out, at heart

---

[29] Kirby, 'From "General Meditations" to "Particular Decisions"', 62.
[30] See Littlejohn, *Peril and Promise*, 147–8.
[31] Shuger, 'Society Supernatural', 116–41.
[32] Hooker, *Laws*, 1:131.6–20; I.15.2. Compare Aquinas, *ST*, I.96.4.

Hooker's ecclesiology recapitulates Luther's soteriological dictum that believers are *simul justus et peccator*, that is to say, they exist simultaneously in the imperfect visible Church as well as in the perfect invisible Church.[33] Hooker distinguishes the inner and outer fora, the supernatural and the political, but also unites them as they commonly participate God through Christ, who is the sapiential source and end of law. As such, Bernard Bourdin adroitly notes that this passage 'demonstrates that Hooker used his borrowings from Aristotelian-Thomist philosophy to serve a reformed ecclesiology first and foremost'.[34]

In Book Three, Hooker develops the dual aspect of the Church and, along reformed lines, carefully distinguishes between 'that Church of Christ which we properly term his body mysticall' and the 'visible Church'.[35] In order to trace out how the visible and mystical aspects of the Church relate to one another, Hooker implicitly turns in Book Three to the first and second features of the grammar of participation. On one hand, Hooker separates the visible from the mystical along lines that recall the two Platonisms of Dionysian mediation and Augustinian immediacy found in the legal ontology of Book One. On the other hand, he also appeals to the Chalcedonian orthodoxy of Book Five in which the human and divine natures of Christ are distinct but also indivisibly co-inhere in his person.[36] Hooker steers the way the mystical and visible aspects of the Church relate, moving 'away from the prevalent fixation on predestination and the elect, and turns towards a Christological vision of the Church as a participatory body within which we can hope for the gradual sanctification of all', as Christopher Insole puts it.[37] Hooker notes that his puritan opponents seem to conflate the visible and mystical aspects of the Church, much like how heretics confused the human and divine natures of Christ. Speaking of how the puritans collapse matters of visible Church order into internal matters of salvation, Hooker echoes Chalcedonian language when he writes how 'the mixture of those thinges by speech which by nature are divided, is the mother of all error', and then commends that 'to take away therefore that error which confusion breedeth, distinction is requisite'.[38] In Chalcedonian fashion, he first distinguishes between mystical and visible aspects, before turning to how they are united in certain regards. Throughout, Hooker takes pains to ensure his Reformed orthodoxy, implying that the radical puritans are they who have abandoned the sound

---

[33] Kirby, *Doctrine of the Royal Supremacy*, 62, 66–74.
[34] Bourdin, *Theological-Political Origins*, 32.
[35] Hooker, *Laws*, 1:194.27–8; III.1.2. Neelands, 'Richard Hooker on the Identity of the Visible Church', 99–110 traces the distinction through Augustine as it gains prominence among Reformers and conciliarists. Although Hooker prefers 'mystical' to 'invisible' he seems to treat them as synonyms, such as in *Laws*, 2:339.3–6; V.67.11 when he writes of the sacraments that they 'mysticallie yeat trulie, invisiblie yeat reallie worke our communion or fellowship with the person of Jesus Christ'.
[36] See Hooker, *Laws*, 2:227.6; V.54.10, where he describes orthodox Christology as teaching that the hypostatic union can be condensed into four words: 'truly, perfectly, indivisibly, distinctly.'
[37] Christopher J. Insole, *The Politics of Human Frailty. A Theological Defence of Political Liberalism* (London: SCM, 2004), 55–6. Indeed, Hooker does not seem to define the mystical Church in terms of predestination or the elect, terms that are more readily referred to as the 'invisible Church' by Augustine, Aquinas and the Magisterial Reformers. See Haugaard, 'Books II, III & IV', in *FLE*, 6 (1): 172–3.
[38] Hooker, *Laws*, 1:209.24–26; III.3.1.

magisterial reformed distinction between Calvin's two fora as well as between Luther's two regiments.[39]

For Hooker, the mystical Church refers to all whom God saves through the alien, external and imputed righteousness of Christ and so contains God's saving activity within the visible Church.[40] This singular, mystical body expresses the divine aspect of the Church as the society of those who are saved across time, immediately through Christ as the *esse* of the invisible Church. It is hypostatically unknowable, having an invisible unifying principle much like the first eternal law, but 'such a real body there is'.[41] This definition fastidiously corresponds with Luther's spiritual regiment and Calvin's inner forum.[42]

The mystical Church cannot simply be identified, however, with the visible Church because the sole and immediate political principle of the mystical Church is Christ, rather than a mediatory and contingent temporal polity such as in the visible Church:

> So fare foorth as the Church is the mysticall body of Christ and his invisible spouse, it needeth no externall politie. That very part of the law divine which teacheth faith and workes of righteousness is itself alone sufficient for the Church of God in that respect.[43]

Just as Christ immediately forms the polity of the mystical Church, the only regulative law of that mystical Church is justification by faith; again, here Hooker remains committed to a key reformed theological tenet. As W. Bradford Littlejohn puts it, Hooker describes 'the mystical church in terms of the passivity of justification, which freely receives and rests on the promises of God by faith'.[44] Hooker appeals to the language of participation to describe the relationship of the mystical Church and Christ: there is an asymmetrical 'inherent copulation' and 'mystical conjunction' between the two such that the saved are raised into the glory of the exalted Christ as far as their human nature permits.[45] The sexualized metaphors – the Church as spouse, copulation and conjunction – portrays the generative renewal of human nature through immediate union with Christ, but the adjective 'mysticall' asymmetrically protects the divine nature from change. The saved therefore recapitulate and receive the analogous benefits of Christ's hypostatic union: 'newness of life' in the renewed relationship with

---

[39] See Kirby, *Doctrine of the Royal Supremacy*, 79–91. Compare W. J. T. Kirby, 'The Paradigm of Chalcedonian Christology in Richard Hooker's Discourse on Grace and the Church', *Churchman* 114, no. 1 (2000): 22–39.

[40] See W. David Neelands, 'Richard Hooker and the Debates about Predestination, 1580–1600', in *Richard Hooker and the English Reformation*, ed. W. J. T. Kirby (Dordrecht: Kluwer Academic Publishers, 2003), 43–61; and Daniel Eppley, 'Richard Hooker and the Un-conditionality of Predestination', in *Richard Hooker and the English Reformation*, ed. W. J. T. Kirby (Dordrecht: Kluwer Academic Publishers, 2003), 63–77.

[41] Hooker, *Laws*, 1:194.33–195.1; III.1.2.

[42] Compare Calvin, *Institutes*, IV.1.7; 2.1021–2; and Luther, *Against the Roman Papacy, an Institution of the Devil*, ed. J. Pelikan and H. Lehmann, trans. Eric Gritsch, in *Works*, vol. 41 (Philadelphia, PA: Fortress, 1966), 259–376.

[43] Hooker, *Laws*, 1:261.25–7; III.11.14.

[44] Littlejohn, *Peril and Promise*, 146.

[45] Hooker, *Laws*, 2:234.31; 2:239.3; V.56.1; V.56.7.

God (both in time and in the *eschaton*) and 'the future restoration of our bodies' in the resurrection.[46] Accordingly, the mystical Church flows out of immediate union with Christ and reveals a divine, atemporal aspect and perspective. David Neelands argues, then, that through this divine aspect Hooker deflates the puritan insistence, which he has laid out in Book Three, that Scripture contains a necessary polity for the visible Church, 'for they have transposed the divine polity of the church *qua* mystical to the church *qua* political.'[47] As such, for Hooker the radical puritans have also misrepresented the orthodoxy that distinguishes between Christ's human and divine natures even while they are personally united, as well as the correlative sound reformed doctrine that clearly distinguishes between (but also relates) inner and outer fora or spiritual and temporal regiments.

In contrast, according to Hooker the visible body of the Church remains marked as a mediatory and contingent 'publique Christian societie' analogous to any political gathering. Hooker's idea of a 'sensible knowne compagnie' corresponds with Luther's temporal regiment and Calvin's external forum. Entry into the visible Church is through the Pauline public profession of one faith, one Lord, one baptism; it contains a broad swathe of people, even those in grievous sin.[48] The visible Church reveals a temporal and earthly aspect which requires mediating structures: 'as the Church is a visible societie and body politique, laws of polities it cannot want.'[49] While Christ remains its spiritual head, the visible Church constitutes a mediatory body, rooted in contingent history, but disposed towards the end of sacramental union with Christ through sanctification.[50] The variety of historical circumstances facing the visible *ecclesia* corresponds with the possibility that there is more than one valid ecclesial polity.[51] Hooker therefore distinguishes between matters necessary to salvation and the *adiaphora* of discipline and government: some things are 'meerely of faith' and must be believed, while other things are 'accesorie and appendent onely.'[52] Just as multiple, valid secondary moral principles can be derived from primary moral axioms, the same is true for church government. Hooker's puritan opponents, he alleges, confuse necessity and variety and 'misdistinguish' between matters of discipline and matters of faith or salvation, stretching Scripture beyond its appointed end of salvation in supposing it

---

[46] Ibid., 2:242.1–2; V.56.10.
[47] Neelands, 'Richard Hooker on the Identity of the Visible Church', 108. See also Lake, *Anglicans & Puritans?*, 31.
[48] Hooker, *Laws*, 1:196.5–7; 1:198.7–33; III.1.3; III.1.7–8.
[49] Ibid., 1:261.28–30; III.11.4.
[50] Ibid., 1:195.22–6; III.1.3. On the consonance with Luther and Calvin, see Littlejohn, *Peril and Promise*, 146.
[51] Hooker, *Laws*, 1:3–12; Pref.2.1–10 considers the origins of Calvin's 'new discipline' in Geneva. Despite some caustic remarks about those who follow (or wish to emulate) Calvin, Hooker sees Calvin's reforms of the Church in Geneva as historically conditioned and as a contingently appropriate course of action: 'I see not how the wisest at that time lyving could have bettered, if we duely consider what the present estate of Geneva did then require.' Hooker takes great care not to 'de-church' the Protestant churches even where he also wishes to defend episcopacy as a fitting polity for the English Church.
[52] Hooker, *Laws*, 1:210.3; 1:211.4–25. III.3.2–3. On the background to Hooker's account of *adiaphora*, see: Bernard J. Verkamp, *The Indifferent Mean: Adiaphorism in the English Reformation to 1554* (Athens and Detroit: Ohio University Press and Wayne State University Press, 1977). On Hooker's political use of permissive natural law, see Tierney, *Liberty and Law*, 172–90.

must contain binding directions over indifferent matters. Thus, 'the scripture of God leaveth unto the Churches discretion in some thinges, including the form of church government, decided through the wit of man', meaning through right reason (a power conditioned by cognitive participation in God), taking into account the broad axioms of Scripture.[53] Indeed, while God had established one form of religious government in the Old Testament, in the New the contrary holds true: 'Christ did not mean to set down particular positive laws for all things in such sort as Moses did.'[54] For Hooker, radical puritan claims about biblical omnicompetency flatten creation, denuding and denying the rich cognitive ecology of the architecture of participation in which human beings are creative sharers in the making of laws through the participation of God. As such, the puritans disturb the sound legal basis in the English Reformation for the 'yoke of human power' to subject the visible Church as a human 'politique society'.[55] Furthermore, unlike Hooker, the radical puritans also stand outside of magisterial Reformed orthodoxy: Luther, Melanchthon, Calvin and the Zurich divines largely held that the marks of a true visible Church (*the notae ecclesiae*) included the preaching of the Word and administration of the sacraments, but not any particular form of church government.[56]

After distinguishing the mystical and visible aspects of the Church through the twin Platonisms of Augustinian immediacy and Dionysian mediation, Hooker then explores their unity through the logic of Chalcedonian orthodoxy. The authority of the positive laws made by the visible Church stems from a *communicatio idiomatum* with the mystical Church, echoing Chalcedonian orthodoxy in which divine attributes can loosely be said to also belong to Christ's human nature. The visible Church receives authority when it displays continuity with the divine law of the mystical Church:

> So that lawes humane must be made according to the generall lawes of nature, and without contradiction unto any positive law in scripture. Otherwise they are ill made. Unto lawes thus made and received by a whole Church, they which live within the bosome of that Church, must not thinke it a matter indifferent either to yeeld or not to yeeld obedience .... It doth not stand with the duty which we owe to our heavenly father, that to ordinances of our mother the Church we should shew ourselves disobedient. Let us not say we keepe the commandments of the one, when we break the law of the other: For unlesse we observe both, we obey neither.[57]

---

[53] Hooker, *Laws*, 1:207.19–21; 1:210.22–6; 1:212.26–213.7; III.2.1; III.3.3; III.4.1.
[54] Ibid., 1:249.9–12; III.11.5.
[55] Hooker, *Laws*, 3:395.28–396.6; VIII.6.9. Hooker here refers to the Anabaptists, but the polemical implication remains clear: the puritans are guilty by theological association with the opinion that Church and Commonwealth exclude one another, thereby threatening the theological ground for lay ecclesiastical supremacy.
[56] Hooker, *Laws*, 1:208.12–209.20; III.2.2. Cartwright certainly stands within the reformed tradition of Bucer and Beza who held that a scriptural form of church government was a mark of the true Church. Yet, Hooker offers a conservative defence of broader magisterial reformed thought. See Kirby, *Doctrine of the Royal Supremacy*, 86.
[57] Hooker, *Laws*, 1:237.28–238.7; III.9.3.

While the visible and mystical remain distinct, they are united under the second eternal law as it unfolds divine wisdom in history, the *ratio* and telos of which is participation in Christ. The ecclesial aspects of visible and mystical are not confused or mixed, but they have a real relationship and the latter mediates authority to the former. Indeed, 'that which inwardly each man should be, the Church outwardly ought to testify'.[58] When Hooker objects, then, in Book Three to Thomas Cartwright's critique of the visible Church established under law in England, he does so because it 'misdistinguishes' the aspect of the mystical with that of the visible. For Cartwright and the radical puritans, ecclesiastical polity should be drawn from a divinely appointed, scriptural form where Christ's authority is immediately present. In addition to Word and Sacrament, Cartwright argues that a scriptural form of church government was another mark of the Church (*notae ecclesiae*).[59] Cartwright expects a golden age of reformed purity when 'our Saviour Christ sitteth wholly and fully not only in his chair to teach but also in his throne to rule, not alone in the hearts of everyone by the spirit, but also generally and in the visible government of the church, by those laws of discipline he hath prescribed'.[60] For Hooker, this is to sink the mystical Church into the visible, at great peril to the penultimate status of the visible Church, confusing the inner and outer fora, the spiritual and the temporal regiments.[61] Rather, the visible Church as a 'politique society' functions within positive human law. Scripture may work 'immutably on matters that are *coram Deo*', as Littlejohn argues, but only 'to some extent mutably on matters *coram hominibus*'.[62] Thus, the puritans miss the mark and should yet subject themselves to the established Church as that which remains consonant with magisterial reformed ecclesiology, upholding a firm distinction between the inner and outer, the visible and invisible. Indeed, for Hooker, the established visible Church gains contingent, mediate and historical authority from a yet greater mystical body participating immediately in Christ, rather than from the confusion of the two fora or regiments.

Yet, whatever its contingency, the visible Church remains, however, a vital 'instrument' for the participation of divine nature. Pace Shuger, Hooker does not merely think of the visible Church 'as a judicial body necessary for dealing with heretics and schismatics', as a 'coercive institution', or as an institution that 'performed a functional and administrative role'.[63] Rather, for Hooker sanctification unfurls through time and materiality: Christ transforms the recipient of grace 'by steppes and degrees' from sinfulness towards eschatological glory through the practices of the visible Church.[64] Accordingly, sacramental participation forms the heart of the visible Church's activity. Baptism acts as the means through which the believer 'is incorporated

---

[58] Ibid., 2:33.26–7; V.6.2.
[59] On the *notae ecclesiae*, Hooker quotes Cartwright in a lengthy footnote in *Lawes*, 1:208.s; III.2.2.
[60] John Whitgift, *The Works of John Whitgift*, ed. J. Ayre (Cambridge: Parker Society, 1851-3), 3.315. Hooker parodies this disciplinarian position in *Laws*, 1:265.8–16; III.11.17.
[61] Hooker, *Laws*, 3:376.13–22; VIII.4.9.
[62] Littlejohn, *Peril and Promise*, 147–8. See Hooker, *Laws*, 1:130.26–8; I.15.1.
[63] Shuger, *Habits of Thought*, 133–5.
[64] See Lake, *Anglicans & Puritans?*, 165, 169, 196. Littlejohn, *Peril and Promise*, 166–72 illustrates how one must take care to avoid Lake's elision of justification and sanctification in order to preserve Hooker's two-realm distinction.

into Christ' and outwardly receives both imputed righteousness (the alien, external justification wrought by Christ) as well as the beginning of imparted righteousness (sanctification).[65] The visible Church becomes a mediated immediacy: baptism 'is admission into the visible church', but this also, through a communication of idioms, brings the visible Church very close to the mystical as it reveals in time the atemporal imputation of righteousness by Christ.[66] Baptism unveils how the visible Church and baptisand participate in God's saving action.[67] Sanctification occurs (although is not guaranteed) through Eucharistic participation: the liturgical reception of Christ's body and blood is necessary for growth in grace, reconciling extrinsic justification with intrinsic sanctification as a prolepsis of eschatological glory.[68] At these moments, the mediatory visible Church once again bears a close resemblance to the mystical Church as it immediately joins with Christ in the visceral 'participation of the bodie and blood of Christ'. As it relates to a supernatural society, the visible Church theurgically tends towards communion with 'God, Angels, and holie men' through the sacraments.

As the previous chapter showed, Hooker defends the established public liturgy because it lifts up, shapes and manuducts human desires into a likeness of the angelic law, satiated with divine love. The visible Church dynamically participates in God's saving action, an eschatological *viator* awaiting the fulfilment of desire in the final union with Christ. While the radical puritans attempt to extract the 'godly elect' from the 'ungodly' on this temporal side of the eschatological kingdom, Hooker refuses any slippage between the visible and mystical. As he writes in his *First Sermon Upon Part of S. Jude*, 'we cannot examine the hearts of other men, [but] we may our own' and so we 'must leave the secret judgment of every servant to his own Lord'.[69] Hooker therefore portrays a visible Church that includes everyone and which, over the recalcitrant but certain passing of time, grows towards the mystical body as sacramental grace ameliorates those whom it touches. Perhaps this explains why Hooker conflates in Book Five the dual aspect of the Church: in the public prayer that we share across time and space with those people and angels whom God alone calls, 'we are joined as parts to that *visible mystical* body which is his Church'.[70] As Insole remarks, Hooker's ecclesiology seems to 'harbour the suggestion . . . that the entire historical visible Church may actually be *smaller* than the invisible; or at least, that in its glory and consummation in Christ, the invisible Church may be more universal and inclusive than we dare to hope'.[71] For Hooker, God's grace raises up the broad visible Church into the mystical, rather than descending the mystical into the visible in order to limit it, as the puritans contend.

The grammar of the architecture of participation therefore helps Hooker chart not only the difference but also the union between the visible and the invisible or mystical. Despite the perspectival distinction between the mystical and visible Church, a real relationship

---

[65] Hooker, *Laws*, 2:254.23–255.13; V.60.2.
[66] Ibid., 1:196.7; III.1.4.
[67] Ibid., 2:280.22–281.3; V.62.15.
[68] Ibid., 2:230.19–29; V.55.6.
[69] Hooker, *Jude*, First Sermon, 11–13, in *FLE*, 5:26.3–4; 5:28.10–11.
[70] Hooker, *Laws*, 2:111.26–7; V.24.1.
[71] Insole, *Politics of Human Frailty*, 56.

and union obtains between the two ecclesial aspects: in Chalcedonian fashion, and in accordance with the system of laws, they co-inhere through their telos (union with Christ), profession (one Lord, one faith, one baptism), and causal relation to Christ as spiritual head.[72] Thus, Hooker states that 'our being in Christ by eternall foreknowledge saveth us not without our actuall and reall adoption into the fellowship of his sainctes in this present world'.[73] As William Covell put it in 1603, Hooker insists that 'visible and invisible maketh not two churches; but the diverse State and condition of the same church'.[74] The mystical Church remains clouded in apophatic mystery: Hooker writes that 'onely our mindes by intellectuall conceipt are able to apprehend' the membership which only God knows. Rather than election or predestination, then, Hooker's real concern in the *Laws* remains sanctification, the spiritual regeneration and growth of believers through the Holy Spirit in the visible Church. The goal of sanctification is participation in Christ. Participation begins in the passive, immediate, external, alien and atemporal imputation of Christ's merits; participation also temporally and mediately unfolds through baptism and through the life of the visible Church:

> From hence it is that they which belonge to the mysticall bodie of our Savior Christ and be in number as the starres of heaven, devided successivelie by reason of their mortall condition unto manie generations, are notwithstandinge coupled everie one to Christ theire head and all unto everie particular person amongst them selves, in as much as the same Spirit, which anointed the blessed soule of our Savior Christ, doth so formalize unite and actuate his whole race, as if both he and they were so many limmes compacted unto one bodie, by being quickned all with one and the same soule.[75]

The apophatic limits of human knowledge mean that, beyond knowing the reality of a divinely ordered *ecclesia* atemporally and immediately united with Christ, all that can truly be spoken of remains the visible Church because the saved are known only to God.[76] In fact, since the visible Church overlaps the invisible Church, there can be no perceptible difference until the *eschaton*. As such, the visible Church truly proffers grace and becomes sacralized, but remains penultimate to the revelatory reality of the mystical Church. Kirby rightly points out, then, the 'close interlocking of soteriology and ecclesiology' in the *Laws*.[77] The grace of justification calls the mystical Church to be immediately 'in Christ', while the grace of sanctification unfolds through the

---

[72] See Bourdin, *Theological-Political Origins*, 34.
[73] Hooker, *Laws*, 2:238.27–9; V.56.7. This seems to be Hooker's version of the principle '*extra ecclesiam nulla salus*' ['no salvation outside of the Church']. The same principle was also accepted by Luther and Calvin, as well as by Roman Catholic apologists. Protestant or Reformed scholastics in the late sixteenth century typically upheld the principle so long as the Church in question possessed the marks of the Church (*notae ecclesiae*), typically meaning the Word and Sacraments. See Muller, *Dictionary*, 112.
[74] William Covell, *A Just and Temperate Defence* (Lampeter: Edwin Mellen Press, 1998), 66.
[75] Hooker, *Laws*, 2:243.14–23; V.56.11.
[76] See J. Gascoigne, 'Church and State Unified: Hooker's Rationale for the English Post-Reformation Order', *Journal of Religious History* 21 (1997): 23–34 (esp. 29–30).
[77] Kirby, *Doctrine of the Royal Supremacy*, 73.

mediation of the visible Church whereby Christ is 'in us'.[78] The double aspect of the Church remains united through participation in Christ, 'that mutuall inward hold which wee have of him and he of us.' Grace remains one in its unitive source, but reflects the multiplicity of a participatory order. The union and distinction of the visible and mystical Church relates to the two modes of participation in Christ, namely imputed and infused righteousness: participation involves atemporal immediacy and also temporal mediation in the one Church, the participated Body of Christ. Christ therefore wields authority over the mystical and political bodies at the same time, giving the Church as his Body the character of unity in duality.[79]

If the grammar of Hooker's architecture of participation helps him to articulate a coherent ecclesiology in Books One and Three, then it also aids him in Book Seven to make what A. S. McGrade calls 'a clear, strong case for episcopacy as divinely instituted or approved, historically well tested, yet not immutably fixed as the only possible legitimate form of church government'.[80] McGrade here encapsulates the problem over Hooker's logical cohesiveness for other scholars like Rory Fox and W. Speed Hill: a divinely instituted form of church government seems to contradict Hooker's emphasis in Book Three on the indifference of ecclesial polity. As already noted, McGrade also offers, however, a solution: each part of the *Laws* presents different aspects of the whole argument, reflecting the various practical and polemical pressures on Hooker's apologia. In Book Three, Hooker responds to the radical puritan claim that Scripture mandates an unalterable form of church government and remains competent in all matters. For Hooker, his opponents hereby evacuate creation of divine influence, flatten out the manifold systems of laws that share in eternal law, and so cut the participatory cord that suspends everything (including the English Reformation) from God. Hooker therefore stresses mutability, contingency and the multiplicity of divine influence within the participatory order, maintaining room for human lawmaking such as that which instituted the English Reformation. In contrast, when Hooker later defends episcopacy as constituting the *bene esse* of the *ecclesia* in Book Seven, he responds to disciplinarian calls for 'further reformation' along Genevan lines. Yet, his defence still depends upon the participatory contours of earlier books. Two aspects of the grammar of participation play a key role in this endeavour. First, Hooker employs scholastic notions of causality, typically found in post-Reformation orthodox thinkers, where secondary, temporal, contingent, instrumental causes participate in divine perfections and receive divine approval. In short, history takes on a providential character, just as it has in his metaphysics and epistemology. Hooker defends episcopal orders, then, as the contingent and historic development of church polity that also receives divine approbation (if not actually divine appointment) since God is the author of 'all good things'.[81] Second, Hooker's logic of desire also casts the bishop as a hierarch

---

[78] Hooker, *Laws*, 2:234.29–30; 2:242.28–243.9; V.56.1; V.56.10–11.
[79] Ibid., 3:362.10–13; VIII.4.5.
[80] A. S. McGrade, 'Episcopacy', in *A Companion to Richard Hooker*, ed. W. J. T. Kirby (Leiden: Brill, 2008), 485.
[81] Patrick Collinson, 'Hooker and the Elizabethan Establishment', in *Richard Hooker and the Construction of Christian Community*, ed. A. S. McGrade (Tempe: Medieval and Renaissance Texts and Studies, 1997), 149–81 notes that Hooker remains the strongest critic of episcopal abuses and

who mediates divine goodness in some diminished form in the life of the visible Church. Here, Hooker maintains that God remains the immediate source of power and authority, but mediates them through episcopal orders as a fitting or convenient polity for the outward political regiment of the Church in a well-ordered Commonwealth as it pursues holiness.

The first of these grammatical aspects of the architecture of participation, namely scholastic notions of causality, allows Hooker to balance in Book Seven the contingency of episcopal orders with their binding divine approval.[82] Hooker begins by contesting the puritans' claim that contemporary bishops depart from what was originally meant by 'bishop' in the early Church, namely 'presbyters' simply in charge of a local congregation. The fifth chapter of Book Seven acts as an historical enquiry into the 'time and cause of instituting every where Bishops with restraint', by which he means within the geographical limits of dioceses. Hooker defines a bishop as follows:

> A Minister of God, unto whom with permanent continuance, there is given not onely power of administring the Word and Sacraments, which power other Presbyters have; but also a further power to ordain Ecclesiastical persons, and a power of Chiefty in Government over Presbyters as well as Lay men, a power to be by way of jurisdiction a Pastor even to Pastors themselves.[83]

This definition allows Hooker to portray the apostles as bishops: the distinctive essence of a bishop is the power to ordain; the historic wealth and territorial extent of historic bishops are incidental and develop as such over time.[84] Thus, the apostles were bishops 'at large' whereas later bishops have a limited geographical compass in the diocese and so minister 'with restraint'; but they are all bishops in the essential sense. Indeed, quoting Cyprian, Hooker recalls how 'it was the general received perswasion of the ancient Christian world, that *Ecclesia est in Episcopo*, the outward being of a Church consisteth in the having of a Bishop.'[85]

In relation to episcopal orders, Hooker displays a sense of historical pragmatism but also gives history a providential texture as it creatively participates in and unfolds eternal law like an effect from a First Cause mediated through temporal human acts. In the fifth chapter of Book Seven, he accepts that a presbyteral model of local congregations governed the primitive church, but argues that an Ignatian monarchical episcopacy took precedence in order to protect doctrinal unity by the end of the apostolic age. Hooker also accepts that the visible Church exists as a corporation, a political body in which certain kinds of laws, including those of order, can be mutable or changeable 'as need may require'.[86] All forms of government, even those of the visible

---

failures, but nevertheless sees the office as being of immense theological and social value. See also McGrade, 'Episcopacy', 482–4; and Shuger, *Habits of Thought*, 128–30.

[82] Sommerville, 'Richard Hooker and his Contemporaries on Episcopacy', 179 notes that Hooker was hardly unique in this balancing act; but Hooker certainly is unique in the metaphysical underpinning of how contingency relates to divine approval.

[83] Hooker, *Laws*, 3:152.19–25; VII.2.3.

[84] Ibid., 3:155.17–160.31; VII.4.1–5.2.

[85] Ibid., 3:160.29–31; VII.5.2.

[86] Ibid., 3:219.30–220.4; VII.14.3. Compare ibid., 3:226.20–2; 3:227.29–31; VII.14.11.

Church, are matters of positive law and remain subject to change when their original basis has become eroded and there is no divine commandment to the contrary. Thus,

> the whole body of the Church, hath power to alter with general consent and upon necessary occasions, even the positive laws of the Apostles, if there be no commandment to the contrary, and it manifestly appears to her, that change of times have clearly taken away the very reason of Gods first institution.[87]

Yet, Hooker suspends such contingency from divine providence: God sits behind history as the primary cause and author of all perfective secondary acts. Indeed, 'of all good things God himself is Author and consequently an approver of them'. The fittingness of monarchical episcopacy was, therefore, divine in origin insofar as it protected the peace and order of the Church: 'if any thing in the Churches Government, surely the first institution of Bishops was from Heaven, was even of God, the Holy Ghost was the Author of it.'[88] Indeed, 'the Apostles who began this order of Regiment by Bishops, did it not but by divine instinct.'[89] Within this divine authorship, since the fittingness of the office persists, any bishop is 'lawful, divine and holy', which is formed according to divine reason, imitative of God, and set apart for special service to the Church.[90]

Accordingly, the grammar of participatory causality allows Hooker to delineate how God authors the law of nature, the law of Scripture and the law of reasonable activity such that the contingent development of the office of bishops remains 'truely derived from God, and approved of him'.[91] Yet, Hooker blends Aristotelian notions of causality with Reformed commitments, as was typical of theologians within Reformed orthodoxy, perhaps with Peter Martyr Vermigli being the most obvious influence, as Littlejohn argues.[92] For Hooker, as with the medieval scholastics and theologians inside Reformed orthodoxy, all secondary causes are suspended from God as First Cause, saturating history and human actions with divine influence. Far from contradicting Book Three, then, Hooker's affirmation of episcopal orders as divinely mandated does not entail its immutability or necessity. Episcopal orders form part of a contingent order hypostatically distinct from the immutability of God and founded on custom and consent rather than explicit divine command. In Book Seven, Hooker quotes Jerome that bishops ought to know that 'custom, rather than the truth of any Ordinance of the Lords maketh them greater than the rest', and so 'they must acknowledge that the Church hath power by universal consent upon urgent cause to take it away, if thereunto she be constrained through the proud, tyrannical, and unreformable dealings of her bishops'.[93] As it establishes a custom such as an ecclesiastical polity, human reason (inspired by the Holy Spirit) leads the visible Church; as in earlier books of the *Laws*,

---

[87] Ibid., 3:167.7–12; VII.5.8.
[88] Ibid., 3:170.17–20; VII.5.10.
[89] Ibid., 3:169.30–1; VII.5.10.
[90] Ibid., 3:153.2–3; VII.2.3.
[91] Ibid., 3:210.4–211.16; VII.11.9–10.
[92] W. Bradford Littlejohn, '"More than a swineherd": Hooker, Vermigli, and an Aristotelian Defence of the Royal Supremacy', *Reformation & Renaissance Review* 15, no. 1 (2013): 68–83.
[93] Hooker, *Laws*, 3:166.16–168.35; VII.5.8.

the utility, benefit and popularity of a custom testifies to its provisional truth and, through a communication of idioms, lends to it divine authority as the mediation through which eternal law reads itself into the world. The laws of the Church are then said to be authored by God, where the life of the Church demonstrably conforms to the activity of the Holy Spirit. The authority of the bishops springs from the fact that the Church 'hath found it good and requisite to be so governed' for the purpose of peace and unity.[94] As a fitting institution, the development of monarchical episcopacy, while historically contingent, thereby also reveals for Hooker 'Divine appointment beforehand' or at the very least 'Divine approbation afterwards'.[95] Seen from the unitive perspective of eternal law, episcopacy is fitting for peace and unity within the visible Church, making it into a providential office. For Hooker, the 'pretended Reformers' in the puritan camp lack urgent cause, universal consent and reason to remove the office of bishops, producing only seditious disquiet with the 'fruitless jars and janglings' of their 'contentious Disputes'.[96]

The episcopal polity of the visible Church derives, then, from human positive law, a reflective process of rational discernment within contingent and mutable circumstances. Nevertheless, the scholastic notion that secondary perfective acts are contained within God's causality means that episcopal orders participate in eternal law. Returning to the legal ontology of Book One, Hooker puts up a high bar for the radical puritans when he claims only general consent and extreme duress can allow episcopal orders to be replaced in favour of presbyterianism. What Hooker means by general consent evokes his earlier discussion in Book One of the *ius gentium* as a particular kind of participation in eternal law. The particular fittingness of episcopal orders becomes clearer when held up against Hooker subtle discussion of *ius gentium* as a form of human positive law dealing with community, the natural inclination 'to have a kind of society or fellowship even with all mankind'.[97] Turning, then, to the relations between visible ecclesial bodies, Hooker produces a conciliarist call for the renewal of General Councils:

> The urgent necessity of mutual communion for preservation of our unity in these things [i.e. doctrinal unity], as also for order in some things convenient to be every where uniformly kept, maketh it requisite that the church of God here on earth have her laws of mutual commerce between Christian nations, laws by virtue whereof all Churches may enjoy freelie the use of those reverend religious and sacred consultations which are termed councels generall.[98]

The implication for his opponents remains clear: since in Book Seven Hooker states that 'Councils do all presuppose bishops', episcopal orders thereby become a normative requirement of the *ius gentium* as it relates to the Church, notwithstanding issues of egregious abuse in which episcopal orders have therefore been rescinded, such as in

---

[94] Ibid., 1:328.18–20; 1:31.32–3; IV.13.2; Pref.6.3.
[95] Ibid., 3:161.5–18; VII.5.2.
[96] Ibid., 3:228.21–230.10; VII.14.12–13.
[97] Ibid., 1:107.3–108.2; I.10.12.
[98] Ibid., 1:109.10–17; I.10.13. Compare ibid., 3:347.23–348.9; VIII.2.17.

Geneva.⁹⁹ Accordingly, it can never ordinarily be proper to replace episcopal orders as they are a necessary part of the participatory legal structures that providentially govern God's creation. As Alan Cromartie argues, Hooker's use of the *ius gentium* means that 'it could never be legitimate wilfully to replace the existing order' without common consent under extreme provocation.¹⁰⁰

Hooker's conciliarism and appeal to the *ius gentium* as it relates the Church of England to the Roman Catholic Church and to the Council of Trent does not produce, however, the kind of ecclesiastical incoherency in the *Laws* that Rory Fox alleges.¹⁰¹ Fox writes that if Hooker's 'use of authority against the puritans really has any merit at all then it is very difficult to see how he can escape having to accept the validity of the same Roman Catholic appeal to authority against Anglicanism'.¹⁰² Yet, far from suggesting that the Church of England must (by the logic of an argument from authority presented to the puritans) submit to the higher, universal authority of Rome, Hooker's argument remains far more nuanced than Fox allows. For Hooker, the Church of England need not yield to the episcopal command of the papacy because only Parliament and Convocation represent the reasoned consensus of the Christian community within the geographical limits of the Commonwealth.¹⁰³ As such, neither the puritans nor the papacy has any claim to supervene over the positive ecclesial laws that the Crown-in-Parliament and Convocation have promulgated. Similarly, the Church of England should not conform to the decrees of the Council of Trent because it was not truly a General Council. For Hooker, the Council of Trent cannot represent the reasoned consensus of the universal Church: as a clerical gathering, it lacked both authority and representatives from the lay faithful and from reformed English Christians; as such, it cannot bind the Christian conscience.¹⁰⁴ The same reservation does not hold true for the Crown-in-Parliament and Convocation, which can accordingly bind the conscience and practice of the English Christian through its legislation; to 'despise them is to despise in them' also the God who remotely authors such human laws through their participation in eternal law.¹⁰⁵ Here, the architecture of participation and its grammar allows Hooker to develop a politicized metaphysics. This development yields a strong and coherent account of the role of law, reason, consent and episcopacy, as he understands it, against his puritan adversaries. In his politicized metaphysics, Hooker suspends the Church of England from the *ratio* of eternal law mediated through history, casting the radical puritans as both unreasonable and as potentially treasonous to the lawful and holy English Church.

Despite Hooker's apparently radical authoritarianism in these texts, he does not quite claim, as some scholars suggest, any unmitigated or unreflective authority

---

[99] Ibid., 3:161.28; VII.5.3.
[100] See Alan Cromartie, 'Theology and Politics in Richard Hooker's Thought', *History of Political Thought* 21, no. 1 (2000): 41–66 (60).
[101] For a detailed rejection of Rory Fox's claims, see Daniel Eppley, 'Royal Supremacy', in *A Companion to Richard Hooker*, ed. W. J. T. Kirby (Leiden: Brill, 2008), 520–30.
[102] Fox, 'Richard Hooker and the Incoherence of the *Ecclesiastical Polity*', 57.
[103] Hooker, *Laws*, 3:401.22–8; 3:405.21–5; VIII.6.11. See Littlejohn, *Peril and Promise*, 184–90.
[104] Hooker, *Laws*, 3:394.8–16; VIII.6.7.
[105] Ibid., 3:395.26–8; VIII.6.8.

for Parliament as the voice of Christian rationality over all aspects of Christian life. For example, Timothy Rosendale argues that Hooker's 'ideology of order demands the uniform and universal submission of all private concerns to the public order'.[106] Ethan Shagan similarly writes of 'Hooker's strangely authoritarian constitutionalism, his gift of *public consent* to all members of the body politic so that their capacity for *private conscience* could be taken away'.[107] Yet, Hooker's participatory epistemology has already located rationality fully in the individual participating in divine reason; the public scrutiny of church authorities simply is there to determine whether particular claims to special spiritual illumination truly demonstrate a consonance between Word and Spirit.[108] Hooker qualifies the authority of the Church since 'what scripture doth plainlie deliver, to that first place both of credit and obedience is due; the next whereunto is whatsoever anie man can necessarelie conclude by force of reason; after these the voice of the Church succeedeth'.[109] As Daniel Eppley points out, in the same passage, while this hierarchy seems perfectly straightforward, Hooker also establishes the church authorities as the arbiter of what counts as demonstrative reasoning, subverting the apparent hierarchy between reason and the Church about where obedience is due.[110] If Hooker errs, however, it is not perhaps in paving the way thereby for radical authoritarianism, but in assigning too sanguine an appraisal that public scrutiny would yield to or recognize rational persuasion, namely, that the church authorities would indeed uphold the standard of applying and assenting to demonstrative reasoning. Such a sanguine appraisal permits Hooker to advance a creative fiction, which Eppley labels as 'dissent without disloyalty' or 'critically thinking loyalty'.[111] Rather than silencing his puritan opponents, Hooker challenges them both to 'recognize the essential validity of the established church' and also 'to continue actively seeking to understand God's will for the church more fully and when appropriate to work for reform within the structures of the church'.[112] The appropriate way remains, of course, to show through rational argument the case for reform, the very call Hooker gives in the preface to the *Laws* to 'resolve the conscience' when he asks to examine whether his opponents can show 'reasonable cause' or the 'force of reason'. If that reasoned case could be given, then Hooker seems to believe sincerely that he and the whole Church of England would 'embrace together with you the selfe same truth'.

---

[106] Timothy Rosendale, *Liturgy and Literature in the Making of Protestant England* (Cambridge: Cambridge University Press, 2007), 58.

[107] Ethan Shagan, *The Rule of Moderation: Violence, Religion, and the Politics of Restraint in Early Modern England* (Cambridge: Cambridge University Press, 2011), 147, emphasis in the original. Compare Almasy, 'Language and Exclusion', 227–42.

[108] On the relation of private conscience to public scrutiny, and the role of church authorities as the public arbiter of what private claims actually display demonstrative reasoning, see Daniel Eppley, *Defending Royal Supremacy and Discerning God's Will in Tudor England* (Aldershot: Ashgate, 2007), 163–222 (esp. 187–204).

[109] Hooker, *Laws*, 2:39.6–11; V.8.2.

[110] Eppley, *Defending Royal Supremacy*, 198–202. Compare Voak, *Reformed Theology*, 256–64.

[111] Daniel Eppley, *Reading the Bible with Richard Hooker* (Minneapolis, MN: Fortress Press, 2016), 188–218. Eppley points out royal prerogative quashed dissent, casting Hooker in a comparatively favourable light, even if his creative fiction never garnered traction.

[112] Ibid., 189.

Having justified the institution of bishops, Hooker turns in the rest of Book Seven to another aspect of the grammar of the architecture of participation, namely the logic of desire, in order to cast the figure of the bishop as a divine hierarch who dispositively mediates participation in God's goodness. As such, the faithful ought to esteem the episcopal office. Hooker yokes the benefits of episcopacy to its capacity to yield two levels of participation. For Hooker, the episcopacy yields horizontal participation across the Church and Commonwealth in terms of social and political participation, with demonstrable and pragmatic benefits. It also yields vertical participation by imitating divine authority and leading the spiritual desire to share in God's nature towards holiness. The bishop simultaneously represents, then, a social functionary but also a divinely appointed hierarch directing the logic of desire towards penultimate political goods as well as towards its final end of loving union with God.

On the one hand, then, when Hooker considers in chapter eighteen of Book Seven 'what good doth publiquely grow from the Prelacy', he surveys six particular instances of benefit for the horizontal, political well-being of English society. A. S. McGrade writes that, taken together, these benefits 'present episcopacy as an important tempering and harmonising institution'.[113] The benefits revolve around the fittingness of episcopal orders in fairly quotidian matters: the country's reputation abroad benefits from the 'higher place and calling' of episcopal ministers; the 'successions, doings, sufferings, and affairs of Prelates' provide salutary historical guidance to society; clergy require a greater authority to settle disputes with congregations and give them support; when 'twined together', prelacy and nobility balance society with wisdom and valour respectively; and rulers need the moral guidance of clergy 'whose greater and higher callings do somewhat more proportion them unto that ample conceit and spirit, wherewith the minde of so powerful persons are possessed'. Yet, for all that such benefits are seemingly pragmatic and quotidian, through them the prelacy becomes 'the temperature of excesses in all estates, the glew and soder of the Publique weal, the ligament which tieth and connecteth the limbs of the Body politique each to the other'.[114] The social function of bishops remains vital. In Book Eight, Hooker avers that 'in all commonwealths things spirituall ought above temporall to be provided for' and the 'of things spirituall the chiefest is *Religion*'.[115] Episcopacy acts as a pragmatic social glue guaranteeing and mediating public order for the common good, as well as equipping public society to be properly oriented to its ultimate spiritual end.

On the other hand, the bishop (like all persons and things employed in religious matters) becomes 'by an excellencie termed *Spirituall*'. He reflects not merely pragmatism but emerges as a particular kind of participation in the providential ordering of creation. As Corneliu Simut puts it, Hooker 'works from the assumption that all things pertaining to Christian ministry have a firm anchor in the being of God'.[116] Christ gives spiritual authority to bishops; their spiritual jurisdiction has to do with the Church as a supernatural community governed by divine law and as a political

---

[113] McGrade, 'Episcopacy', 495.
[114] Hooker, *Laws*, 3:263.20–31; VII.18.12.
[115] Ibid., 3:321.15–18; VIII.1.4.
[116] Corneliu Simut, 'Orders of Ministry', in *A Companion to Richard Hooker*, ed. W. J. T. Kirby (Leiden: Brill, 2008), 403–34 (403).

society under positive law, both types of participation in God.[117] The bishop leads the visible society of the Church to its desirous end: that which is 'most desirable', Hooker argues in Book One, is that 'wherin ther is infinitie of goodness', and since 'no good is infinite but only God', our greatest desire is to be 'unto God united'.[118] Accordingly, then, the bishop becomes a mediatory analogue of the angels as they are desirously oriented to God and cooperate with humankind to bring creation to salvation. Hooker links esteem for a bishop with virtue, and understands virtue in desirous terms echoing the angelic law of Book One: a 'Bishops estimation doth grow from the excellency of vertues suitable unto his place'. The chief episcopal virtues are 'devotion and the feeling sence of Religion'. These virtues humble the powerful and 'frameth their hearts to a stooping kind of disposition', allowing bishops to 'shine . . . as Angels of God in the midst of perverse men'.[119] Hooker uses the parallel image of bishops as 'angels among men' three times in Book Seven.[120] Hooker does not spell out what he means by 'devotion and the feeling sence of Religion', but it remains allusive to the logic of desire in angelic law and the participation in Christ through prayer and the sacraments found in Book One and Book Five respectively. Where bishops exist, people can see how

> [in] the powers and faculties of whose souls God hath possest, those very actions the kind whereof is common unto them with other men, have notwithstanding in them a more high and heavenly form, which draweth correspondent estimation unto it, by vertue of that celestial impression, which deep meditation of holy things, and as it were conversation with God doth leave in their mindes.[121]

Just an the angels act as intermediaries and helpers for humanity, desirous that all of creation shares in God's self-diffusive plenitude, so too do bishops show a 'fatherly affection toward the flock of Christ', thereby shining as 'Angels of God'.[122]

Hooker also at times turns the bishop into an analogue of God. In Book Six, Hooker explains the purpose of a church is to lead souls to felicity and to restrain the impious. Within this purpose, the Bishop 'doth beare the Image of God and of Christ' because he rules and administers holy things respectively.[123] Hooker here cites Ignatius of Antioch, the theological progenitor of monarchical episcopacy, and he repeatedly does so in what follows, invoking the sense that the *esse* of a bishop is the participatory image of the Trinity. Together with the more commonly used analogy between bishops and angels, Hooker thereby extends (as a *communicatio idiomatum*) divine illumination from the eschatological realm into the polity of the visible Church, thereby sacralizing it and its bishops while maintaining their human contingency. Feisal Mohamed rightly locates this element of Hooker's thought in the Neoplatonism

---

[117] Hooker, *Laws*, 3.5.28–33; VI.2.2.
[118] Ibid., 1:112.7–20; I.11.2.
[119] Ibid., 3:299.1–25; VII.24.15.
[120] Ibid., 3:146.31; 3:205.24; 3:303.24; VII.1.3; VII.11.3; VII.24.18.
[121] Ibid., 3:299.14–20; VII.24.15.
[122] Ibid., 3:299.22–4; VII.24.15.
[123] Ibid., 3:4.8–5.7; VI.2.1-2.

of Pseudo-Dionysius and brings to the fore two pertinent examples.[124] First, when Hooker defends the English Church from the accusation that it is 'corrupted with Popish orders', he does so with an explicit quotation from Pseudo-Dionysius. This quotation extends illumination from the celestial order into the material world of the visible Church: '*The sensible things which religion hath hallowed, are resemblances framed according to things spiritually understood, whereunto they serve as a hand to lead and a way to direct*'.[125] The long usage of things by the Church becomes imbued with divine power that leads by the hand (*manuductio*) and directs material creatures back to their Creator. Much as in Pseudo-Dionysius's thought, for Hooker, the clergy possess a special kind of illumination, both by virtue of their office and through their *theurgia*, the holy works that Pseudo-Dionysius claims allow divinity to pass down through the mediation of the celestial and ecclesiastical hierarchies. Second, Mohamed traces how Hooker accordingly sacralizes ordination and the episcopacy in a Dionysian fashion. In ordination, clergy receive power from Christ and become direct agents of the Holy Spirit, thereby possessing a special, unique illumination:

> To whome Christ hath imparted power both over that mysticall bodie which is the societie of soules, and over that naturall which is him selfe for the knitting of both in one (a worke which antiquitie doth call the making of Christes bodie) the same power is in such not amisse both termed a kind of marke or character and acknowledged to be indeleble. Minsiteriall power is a mark of separation, because it severeth them that have it from other men and maketh them a special *order* consecrated unto the service of the most high in thinges wherewith others may not meddle.... [W]hen wee take ordination wee also receive the presence of the holy Ghost partlie to guide direct and strengthen us in all our waies, and partlie to assume unto itself for the more authoritie those actions that apperteine to our place and calling.... Whether wee preach, pray, baptise, communicate, condemne, give absolution, or whatsoever, as disposers of Gods misteries, our wordes, judgmentes, actes, and deedes, are not ours but the holie Ghostes.[126]

It is within this Dionysian context that a presbyter is 'he unto whome our Savior Christ hath communicated the power of spirituall procreation' and that a bishop is 'the Image of God and of Christ' as well as 'like unto an angel'.[127] Dionysian hierarchy elevates the bishop into a particularly important mediatory role: 'the apostles peculiar charge was to publish the gospel of Christ unto all nations, and to deliver them his ordinances received by immediate revelation from himself', a role filled 'afterwardes in stead of Apostles [by] Bishops'.[128]

---

[124] Mohamed, 'Renaissance Thought on the Celestial Hierarchy', 559–82. See also: Peter Marshall and Alexandra Walsham (eds), *Angels in the Early Modern World* (Cambridge: Cambridge University Press, 2006), ch. 1; and Feisal Mohamed, *In the Anteroom of Divinity: The Reformation of the Angels from Colet to Milton*. (Toronto: University of Toronto Press, 2008), ch. 2.
[125] Hooker, *Laws*, 1:275.21–4; IV.1.3, emphasis in the original. On the role of the Holy Spirit in ministry, see Simut, 'Orders of Ministry', 406–7.
[126] Hooker, *Laws*, 2:425.14–430.22; V.77.2–8.
[127] Ibid., 2:439.27–9; V.78.3.
[128] Ibid., 2:440.7–9; 2:446.7–8; V.78.4; V.78.9.

Accordingly, the architecture of participation and its grammar coherently and systematically informs and structures Hooker's ecclesiology throughout the *Laws*. The idea of the visible Church as a political body bound by positive as well as divine law does not evacuate it of divine agency, reducing it or its bishops merely into being a locus of repressive temporal authority. Rather, the political character of the visible Church ennobles it and its orders as a creative co-participant in the unfolding of the eternal law in the world and the contiguous desire to participate in God. As such, the visible intersects with the mystical and, just as 'grace hath use of nature' and 'nature hath need of grace', so too does the natural Church prove of use to, as well as having need of, the supernatural Church. Charles Miller rightly notes, therefore, that Hooker's use of the 'visible' and 'mystical' couplet attempts to 'recapture the dynamism found in, say, Augustine and Aquinas, for whom the church, while a concrete reality in time and space, is chiefly defined in – for a lack of better words – invisible terms'.[129] Yet, pace Miller and Lake, such an ecclesiology represents neither a departure from Continental Reformed orthodoxy nor an attempt to locate the Church of England as some kind of via media between Geneva and Rome.[130] The grammar of participation allows Hooker to weave a tapestry of claims that distinguish between (as well as clearly relate) the natural and supernatural, the visible and the mystical or invisible, in accordance with magisterial Reformed assumptions about the Church, as well as scholastic concepts about causality that suspend creation from divine influence. Such participatory grammar simultaneously humanizes and sacralizes the reformed Church of England. The visible Church is a mediatory, penultimate and historically contingent institution open to creative variety and change. It is also a participant in the providential and ultimate *ratio* of God, the end of which is heavenly union and the present of which is temporal authority. As James Turrell puts it, 'as the Body of Christ, the Christian assembly took on a mystical significance ... that transcended time and space.... Through the corporate body ... believers participated in communion with Christ himself.'[131]

'Lovingly dwell together in one subject': The grammar of royal supremacy

As with Hooker's ecclesiology, the grammar of participation informs and structures how Hooker defends the 'dominion' of lay ecclesiastical supremacy in Book Eight of the *Laws* against attacks from Roman Catholics and radical puritans. Although they represented strange bedfellows, both of these groups argued that lay ecclesiastical supremacy deviated from religious orthodoxy by stripping the Church of its autonomy and by setting up the monarch in place of Christ as the head of the Church.[132] Hooker summarizes the objections of his opponents as follows: 'unto no Civill Prince or

---

[129] Miller, *Vision of God*, 224.
[130] Ibid., 238. Compare Lake, *Anglicans & Puritans?*, 159–60.
[131] Turrell, 'Uniformity and Common Prayer', 357. Compare Kirby, 'Angels Descending and Ascending', 118–19.
[132] Hooker mentions Thomas More and Jean Calvin as respective representatives of the Catholic and Reformed Protestant opposition to the Henrician royal supremacy in *Laws*, 3:380.6–381.18; VIII.4.12.

Governour there may be given such power of Ecclesiastical Dominion as by the Lawes of this Land belongeth unto the Supreme Regent thereof.'[133] Through the grammar of participation, Hooker unfolds both the distinction and union of the spiritual and the temporal regiments in the concrete human person, and particularly in the person of the monarch as hierarch.[134] First, as Kirby has shown, Hooker uses the Chalcedonian logic of Christ's hypostatic union in order to distinguish between, but also connect, the Church and Commonwealth as aspects of a 'politique societie' in which both can 'lovingly dwell together in one subject', just as Christ's two distinct natures co-inhere in his person.[135] Such language allows Hooker to undercut the unequivocal, perpetual separation between Church and Commonwealth insisted on by his opponents, as well as their refusal of the title 'head' to anyone except Christ. For Hooker, 'headship' belongs to the monarch insofar as he or she analogically participates in Christ, to whom the title of 'head' properly belongs in an unrestricted sense as the primary, participated analogate. Second, as Kirby has also demonstrated, Hooker uses the two Platonisms of Augustinian immediacy and Dionysian mediation found in his system of laws in order to distinguish between Christ's authority and the monarch's power, but also to connect them since the monarch is 'God's lievtenant' and 'highest uncommanded Commander'.[136] Here, Hooker suggests that every separation forms a link. As in his account of episcopal orders, Hooker employs scholastic notions of God's prime causality, as well as the logic of desire, in order to portray the monarch as a mediatory divine hierarch who manuducts ('leads by the hand') society towards the common good and so to the participation of God.

This part considers these two features in turn: the opening half unpacks Hooker's use of Chalcedonian Christology in relation to lay ecclesiastical supremacy; the second half unpacks how Hooker portrays the monarch as a diminished, public, participatory analogue of God's *ratio* found perfectly in Christ as head of the Church. Through the grammar of participation, Hooker accordingly both deflates and elevates the terms of lay ecclesiastical supremacy, placing Christ as the key to unlock the relationship between visible and invisible political orders. On one hand, the power of the monarch shares in divine power in a subordinate sense, and as such should remain limited by law like all other creatures. On the other hand, however, the monarch is a divine hierarch or 'instrument' and 'subjection is due unto all such powers in as much as they are of God's owne institution even when they are of mans creation'.[137] On both sides, using 'grammatical' aspects of the architecture of participation developed in his metaphysics and epistemology, Hooker challenges the doctrinal orthodoxy, reformed credentials, and biblicism of his radical puritan opponents. The parameters of lay ecclesiastical supremacy follows an orthodox Chalcedonian Christology, immaculately respects reformed commitments to Luther's two regiments or Calvin's two fora, and derives its

---

[133] Ibid., 3:315.3–7; VIII.Title.
[134] See McGrade, 'The Coherence of Hooker's Polity', 176.
[135] Kirby, *Doctrine of the Royal Supremacy*, 51–2; 74–9. See also Kirby, *Reformer and Platonist*, 79–96.
[136] See Kirby, '"Law Makes the King"', 274–88. See also Kirby, 'From "General Mediations" to "Particular Decisions"', 41–63.
[137] Hooker, *Laws*, 3:398.25–8; VIII.6.9. Hooker here interprets Rom. 13.1.

authority or *cura religionis* ('oversight of religion') from natural and human law, rather than simply from divine law, as they share in eternal law.

As both Kirby and Bourdin comment, Hooker employs one particular feature of his grammar of participation in order to argue for a personal unity of Church and Commonwealth: namely, the logic of Chalcedonian Christology developed in Book Five that both distinguishes between Christ's human and divine natures, but also unites them as they co-inhere in Christ's person.[138] The analogous unity between the visible Church and Commonwealth as 'personallie one societie' in turn justifies that there is only one visible head over both, namely the monarch who wields lay ecclesiastical supremacy. As such, Hooker puts allegiance to the royal supremacy as a test of doctrinal orthodoxy consistent with the reformed ecclesiology he has already defended in earlier books of the *Laws*. The personhood of Christ forms the key by which Hooker unlocks the distinction but also the unity of invisible spiritual and visible secular power.

Hooker's political use of the Chalcedonian logic of distinction and union has, of course, a specific polemical purpose and context, responding directly to the earlier Elizabethan debates over the royal supremacy between Cartwright and Bishop John Whitgift in the Admonition Controversy of the 1570s.[139] The latter defended the title of 'head' as applied to the monarch governing the visible Church by appealing to the commonplace motif of reformed ecclesiology, namely, the distinction between 'spiritual regiment' (exclusively the invisible power of Christ 'reigning in the consciences of the faithful') and 'external regiment' (mediated by Christ's visible representatives).[140] The former figure, however, followed Calvin's criticism of the royal supremacy. Cartwright argued that civil and ecclesiastical spheres ought to remain separate, grounding his argument in the Chalcedonian distinction between Christ's two natures.[141] Cartwright employed this Chalcedonian distinction in order to distinguish perpetually between Church and Commonwealth, offering a doctrinal rationale for opposing lay ecclesiastical supremacy since the 'spirituall regiment' of Christ is identical with the so-called *Disciplina*, the outward form of the Church that can suffer no other head than Christ.[142] Cartwright opposed Whitgift's 'absurde distinction' between inner and outer fora that seemed to 'overthrowe this doctrine that Christe alone is Head of his Church' by allowing the monarch to have authority over the external regiment of the Church. Cartwright penned:

---

[138] Kirby, *Doctrine of the Royal Supremacy*, 51–2; 74–9; Bourdin, *Theological-Political Origins*, 30–44. See also Eppley, 'Royal Supremacy', 516–17.

[139] Kirby, *Doctrine of the Royal Supremacy*, 54–8; 98–105. Kirby convincingly argues that Hooker depends upon and takes up unresolved issues from the Admonition Controversy. See also W. J. T. Kirby, '*Supremum Caput*: Richard Hooker's Theory of Ecclesiastical Dominion', *Dionysius* 12 (1988): 69–110.

[140] Whitgift, *Works*, 2:83–4.

[141] Hooker references Calvin's complaint, seeing it as misinformed, in *Laws*, 3:380.23–381.4; VIII.4.12, also cited by Thomas Cartwright, *The Second Replie of Thomas Cartwright against Maister Doctor Whitgiftes Second Answer, Touching the Church Discipline*. (Heidelberg: Michael Schirat, 1575), 2:414. Compare Calvin, *Commentaries on the Twelve Minor Prophets*, trans. John Owen, 5 vols. (Edinburgh: Calvin Translation Society, 1844–59), 2:349–50.

[142] See Whitgift, *Works*, 2:82 and Cartwright, *The Second Replie*, 2:411, referenced in Hooker, *Laws*, 3:357.10–28; VIII.4.2.

> The other faulte of this distinction is / that yt confoundeth and shuffleth together the authoritie of our Saviour Christ / as he is the sonne off God onely before all worldes / coequall with his father: with that which he hath gyven off his father and which he exerciseth in respecte he is mediator betwene God and us. For in the governement off the church / and superiorytie over the officers off it / our Saviour Christ himselfe hath a superior / which is his father: but in the governement off kingdoms / and other commonwealths / and in the superiority which he hath over kings / and judges / he hath no superior / but immediate authoritie with his father. Therfore the mouldinge upp off the two estates / and governementes together / is to lay the foundations of many errors.[143]

For Cartwright, just as Christ's sovereignty is distinguished in a twofold manner (qua his humanity and qua his divinity), so too must the Church and Commonwealth be separated. Cartwright roots the perpetual separation in the double function of Christ. On one hand, Christ rules the Church as Son of Man and Redeemer, meaning through his humanity 'subordinate to the Father'. On the other hand, the Commonwealth receives its rule from Christ as the Son of God, consubstantial and 'coequall with his Father and the Holy Spirit'. Cartwright held that the 'externall governement off Christ in his church is spirituall', fusing the outward polity of the Church with Christ's direct authority as Redeemer, precluding lay ecclesiastical supremacy since that would seem to abrogate Christ's spiritual regiment.[144] Cartwright simultaneously reifies the two regiments in such a way that the visible Church becomes a sacralized political institution alongside or in place of natural political communities, but also that natural political community such as the Commonwealth becomes 'de-Christianised', as Kirby puts it.[145] Cartwright and his puritan allies strangely advocate, in the pithy words of Littlejohn, both an 'overreaching biblicism and [an] incipient secularism'.[146]

Hooker's response to Cartwright expands that of Whitgift in the Admonition Controversy but seizes on the participatory grammar of Chalcedonian Christology developed in Book Five of the *Laws* as the singular key to unlock the right, reformed relationship between the spiritual and the external regiments or inner and outer fora in the political and ecclesial realms. For Hooker, Cartwright's political Christology brings his opponents close to a form of political and ecclesiological Nestorianism, which viewed the Incarnation merely as a moral union of 'two persons linked in amity'.[147] It also violates the reformed distinctions between inner and outer fora, spiritual and temporal regiments, which nevertheless enjoy a real participatory relationship. The participatory textures of visible and invisible, spiritual and temporal, so key to Hooker's reformed ecclesiology, re-emerge in his account of the royal supremacy over the visible Church. The participatory grammar of distinction and union allows him both to defend and also to define lay ecclesiastical supremacy as contingent and penultimate, but also as the providential mediation of, and participation in, the invisible authority of Christ.

---

[143] Cartwright, *The Second Replie*, 2:411–414.
[144] Ibid., 2:410, 417.
[145] Kirby, *Doctrine of the Royal Supremacy*, 106.
[146] Littlejohn, *Peril and Promise*, 194.
[147] See Hooker, *Laws*, 2:212–13; V.52.2 for Hooker's account of Nestorius.

In this regard, Hooker's political vision clearly exhibits a systematic homology with his architecture of participation and its grammar established in earlier books of the *Laws*.

Hooker responds to Cartwright in Book Eight of the *Laws* by turning the doctrinal tables on him and, by extension, the radical puritans en masse. As Hooker puts it, the radical puritans object that, by exercising supremacy over the visible Church, 'kings, being meer lay persons... exceed the lawfull boundes of their calling', therefore arguing for a 'necessarie separation perpetuall and personal between the *Church* and *Commonwealth*'.[148] Yet, for Hooker, those who oppose lay ecclesiastical supremacy, supposing it entails no limits on royal dominion or subjection to God, are 'brainsick'. Hooker therefore pragmatically defines what 'Church' and 'Commonwealth' mean in the case of a Christian nation. Hooker's account recalls the Chalcedonian logic of separation and union recounted in Book Five, as well as the ecclesiology of Book Seven and its distinctions between visible and invisible, inner and outer, spiritual and temporal. While he grants that Church and Commonwealth are 'thinges in nature the one distinguished from the other', he goes on to describe their personal unity in the English context:

> [T]he name of a *Church* importeth only a *Societie* of men first united into some publique forme of regiment and secondly distinguished from other *Societies*, by the vertue of *Christian* religion ... [S]eeing there is not any man of the *Church of England*, but the same man is also a member of the *Commonwealth*, nor any man a member of the *Commonwealth* which is not also of the *Church of England*, therefore as in a figure *triangular* the base doth differ from the sides thereof, and yet one and the self same line, is both a base and also a side; a side simplie, a base if it chance to be the bottome and underlie the rest: So albeit properties and actions of one kinde doe cause the name of a Commonwealth, qualities and functions of an other sort the name of a *Church* to be given unto a multitude, yet one and the self same multitude may in such sort be both and is so with us, that no person appertaining to the one can be denied to be also of the other.[149]

Hooker distinguishes between Church and Commonwealth, but denies that they need to be (or in fact are) essentially and perpetually separated.[150] The difference between the two (one defined by true religion, the other by a certain political arrangement) remains accidental, 'and such accidentes as may and should always lovingly dwell together in one subject.'[151] Indeed, the Church and Commonwealth co-inhere in every English subject.[152] Both Church and Commonwealth therefore share the Aristotelian telos of rightly ordering community towards the common good. To a far greater degree

---

[148] Ibid., 3:317.21–318.2; VIII.1.2.
[149] Ibid., 3:319.6–27; VIII.1.2, emphasis in the original.
[150] Hooker follows Stephen Gardiner's *De Vera Obedientia* (1535) in casting Church and Commonwealth as a personal unity in the reformed English context. See Rosenthal, *Crown Under Law*, 100–3.
[151] Hooker, *Laws*, 3:325.1–326.10; VIII.1.5.
[152] Ibid., 3:318.21–6; VIII.1.2.

than Aristotle, however, Hooker makes religion the primary duty of politics since the aim of any society

> is not simplie to live, nor the duetie so much as to provide for life as for meanes of living well, and that even as the soule is the worthier part of man, so humane societies are much more to care for that which tendeth properly unto the soules estate then for such temporall thinges as this life doth stand in need of.[153]

Church and Commonwealth are 'in this case personallie one societie' living under various laws and with a complex web of dependency and interaction.[154] As such, Hooker employs one grammatical feature of his architecture of participation (the logic of Chalcedonian Christology) in order to lay the basis for the royal supremacy and its authority in the external, temporal regiment of the Church. To oppose the order of such supremacy is, for Hooker, tantamount to sedition since 'out of such division [follows] inevitable destruction'.[155]

Hooker responds, after such prolegomena, to the particular theological objections against the 'title of Headship which we give to the kings of England in relation unto the church'.[156] For Cartwright, the title could only belong to Christ through his priestly, mediatorial function as Son of Man. In response, however, Hooker employs the participatory grammar of Chalcedonian Christology in order to defuse Cartwright's doctrinal objections, offering a nuanced, coherent and orthodox account of royal ecclesiastical dominion. Following Whitgift, Hooker distinguishes between 'two kindes of power', namely the 'external regiment' of the visible Church and the 'secret inward influence of grace', thereby maintaining the reformed distinction between the visible and invisible kingdoms.[157] Yet, within his architecture of participation, every separation remains a link. Hooker qualifies the title of headship by reminding his readers that while it only belongs by nature to Christ as head of the Church,[158] the monarch can participate in that headship as a diminished similitude who differs in order, measure and kind from Christ, just as Christ's human nature enjoys union with the divine nature while remaining distinctly human.[159] Here, Hooker (building on Whitgift's account in the Admonition Controversy) immaculately maintains the sense of Luther's two regiments or Calvin's two fora. More broadly, the relationship of the civil magistrate to the source of divine authority also recalls, of course, the basic relationship that obtains between a participant with that which it participates in: an effect participates in its cause and exhibits a diminished and dependent similitude to that cause. Hooker distinguishes headship in terms of order, measure and kind, but

---

[153] Ibid., 3:321.7–13; VIII.1.4.
[154] Ibid., 3:323.16–23; VIII.1.4. Compare ibid., 3:325.25–326.5; VIII.1.5.
[155] Ibid., 3:331.11–13; VIII.2.1.
[156] Ibid., 3:356.19-358.17; VIII.4.1–2. Hooker could have, of course, simply defended the Elizabethan title of 'supreme Governor' but chooses the more provocative Henrician title of 'Supreme Head' in order to show that what is really at stake is the notion of secular political authority: the puritans would deny not only the title but any kind of lay supremacy over the visible Church.
[157] Ibid., 3:362.4–263.6; 3:374.6–376.6; VIII.4.5; VIII.4.8.
[158] Ibid., 3:357.27–9; 3:377.11–28; VIII.4.2; VIII.4.9.
[159] Ibid., 3:359.16–361.13; VIII.4.3–4.5.

sees the civil magistrate as a participant in Christ's headship. In terms of order Christ suffers no subordination, 'whereas the power which others have is subordinated unto his'. In terms of measure, there is not 'any kinde of lawe which tyeth him [i.e. Christ] but his own proper will and wisedome; his power is absolute'. In contrast, monarchs are restrained by external laws and geographical limits in ecclesiastical headship, even though 'the largnes of power wherin neither man nor Angell can be matched or compared with him'.[160] Finally, in terms of kind, Christ exercises the immediate, internal and spiritual headship over the Church (visible and mystical), whereas the monarch forms the mediate, visible and external power to order the visible Church. Using a Platonic image, Christ remains the unitive 'fountaine of sense, of motion, the throne where the guide of the soule doth raign, the court from whence direction of all thinges humane proceedeth'.[161]

In measure, order and kind, therefore, royal headship participates in and mediates Christ's headship like an effect from its cause, but remains fundamentally distinct, just as created laws share in the eternal law, or just as Christ's human nature unites with but remains distinct from his divine nature. Christ is the participatory origin and animator of human life; the king, whatever his temporal headship, remains penultimate to the unfolding and eternal rule of Christ, as does the visible Church.[162] Thus, there are two kinds of dominion: that of Christ as the primary analogate or the 'fountaine of life' and 'welspringe of spiritual blessings'; and that of monarchs who, as analogues of Christ, are 'his principall instrumentes for the *Churches* outward government'.[163] In what Kirby labels as an 'irenical gesture', Hooker distinguishes between two modes of 'spirituall regiment': the inward, invisible and direct authority of Christ 'in his own person'; and the outward, visible and mediated power of those given charge of the temporal Church through Christ's 'influence'.[164] The first distinction appeals to the puritan notion of Christ's singular authority, while the latter sees the outer forum or regiment as distinct from, but contained within and permitted by, the spiritual regiment of Christ.

Hooker's grammar of participation, especially the Chalcedonian logic of Christ's two natures, allows him to rebut and rebound puritan attacks on the royal supremacy, casting their argument as a heterodox development that divides Christ's sovereignty. Hooker describes the doctrinal assumptions underneath Cartwright's attacks as follows:

> Of the *Church* he [i.e. Christ] is *Head* and governour only as the sonne of man, *Head* and governour over *Kingdomes* only as the sonne of God. In the *Church* as

---

[160] Ibid., 3:361.8–362.3; VIII.4.5.
[161] Ibid., 3:362.7–9; VIII.4.5. Hooker bases the images from Plato's 'Timaeus' (362.g) about how a body is constituted out of the head.
[162] Hooker, *Laws*, 3:363.7–364.4; VIII.4.6: 'First that as *Christ* being Lord or *Head* over all doth by vertue of that Soveraigntie rule all, so he hath no more a superior in governing his *Church* then in exercising soveraigne Dominion upon the rest of the world besides. Secondly, that all authoritie as well civill as Ecclesiastical is subordinate unto his: And thirdly that the *Civill Magistrate* being termed *Head* . . . it followeth that he is an *Head* even subordinated of and to *Christ*', emphasis in the original.
[163] Ibid., 3:374.10–14; VIII.4.8.
[164] Kirby, *Doctrine of the Royal Supremacy*, 56–7. See Hooker, *Laws*, 3:377.3–10; VIII.4.9.

man he hath officers under him, which Officers are *Ecclesiastical* persons. As for the Civill Magistrate his office belongeth unto *Kingdomes* and Commonwealthes, neither is he therein an under or subordinate *Head of Christ* considering that his authoritie commeth from God simplie and immediately even as our *Saviour Christs* doth.[165]

For Hooker, Cartwright and the radical puritans mistakenly separate out the ecclesial and political spheres, the former receiving authority from Christ as human, and the latter immediately from the divine nature. Since this is the doctrinal basis for the argument against lay ecclesiastical supremacy, Hooker immediately attacks these divisions. He argues that Cartwright here introduces a form of subordinationism into the Trinity and a form of Nestorianism into his Christology, producing an unwarranted division of divine activity and of Christ's two natures:

> In what Evangelist, Apostle, or Prophett is it found, that *Christ Supreme Governour of the Church* should be so unequall to himself as he is supreme Governour of *Kingdomes*? . . . Surely if *Christ as God and man have ordayned certaine meanes for the gathering and keeping of his Church* . . . it must in reason follow I think that as *God* and *man* he worketh in *Church* regiment . . . . [T]here is no remedie but to acknowledg it a manifest errour that *Christ* in the government of the world is equall unto the Father but not in the government of the *Church*.[166]

According to Hooker, Cartwright distorts Trinitarian dogma by making Christ subordinate to the Father in relation to the Church, and he rigidly separates Christ's two natures. Upholding Calvin's distinctions between the kingly, priestly and prophetic roles on Christ, Hooker locates Cartwright's principal error as a confusion of the first two of these offices.[167] As such, 'dominion' of any kind belongs to Christ's kingly office, and Christ exercises dominion in the unity of his person rather than simply through one or the other of his natures. For Hooker, in both the visible Church and the Commonwealth, authority is 'from God' but 'mediately through Christ' and with 'subordination to Christ' such that 'Christ hath supreme dominion over the whole universal world'. Christ's universal headship indissolubly encompasses both his divine and human natures. The differences in order, measure and kind between the monarch's and Christ's headship do not lessen the real relationship between visible secular power and its invisible divine approbation. In fact, the unity of Christ's natures logically implies the universality of his power. Since visible structures mediates that invisible power, the nature of ecclesiastical dominion (and who wields it) becomes the next issue for Hooker to explore.

Indeed, maintaining Luther's distinction between spiritual and temporal regiments, as well as Calvin's separation between inner and outer fora, Hooker explores how Christ's

---

[165] Hooker, *Laws*, 3:363.9–22; VIII.4.6.
[166] Ibid., 3:366.10–367.6; VIII.4.6, emphasis in the original.
[167] Ibid., 3:364.26–365.3; VIII.4.6. Compare Calvin, *Institutes*, 2.14.1; 15.1–6. See Kirby, '*Supremum Caput*', 98–100.

government remains invisible and so requires external, mediatory government because his human nature is not ubiquitous. Recalling the rejection of Lutheran accounts about the ubiquity of Christ's physical presence in Book Five, Hooker reminds his readers that although Christ is 'spiritually alwayes united unto every part of his body which is the Church', his 'corporall presence is removed as farr as heaven from earth is distant'.[168] In Book Five, however, Hooker also argues that, even though it is not ubiquitous, since Christ's body 'is presently joyned unto deitie' it also has 'presence of force and efficacie throughout all generations of men' and is 'infinite in possibilitie of application'.[169] The sacraments therefore form a mediated immediacy, a mediatory but necessary and external cooperation with divine grace. Similarly, in Book Eight the structures and forms of political life, though contingent, participate in a nuanced manner in Christ. Hooker here appeals to something like the so-called *extra calvinisticum*, the distinction between the Word incarnate and the eternal Word. Just as '*Christ* touching visible and corporall presence is removed as far as heaven from earth is distant', such distance requires a 'visible and corporall' subordinate who mediates in some diminished form Christ's spiritual authority.[170] So, 'visible government is a thing necessarie for the *Church*' and '*Heads* indued with supreme power unto a certain compasse are for the exercise of visible regiment not unncessarie'.[171] Yet, since such power is external, it is also limited, provisional, dependent on, and distinct from Christ's immediate, internal rule: 'We doe not therefore vainly imagine but truly and rightly discerne a power externall and visible in the *Church* exercised by men and severed in nature from that *spirituall* power of Christes own regiment'.[172] The monarch as visible spiritual head becomes Christ's 'principal instrument', participating like any secondary cause or instrument in divine providence. Crucially, unlike the radical puritans, Hooker includes the administration of 'the word, sacraments, and discipline' as constituents of the external polity of the Church, giving the monarch responsibility for such matters under human law, such as was established in the Henrician and Elizabethan Acts of Supremacy. The magistrate's *cura religionis* derives from and shares in Christ's spiritual regiment without being identical to it or requiring explicit scriptural mandate. As such, the ecclesiastical dominion of the monarch is one thread in a vast participatory tapestry that reveals the manifold ways creation shares in God. As Kirby puts it, 'the two regiments are invisibly unified in Christ, their source; they are visibly unified through the royal supremacy'.[173]

Hooker's doctrinal defence of lay ecclesiastical supremacy shows, then, two crucial features. First, his political vision displays a close logical connection between the metaphysical 'mini-treatise' of Book Five and the political concerns of Book Eight, suggesting the systematic role of gesture and order across the *Laws*. Second, the role of participation in particular remains central in establishing such homology: the participatory grammar of Chalcedonian Christology gives Hooker clear doctrinal grounds to justify lay ecclesiastical supremacy and chart out what he sees as the proper

---

[168] Hooker, *Laws*, 3:370.18–23; VIII.4.7.
[169] Ibid., 2:233.28–30; 2:234.7–10; V.55.8–9.
[170] Ibid., 3:370.18–23; VIII.4.7, emphasis in the original.
[171] Ibid., 3:370.23–371.4; VIII.4.7, emphasis in the original.
[172] Ibid., 3:378.8–11; VIII.8.9, emphasis in the original.
[173] Kirby, *Doctrine of the Royal Supremacy*, 113.

reformed orthodox relationship between the two reigns of Luther's thought or two fora of Calvin's theology. The unity of Christ's person under the formula of Chalcedon allows Hooker to distinguish in order to unite. The universal dominion exercised by the unity of Christ's distinct natures analogously suspends the monarch's dominion over the visible Church from its transcendent origin. The monarch subordinately and provisionally mediates the immediate spiritual dominion of Christ. Although Hooker sets out to undermine Cartwright's theological credibility as a reformed thinker, he also offers a sound doctrinal basis for, as well as an irenic call to support, lay ecclesiastical supremacy through the established commitments of patristic, conciliar and Reformed orthodoxy acknowledged by all Elizabethan reformed groups. Once again, Christ is the key to Hooker's thought in this regard.

Hooker goes even further in Book Eight of the *Laws* and argues that lay ecclesiastical supremacy is not merely doctrinally sound but also exhibits a providential fittingness to which obedience is due for the common good. Indeed, monarchs under law work as godly hierarchs, acting as 'Godes Livetenantes' and God's 'principall instrumentes' in the visible political realm. This high evaluation in Book Eight of the monarch's dominion and status occasions, however, the modern critical allegations of inconsistency and incoherency in Hooker's thought outlined in the introduction to this chapter. In Book Eight of the *Laws*, the argument goes, Hooker strains to square the historical political contingencies of the Tudor world with his legal ontology. In this line of criticism, a kind of 'Tudor Averroism' in Book Eight replaces Hooker's earlier Thomistic commitment to the rule of law with a kind of Marsilian political voluntarism where the will of the Crown becomes law and the monarch properly controls the governance of the national church by 'divine right' in lay ecclesiastical supremacy. Yet, the presence of two grammatical aspects of the architecture of participation in Book Eight deflates such accusations, revealing a kind of homology between Hooker's political vision and the epistemological and ecclesiological commitments of Books Three and Seven in particular. As such, the *Laws* remains a coherent whole. Just as he appeals to the grammar of participation in order to undercut the radical puritans' doctrinal opposition to the royal supremacy, Hooker also rejects their biblicism through reformed scholastic notions of causality and the logic of desire drawn from the same grammar. Hooker casts lay ecclesiastical supremacy as the result of natural law mediated through the changeable contingencies of human law and history. Hooker employs reformed scholastic notions of causality in order to describe how visible human political agents can be said to be creative participants in the invisible power of God. The human political agent is a homo faber, a fabricating animal whose public laws and figures are 'instruments to work by', caught up in the work of God but also dependent upon it as their ultimate cause and fulfilment. The Neoplatonic return to God (*reditus*) is no mere passive act. Far from emptying agency from the created 'middle' between creative exit and redemptive reversion, Hooker implicitly follows the Proclean Neoplatonic structure of *monē-proodos-epistrophē* that honours the suspended middle between exit and return. If *monē* and *monos* describes the unitary source of emanation, and *epistrophē* describes the reversion of the many to the One, then the *proodos* identifies the rise of every being into its own determinate being. As such, the *proodos* describes the dynamic sharing of the many in the productive capacity of the *monos*. Just as was the case with Hooker's defence of episcopal orders, lay ecclesiastical supremacy can be seen to be contingent and yet caught up in the providential texture of history, lending a sense of fittingness but not necessity. Indeed, the logic of desire in the architecture of participation sets the monarch as a divine agent or hierarch guiding, alongside bishops, the political fulfilment of temporal and spiritual goods in the Commonwealth.

As André Gazal persuasively argues, before the legal ontology of Hooker's *Laws* cut through the stranglehold of biblicism, both conformist apologists and radical puritans were typically committed to the priority of Scripture in political discourse, emphasizing the warrant of scriptural arguments either for or against lay ecclesiastical supremacy.[174] Hooker's architecture of participation generates a profound shift in Book Eight of the *Laws* away from this common Elizabethan emphasis on biblical authority. The kind of philological and historical analysis developed in his participatory epistemology allows Hooker to dismiss any putative isomorphism of past and present employed by his puritan opponents, namely, their normative use of typological arguments about proper church and political order drawn from scriptural texts.[175] Hooker certainly begins Book Eight with appeals to scriptural narrative, but in Thomistic fashion argues from the convenience or fittingness (*ex convenientia*) of lay ecclesiastical supremacy shown therein rather than from any binding quality of divine law. Accordingly, Hooker lists David, Jehoshaphat, Hezekiah and Josiah as 'the patterne of which example the like power in causes *Ecclesiastical* is by the Laws of this Realme annexed unto the *Crowne*'.[176] The sole dominion of kings exhibited a public 'conveniencie' for the common good since 'the multitude of supreme commanders is troublesome' and '*No man* (sayth our Saviour) *can serve two masters*'.[177] The joining of civic and ecclesiastical powers in the royal supremacy followed the 'example or patterne' of Moses who 'deriving so great a part of his burden in government unto others did notwithstanding retained to himself universall supremacie'.[178] These scriptural examples or patterns have no regulative force in themselves, however, but simply lend aesthetic weight to the legality of the English Reformation.

Having relegated the biblicism of his radical puritan opponents in political discourse, Hooker's architecture of participation allows him to cast the positive human laws that established the royal supremacy both as contingently mutable and yet also as sharing in divine wisdom, 'which shineth in the bewtifull varietie of all things, but most in the manifold and yet harmonious dissimilitude of those ways, whereby his Church upon earth is guided from age to age.'[179] Hooker again puts to play scholastic notions, whereby secondary acts depend upon the primary causality

---

[174] André Gazal, *Scripture and Royal Supremacy in Tudor England* (Lewiston, Queenston, Lampeter: Edwin Mellen Press, 2013), 495–519.
[175] See Shuger, *Habits of Thought*, 30–5.
[176] Hooker, *Laws*, 3:316.9–317.21; VIII.1.1–2.
[177] Ibid., 3:350.1–2; VIII.3.4, emphasis in the original.
[178] Ibid., 3:350.11–19; VIII.3.5. See Paul Dominiak, 'Moses the Magistrate: The Mosaic Theological Imaginary of John Jewel and Richard Hooker in Elizabethan Apologetics', in *Defending the Faith: John Jewel and the Elizabethan Church*, ed. Angela Ranson, André Gazal and Sarah Bastow (University Park: Pennsylvania State University Press, 2018), 161–82.
[179] Hooker, *Laws*, 1:253.15–20; III.11.8.

of God insofar as they participate in God. Just as with his defence of episcopal orders, Hooker therefore has an exalted but historically grounded conception of monarchy. Hooker argues that neither monarchy nor lay ecclesiastical supremacy are necessary or commanded by Scripture, but are rather historically contingent.[180] Monarchy and the royal supremacy emerge out of particular human arrangements, and human positive law remains competent to make a political order suitable for its variable contexts, a position entirely compatible with his account of human freedom to make laws of polity in Books One and Three.[181] As with episcopal orders, however, God ratifies the fitting benefits of monarchy and so, through a providential *communicatio idiomatum*, authors it:

> That the Christian world should be ordered by kingly regiment, the law of God doth not any where command; and yet the law of God doth give them right, which once are exalted to that estate, to exact at the hands of their subjects general obedience in whatsoever affairs their power may serve to command. So God doth ratify the works of that sovereign authority which kings have received by men.[182]

All authority comes from God (directly or otherwise) and so civic magistrates share in God's power and authority.[183] Thus, English Christians have historically 'condescended unto [monarchy] for their own most behoof and securitie', but God ratifies that consent as providential. The same dynamic holds true for lay ecclesiastical supremacy: Scripture does not dictate that all monarchs should or should not have it, but when monarchs are lawfully granted such dominion, 'we by the law of God stand bound meekly to acknowledg them for *Godes Livetnenates*'. For Hooker, even if (following Aristotle) human beings are naturally social, government is nevertheless a product of artifice, a matter of human positive law which, as it variably shares in eternal law, also can be said to participate in God despite its contingency. Hooker hereby sacralizes the practical law-making capacity of human societies. Human beings make positive human laws through using their rational faculties which participate in God, rendering them as not only made in the *imago dei* but as homo faber, co-creative participants in God's Wisdom, the divine *Logos* who is 'that law which hath been the pattern to make, and is the card to guide the world by'. As such, the royal supremacy, as it exhibits the scholastic notion of fittingness or 'conveniency', also displays the Thomistic aesthetic notion of how contingency relates to transcendence, or of how history unveils providence. The legal character of the royal supremacy demonstrates an aesthetic fittingness in accordance with the rational character of eternal law. Accordingly, it shares in the binding character of divine wisdom, refusing the Catholic and Puritan objections to its legitimacy.

By suspending the royal supremacy from God's influence with such participatory cords, Hooker develops a nascent constitutionalism, meaning that Book Eight acts as 'a crucial bridge between medieval and modern political theory', as Alexander Rosenthal

---

[180] Ibid., 3:335.5–9; VIII.2.5.
[181] Ibid., 3:334.13–28; VIII.2.5. Compare ibid., 1:100.16–19 ; 1:236.3–8; I.10.4; III.9.1.
[182] Ibid., 3:336.9–15; VIII.3.1.
[183] Ibid., 3:335.2–4; VIII.2.5.

suggests.[184] Pace Munz and Kearney, Hooker's participatory account of law, consent and the compact of sovereignty put him in marked contrast to contemporary proponents of royal absolutism like Hadrian Saravia or Jean Bodin. Instead, Hooker here stands in continuity with the medieval and reformed English tradition of legal constitutionalism, including figures like Henry Bracton, Sir John Fortescue, Christopher St Germain and Sir Thomas Smith.[185] More surprisingly, he also finds sympathetic allies in the early modern Spanish scholastic school of Salamanca (including Francisco Suàrez, Luis de Molina, Thomas de Vitoria and Domingo de Soto) that advanced constitutional Thomistic models of government against the emergent absolutists.[186] For Hooker, the rule of the monarch derives its legitimacy from historic consent, depends upon a social compact with the entire body politic, and is limited by the species of laws that participate in eternal law, as developed in Book One.[187] As such, monarchical authority is rationally limited from above by God and eternal law, as well as from below by the body politic since sovereignty belongs to the community as a whole. Such dependency both subordinates and subjects the monarch to God (through eternal law) and the visible body politic (through the species of laws participating in eternal law).[188] After celebrating in chapter six of Book Eight the legislative competence of Parliament and Convocation which historically and personally represent the entire body politic, Hooker writes in chapter eight in relation to the Crown's dominion:

> What power the *King* hath he hath it by law, the boundes and limites of it are knowne. The entire communitie giveth generall order by law how all things publiquely are to be done and the *King* as head thereof the highest in authoritie over all causeth according to the same lawe every particuler to be framed and ordered thereby. The whole body politique maketh laws which laws give power unto the *King* and the *King* having bound himself to use according unto lawe that power, it so falleth out that the execution of the one is accomplished by the other in most religious and peaceable sort.[189]

Hooker therefore defends a version of royal supremacy grounded and limited under law, as A. S. McGrade notes.[190] The monarch as hierarch is subsumed by the hierarchical superiority of the whole body politic and its variegated species of laws suspended from God through participation in eternal law. Hooker strings together a

---

[184] Rosenthal, *Crown under Law*, 84, 103–11. See also: Lake, *Anglicans & Puritans?*, 201–12; O'Donovan, *Law and Authority*, 43–54, 67–80, 129–54; John E. Booty, 'Book V', in *FLE*, 6 (1): 244–6; and A. S. McGrade, 'Book VIII', in *FLE*, 6 (1): 358–9, 364–75.

[185] For an account comparing Hooker's genealogy to accounts of royal absolutism, and their divergence, see Harold J. Berman, *Law and Revolution II. The Impact of the Protestant Reformations on the Western Legal Tradition* (Cambridge: Belknap Press, 2003), 231–48.

[186] Rosenthal, *Crown under Law*, 110.

[187] See Hooker, *Laws*, 1:99.13–27; 1:103.21–7; 1:106.24–9; 1:136.4–15; 1:139.13–26; I.10.4; I.10.8; I.10.11; I.16.2; I.16.5. See Littlejohn, *Peril and Promise*, 181–4, 187–8 on consent and government as a corporate exercise of reason.

[188] Hooker, *Laws*, 3:339.4–9; VIII.2.9.

[189] Ibid., 3:434.23–435.4; VIII.8.9.

[190] McGrade, 'Classical, Patristic, and Medieval Sources', 77–82. See Eccleshall, 'Richard Hooker and the Peculiarities of the English', 63–117.

series of allusive statements drawn (or rewritten) from classical, patristic and medieval sources to support this legal vision: from the Hellenistic Stobæus, 'Happier that people, whose lawe is their *King* in the greatest thinges then that whose *King* is himself their law';[191] from St Ambrose, '*Kings* have dominion to exercise in *Ecclesiastical* causes but according to the lawes of the *Church*';[192] and from the medieval jurist Henry Bracton, '*The King is major singulis universis minor*', '*attribuat Rex Legi quod Lex attribuit ei potestam et Dominum*', '*Rex no debet esse sub homine, sed sub Deo et Lege*', and '*Lex facit Regem*'.[193] The power of the king is best limited such that the law guides and restrains the king (*lex facit regem*), rather than the king being the law. Echoing the notion from Book One that law is a rule (*regula*) and measure (*measura*) for right action, so is the 'power of the *King* over all and in all limited that unto all his proceedings the lawe itself is a rule'.[194] Therefore, 'limited power is best . . . [as] tyed unto the soundest and perfectest and most indifferent rule; which rule is the law'.[195] Since law has its metaphysical roots in the divine nature, Hooker remains clear that the visible political realm remains subject to God's dominion and order.

Hooker's architecture of participation entails, therefore, a constitutionally limited form of monarchy in which the monarch ought to serve the common good ('commonweal') as a godly hierarch under the system of laws that share in eternal law. Accordingly, the royal supremacy, whatever its providential contours, remains mediated through Parliament and Convocation – 'the very essence of all government within this kingdome' – and no ecclesiastical law can be made 'without consent of the highest power and under the guidance of Scripture and the General Councils'.[196] The spiritual dominion of the monarch is 'universall dominion, but with dependence upon that whole entier body over the severall partes whereof he hath dominion'.[197] Indeed, the co-inherence of Commonwealth and Church in the personal dominion of the monarch itself becomes parsed through the type of harmony envisaged by the legal metaphysics of participation of Book One:

> Where the *King* doth guide the state, and the lawe the *King*, that commonwealth is like an harpe or melodious instrument, the stringes whereof are tuned and handled all by one, following as lawes the rules and canons of Musicall science.[198]

In short, the monarch, though visible head of the Commonwealth and Church, remains (or should remain) at the service of the whole community for its common good. Indeed, in Aristotelian fashion, 'the end whereunto all government was instituted was

---

[191] Hooker, *Laws*, 3:341.25–342.1, emphasis in the original; VIII.2.12 (his own version of the Greek philosopher Archytas's dictum '*The king ruling by Lawe the magistrate following, the subject free and the whole society happie*' in ibid., 3:342.5–14.d; VIII.2.12), emphasis in the original.
[192] Ibid., 3:347.12–15; VIII.2.17, emphasis in the original.
[193] Ibid., 3:332.22–4; 3:342.19–21; 3:336.28–337.1; VIII.2.3; VIII.2.13; VIII.2.8, emphasis in the original.
[194] Ibid., 3:342.14–19; VIII.2.13.
[195] Ibid., 3:341.19–25; VIII.2.12. Compare ibid., 1:100.25–6; 1:102.22–33; I.10.5; I.10.8.
[196] Ibid., 3:348.9–18, 3:410.22–8, 3:393.8–11; VIII.3.3; VIII.6.14; VIII.6.7.
[197] Ibid., 3:336.26–8; VIII.3.2. Compare ibid., 1:96.16–23; I.10.1.
[198] Ibid., 3:342.2–3; VIII.2.12.

bonum publicum, the universal or common good' and 'the good which is proper unto each man belongeth to the common good of all as a part of the wholes perfection'.[199] The 'competent authoritie' of Parliament grounds the royal supremacy in legal consent, lending it the legitimacy but also the limits of a political form participating in eternal law. While lay ecclesiastical supremacy appeared within the contingencies of history, the implication remained clear: God loosely could be said to author and ratify it, just as much as episcopacy and monarchy, because it providentially shared in the *ratio* of eternal law.

Finally, in the remaining fifth through ninth chapters of Book Eight, Hooker explores the powers and prerogatives of the royal ecclesiastical supremacy within such nascent constitutionalism. The logic of desire found in the architecture of participation provides the grammar through which he parses such powers and prerogatives. Debora Shuger goes too far, therefore, when she insists that 'Hooker virtually never thinks of royal power as participation in the divine but as an authority able to constrain people to perform their duties'.[200] The opposite is true. Pace Shuger, Hooker does not simply separate out the mystical, inward, invisible, participatory, and private life of faith from the 'visible arenas of history and institutions' which are 'analyzed in terms of coercion, politics, contingency, and secondary causality' and 'no longer serve as carriers of ultimate value or signification'. Rather, the visible political regiment remains freighted with, and suspended from, divinity; that is to say, Hooker intimately nestles lay ecclesiastical supremacy within the architecture of participation. Whatever the limits ideally placed by law upon the monarch-in-parliament as the practical authority in the Church, Hooker emphasizes that the monarch nevertheless acts as participatory hierarch who, along with bishops, shapes and guides or manuducts social desires towards divine ends. As such, the monarch combines hierarchical and representative aspects.

On one hand, while Hooker rejects the notion that the monarch can 'participate that sanctified power [with] which God hath endued his clergy', he simply maintains the distinction drawn by John Jewel, his former patron and conformist hero. Jewel remained clear that the monarch did not have the power of orders (*potestas ordinis*), only the power of authority (*potestas jurisdictionis*) to see that religious duties 'be done, and orderly and truly done, by the bishops'.[201] Hooker concurs. Monarchs delegate civil coercive powers to bishops, but bishops remain jurisdictionally subordinate to monarchs. The proper relationship between sacerdotal and temporal power, then, is that monarchs should take counsel from clergy, especially on matters of piety and religion, and use their coercive power accordingly.[202] Yet, the monarch, rather than the clergy, has supreme visible dominion over how the Church exercises 'the word,

---

[199] Ibid., 3:349.19–25; VIII.3.4. See Gascoigne, 'Church and State Unified', 23–34.
[200] Shuger *Habits of Thought*, 136, 140–1.
[201] John Jewel, *The Works of John Jewel*, ed. John Ayre, 4 vols. (Cambridge: Cambridge University Press, 1845–50), 4:959. Sacred kingship made the distinction between *potestas ordinis* with *potestas jurisdictionis* a somewhat grey area even in the English Reformation. See Rémi Brague, *The Law of God: The Philosophical History of an Idea*, trans. Lydia Cochrane (Chicago: University of Chicago Press, 2007), 136–40. Also see Malcolm B. Yarnell, *Royal Priesthood in the English Reformation* (Oxford: Oxford University Press, 2013), 12, 41–84, 123–50.
[202] Hooker, *Laws*, 3:256.28–35, 3:354.14–355.4, 3:403.13–17 ; VII.18.5; VIII.3.4; VIII.6.11.

sacraments, and discipline'. As such, Hooker's polity is not crudely Erastian: royal dominion derives from the historic body politic below but also from God above; it includes and visibly represents voices from the Convocation of clergy as well as from divine law.

On the other hand, the provision of godly religion exists as the most important spiritual and political responsibility of the monarch for the common good since 'godliness' represents the 'welspring of all true virtues'. Hooker may refuse to the monarch any sacerdotal characteristics, but he certainly therefore sacralizes the monarch as a mediatory, visible analogue of God's invisible dominion in Christ. Hooker calls the monarch an 'uncommanded Commander' and 'general mover' in the body politic, evoking the Aristotelian and scholastic idea of God as First Mover. In a footnote appended to his discussion of monarchs as 'Godes Livetenantes' in the context of an exegesis of Rom. 13, Hooker quotes from Hellenistic passages where kingship is likened to divine kingship, as well as Henry Bracton's notion that the Crown is a power delegated by God.[203] Later in Book Eight, Hooker goes even further and sets the monarch above visible and invisible natural orders: within the geographical and legal limits of dominion, the sovereign enjoys 'the largnes of power wherin neither man nor Angell can be matched or compared with him'.[204] While Hooker certainly transmits a form of constitutionalism from the medieval to the modern period, he also appropriates within this commitment aspects of Hellenistic (especially Pythagorean) and Dionysian thought that stress a hierarchy of mediated power as well as the mystical likeness of human to divine kingship. Pace Frederick Beiser and Frank Furedi, then, who respectively charge that Hooker 'lapses into the kind of authoritarianism that he hoped to avoid' and cultivates the 'secularisation and politicisation of power' in the Elizabethan period, for Hooker the desirable natural public goods retain a transcendent orientation.[205] As such, the monarch does not merely concern him or herself with the temporal and material well-being of his or her subjects. Just as human nature has a hierarchy of natural, material and moral goods, all of which remain subordinate to the final spiritual participation of God, so too are the temporal perfections of the body politic penultimate and subordinate to the highest goods of religion. The monarch, as visible head of the body politic and guide of its political desires, therefore fosters two levels of participation. On a horizontal plane, the monarch as a mediatory hierarch nurtures a social ethos of mutuality and interdependency, otherwise known as the common good, through exercising dominion in the ecclesiastical polity. On a vertical plane, the monarch also has a duty to draw out and craft the inward cosmic draw to spiritual union with God through Christ in the visible *cura religionis*. These two aspects of Hooker's thought suggest, of course, that God ultimately suspends the horizontal political participation of the body politic and its pursuit of the common good from the vertical and final participation of the divine nature, rendering any notion of an autonomous secular politics impossible.

---

[203] Ibid., 3:335.s-t; VIII.2.5–6.
[204] Ibid., 3:361.14–362.3; VIII.4.5.
[205] Frederick Beiser, *The Sovereignty of Reason: The Defense of Rationality and the Early English Enlightenment* (Princeton, NJ: Princeton University Press, 1996), 83; Frank Furedi, *Authority: A Sociological History* (Cambridge: Cambridge University Press, 2013), 161.

'Under God and under the law': The two Platonisms of the ecclesiastical polity

This chapter has explored how, above all else, the controversies in the Elizabethan polity implied the relation between God and the world, addressing what transcendent source constituted the power of social institutions. As Debora Shuger sagely notes, 'such controversies inevitably centred on the question of participation – the mystical relation between the apparently separate.'[206] Far from desacralizing, however, episcopal orders and lay ecclesiastical supremacy, as Shuger suggests, Hooker freights them both with divinity, albeit by carefully limiting them as diminished and dependent analogues 'under God and under the law'. Indeed, the architecture of participation theonomously suspends creation from God as source and goal, including the visible political structures of the royal supremacy. As Kirby concludes, here 'Hooker anchors his elaborate exposition and defense . . . in a metaphysical theory of law which itself assumes a Neoplatonic ontology of "participation" in the Proclean tradition'.[207] In the Proclean tradition of participation, the highest cause remains the fundamental but non-competitive cause at work in every other secondary cause. Hooker regularly talks of 'God's influence', recalling the Neoplatonic notion of *influentia*, as that which underwrites and suspends all of creation. For Hooker, the unity of natures in Christ's divine personhood means that he personally influences everything, moving all of creation from within. Across the *Laws*, Christ forms the key who unlocks the distinct but related textures of nature and grace. As this chapter has shown, such divine influence undergirds episcopal orders and lay ecclesiastical supremacy, giving a Christological character to both as godly hierarchs, but also maintaining their visible authority as provisional and subordinate to Christ's absolute dominion. Through the grammar of the architecture of participation developed in earlier books of the *Laws*, Hooker remains able in the books of power to meticulously observe the reformed distinction between the two regiments or fora, grounding their distinction and unity in the unitary person and work of Christ.

As he distinguishes and relates lay and clerical power, Hooker turns full circle in the books of power to the first grammatical aspect of his architecture of participation developed in Books One and Five, namely the two Platonisms of Augustinian immediacy and Dionysian mediation. Hooker accordingly sets out, then, a deeply hierarchical view of political society, but one that participates in the immediacy of the eternal *ratio* by steps and degrees. He roots visible political order and the need for conformity in the Dionysian *lex divinitatis* [law of divinity]:

> Without order there is no living in publique societie, because the want thereof is the mother of confusion, whereupon division of necessitie followeth, and out of division inevitable destruction . . . For order is a graduall disposition. The whole world consisting of so partes so manie so different is by this one thing upheld,

---

[206] Shuger, *Habits of Thought*, 124.
[207] W. J. T. Kirby, *Persuasion and Conversion: Essays on Religion, Politics, and the Public Sphere in Early Modern England* (Leiden: Brill, 2013), 168.

he which framed them hath sett them in order. Yea the very deitie it self both keepeth and requireth for ever this to be kept as a law, that wheresoever there is a coagmentation of many, the lowest be knit to the highest by that which being interjacent may cause each to cleave unto other and so all continue one.[208]

Whereas in the traditional Dionysian *lex divinitatis*, temporal power ought to yield to the spiritual authority of the Church, Hooker radically inverts the relationship, refusing to sink the invisible forum of divine power into the visible regiment of spiritual association as he thinks his radical puritan and Catholic opponents do.[209] As such, Hooker gives one example of the Renaissance reaction against the Pope's claim to the *plenitudo potestatis* [plenitude of power] through the *lex divinitatis*, as well as the conformist critique of the radical puritans.[210] The result inverts the Catholic claim, investing the monarch with supreme dominion within the geographical boundaries of the Commonwealth. It also divests final authority from the visible Church, *contra* the radical puritans, framing the visible Church as subject to the external political order that is itself subordinate to, and dependent upon, God's ultimate power.

Yet, herein lies the root of the problem for interpreters of Hooker like Peter Munz. The Thomistic dispositive understanding of the *lex divinitatis* secures the priority of the Church over civil power, just as nature remains subordinate to grace. For Munz, Hooker's inversion of the *lex divinitatis* in Book Eight therefore contradicts the Thomistic legal ontology of Book One. In its place, Munz argues, Hooker embraces the thought of Marsilius of Padua in the *Defensor Pacis*, subordinating the Church to the secular powers in both religious and civic matters. Munz incorrectly assumes, however, that Hooker only reproduces a Thomistic dispositive account of law in Book One. Kirby conversely argues that Book Eight actually 'is nothing less than the practical completion of [Hooker's] argument, the necessary fulfilment of his nomos-theology' found at the beginning of the *Laws*.[211] As Kirby illustrates, while all laws detailed in Book One dispositively participate in the second eternal law, they nevertheless remain hypostatically distinct from the first eternal law. While participation in the second eternal law is hierarchical and dispositive insofar as creatures share in God as diminished analogues, the first eternal law describes eternal law from God's perspective, securing the radical otherness of God. Hooker's two Platonisms hereby both distinguish but also relate the spiritual and temporal realms, just as they secure the distinction and relationship between grace and nature. Thus, in the books of power Christ rules immediately in the invisible mystical sphere, but mediates his authority through penultimate visible hierarchies. Even though Christ is the unitive source of

---

[208] Hooker, *Laws*, 3:331.10–332.1; VIII.2.1–2.
[209] See the commentary notes in *FLE*, 6 (2): 1080–1, which refers Hooker's use back to Boniface VIII's papal bull *Unum Sanctum* (1302) incorporated into medieval canon law. Compare Hooker, *Autograph Notes*, in *FLE*, 3:494.10–14 where he quotes almost verbatim from *Unum Sanctum*. On the Protestant awareness and use of Roman Catholic canon law, see R. H.Helmholz, *Roman Canon Law in Reformation England* (Cambridge: Cambridge University Press, 1990).
[210] See Paolo Prodi, *The Papal Prince: One Body and Two Souls. The Papal Monarchy in Early Modern Europe* (Cambridge: Cambridge University Press, 1987), esp. 1–16.
[211] Kirby, '"Law Makes the King"', 281. See also Kirby, 'From "Generall Meditations" to "Particular Decisions"', 43–65.

both spheres, being 'severed in nature' these two kinds of power are incommensurable and not dispositive, just as the second eternal law is hypostatically distinct from the first. In a similar fashion, as we have seen, unlike both Roman Catholics and radical puritans, Hooker distinguishes the visible Church from the mystical, rendering the former as part of the 'politic society', itself hypostatically distinct from (if still subordinate to) Christ's immediate authority. As such, the temporal power subordinates the visible Church within the hierarchical *dispositio*. The visible Church remains under the monarch's *cura religionis* when and where the identity of the visible Church and Commonwealth coincide. While English bishops have, therefore, certain spiritual powers (such as ordination) which do not belong to the monarch, only the latter properly has 'authoritie and power to command even in matters of *Christian Religion*' in the temporal, visible, external sphere. In the mystical, invisible and inward sphere, however, Christ's immediate, universal and final authority suffers no possible abrogation.

While Kirby and Miller claim, like Munz, that Hooker's argument from these two Platonisms closely resembles the political theology of Marsilius of Padua, this seems unlikely, both on textual and theological lines.[212] Textually, Hooker's sole reference to Marsilius's *Defensor Pacis* is in Book Eight, where Hooker strenuously opposes his attack on the authority of bishops. Cargill Thompson casts doubt on the provenance even of that sole quotation.[213] Even though both Marsilius and Hooker attack papal jurisdiction, subordinate the visible Church to secular authority, and discuss consent, the singular lack of other references to Marsilius in the *Laws* make him, at best, a highly speculative influence. Instead, the architecture of participation, as well as its grammar, seems a more parsimonious theological and philosophical frame of reference.[214] Indeed, participation lies behind every major claim Hooker makes in relation to metaphysics, epistemology and politics, drenching human activity with deity and refusing any 'de-Christianization' of the secular political order.

As this chapter has shown, therefore, the architecture of participation structures Hooker's commitments to patristic, as well as reformed, doctrinal orthodoxy as he defends episcopal orders and lay ecclesiastical supremacy. It singularly explains the gestures made back and forth across the *Laws*, suggesting the systematicity, coherency and success of Hooker's desire to move from 'general meditations' in Book One to the disputed 'particulars' of the Tudor ecclesiastical polity in the books of power. Just as for Hooker, Christ is the key who unlocks the participatory relation between nature and grace, the architecture of participation forms the key that unlocks the integrity of Hooker's thought.

---

[212] See Miller, *Vision of God*, 254–6.
[213] W. D. J. Cargill Thompson, 'The Source of Hooker's Knowledge of Marsilius of Padua', *Journal of Ecclesiastical History* 25, no. 1 (1974): 75–81.
[214] See Rosenthal, *Crown under Law*, 98–103.

5

'To resolve the conscience': Revisiting the architecture of participation

Having demonstrated the homology that Hooker's architecture of participation generates across metaphysics, epistemology and politics, this final chapter returns to the provocations mooted in the opening chapter. Just as in the *Laws* Hooker's 'whole endevor is to resolve the conscience' of his opponents, this work has addressed those modern scholarly voices who either fail to see the systematic aspect of Hooker's architecture of participation in the *Laws*, or who argue that Hooker's thought falls into one form of incoherency or another.[1] This final chapter accordingly determines in what sense Hooker's thought is systematic and coherent, allaying accusations to the contrary.

The opening chapter discussed just how contested Hooker's place as a coherent and systematic thinker remains in modern scholarly circles. It suggested two basic hermeneutical principles to adjudicate between seemingly intractable appraisals of Hooker's thought. First, Hooker's thought would be coherent to the degree that the metaphysical, epistemological and political claims of the *Laws* avoid blatant contradiction but not necessarily tension, while also implying each other. Second, Hooker's thought would be systematic, if it unveiled in each of its parts a series of gestures back and forth which measured, shaped or informed other moments.

This work has explored how, as Hooker moves in the *Laws* from 'general meditations' to the 'particular decisions' that govern the Elizabethan Religious Settlement, the architecture of participation indeed structures, informs and unites his varied arguments into a coherent and systematic vision. Demonstrably, the architecture of participation yields a strong homology between his metaphysics, epistemology and politics. Each chapter in this work has laid out the following gestures around the idea of participation across Hooker's *Laws*.

The second chapter demonstrated how two mini-treatises in Books One and Five of the *Laws* describe extensive and intensive modes of participation, with Christ the 'woord or Wisdom' of God relating and unlocking natural and supernatural orders. The extensive mode of participation found in Book One describes how manifold species of laws participate in eternal law. In this extensive mode, Christ acts as the

---

[1] Hooker, *Laws*, 1:34.20; Pref.7.1.

rational, divine pattern who freely, wisely and lovingly makes creatures as extensive, diminished, hierarchical and formal analogues of divine being. The intensive mode found especially in Book Five describes the saving return of human beings to God through participation in Christ. Christ's Incarnation restores the integrity of nature, allowing believers ultimately to enjoy through grace an intensive (re)union with God. Across both modes, Hooker balances the integrity of nature and the gratuity of grace. Theonomous participation in eternal law renders the integrity of nature as possible, refusing to evacuate creation of its own agency in unfolding the eternal law into the world. Instead, human beings are fellow workers with God; human intellective capacities reflect a diminished but real image of God's perfection and Christ as eternal creative *Logos*. Here, the human capacity for creativity flows from and reflects the divine act of creation. In turn, Hooker doubly secures the gratuity of grace, seeing creation and salvation as God's free and gratuitous act through Christ, and refusing to evacuate any created space of divine influence. In this way, Hooker understands creation under the system of laws that participates in eternal law as logical, dynamic and open to self-transcendence. In short, creation is suspended from God and imbued with God's influence. As such, creation inherently discloses the grace of God, which invites creation through love to share in the inner life of the Trinity, an invitation finally fulfilled through the gift of salvation.

The third chapter then showed how, in Hooker's epistemology, reason and desire emerge from Hooker's participatory metaphysics to become the constellating categories for a mixed cognitive ecology in Books Two through Five. This ecology circumscribes both natural and supernatural forms of cognitive participation in God, moments which Christ as 'woord or Wisdom' again unites and unlocks. Divine influence undergirds and illumines the integrity of created intellective capacities, leading them to natural fulfilment and ultimately lifting them into supernatural beatitude through participation in Christ. Alongside Scripture, human nature inherently discloses the 'sundry' causal influences of divine Wisdom, and (as it is attuned to the world around it) leads human beings under the influence of grace to the extensive and intensive 'participation of God himselfe.' As such, reason and Scripture are correlative acts of divine disclosure. Human creativity in the making of laws and in cultural artifice flow out of the created status of human beings as made in the *imago dei*. Since Hooker sees human beings as homo faber, human creativity reflects the rational participation in God's own creativity. For Hooker, Christ (as 'woord or Wisdom') acts as the sapiential, personal principium who informs reason, Scripture and desire alike as first and final cause.[2] Worship (especially sacramental participation) acts as a training school that mediates supernatural illumination and re-forms both right reason and right desire as

---

[2] See R. A. Muller, *After Calvin: Studies in the Development of a Theological Tradition* (Oxford: Oxford University Press, 2003), 97–8, which distinguishes between the 'soteriological christocentrism' of Calvin that places Christ as the sole mediator of redemption, and the 'principial christocentrism' of the nineteenth and twentieth centuries, which has a more synergistic account. Hooker's sapiential, personal christocentrism suspends creation and believers from the personhood of Christ, the former as *eternal* Logos and the latter as the personal union of the divine nature with a specific human nature. As such, Hooker holds together the possibilities of both of Muller's models, protecting the priority of Christ but also maintaining the agency of creation as it participates in its highest cause.

a participation in God as source and goal through sacramentally sharing in Christ. The established forms of worship acts as a repository of spiritual formation preparing the habits of the body and mind to be fit for heaven as their final beatitude.

Next, the fourth chapter showed how these prior arguments generate a grammar of participation that structures how Hooker defends episcopal orders and lay ecclesiastical supremacy. The grammar of the architecture of participation allows Hooker to parse both the ecclesiastical polity and lay supremacy of the Church of England as contingent products of human history and yet also as binding participations in the divine 'woord or Wisdom' of God. The natural integrity of human societies to order themselves stems from the intellectual status of humankind as not only being made in the *imago dei* but also as being co-creative participants in God's providential ordering of creation. Far from being passive recipients evacuated of political agency, simply caught between the creative exit from and salvific return to God, human beings are co-creative participants in God, cultivating the metaphysical becoming of the world as it is drawn towards union with God. As they use their rational capacities to create laws, human beings are homo faber, makers who read divine wisdom into the world through the 'divine power of the soule'. As co-workers with God, human political agents participate in the ongoing, dynamic, ecstatic process of creation and redemption. Yet, such natural integrity is undergirded by divine influence, which is to say human politics remain suspended from, contingent upon, and penultimate to God's sapiential ordering of history for the common good. Hooker here refuses simply to sink the invisible into the visible order as he thinks his opponents do, but also charts out their relationship as the former constitutes the authority of the latter. Once again, Christ forms the key to unlock the relationship between the visible political order of the Church and Commonwealth and the transcendent, invisible source of power. All powers, visible and invisible, are distinguished only in order to be united through Christ's universal dominion, just as his two natures remain distinct but co-inhere in his person.

Each of these chapters present a strong case for seeing Hooker as both coherent and systematic in the senses already suggested. Hooker's metaphysical, epistemological and political claims across the *Laws* consistently appeal to elements drawn from the heuristic architecture of participation and its grammar. The various parts of Hooker's argument in the *Laws* show remarkable consistency and logical arrangement, drawing connections across disparate arguments, even as they explore the tensions between nature and grace, or the visible and the invisible. As such, they exhibit a rich form of coherency. Hooker remains remarkably aware, of course, that his legal arguments in the *Laws* are not indubitable but rather are provisional and open to change with the vagaries of history. The royal supremacy has its legal basis in human law, a particular positive application of the natural law of reason that can find examples and motives in divine law to support it. All such laws are suspended, however, from eternal law through the legal metaphysics of participation. The royal supremacy is thus binding within the contingencies of history: it is not unconditionally necessary, but it is conditionally compulsive for it shows the aesthetic convenience of the magisterial duty to order religion as the wellspring of public virtue, drawing the Commonwealth towards God. Hooker's arguments across the *Laws*, framed by an architecture of participation, accordingly seek to imitate the divine self-disclosure and draw people into divine participation, making him confident that his contemporaries ought to be 'led by great reason' to support the ecclesiastical laws of the Elizabethan Church, for they are fit to lead the people to godliness.

Similarly, Hooker intends the argument of the *Laws* to be systematic, endeavouring that 'that every former part might give strength unto all that followe, and every later bring some light unto all before.' Such an account is systematic insofar as each move acts like a jigsaw piece: though a complete picture of Christian doctrine may be absent, each individual piece gestures towards linkage and a unifying picture. Participation illumines the entirety of the *Laws*: it is the principle behind and implied in every argument; all of Hooker's claims must be read in light of his commitment to participation. The architecture of participation forms a picture of associated ideas that, at various points, individually emerge to structure and justify both Hooker's particular claims as well as his overall argument. No one piece fully explains or contains the entirety of this Christian vision, but each witnesses and contributes to the presence and force of it. Across the *Laws*, the architecture of participation stands behind and informs every major claim, generating relations between ideas that mutually gesture back and forth towards each other. The architecture of participation both structures his particular arguments, but also describes the rhetorical tone and purpose of the *Laws*. Just as divine influence manuducts creation towards its beatitude through natural and supernatural means, Hooker's *Laws* attempts to induce his opponents not only to obey the ecclesiastical polity of the Church of England, but also to freely embrace it as the mediating aspect of God's call to heal and restore creation in Christ. As such, the *Laws* certainly both contains and displays a system (the architecture of participation), allowing us to classify Hooker a systematic theologian. In Hooker's systematics, of course, the person of Jesus Christ represents the key who unlocks the separation but also the link between nature and grace in the architecture of participation. Across the *Laws*, Hooker develops a Christ-centred theological vision that he uses to explore the matters at hand in an integrated way, sufficiently confident about what it illumines (namely the architecture of participation) that he employs and advocates it. Indeed, Hooker's very method in the *Laws* is, as Andrea Russell puts it, 'intensely participative' since it imitates (as a text seeking to 'resolve the conscience') the manuduction by God of a broken world such that it enjoys the peace and order that is the 'participation of God himselfe'.[3]

This work opens up two future avenues for an ecumenical and political *ressourcement* of participation using Hooker's thought.

On the one hand, Hooker's architecture of participation yields two ecumenical possibilities. First, Hooker's *Laws* provides one significant Western trace of what Paul Collins calls the 'metaphor of deification'.[4] The strong, intensive return to God within the architecture of participation, imaged as union with God, leads Hooker unabashedly to use the language of deification. In the *Laws*, he gives an analogical but also realistic account of deification as a kind of Christification, imaging the ontological

---

[3] Russell, *Beyond Certainty*, 101–2.
[4] Collins, *Partaking in Divine Nature*, 111–12.

and ethical transformation of the believer sharing in Christ. The words of Catherine Mowry LaCugna might very well summarize Hooker's intensive mode of participation:

> Since *theōsis* means the true union of human and divine, the model for which is Jesus Christ, in a theanthroponomous ethic persons are defined neither autonomously nor heteronomously but with reference to the conincidence of divine and human, Jesus Christ. The ultimate good of human beings is to achieve *theōsis*, to realise the fullness of our humanity in union with the Trinity.[5]

While Hooker's account of *theōsis* is thematic rather than doctrinal, meaning that it would be a stretch to describe Anglicanism as it developed as a 'Western Orthodoxy', Anglican-Orthodox dialogue can and should nevertheless comfortably move to a rich and productive level of common agreement about deification as a shared theological emphasis for the Christian life. Second, in a different direction, while scholarship has until the seminal work of W. J. T. Kirby contested within what theological taxonomy to place Hooker, the emerging consensus that now identifies Hooker as a Reformed orthodox and scholastic thinker opens up a range of possibilities for dialogue between the Anglican and Reformed churches.[6] The *ressourcement* of participation in Hooker's work also contributes to what Boersma calls a 'genuine rapprochement between evangelicals and Catholics' against the 'onslaught of a desacralized modernity'.[7] Further critical scholarly and ecumenical engagement, especially in relation to the role of participation, should prove productive in these regards. It will help in seeing Reformed orthodoxy as a fertile and protean sensibility within which Hooker operates, as well as in breaking down an overly simplistic dualism between 'Reformed' and 'medieval' or 'Catholic' thought in relation to modernity.

On the other hand, then, further study of Hooker's architecture of participation could critically feed into the broader *ressourcement* of participatory metaphysics in relation to political theology. Hooker represents a 'Janus-like figure' who connects both medieval and modern political visions.[8] Hooker's nuanced account of nature and grace within an architecture of participation underpins his entire political theology, or (as might be better said), his politicized metaphysics. Hooker remains sanguine about the incipient rational capacity and broken nature of humankind from within which grace works. As such, Hooker's architecture of participation unfurls the central role for what Bradford Littlejohn calls a political 'culture of persuasion', rather than one of dogmatic absolutes.[9] A character of humility marks the former culture, recognizing the 'root of human frailty and corruption' in political society. Again, Christ is the key for Hooker. In Christ, the union of his divine nature with his human nature becomes a source of participable perfection to recreate human nature as we embody it, as individuals and as communities. Churches and nations are immediately under the kingship of

---

[5] Catherine Mowry LaCugna, *God for Us: The Trinity and Christian Life* (New York: HarperCollins, 1991), 284.
[6] See Littlejohn, 'The Search for a Reformed Hooker', 62–82.
[7] Boersma, *Heavenly Participation*, 10–11.
[8] See D'Entrèves, *The Medieval Contribution to Political Thought*, 88–90.
[9] See Littlejohn, *Peril and Promise*, 237.

Christ. Yet, they also share in the unfolding of the perfection to which nature draws us – namely, in Hooker's context, to a commonwealth secured by a public religion. Such political mediation remains, however, contingent upon, and secondary to, the immediacy of Christ's rule as the beatific vision completes it eschatologically. Such immediacy ought never to be sunk into the visible regiment, which is itself always marked in time by frailty, fallenness and complexity. As Hooker thinks the radical puritans fail to recognize, the 'stains and blemishes' of human life together 'springing from the root of human frailty and corruption, not only are, but have been always more or less, yea and (for any thing we know to the contrary) will be till the world's end complained of, what form of government soever take place'.[10]

Hooker's politicized metaphysics can neither simply be transplanted into a fully modern context, nor can he be seen as a political liberal in any direct sense. Yet, his architecture of participation certainly stands within the genealogy of modern constitutionalism, as Alexander Rosenthal argues.[11] As John Rawls points out, 'the historical origin of political liberalism' begins with 'the Reformation and its aftermath, with the long controversies over religious toleration in the sixteenth and seventeenth centuries'.[12] Accordingly, any modern retrieval of participation will do well to pay careful attention to Hooker. In contrast to the agonistic dualism of the loose sensibility known as 'Radical Orthodoxy', seeing (as it does) a dangerous and debilitating 'unhooking' of the world from God in the modern period, Hooker (as unlikely a candidate as he might seem) offers resources for modern thinkers in what Christopher Insole calls a 'theological defence of liberalism'. As a representative of Radical Orthodoxy, John Milbank offers an alternative to political liberalism that might rightly alarm a reader sensitive to Hooker's architecture of participation. 'True society', Milbank writes, 'implies absolute consensus, agreement in desire, and entire harmony amongst its members, and this is exactly (as Augustine reiterates again and again) what the Church provides, and that in which salvation, the restoration of being, consists.'[13] Hooker would likely in some sense agree with this sentiment, as well as with the centrality afforded to participation in its vision. Yet, he would disagree strongly with the sinking of the invisible into the visible, the conflation of the eternal gratuitous donation of the beatific vision with the temporal (and temporary) mediations of the world. Despite his own apparent authoritarianism, Hooker offers a perspicacious embodiment of trying to manuduct ('lead by the hand') competing visions of the good towards a sense of peace and harmony that contains and even welcomes dissent as part of public enquiry. As Insole puts it, Hooker sees the 'danger and hubris' of conflating the invisible and visible Church, a sight which is at 'the heart of the theological defence of political liberalism'.[14] Therefore, as Insole points out, 'Hooker's call to self-examination, moderation and charity provides a theological reason for the sort of self-restraint and consideration to others' central to certain traditions within political liberalism. It may well be that political liberalism, far from being simply individualist, relativist and hubristic, has the

---

[10] Hooker, *Laws*, 1:15.29–16.1; Pref.3.7–8.
[11] Rosenthal, *Crown under Law*, 245–66.
[12] John Rawls, *Political Liberalism* (New York: Columbia University Press, 1993), xxvi.
[13] Milbank, *Theology and Social Theory*, 402.
[14] Insole, *The Politics of Human Frailty*, 59.

theological resources within itself for a renaissance rather than needing a revolution.[15] Hooker's architecture of participation offers one such resource, and it ought to be explored so that, as he writes at the beginning of the *Laws*, 'posteritie may know we have not loosely through silence permitted things to passe away as in a dreame.'[16]

'Posteritie' is indeed perhaps Hooker's most significant intended audience in the *Laws*. In and beyond the immediate historical provocations of the Elizabethan Church, Hooker transmits through the architecture of participation a vision that saturates all of our being, knowing, and doing with a sense of divinity. Participation in God constitutes the human self, immersing it in the contingencies of the world, and drawing it to eternity. All of creation represents a divine gift. Seeing the world as suspended from God means that creation inherently discloses God. The self and its understanding is mediated through sharing in the personal reality of the Trinity as it creates, sustains and redeems. Such a theonomous rendering of the human self undercuts both autonomy and heteronomy, making instead every separation between creation and God into an intimate point of connection. It also fundamentally casts the self in terms of relationship, whether with other human beings, angels or God. Christ forms the key to unlock the distinctions and relations between creation and Creator. As Word, Christ mediates God's presence, making the reality and sense of all that exists. As Wisdom, Christ participates us and we participate him, enabling us to know, enjoy and love both the multiplicity of creation and God. Such Wisdom flows from God into the multiplicity of a created order so that the world might flow back to God through the many tributaries of Wisdom. Paradoxically, then, human selves and communities exhibit their integrity only in dynamic relation to some Other; the deification of humanity is that which exceeds human nature as the Other descends into it in order to restore and elevate; and human communities are constituted and yet ruptured by the Other. None of this suggests, however, impassivity for Hooker. Rather, it is the dynamic pursuit of the participation of God built into the very hollow of our being, driving us from restless desire towards our final rest.

---

[15] See Littlejohn, *Peril and Promise*, 238–71.
[16] Hooker, *Laws*, 1:1.9–10; Pref.1.1.

Bibliography

Primary texts

Aquinas, Thomas. *Compendium Theologiae ad Fratrem Reginaldum*. English translation in *Compendium of Theology*, trans. Cyril Vollert. St Louis: Herder, 1947.

Aquinas, Thomas. *De Veritate*. English translation in *Truth*, trans. N. T. Bourke. Chicago: University of Chicago Press, 1952–4.

Aquinas, Thomas. *In octo libros Physicorum expositio*. English translation in *Commentary on Aristotle's Physics*, trans. R. J. Blackwell, Richard J. Spath and W. Edmund Thirlkel. Notre Dame: Dumb Ox, 1999.

Aquinas, Thomas. *Summa Theologiae*. Latin and English dual text. New York: Blackfriars, 1964–81.

Aquinas, Thomas. *Summa contra Gentiles*. Trans. A. Pegis and V. Bourke. Notre Dame, IN: University of Notre Dame Press, 1975.

Aquinas, Thomas. *In duodecim libros Metaphysicorum expositio*. English translation in *Commentary on Aristotle's Metaphysics*, trans. John P. Rowan. Notre Dame: Dumb Ox, 1995.

Aquinas, Thomas. *Expositio libri Boetii de Hebdomadibus*. English translation in *An Exposition of the 'On the Hebdomads' of Boethius*, trans. J. Schultz and E. Synan. Washington: Catholic University of America Press, 2001.

Aquinas, Thomas. *Scriptum super libros Sententiarum*. English translation in *On Love and Charity: Readings from the Commentary on the Sentences of Peter Lombard. Thomas Aquinas in Translation*, trans. Peter A. Kwasniewski, Thomas Bolin and Joseph Bolin. Washington: Catholic University of America Press, 2008.

Aristotle. *The Complete Works of Aristotle*, ed. Jonathan Barnes, 2 vols. Princeton, NJ: Princeton University Press, 1995.

Athanasius. *De Incarnatione Verbi Dei*. English translation in *Nicene and Post-Nicene Fathers*, ed. Philip Schaff and Henry Wace, second series, 14 vols. Vol. 4. Peabody: Hendrickson, 1994.

Augustine. *Confessiones*. English translation in *Nicene and Post-Nicene Fathers*, ed. Philip Schaff and Henry Wace, first series, 14 vols. Vol. 1. Peabody: Hendrickson, 1994.

Augustine. *Contra epistulam Manichaei quam vocant fundamenti*. English translation in *Nicene and Post-Nicene Fathers*, ed. Philip Schaff and Henry Wace, first series, 14 vols. Vol. 4. Peabody: Hendrickson, 1994.

Augustine. *De civitate Dei*. English translation in *Nicene and Post-Nicene Fathers*, ed. Philip Schaff and Henry Wace, first series, 14 vols. Vol. 2. Peabody: Hendrickson, 1994.

Augustine. *De doctrina Christiana*. English translation in *Nicene and Post-Nicene Fathers*, ed. Philip Schaff and Henry Wace, first series, 14 vols. Vol. 2. Peabody: Hendrickson, 1994.

Barth, Karl. *The Christian Life: Church Dogmatics, IV, 4, Lecture Fragments*, trans. G. W. Bromiley. Grand Rapids, MI: Eerdmans, 1981.
Bullinger, H. *Ad Ioannis Cochlei d Canonicare Scripturae . . . authoritate labellum responsio*. Tiguri [Zurich]: Froschouer, 1544.
Calvin, Jean. *Commentaries on the Twelve Minor Prophets*, trans. John Owen, 5 vols. Edinburgh: Calvin Translation Society, 1844–59.
Calvin, Jean. *Institutes of the Christian Religion*, trans. F. Battles, 2 vols. Louisville, KY: Westminster John Knox Press, 2006.
Cartwright, Thomas. *The Second Replie of Thomas Cartwright against Maister Doctor Whitgiftes Second Answer, Touching the Church Discipline*. Heidelberg: Michael Schirat, 1575.
Covell, William. *A Just and Temperate* Defence. Lampeter: Edwin Mellen Press, 1998.
Duns Scotus. *Lectura*, lib. III. Vols 20–1. Ediz. Vaticana, 2003–4.
Duns Scotus. *Ordinatio*, lib. III. Vol. 9. Ediz. Vaticana, 2006.
Eriugena, John Scotus. *Periphyseon: the Division of Nature*, trans. John O'Meara. Montreal: Bellarmin, 1987.
Hooker, Richard. *The Works of . . . Mr. Richard Hooker: With an Account of His Life and Death by Izaac Walton*, ed. John Keble, 7th edn, rev. R. W. Church and F. Paget, 3 vols. Oxford: Clarendon Press, 1888.
Hooker, Richard. *The Folger Library Edition of the Works of Richard Hooker*, ed. W. Speed Hill, 7 vols. Vols 1–5, Cambridge: Belknap Press, 1977–90. Vol. 6, Binghamton: Belknap Press, 1993. Vol. 7, Tempe: Medieval and Renaissance Texts and Studies, 1998.
Irenaeus. *Adversus omnes haereses*. English translation in *Ante-Nicene Fathers*, ed. Alexander Roberts and James Donaldson, 10 vols. Vol. 1. Peabody: Hendrickson, 2004; and *Irenaeus of Lyons*, trans. Robert M. Grant, 55–186. London: Routledge, 1997.
Jewel, John. *The Works of John Jewel*, ed. John Ayre, 4 vols. Cambridge: Cambridge University Press, 1845–50.
Luther, Martin. *Against the Roman Papacy, an Institution of the Devil*, ed. J. Pelikan and H. Lehmann, trans. Eric Gritsch. In *Works*, vol. 41. Philadelphia, PA: Fortress, 1966.
Luther, Martin. *Selected Writings of Martin Luther*, ed. G. Tappert, trans. J. J. Schindel, 4 vols. Minneapolis, MN: Fortress, 2007.
Plato: *Complete Works*, ed. John M. Cooper, 2 vols. Indianapolis and Cambridge: Hackett 1997.
Plotinus. *Enneads*, trans. Stephen MacKenna. London: Penguin, 1991.
Proclus. *The Elements of Theology*, trans. E. R. Dodds. Oxford: Clarendon Press, 2004.
Pseudo-Dionysius. *Pseudo-Dionysius: The Complete Works*, trans. Colm Luibheid. New York: Paulist Press, 1987.
Voetius, G. *Disputationes Selectae*, 3 vols. Utrecht: J. Waesberge, 1648–59.
Whitgift, John. *The Works of John Whitgift*, ed. J. Ayre, 3 vols. Cambridge: Parker Society, 1851–3.

Ecumenical texts

Anglican-Orthodox Joint Doctrinal Commission. *Anglican-Orthodox Dialogue 1976: Moscow Agreed Statement*. London: SPCK, 1977.

Anglican-Orthodox Joint Doctrinal Commission. *Anglican-Orthodox Dialogue 1984: Dublin Agreed Statement*. London: SPCK, 1985.

International Commission for Anglican-Orthodox Theological Dialogue. *Church of the Triune God: Cyprus Statement Agreed by the International Commission for Anglican-Orthodox Theological Dialogue 2006*. London: Anglican Communion Office, 2006.

International Commission for Anglican-Orthodox Theological Dialogue. *In the Image and Likeness of God: A Hope-Filled Anthropology. The Buffalo Statement Agreed by the International Commission for Anglican-Orthodox Theological Dialogue*. London: Anglican Communion Office, 2015.

World Council of Churches. *Growth in Agreement*, 3 vols. Geneva: WCC, 2000–7.

Secondary texts

Aertsen, J. 'The Convertibility of Being and Good in St. Thomas Aquinas'. *New Scholasticism* 59 (1985): 449–70.

Aertsen, J. *Medieval Philosophy and the Transcendentals: The Case of Thomas Aquinas*. Leiden: Brill, 1996.

Allchin, A. M. *Participation in God: A Forgotten Strand in Anglican Tradition*. London: Darton, Longman & Todd, 1988.

Allen, R. E. 'Participation and Predication in Plato's Middle Dialogues'. *Philosophical Review* 69 (1960): 147–83.

Almasy, Rudolph. 'The Purpose of Richard Hooker's Polemic'. *Journal of the History of Ideas* 39, no. 2 (1978): 251–70.

Almasy, Rudolph. 'Language and Exclusion in the First Book of Hooker's Politie'. In *Richard Hooker and the English Reformation*, ed. W. J. T. Kirby, 227–42. Dordrecht: Kluwer, 2003.

Almasy, Rudolph. 'Rhetoric and Apologetics'. In *A Companion to Richard Hooker*, ed. W. J. T. Kirby, 121–50. Leiden: Brill, 2008.

Annice, M. 'Historical Sketch of the Theory of Participation'. *New Scholasticism* 26 (1952): 49–79.

Arblaster, John and Rob Faesen (eds). *Mystical Doctrines of Deification: Case Studies in the Christian Tradition*. Oxford: Routledge, 2018.

Atkinson, Nigel. *Richard Hooker and the Authority of Scripture, Tradition and Reason*. Carlisle: Paternoster Press, 1997.

Audi, Robert. *The Architecture of Reason: The Structure and Substance of Rationality*. Oxford: Oxford University Press, 2001.

Avis, Paul. *Anglicanism and the Christian Church*. Edinburgh: T&T Clark, 1989.

Bagchi, David. ' "The Scripture moveth us in sundry places": Framing Biblical Emotions in the Book of Common Prayer'. In *The Renaissance of Emotion: Understanding Affect in Shakespeare and His Contemporaries*, ed. Richard Meek and Erin Sullivan, 45–64. Manchester: Manchester University Press, 2015.

Bartos, Emil. *Deification in Eastern Orthodox Theology*. Eugene: Wipf and Stock, 2007.

Bauerschmidt, F. C. *Thomas Aquinas: Faith, Reason, and Following Christ*. Oxford: Oxford University Press, 2013.

Baur, Michael. 'Law and Natural Law'. In *The Oxford Handbook of Aquinas*, ed. Brian Davies and Eleanore Stump, 238–54. Oxford: Oxford University Press, 2014.

Beiser, Frederick. *The Sovereignty of Reason: The Defense of Rationality and the Early English Enlightenment*. Princeton, NJ: Princeton University Press, 1996.

Bell, Daniel. *Liberation Theology after the End of History: The Refusal to Cease Suffering*. London: Routledge, 2001.

Berman, Harold J. *Law and Revolution II. The Impact of the Protestant Reformations on the Western Legal Tradition*. Cambridge: Belknap Press, 2003.

Bigger, Charles P. *Participation: A Platonic Inquiry*. Baton Rouge: Louisiana State University Press, 1968.

Billings, J. Todd. *Calvin, Participation, and the Gift: The Activity of Believers in Union with Christ*. Oxford: Oxford University Press, 2007.

Boersma, Hans. *Heavenly Participation: The Weaving of a Sacramental Tapestry*. Grand Rapids, MI: Eerdmans, 2011.

BonJour, Laurence. *The Structure of Empirical Knowledge*. Cambridge: Harvard University Press, 1985.

BonJour, Laurence. 'Coherence Theory of Truth'. In *The Cambridge Dictionary of Philosophy*, ed. Robert Audi, 153–4. Cambridge: Cambridge University Press, 2001.

Bonner, Gerald. 'Deification, Divinization'. In *Augustine through the Ages: An Encyclopedia*, ed. Allan D. Fitzgerald, 265–6. Grand Rapids, MI: Eerdmans, 1999.

Booty, John E. 'Richard Hooker'. In *The Spirit of Anglicanism*, ed. William J. Wolf, John E. Booty and Owen C. Thomas, 1–45. Wilton: Morehouse Barlow, 1979.

Booty, John E. 'Book V'. In *The Folger Library Edition of the Works of Richard Hooker*, ed. W. Speed Hill, 7 vols., vol. 6 (1), 183–231. Vols 1–5, Cambridge: Belknap Press, 1977–90; vol. 6, Binghamton: Belknap Press, 1993; vol. 7, Tempe: Medieval and Renaissance Texts and Studies, 1998.

Booty, John E. 'The Spirituality of Participation in Richard Hooker'. *Sewanee Theological Review* 38, no. 1 (1994): 9–20.

Booty, John E. *Reflections on the Theology of Richard Hooker*. Sewanee: University of the South Press, 1998.

Boquet, Damien and Piroska Nagy. *Medieval Sensibilities. A History of Emotions in the Middle Ages*, trans. Robert Shaw. Cambridge: Polity, 2018.

Bourdin, Bernard. *The Theological-Political Origins of the Modern State*. Washington: Catholic University of America Press, 2011.

Bousset, W. *Kyrios Christos: A History of the Belief in Christ from the Beginnings of Christianity to Irenaeus*. Nashville, TN: Abingdon, 1970.

Bouwsma, William J. 'Hooker in the Context of European Cultural History'. In *Richard Hooker and the Construction of Christian Community*, ed. A. S. McGrade, 41–58. Tempe: Medieval and Renaissance Texts and Studies, 1997.

Bozeman, Theodore Dwight. *The Precisianist Strain: Disciplinary Religion and Antinomian Backlash in Puritanism to 1638*. Chapel Hill: University of North Carolina Press, 2004.

Braaten, Carl E. and Robert W. Jenson (eds). *Union with Christ: The New Finnish Interpretation of Luther*. Grand Rapids, MI: Eerdmans, 1998.

Bradley, Denis J. *Aquinas on the Twofold Human Good: Reason and Human Happiness in Aquinas's Moral Science*. Washington: Catholic University of America Press, 1999.

Bradshaw, David. *Aristotle East and West: Metaphysics and the Division of Christendom*. Cambridge: Cambridge University Press, 2008.

Brague, Rémi. *The Law of God: The Philosophical History of an Idea*, trans. Lydia Cochrane. Chicago: University of Chicago Press, 2007.

Brown, Raymond. *The Gospel and Epistles of John*. Collegeville: Liturgical Press, 1992.

Brydon, Michael A. *The Evolving Reputation of Richard Hooker. An Examination of Responses 1600–1714*. Oxford: Oxford University Press, 2006.
Burnhart, Bruno. 'One Spirit, One Body: Jesus' Participatory Revolution'. In *The Participatory Turn: Spirituality, Mysticism, Religious Studies*, ed. Jorge N. Ferrer and Jacob H. Sherman, 265–91. Albany: State University of New York Press, 2008.
Candler, Peter. *Theology,Rhetoric, Manuduction, or Reading Scripture Together on the Path of God*. London: SCM Press, 2011.
Capps, Walter. *Religious Studies: The Making of a Discipline*. Minneapolis, MN: Fortress Press, 1995.
Cargill Thompson, W. D. J. 'The Philosopher of the Politic Society: Richard Hooker as a Political Thinker'. In *Studies in Richard Hooker*, ed. W. Speed Hill, 3–76. Cleveland and London: Case Western Reserve University Press, 1972.
Cargill Thompson, W. D. J. 'The Source of Hooker's Knowledge of Marsilius of Padua'. *Journal of Ecclesiastical History* 25, no. 1 (1974): 75–81.
Chapman, Mark D., Sathianathan Clarke and Martyn Percy (eds). *The Oxford Handbook of Anglican Studies*. Oxford: Oxford University Press, 2016.
Christensen, Michael J. 'John Wesley: Christian perfection as Faith Filled with the Energy of Love'. In *Partakers of the Divine Nature: The History and Development of Deification in the Christian Traditions*, ed. M. J. Christensen and Jeffrey A. Wittung, 219–33. Grand Rapids, MI: Baker, 2007.
Clarke, W. N. 'The Meaning of Participation in St. Thomas'. *Proceedings of the American Catholic Philosophical Association* 26 (1952): 150–2.
Coakley, Sarah. '"Mingling" in Gregory of Nyssa's Christology: A Reconsideration'. In *Who Is Jesus Christ for Us Today? Pathways to Contemporary Christology*, ed. Andreas Schuele and Gunter Thomas, 72–84. Louisville, KY: Westminster John Knox, 2009.
Coakley, Sarah. *God, Sexuality, and the Self: An Essay 'On the Trinity'*. Cambridge: Cambridge University Press, 2013.
Collins, Paul M. 'An Investigation of the Use of the Metaphor of Deification in the Anglican Tradition'. *Studia Theologia Orthodoxa* 1 (2010): 205–17.
Collins, Paul M. *Partaking in Divine Nature: Deification and Communion*. London: T&T Clark, 2012.
Collins, Stephen. *From Divine Cosmos to Sovereign State: An Intellectual History of Consciousness and the Idea of Order in Renaissance England*. Oxford: Oxford University Press, 1989.
Collinson, Patrick. *The Religion of Protestants: The Church in English Society 1559–1625*. Oxford: Clarendon Press, 1982.
Collinson, Patrick. 'Hooker and the Elizabethan Establishment'. In *Richard Hooker and the Construction of Christian Community*, ed. A. S. McGrade, 149–81. Tempe: Medieval and Renaissance Texts and Studies, 1997.
Cooper, Adam G. *Naturally Human, Supernaturally God: Deification in Pre-conciliar Catholicism*. Minneapolis, MN: Fortress Press, 2014.
Cooper, Jordan. *Christification: A Lutheran Approach to Theosis*. Eugene: Wipf & Stock, 2014.
Cromartie, Alan. 'Theology and Politics in Richard Hooker's Thought'. *History of Political Thought* 21, no. 1 (2000): 41–66.
Cross, F. L. and E. A. Livingstone. 'Deification'. In *The Oxford Dictionary of the Christian Church*, ed. F. L. Cross and E. A. Livingstone, 465. Oxford and New York: Oxford University Press, 2005.
Davies, Brian. 'Is Sacra Doctrina Theology?'. *New Blackfriars* 71 (1990): 141–7.

Davies, Charles Watterson. '"For conformities sake": How Richard Hooker Used Fuzzy Logic and Legal Rhetoric against Political Extremes'. In *Richard Hooker and the Construction of Christian Community*, ed. A. S. McGrade, 332–49. Tempe: Medieval and Renaissance Texts and Studies, 1997.

Davison, Andrew. *Participation in God: A Study in Christian Doctrine and Metaphysics*. Cambridge: Cambridge University Press, 2019.

De Lara, Dionisio. 'Richard Hooker's Concept of Law'. *Anglican Theological Review* 44 (1962): 380–9.

D'Entrèves, A. P. *The Medieval Contribution to Political Thought: Thomas Aquinas, Marsilius of Padua, Richard Hooker*. Oxford: Oxford University Press, 1939; repr. New York: Humanities Press, 1959.

Devine, Joseph G. 'Richard Hooker's Doctrine of Justification and Sanctification in the Debate with Walter Travers, 1585–1586'. PhD thesis, Hartford: Hartford Seminary Foundation, 1976.

Dixon, Thomas. *From Passions to Emotions: the Creation of a Secular Psychological Category*. Cambridge: Cambridge University Press, 2003.

Dixon, Thomas. 'Revolting Passions'. In *Faith, Rationality, and the Passions*, ed. Sarah Coakley, 181–96. Chichester: Wiley-Blackwell, 2012.

Dominiak, Paul. '"From the Footstool to the Throne of God": *Methexis*, *Metaxu*, and *Eros* in Richard Hooker's *Of the Lawes of Ecclesiastical Polity*'. *Perichoresis* 12, no. 1 (2014): 57–76.

Dominiak, Paul. 'Hooker, Scholasticism, Thomism, and Reformed Orthodoxy'. In *Richard Hooker and Reformed Orthodoxy*, ed. Scott Kindred-Barnes and W. Bradford Littlejohn, 101–26. Göttingen, Bristol: Vandenhoeck & Ruprecht, 2017.

Dominiak, Paul. 'Moses the Magistrate: The Mosaic Theological Imaginary of John Jewel and Richard Hooker in Elizabethan Apologetics'. In *Defending the Faith: John Jewel and the Elizabethan Church*, ed. Angela Ranson, André Gazal and Sarah Bastow, 161–82. University Park: Pennsylvania State University Press, 2018.

Drewery, B. 'Deification'. In *Christian Spirituality: Essays in Honour of Gordon Rupp*, ed. Peter Brooks, 49–62. London: SCM, 1975.

Dunn, James D. G. *Christology in the Making: A New Testament Inquiry into the Origins of the Doctrine of the Incarnation*. Grand Rapids, MI: Eerdmans, 1996.

Ebbersmeyer, Sabrina. 'The Philosopher as a Lover: Renaissance Debates on Platonic *Eros*'. In *Emotion & Cognitive Life in Medieval & Early Modern Philosophy*, ed. Martin Pickavé and Lisa Shapiro, 133–55. Oxford: Oxford University Press, 2012.

Eccleshall, Robert 'Richard Hooker and the Peculiarities of the English'. *History of Political Thought* 2, no. 1 (1981): 63–117.

Edwards, Mark and Elena Ene D-Vasilescu (eds). *Visions of God and Ideas on Deification in Patristic Thought*. Oxford: Routledge, 2016.

Enos, Theresa (ed.). *Encyclopedia of Rhetoric and Composition: Communication from Ancient Times to the Information Age*. Abingdon: Routledge, 2010.

Eppley, Daniel. 'Richard Hooker and the Un-conditionality of Predestination'. In *Richard Hooker and the English Reformation*, ed. W. J. T. Kirby, 63–77. Dordrecht: Kluwer, 2003.

Eppley, Daniel. *Defending Royal Supremacy and Discerning God's Will in Tudor England*. Aldershot: Ashgate, 2007.

Eppley, Daniel. 'Royal Supremacy'. In *A Companion to Richard Hooker*, ed. W. J. T. Kirby, 503–34. Leiden: Brill, 2008.

Eppley, Daniel. *Reading the Bible with Richard Hooker*. Minneapolis, MN: Fortress Press, 2016.

Fabro, C. 'The Intensive Hermeneutics of Thomistic Philosophy: The Notion of Participation'. *Review of Metaphysics* 27 (1947): 465–9.
Fabro, C. *Participatio et causalité selon S. Thomas d'Aquin*. Paris: Louvain, 1961.
Faulkner, Robert. 'Reason and Revelation in Hooker's Ethics'. *The American Political Science Review* 59 (1965): 680–90.
Faulkner, Robert. *Richard Hooker and the Politics of Christian England*. Berkeley: University of California Press, 1981.
Ferrer, Jorge N. and Jacob H. Sherman (eds). *The Participatory Turn: Spirituality, Mysticism, Religious Studies*. Albany: State University of New York Press, 2008.
Fesko, J. V. 'Richard Hooker and John Owen on Union with Christ'. In *Richard Hooker and Reformed Orthodoxy*, ed. Scott Kindred-Barnes and W. Bradford Littlejohn, 255–72. Göttingen, Bristol: Vandenhoeck & Ruprecht, 2017.
Finlan, Stephen. 'Second Peter's Notion of Divine Participation'. In *Theōsis: Deification in Christian Theology*, ed. Stephen Finlan and Vladimir Kharlamov, 32–50. Eugene: Princeton Theological Monograph Series, 2006.
Finlan, Stephen and Vladimir Kharlamov (eds). *Theōsis: Deification in Christian Theology*. Eugene: Princeton Theological Monograph Series, 2006.
Forte, Paul. 'Richard Hooker's Theory of Law'. *Journal of Medieval and Renaissance Studies* 12 (1982): 135–41.
Forte, Paul. 'Hooker as Preacher'. In *The Folger Library Edition of the Works of Richard Hooker*, 7 vols., e. W. Speed Hill, vol. 5, 657–82. Vols 1–5, Cambridge: Belknap Press, 1977–90; vol. 6, Binghamton: Belknap Press, 1993; vol. 7, Tempe: Medieval and Renaissance Texts and Studies, 1998.
Fox, Rory. 'Richard Hooker and the Incoherence of "Ecclesiastical Polity"'. *Heythrop Journal* 44, no. 1 (2003): 43–59.
Fulford, Andrew. '"A Truth Infallible": Richard Hooker and Reformed Orthodoxy on Autopistos'. In *Richard Hooker and Reformed Orthodoxy*, ed. Scott Kindred-Barnes and W. Bradford Littlejohn, 203–20. Göttingen, Bristol: Vandenhoeck & Ruprecht, 2017.
Furedi, Frank. *Authority: A Sociological History*. Cambridge: Cambridge University Press, 2013.
Gascoigne, J. 'Church and State Unified: Hooker's Rationale for the English Post-Reformation Order'. *Journal of Religious History* 21 (1997): 23–34.
Gavrilyuk, Paul L. 'The Retrieval of Deification: How a Once-Despised Archaism Became an Ecumenical Desideratum'. *Modern Theology* 25, no. 4 (2009): 647–59.
Gazal, André. *Scripture and Royal Supremacy in Tudor England*. Lewiston, Queenston, Lampeter: Edwin Mellen Press, 2013.
Gazal, André. '"By force of participation and conjunction with him": John Jewel and Richard Hooker on Union with Christ'. *Perichoresis* 12, no. 1 (2014): 39–56.
Geiger, L. B. *La participation dans la philosophie de Thomas d'Aquin*. Paris: J. Vrin, 1953.
Gibbs, Lee. 'Richard Hooker's *Via Media* Doctrine of Justification'. *Harvard Theological Review* 74, no. 2 (1981): 211–20.
Gibbs, Lee. 'Theology, Logic, and Rhetoric in the Temple Controversy between Richard Hooker and Walter Travers'. *Anglican Theological Review* 55 (1983): 177–88.
Gibbs, Lee. 'The Source of the Most Famous Quotation from Richard Hooker's Law of Ecclesiastical Polity'. *Sixteenth Century Journal* 21, no. 1 (1990): 77–86.
Gibbs, Lee. 'Book I'. In *The Folger Library Edition of the Works of Richard Hooker*, ed. W. Speed Hill, 7 vols, vol. 6 (1), 81–124. Vols. 1–5, Cambridge: Belknap Press, 1977–90; vol. 6, Binghamton: Belknap Press, 1993; vol. 7, Tempe: Medieval and Renaissance Texts and Studies, 1998.

Gorman, Michael J. *Inhabiting the Cruciform God: Kenosis, Justification, and Theosis in Paul's Narrative Soteriology*. Grand Rapids, MI: Eerdmans, 2009.
Grace, Damian. 'Natural Law in Hooker's *Of the Lawes of Ecclesiastical Polity*'. *Journal of Religious History* 21, no. 1 (1997): 10–22.
Grislis, Egil, 'Richard Hooker's Image of Man'. *Renaissance Papers: The Southeastern Renaissance Conference* (1964): 73–84.
Grislis, Egil. 'The Hermeneutical Problem in Hooker'. In *Studies in Richard Hooker*, ed. W. Speed Hill, 159–206. Cleveland and London: Case Western Reserve University Press, 1972.
Grislis, Egil. 'The Role of Sin in the Theology of Richard Hooker'. *Anglican Theological Review* 84, no. 4 (2002): 881–4.
Grislis, Egil. 'Richard Hooker and Mysticism'. *Anglican Theological Review* 87, no. 2 (2005): 253–71.
Grislis, Egil. 'Jesus Christ – The Centre of Theology in Richard Hooker's *Of the Lawes of Ecclesiastical* Polity, Book V'. *Journal of Anglican Studies* 5, no. 2 (2007): 227–51.
Grislis, Egil. 'Scriptural Hermeneutics'. In *A Companion to Richard Hooker*, ed. W. J. T. Kirby, 297–301. Leiden: Brill, 2008.
Gross, Jules. *The Divinisation of the Christian According to the Greek Fathers*, trans. Paul A. Onica. Anaheim: A & C Press, 2002.
Grube, G. M. *Plato's Thought*, 2nd edn. London: Athlone Press, 1980.
Hadot, Pierre. *Plotinus or the Simplicity of Vision*, trans. Michael Chase. Chicago: University of Chicago Press, 1993.
Hall, M. S. and R. W. Hall. 'Platonism in Hooker'. *Apeiron: A Journal for Ancient Philosophy and Science*, 17 (1983): 48–56.
Hallonsten, Gösta. 'Theōsis in Recent Research: A Renewal of Interest and a Need for Clarity'. In *Partakers of the Divine Nature: The History and Development of Deification in the Christian Traditions*, ed. M. J. Christensen and Jeffrey A. Wittung, 281–93. Grand Rapids, MI: Baker, 2007.
Hankey, Wayne J. *God in Himself: Aquinas' Doctrine of God as Expounded in the Summa Theologiae*. Oxford: Oxford University Press, 1987.
Hankey, Wayne J. 'Augustinian Immediacy and Dionysian Mediation in John Colet, Edmund Spenser, Richard Hooker and the Cardinal de Bérulle'. In *Acts of the 1996 Kolloquium Augustinus in der Neuzeit*, ed. Kurt Flasch and Dominique de Courcelles, 125–60. Turnhout: Editions Brepols, 1998.
Hankey, Wayne J. and Douglas Hedley (eds). *Deconstructing Radical Orthodoxy: Postmodern Theology, Rhetoric, and Truth*. Abingdon: Routledge, 2005.
Hardy, Daniel W. *Wording a Radiance: Parting Conversations about God and the Church*. London: SCM Press, 2010.
Harnack, Adolf von. *History of Dogma*, 7 vols. London: Williams & Norgate, 1896–9.
Harrison, William H. 'Prudence and Custom: Revisiting Hooker on Authority'. *Anglican Theological Review* 84, no. 4 (2003): 897–913.
Harrison, William H. 'Powers of Nature and Influences of Grace'. In *Richard Hooker and the English Reformation*, ed. W. J. T. Kirby, 15–24. Dordrecht: Kluwer, 2003.
Harrison, William H. 'The Church'. In *A Companion to Richard Hooker*, ed. W. J. T. Kirby, 305–36. Leiden: Brill, 2008.
Haugaard, William. 'The Preface'. In *The Folger Library Edition of the Works of Richard Hooker*, ed. W. Speed Hill, 7 vols, vol. 6 (1), 1–80. Vols 1–5, Cambridge: Belknap

Press, 1977–90; vol. 6, Binghamton: Belknap Press, 1993; vol. 7, Tempe: Medieval and Renaissance Texts and Studies, 1998.
Haugaard, William. 'Books II, III, & IV' In *The Folger Library Edition of the Works of Richard Hooker*, ed. W. Speed Hill, 7 vols, vol. 6 (1), 125–82. Vols 1–5, Cambridge: Belknap Press, 1977–90; vol. 6, Binghamton: Belknap Press, 1993; vol. 7, Tempe: Medieval and Renaissance Texts and Studies, 1998.
Heide, Gale. *Timeless Truth in the Hands of History. A Short History of System in Theology*. Cambridge: James Clarke, 2012.
Helmholz, R. H. *Roman Canon Law in Reformation England*. Cambridge: Cambridge University Press, 1990.
Hemming, Laurence Paul (ed.). *Radical Orthodoxy? – A Catholic Enquiry*. Aldershot: Ashgate, 2000.
Hermann, Fritz-Gregor. 'μετέχειν, μεταλαμβάνειν and the Problem of Participation in Plato's Ontology'. *Philosophical Inquiry* 25, nos 3–4 (2003): 19–56.
Hill, W. Speed. 'The Doctrinal Background of Richard Hooker's Laws of Ecclesiastical Polity'. PhD thesis, Cambridge: Harvard University, 1964.
Hill, W. Speed. 'Hooker's Polity. The Problem of the "last three books"'. *Huntingdon Library Quarterly* 24, no. 4 (1971): 317–36.
Hillar, Marian. *From Logos to Trinity: The Evolution of Religious Beliefs from Pythagoras to Tertullian*. Cambridge: Cambridge University Press, 2012.
Hillerdal, Gunnar. *Reason and Revelation in Richard Hooker*. Lund: Gleerup, 1962.
Holmer, Paul. *The Grammar of Faith*. San Francisco, CA: Harper & Row, 1978.
Holtzen, T. C. 'Sacramental Causality in Hooker's Eucharistic Theology'. *Journal of Theological Studies* 62, no. 2 (2011): 607–48.
Hoopes, Robert. *Right Reason in the English Renaissance*. Cambridge: Harvard University Press, 1962.
Ingalls, Ranall. 'Sin and Grace'. In *A Companion to Richard Hooker*, ed. W. J. T. Kirby, 151–84. Leiden: Brill, 2008.
Insole, Christopher J. *The Politics of Human Frailty. A Theological Defence of Political Liberalism*. London: SCM Press, 2004.
Irish, Charles. '"Participation of God himselfe": Law, the Mediation of Christ, and Sacramental Participation in the Thought of Richard Hooker'. In *Richard Hooker and the English Reformation*, ed. W. J. T. Kirby, 165–84. Dordrecht: Kluwer, 2003.
Jager, Eric. *The Book of the Heart*. Chicago: University of Chicago Press, 2001.
James, Susan. *Passion and Action: The Emotions in Seventeenth-Century Philosophy*. Oxford: Oxford University Press, 1997.
Jenkins, John. *Knowledge and Faith in Thomas Aquinas*. Cambridge: Cambridge University Press, 1997.
Joyce, A. J. *Richard Hooker and Anglican Moral Theology*. Oxford: Oxford University Press, 2012.
Karkkainen, Veli-Matti. *One with God: Salvation as Deification and Justification*. Collegeville: Liturgical Press, 2004.
Kavanagh, Robert. 'Reason and Nature in Hooker's Polity'. Unpublished PhD Thesis, University of Wisconsin, 1944.
Keating, Daniel. *Deification and Grace*. Washington: Catholic University of America Press, 2007.
Kearney, H. F. 'Richard Hooker: A Reconstruction'. *Cambridge Journal* 5 (1952): 300–11.
Kenney, J. P. *Mystical Monotheism: A Study in Ancient Platonic Theology*. Hanover and London: Brown University Press, 1991.

Kimbrough, S. T. 'Theosis in the Writings of Charles Wesley'. *St. Vladimir's Theological Quarterly* 52 (2008): 199–212.
Kimbrough, S. T. *Partakers of the Life Divine: Participation in the Divine Nature in the Writings of Charles Wesley*. Eugene: Cascade, 2016.
King, Peter. 'Emotions in Medieval Thought'. In *The Oxford Handbook of Philosophy of Emotion*, ed. Peter Goldie, 167–88. Oxford: Oxford University Press, 2012.
King, Peter. 'Emotions'. In *The Oxford Handbook of Aquinas*, ed. Brian Davies and Eleanore Stump, 209–26. Oxford: Oxford University Press, 2012.
Kirby, W. J. T. '*Supremum Caput*: Richard Hooker's Theory of Ecclesiastical Dominion'. *Dionysius* 12 (1988): 69–110.
Kirby, W. J. T. *Richard Hooker's Doctrine of the Royal Supremacy*. Leiden: Brill, 1990.
Kirby, W. J. T. 'The Neoplatonic Logic of Richard Hooker's Generic Division of Law'. *Renaissance et Réforme* 22, no. 4 (1998): 49–67.
Kirby, W. J. T. 'The Context of Reformation Thought: The Influence of the Magisterial Reformers on Richard Hooker's Discourse on Natural Law'. In *The Theology of Richard Hooker in the Context of the Magisterial Reformation*, ed. W. J. T. Kirby, 1–21. Princeton, NJ: Princeton Theological Seminary, 2000.
Kirby, W. J. T. 'The Paradigm of Chalcedonian Christology in Richard Hooker's Discourse on Grace and the Church'. *Churchman* 114, no. 1 (2000): 22–39.
Kirby, W. J. T. 'Grace and Hierarchy: Richard Hooker's Two Platonisms'. In *Richard Hooker and the English Reformation*, ed. W. J. T. Kirby, 25–40. Dordrecht: Kluwer, 2003.
Kirby, W. J. T. 'Angels Descending and Ascending: Hooker's Discourse on the Double Motion of Common Prayer'. In *Richard Hooker and the English Reformation*, ed. W. J. T. Kirby, 111–30. Dordrecht: Kluwer, 2003.
Kirby, W. J. T. *Richard Hooker, Reformer and Platonist*. Aldershot: Ashgate, 2005.
Kirby, W. J. T. *The Zurich Connection and Tudor Political Theology*. Leiden: Brill, 2007.
Kirby, W. J. T. 'Creation and Government: Eternal Law as the Fountain of Laws in Richard Hooker's Ecclesiastical Polity'. In *Divine Creation in Ancient, Medieval, and Early Modern Thought*, ed. Willemien Otten, Walter Hannam and Michael Treschow, 405–23. Leiden: Brill, 2007.
Kirby, W. J. T. 'Reason and Law'. In *A Companion to Richard Hooker*, ed. W. J. T. Kirby, 251–72. Leiden: Brill, 2008.
Kirby, W. J. T. 'Law Makes the King: Richard Hooker on Law and Princely Rule'. In *A New Companion to English Renaissance Literature and Culture*, ed. Michael Hattaway, 274–88. Oxford: Blackwell, 2010.
Kirby, W. J. T. 'From "General Mediations" to "Particular Decisions": The Augustinian Coherence of Richard Hooker's Political Theology'. In *Sovereignty and Law in the Middle Ages and Renaissance*, ed. R. Sturges, 43–68. Turnhout: Brepols, 2011.
Kirby, W. J. T. *Persuasion and Conversion: Essays on Religion, Politics, and the Public Sphere in Early Modern England*. Leiden: Brill, 2013.
Kirby, W. J. T. '"Divine Offspring": Richard Hooker's Neoplatonic Account of Law and Causality'. *Perichoresis* 13, no. 1 (2015): 3–15.
Kirby, W. J. T. 'The "sundrie waies of Wisdom": Richard Hooker on the Authority of Scripture and Reason'. In *Richard Hooker. His Life, Work, and Legacy*, ed. Daniel Graves and Scott Kindred-Barnes, 145–60. Bradford: St Osmund Press, 2013.
Kirby, W. J. T. 'Richard Hooker and Thomas Aquinas on defining Law'. In *Aquinas Among the Protestants*, ed. Manfred Svensson and David VanDrunen, 91–108. Chichester: Wiley-Blackwell, 2018.

Kharlamov, Vladimir (ed.). *Theōsis: Deification in Christian Theology, Volume Two*. Cambridge: James Clarke, 2012.
Knuutila, Simo. *Emotions in Ancient and Medieval Philosophy*. Oxford: Oxford University Press, 2004.
Kolb, Robert. *Martin Luther: Confessor of the Faith*. Oxford: Oxford University Press, 2009.
Kristerva, Julia. *Tales of Love*. New York: Colombia University Press, 1987.
LaCugna, Catherine Mowry. *God for Us: The Trinity and Christian Life*. New York: Harper Collins, 1991.
Lake, Peter. *Anglicans & Puritans? Presbyterian and English Conformist Thought from Whitgift to Hooker*. London: Unwin Hyman, 1988.
Lake, Peter. 'The "Anglican Moment"? Richard Hooker and the Ideological Watershed of the 1590s'. In *Anglicanism and the Western Christian Tradition*, ed. Stephen Platten, 90–121. Norwich: Canterbury Press, 2003.
Larchet, Jean-Claude. 'The Mode of Deification'. In *The Oxford Handbook of Maximus the Confessor*, ed. Pauline Allen and Bronwen Neil, 341–59. Oxford: Oxford University Press, 2015.
Lawson, J. *The Biblical Theology of Saint Irenaeus*. London: The Epworth Press, 1948.
LeTourneau, Mark. 'Richard Hooker and the Sufficiency of Scripture'. *Journal of Anglican Studies* 14, no. 2 (2016): 134–55.
Lewis, C. S. *English Literature in the Sixteenth Century, Excluding Drama*. Oxford: Clarendon Press, 1954.
Liddell, H. G., R. Scott and H. S. Jones. *A Greek-English Lexicon*. Oxford: Clarendon Press, 1968.
Littlejohn, W. Bradford. ' "More than a swinehered": Hooker, Vermigli, and an Aristoelian Defence of the Royal Supremacy'. *Reformation & Renaissance Review* 15, no. 1 (2013): 68–83.
Littlejohn, W. Bradford. 'The Edification of the Church: Richard Hooker's Theology of Worship and the Protestant Inward/Outward Disjunction'. *Perichoresis* 12, no. 1 (2014): 3–18.
Littlejohn, W. Bradford. 'The Search for a Reformed Hooker: Some Modest Proposals'. *Reformation and Renaissance Review* 16, no. 1 (2015): 68–82.
Littlejohn, W. Bradford. *Richard Hooker: A Companion to His Life and Work*. Eugene: Cascade, 2015.
Littlejohn, W. Bradford. 'Hooker, Junius, and a Reformed Theology of Law'. In *Richard Hooker and Reformed Orthodoxy*, ed. Scott Kindred-Barnes and W. Bradford Littlejohn, 221–40. Göttingen, Bristol: Vandenhoeck & Ruprecht, 2017.
Littlejohn, W. Bradford. *The Peril and Promise of Christian Liberty. Richard Hooker, the Puritans, and Protestant Political Theology*. Grand Rapids, MI: Eerdmans, 2017.
Litwa, M. David. *We Are Being Transformed: Deification in Paul's Soteriology*. Berlin: Walter de Gruyter, 2012.
Lombardo, Nicholas E. *The Logic of Desire: Aquinas on Emotion*. Washington: Catholic University of America Press, 2011.
Lossky, Vladimir. *The Mystical Theology of the Eastern Church*. Crestwood: St. Vladimir's Seminary Press, 1973.
Louth, Andrew. *The Origins of the Christian Mystical Tradition*. Oxford: Clarendon Press, 1981.
Louth, Andrew. 'The Place of Theōsis in Orthodox Theology'. In *Partakers of the Divine Nature: The History and Development of Deification in the Christian Traditions*, ed. M. J. Christensen and Jeffrey A. Wittung, 32–46. Grand Rapids, MI: Baker, 2007.

Loyer, Olivier. *L'Anglicanisme de Richard Hooker: Thèse Presentée devant l'université de Paris III*, 2 vols. Paris: Université de Paris, 1979.
Luoma, John K. 'Who Owns the Fathers? Hooker and Cartwright on the Authority of the Primitive Church'. *Sixteenth Century Journal* 8, no. 3 (1977): 45–59.
Macaskill, Grant. *Union with Christ in the New Testament*. Oxford: Oxford University Press, 2013.
MacCulloch, Diarmaid. 'Richard Hooker's Reputation'. In *A Companion to Richard Hooker*, ed. W. J. T. Kirby, 563–612. Leiden: Brill, 2008.
Mantzaridis, G. I. *The Deification of Man: St. Gregory Palamas and the Orthodox Tradition*. Crestwood: St. Vladimir's Seminary Press, 1984.
Marenbon, John. *Later Medieval Philosophy*. London: Routledge, 1991.
Marenbon, John. *Pagans and Philosophers: The Problem of Paganism from Augustine to Leibniz*. Princeton, NJ: Princeton University Press, 2015.
Marot, D. H. 'Aux origines de la Théologie anglicaine'. *Irénikon* 33 (1960): 321–43.
Marshall, J. S. *Hooker and the Anglican Tradition: An Historical and Theological Study of Hooker's Ecclesiastical Polity*. London: Adam and Charles Black, 1963.
Marshall, Peter and Alexandra Walsham (eds). *Angels in the Early Modern World*. Cambridge: Cambridge University Press, 2006.
McGrade, A. S. 'The Coherence of Hooker's Polity: The Books on Power'. *Journal of the History of Ideas* 24 (1963): 163–82.
McGrade, A. S. 'Reason'. In *The Study of Anglicanism*, ed. Stephen Sykes, John Booty and Jonathan Knight, 115–30. London: SPCK, 1998.
McGrade, A. S. 'Book VIII'. In *The Folger Library Edition of the Works of Richard Hooker*, 7 vols, ed. W. Speed Hill, vol. 6 (1), 337–83. Vols 1–5, Cambridge: Belknap Press, 1977–90; vol. 6, Binghamton: Belknap Press, 1993; vol. 7, Tempe: Medieval and Renaissance Texts and Studies, 1998.
McGrade, A. S. 'Classical, Patristic, and Medieval Sources'. In *A Companion to Richard Hooker*, ed. W. J. T. Kirby, 51–88. Leiden: Brill, 2008.
McGrade, A. S. 'Episcopacy'. In *A Companion to Richard Hooker*, ed. W. J. T. Kirby, 481–502. Leiden: Brill, 2008.
Meconi, David Vincent. *The One Christ: St. Augustine's Theology of Deification*. Washington: Catholic University of America Press, 2013.
Meconi, David and Carl E. Olson. *Called to Be the Children of God: The Catholic Theology of Human Deification*. San Francisco, CA: Ignatius Press, 2016.
Milbank, John. *Theology and Social Theory: Beyond Secular Reason*. Oxford: Blackwell, 1990.
Milbank, John. 'Materialism and Transcendence'. In *Theology and the Political: The New Debate*, ed. Creston Davis, John Milbank and Slavoj Žižek, 393–426. Durham: Duke University Press, 2005.
Milbank, John and Simon Oliver. 'Radical Orthodoxy'. In *God's Advocates: Christian Thinkers in Conversation*, ed. Rupert Shortt, 103–25. London: Darton, Longman & Todd, 2005.
Milbank, John, Catherine Pickstock and Graham Ward (eds). *Radical Orthodoxy: A New Theology*. London: Routledge, 1999.
Miller, Charles. *Richard Hooker and the Vision of God: Exploring the Origins of 'Anglicanism'*. Cambridge: James Clarke, 2013.
Miller, E. C. *Toward a Fuller Vision: Orthodoxy and the Anglican Experience*. Wilton: Morehouse Barlow, 1984.

Mohamed, Feisal G. 'Renaissance Thought on the Celestial Hierarchy: The Decline of a Tradition'. *Journal of the History of Ideas* 65, no. 4 (2004): 559–82.
Mohamed, Feisal G. *In the Anteroom of Divinity: The Reformation of the Angels from Colet to Milton.* Toronto: University of Toronto Press, 2008.
Morrel, George. 'The Systematic Theology of Richard Hooker'. Unpublished PhD thesis, Pacific School of Religion, 1969.
Moser, Paul K., Dwayne H. Mulder and J. D. Trout. *The Theory of Knowledge: A Thematic Introduction.* Oxford: Oxford University Press, 1998.
Mosser, Carl. 'The Greatest Possible Blessing: Calvin and Deification'. *Scottish Journal of Theology* 55, no. 1 (2002): 36–57.
Mulcahy, Bernard. *Aquinas's Notion of Pure Nature and the Christian Integralism of Henri de Lubac.* New York: Peter Lang, 2011.
Muller, Richard A. *Dictionary of Latin and Greek Theological Terms Drawn Principally from Protestant Scholastic Theology.* Grand Rapids, MI: Baker, 1985.
Muller, Richard A. *Post-Reformation Reformed Dogmatics,* 4 vols. Grand Rapids, MI: Baker, 2003.
Muller, Richard A. *After Calvin: Studies in the Development of a Theological Tradition.* Oxford: Oxford University Press, 2003.
Munz, Peter. *The Place of Hooker in the History of Thought.* London: Routledge & Kegan Paul, 1952.
Murphy, Roland. *The Tree of Life: An Exploration of Biblical Wisdom Literature.* Grand Rapids, MI: Eerdmans, 2002.
Narcisse, Gilbert. *Les Raisons de Dieu: Argument de convenance et esthétique théologique selon saint Thomas d'Aquin et Hans Urs von Balthasar.* Fribourg: Editions universitaires, 1997.
Neelands, David. *The Theology of Grace of Richard Hooker.* PhD thesis, Toronto: Trinity College, University of Toronto, 1988.
Neelands, David. 'Hooker on Scripture, Reason, and "Tradition"'. In *Richard Hooker and the Construction of Christian Community,* ed. A. S. McGrade, 75–94. Tempe: Medieval and Renaissance Texts and Studies, 1997.
Neelands, David. 'Richard Hooker and the Debates about Predestination, 1580–1600'. In *Richard Hooker and the English Reformation,* ed. W. J. T. Kirby, 43–61. Dordrecht: Kluwer, 2003.
Neelands, David. 'Richard Hooker on the Identity of the Visible and Invisible Church'. In *Richard Hooker and the English Reformation,* ed. W. J. T. Kirby, 99–110. Dordrecht: Kluwer, 2003.
Neelands, David. 'Predestination'. In *A Companion to Richard Hooker,* ed. W. J. T. Kirby, 185–220. Leiden: Brill, 2008.
Neelands, David. 'Christology and the Sacraments'. In *A Companion to Richard Hooker,* ed. W. J. T. Kirby, 369–402. Leiden: Brill, 2008.
Neelands, David. 'Hooker on Divinization: Our Participation of Christ'. In *From Logos to Christos: Essays in Christology in Honour of Joanne McWilliam,* ed. Ellen Leonard and Kate Merriman, 137–50. Waterloo: Wilfrid Laurier University Press, 2010.
Neelands, David. 'The Use and Abuse of John Calvin in Richard Hooker's Defence of the English Church'. *Perichoresis* 10, no. 1 (2012): 3–22.
Newey, Edmund. 'The Form of Reason: Participation in the work of Richard Hooker, Benjamin Whichcote, Ralph Cudworth, and Jeremy Taylor'. *Modern Theology* 18, no. 1 (2002): 1–26.

Nichols, Aidan. *The Panther and the Hind: A Theological History of Anglicanism*. Edinburgh: T&T Clark, 1993.
Norris, Frederick W. 'Deification: Consensual and Cogent'. *Scottish Journal of Theology* 49, no. 4 (1996): 411–28.
O' Donovan, Joan Lockwood. *Theology of Law and Authority in the English Reformation*. Atlanta: Scholars Press, 2000.
Olson, Roger E. 'Deification in Contemporary Theology'. *Theology Today* 64 (2007): 186–200.
Ortiz, Jared (ed.). *Deification in the Latin Patristic Tradition*. Washington: Catholic University of America Press, 2019.
Pabst, Adrian. *Metaphysics: The Creation of Hierarchy*. Grand Rapids, MI: Eerdmans, 2012.
Pabst, Adrian and Christoph Schneider (eds). *Encounter between Eastern Orthodoxy and Radical Orthodoxy: Transfiguring the World through the Word*. Farnham: Ashgate, 2009.
Paddison, A. and N. Messer (eds). *The Bible. Culture, Community, Society*. London: Bloomsbury T&T Clark, 2013.
Paget, Francis. *Introduction to the Fifth Book of Hooker's Ecclesiastical Polity*. Oxford: Oxford University Press, 1899.
Paster, Gail Kern, Katherine Rowe, and Mary Floyd-Wilson (eds). *Reading the Early Modern Passions: Essays in the Cultural History of Emotion*. Philadelphia: University of Pennsylvania Press, 2004.
Patterson, Patrick D. M. 'Hooker's Apprentice: God, Entelechy, Beauty, and Desire in Book One of Richard Hooker's *Lawes of Ecclesiastical Politie*'. *Anglican Theological Review* 84, no. 4 (2002): 961–98.
Patterson, W. B. 'Elizabethan Theological Polemics'. In *A Companion to Richard Hooker*, ed. W. J. T. Kirby, 89–120. Leiden: Brill, 2008.
Perkins, Pheme. *First and Second Peter, James, and Jude*. Louisville, KY: Westminster John Knox, 1995.
Pliezier, T., Theo J. and Maarten Wisse. '"As the Philosopher Says": Aristotle'. In *Introduction to Reformed Scholasticism*, ed. Willem J. Van Asselt, 26–45. Grand Rapids, MI: Reformation Heritage Books, 2011.
Popov, Ivan V. 'The Idea of Deification in the Early Eastern Church'. In *Theōsis: Deification in Christian Theology, Volume Two*, ed. Vladimir Kharlamov, trans. Boris Yakimin, 42–82. Cambridge: James Clarke, 2012.
Porter, H. C. 'Hooker, the Tudor Constitution, and the *Via Media*'. In *Studies in Richard Hooker*, ed. W. Speed Hill, 77–116. Cleveland: The Press of Case Western Reserve University, 1972.
Prodi, Paolo. *The Papal Prince: One Body and Two Souls: The Papal Monarchy in Early Modern Europe*. Cambridge: Cambridge University Press, 1987.
Quine, W. V. and J. S. Ullian. *The Web of Belief*, 2nd edn. New York: Random House, 1978.
Rashdall, H. *The Idea of Atonement in Christian Theology*. London: Macmillan, 1919.
Rasmussen, Barry. 'The Priority of God's Gracious Action in Richard Hooker's Hermeneutic'. In *Richard Hooker and the English Reformation*, ed. W. J. T. Kirby, 3–14. Dordrecht: Kluwer, 2003.
Ratzinger, Joseph. *God's Word: Scripture, Tradition, Office*. San Francisco, CA: Ignatius Press, 2008.
Rawls, John. *Political Liberalism*. New York: Columbia University Press, 1993.
Reed, Esther. 'Richard Hooker, Eternal Law, and the Human Exercise of Authority'. *Journal of Anglican Studies* 4, no. 2 (2006): 219–38.
Reid, D. *Energies of the Spirit: Trinitarian Models in Eastern Orthodox and Western Theology*. Oxford: Oxford University Press, 2000.

Rhonheimer, M. *Natural Law and Practical Reason: A Thomist View of Moral Autonomy*, trans. Gerald Malsbary. New York: Fordham University Press, 2000.
Riis, Ole and Linda Woodhead. *A Sociology of Religious Emotion*. Oxford: Oxford University Press, 2010.
Rosendale, Timothy. *Liturgy and Literature in the Making of Protestant England*. Cambridge: Cambridge University Press, 2007.
Rosenthal, Alexander S. *Crown under Law: Richard Hooker, John Locke, and the Ascent of Modern Constitutionalism*. Lanham, MD: Lexington Books, 2008.
Ruether, Rosemary Radford and Marian Grau (eds). *Interpreting Postmodernity: Responses to Radical Orthodoxy*. New York: T&T Clark, 2006.
Russell, Andrea. *Richard Hooker, Beyond Certainty*. Oxford: Routledge, 2016.
Russell, Norman. *The Doctrine of Deification in the Greek Patristic Tradition*. Oxford: Oxford University Press, 2006.
Russell, Norman. *Fellow Workers with God: Orthodox Thinking on Theosis*. New York: St Vladimir's Seminary Press, 2009.
Ryan, Fáinche. *Formation in Holiness: Thomas Aquinas on 'Sacra Doctrina'*. Leuven: Peeters, 2007.
Rziha, John. *Perfecting Human Actions: St. Thomas Aquinas on Human Participation in Eternal Law*. Washington: Catholic University of America Press, 2009.
Sammon, Brendan Thomas. *The God Who Is Beauty: Beauty as a Divine Name in Thomas Aquinas and Dionysius the Areopagite*. Eugene: Pickwick, 2013.
Schindler, David C. 'What's the Difference? On the Metaphysics of Participation in a Christian Context'. *The Saint Anselm Journal* 3, no. 1 (2005): 1–27.
Schoeck, R.J. 'From Erasmus to Hooker: An Overview'. In *Richard Hooker and the Construction of Christian Community*, ed. A. S. McGrade, 59–73. Tempe: Medieval and Renaissance Texts and Studies, 1997.
Schwarz, Robert C. 'Dignified and Commodious: Richard Hooker's "Mystical Copulation" Metaphor'. *Sewanee Theological Review* 43, no. 1 (1999): 16–30.
Scrutton, A. P. *Thinking through Feeling: God, Emotion, and Possibility*. New York: Bloomsbury, 2011.
Sedgwick, Peter. *The Origins of Anglican Moral Theology*. Leiden: Brill, 2019.
Selderhuis, Herman J. (ed.). *A Companion to Reformed Orthodoxy*. Leiden: Brill, 2013.
Shagan, Ethan. *The Rule of Moderation: Violence, Religion, and the Politics of Restraint in Early Modern England*. Cambridge: Cambridge University Press, 2011.
Sherman, Jacob H. 'A Genealogy of Participation'. In *The Participatory Turn: Spirituality, Mysticism, Religious Studies*, ed. Jorge N. Ferrer and Jacob H. Sherman, 81–112. Albany: State University of New York Press, 2008.
Sherman, Jacob H. *Partakers of the Divine: Contemplation and the Practice of Theology*. Minneapolis, MN: Fortress Press, 2014.
Shirley, F. J. *Richard Hooker and Contemporary Political Ideas*. London: SPCK, 1949.
Shuger, Debora. *Sacred Rhetoric: The Christian Grand Style in the English Renaissance*. Princeton, NJ: Princeton University Press, 1988.
Shuger, Debora. 'Society Supernaturall: The Imagined Community of Hooker's *Lawes*'. In *Richard Hooker and the Construction of Christian Community*, ed. A. S. McGrade, 309–29. Tempe: Medieval and Renaissance Texts and Studies, 1997.
Shuger, Debora. 'Society Supernatural: The Imagined Community of Hooker's *Laws*'. In *Religion and Culture in Renaissance England*, ed. Claire McEachern and Debora Shuger, 116–41. Cambridge: Cambridge University Press, 1997.

Shuger, Debora. *Habits of Thought in the English Renaissance*. Toronto: University of Toronto Press, 1997.
Shuger, Debora. 'Faith and Assurance'. In *A Companion to Richard Hooker*, ed. W. J. T. Kirby, 221–50. Leiden: Brill, 2008.
Simut, Corneliu. *Richard Hooker and His Early Doctrine of Justification: A Study of His Discourse on Justification*. Aldershot: Ashgate, 2005.
Simut, Corneliu. *The Doctrine of Salvation in the Sermons of Richard Hooker*. Berlin: Walter de Gruyter, 2005.
Simut, Corneliu. 'Orders of Ministry'. In *A Companion to Richard Hooker*, ed. W. J. T. Kirby, 403–34. Leiden: Brill, 2008.
Skinner, Quentin. 'Meaning and Understanding in the History of Ideas'. *History and Theory* 8, no. 1 (1969): 3–53.
Slater, Jonathan. 'Salvation as Participation in the Humanity of the Mediator in Calvin's Institutes of the Christian Religion: A Reply to Carl Mosser'. *Scottish Journal of Theology* 58, no. 1 (2005): 39–58.
Slocum, Robert B. 'An Answering Heart: Reflections on Saving Participation'. *Anglican Theological Review* 84, no. 3 (2002): 1009–15.
Smith, James K.A. *Introducing Radical Orthodoxy: Mapping a Post-Secular Theology*. Grand Rapids, MI: Baker, 2004.
Sommerville, M. R. 'Richard Hooker and His Contemporaries on Episcopacy. An Elizabethan Consensus'. *Journal of Ecclesiastical History* 35, no. 2 (1984): 177–87.
Spezzano, Daria. *The Glory of God's Grace: Deification According to St. Thomas Aquinas*. Washington: Catholic University of America Press, 2015.
Spinks, Bryan D. *Two Faces of Elizabethan Anglican Theology: Sacraments and Salvation in the Thought of William Perkins and Richard Hooker*. Lanham, Maryland, and London: Scarecrow Press, 1999.
Stafford, John. 'Practical Divinity'. In *A Companion to Richard Hooker*, ed. W. J. T. Kirby, 131–47. Leiden: Brill, 2008.
Stafford, John. 'Richard Hooker's Pneumatologia'. *Perichoresis* 11, no. 2 (2013): 161–86.
Stanwood, P. G. 'Works and Editions I'. In *A Companion to Richard Hooker*, ed. W. J. T. Kirby, 27–39. Leiden: Brill, 2008.
Steel, Richard B. 'Transfiguring Light: The Moral Beauty of the Christian Life According to Gregory Palamas and Jonathan Edwards'. *St. Vladimir's Theological Quarterly* 52 (2008): 403–39.
Strobel, Kyle. 'Jonathan Edwards and the Polemics of Theosis'. *Harvard Theological Review* 105, no. 3 (2012): 259–79.
Studer, Basil. 'Divinization'. In *Encyclopedia of the Early Church*, ed. Angelo Di Beradina, 2 vols, vol. 1, 242. New York: Oxford University Press, 1992.
Svensson, Manfred and David VanDrunen (eds). *Aquinas among the Protestants*. Chichester: Wiley-Blackwell, 2018.
Sweetman, Robert. 'Univocity, Analogy, and the Mystery of Being According to John Duns Scotus'. In *Radical Orthodoxy and the Reformed Tradition: Creation, Covenant, and Participation*, ed. James K. A. Smith and James H. Olthuis, 73–87. Grand Rapids, MI: Baker, 2005.
Tanner, Kathryn. *Christ the Key*. Cambridge: Cambridge University Press, 2009.
Taylor, Charles. 'Reason, Faith, and Meaning'. In *Faith, Rationality, and the Passions*, ed. Sarah Coakley, 13–28. Chichester: Wiley-Blackwell, 2012.
Te Velde, Rudi. *Participation and Substantiality in Thomas Aquinas*. New York: Brill Press, 1995.

Thomas, Stephen. *Deification in the Eastern Orthodox Tradition: A Biblical Perspective*. Piscataway: Gorgias Press, 2008.
Thornton, L. S. *Richard Hooker: A Study of His Theology*. London: SPCK, 1924.
Tierney, Brian. *Liberty & Law. The Idea of Permissive Natural Law, 1100–1800*. Washington: Catholic University of America Press, 2014.
Tollefsen, Torstein Theodor. *Activity and Participation in Late Antique and Early Christian Thought*. Oxford: Oxford University Press, 2012.
Törönen, Melchisedec. *Union and Distinction in the Thought of St Maximus the Confessor*. Oxford: Oxford University Press, 2007.
Tóth, Béata. *The Heart Has Its Reasons: Towards a Theological Anthropology of the Heart*. Eugene: Cascade, 2016.
Trenchard, Warren. *Complete Vocabulary Guide to the Greek New Testament*. Grand Rapids, MI: Zondervan, 1998.
Trimpi, Wesley. *Muses of One Mind: The Literary Analysis of Experience and Its Continuity*. Princeton, NJ: Princeton University Press, 1983.
Turrell, James. 'Uniformity and Common Prayer'. In *A Companion to Richard Hooker*, ed. W. J. T. Kirby, 337–67. Leiden: Brill, 2008.
Underhill, E. *Mysticism: A Study in the Nature and Development of Man's Spiritual Consciousness*. London: Methuen, 1949.
Urban, Linwood. 'A Revolution in English Moral Theology'. *Anglican Theological Review* 53, no. 1 (1971): 5–20.
Valkenberg, W. G. B. M. *Words of the Living God: Place and Function of Holy Scripture in the Theology of St. Thomas Aquinas*. Leiden: Peeters, 2003.
van Asselt, Willem J. 'Reformed Orthodoxy: A Short History of Research'. In *A Companion to Reformed Orthodoxy*, ed. Herman J. Selderhuis, 11–26. Leiden: Brill, 2013.
Van den Belt, Henk. *The Authority of Scripture in Reformed Theology: Truth and Trust*. Leiden: Brill, 2008.
Verkamp, Bernard J. *The Indifferent Mean: Adiaphorism in the English Reformation to 1554*. Athens and Detroit: Ohio University Press and Wayne State University Press, 1977.
Vickers, Brian. 'Introduction 2: Hooker's Prose Style'. In *Of the Laws of Ecclesiastical Polity. An Abridged Edition*, ed. A. S. McGrade and Brian Vickers, 41–59. London: Sidgwick & Jackson, 1975.
Vickers, Brian. 'Public and Private Rhetoric in Hooker's *Lawes*'. In *Richard Hooker and the Construction of Christian Community*, ed. A. S. McGrade, 95–145. Tempe: Medieval and Renaissance Texts and Studies, 1997.
Voak, Nigel. *Richard Hooker and Reformed Theology: A Study of Reason, Will, and Grace*. Oxford: Oxford University Press, 2003.
Voak, Nigel. 'Richard Hooker and the Principle of *Sola Scriptura*'. *Journal of Theological Studies* 59, no. 1 (2008): 96–131.
Voak, Nigel. 'English Molinism in the Late 1590s: Richard Hooker on Free Will, Predestination, and Divine Foreknowledge'. *Journal of Theological Studies* 60, no. 1 (2009): 130–77.
Wall, John N. 'Hooker's "Faire Speeche". Rhetorical Strategies in the *Lawes of Ecclesiastical Polity*'. In *This Sacred History. Anglican Reflections for John Booty*, ed. Donald S. Armentrout, 125–43. Cambridge: Cowley, 1990.
Wallace, Dewey. *Puritans and Predestination: Grace in English Protestant Theology, 1552–1695*. Chapel Hill: University of North Carolina Press, 1982.

Weisheipl, James. 'The Meaning of Sacra Doctrina in *Summa Theologiae* I, q.1'. *Thomist* 38 (1974): 49–80.
Werner, M. *The Formation of Christian Dogma*. New York: Harper, 1957.
Westberg, Daniel. 'Thomistic Law and the Moral Theology of Richard Hooker'. *Catholic Philosophical Quarterly* 68 (1994): 203–14.
Westberg, Daniel. *Right Practical Reason: Aristotle, Action, and Prudence in Aquinas*. Oxford: Oxford University Press, 1994.
Westberg, Daniel. *Renewing Moral Theology*. Downers Grove: IVP Academic, 2015.
Westerman, Pauline. *The Disintegration of Natural Law Theory: Aquinas to Finnis*. New York: Brill 1997.
Whidden III, Daniel L. *Christ the Light: The Theology of Light and Illumination in Thomas Aquinas*. Minneapolis, MN: Fortress, 2014.
Wierzbicka, Anna. *Emotions across Languages and Cultures: Diversity and Universals*. Cambridge: Cambridge University Press, 1999.
Williams, Anna N. 'Deification in the *Summa Theologiae*: A Structural Interpretation of the Prima Pars'. *Thomist* 61, no. 2 (1997): 219–55.
Williams, Anna N. 'Mystical Theology Redux: The Pattern of Aquinas' *Summa Theologiae*'. *Modern Theology* 13, no. 1 (1997): 53–74.
Williams, Anna N. *The Ground of Union: Deification in Aquinas and Palamas*. New York: Oxford University Press, 1999.
Williams, Anna N. *The Divine Sense: The Intellect in Patristic Theology*. Cambridge: Cambridge University Press, 2007.
Williams, Anna N. *The Architecture of Theology: Structure, System & Ratio*. Oxford: Oxford University Press, 2011.
Williams, Raymond. *Keywords: A Vocabulary of Culture and Society*, rev. edn. London: Fontana, 1976.
Williams, Rowan. 'Deification'. In *A Dictionary of Christian Spirituality*, ed. Gordon S. Wakefield, 106–8. London: SCM Press, 1983.
Williams, Rowan. *Anglican Identities*. London: Darton, Longman & Todd, 2009.
Willis, Jonathan. 'Protestant Worship and the Discourse of Music in Reformation England'. In *Worship and the Parish Church in Early Modern Britain*, ed. Natalie Mears and Alec Ryrie, 131–50. Farnham: Ashgate, 2013.
Wippel, J. *The Metaphysical Thought of Thomas Aquinas: From Finite Being to Uncreated Being*. Washington: Catholic University of America Press, 2000.
Withrow, Brandon G. *Becoming Divine: Jonathan Edwards's Incarnational Spirituality within the Christian Tradition*. Cambridge: Lutterworth, 2017.
Yarnell, Malcolm B. *Royal Priesthood in the English Reformation*. Oxford: Oxford University Press, 2013.

Index

abduction 114, 148
absolute power (*potentia absoluta*) 43 n.49
  see also God
active intellect 100–1 *see also* passive intellect
Adamic Christology 69–70 *see also* Christ
Admonition Controversy 174, 175, 177
adoption 5–7, 15, 27, 64, 65, 69, 70, 88, 162
  see also Christ
affections 129–32, 141, 143, 148 *see also* emotions; passions
Ambrose 83, 185
Anabaptists 117, 117 n.214, 132
analogy *see* Aquinas, Thomas
Anaxagoras 95
angelic law 39, 53, 161, 170 *see also* law
angels 48, 53–6, 59, 80, 86, 96, 109, 131–2, 132 n.307, 136, 142, 146, 150, 155, 161, 170, 197
Anglican-Orthodox relations 15–16, 15 n.66, 16 n.67, 36, 39, 53, 54, 195
anthropology 7, 24, 127
  Aristotelian-Thomistic 55, 133
  faculty-based 93
  heart 127, 137–8, 140, 148
  homo creator 10
  homo faber 10, 152, 181, 183, 192–3
  imago dei 94–6, 105, 148, 152, 183, 192–3
Apostles 103, 164, 165, 171
apotheōsis 5 *see also* deification
appetite *see* desire
Aquinas, Thomas 2, 2 n.7, 7–11, 7 n.32, 9 n.36–9, 17, 20, 31, 45–8, 51, 52, 64, 80, 81, 84, 93–102, 107, 108, 120, 129–38, 172
  analogy 40, 94
  Aristotelian-Thomist philosophy 9, 26, 41, 46, 55, 109, 125, 133, 149, 156
  definition of grace 80
  emotions 129–132
  faith, formed by love 139
  grace perfects nature 27, 60 n.156–7, 97, 108
  Incarnation 64
  intellect, passive and active 97–102
  legal and teleological tradition 44, 52
  per se nota 107, 115, 119–21
  political nature 155
  rationality 93, 97–102, 105, 108, 151
  reduplicative strategy 66
  sacra doctrina 107
  subalternation 107–8
  subsistens 65
  theological virtues 138
  transcendentals 45
Aristotle 9, 155, 177
  Aristotelian revolution 129
  Aristotelian-Thomist philosophy 9, 26, 41, 46, 55, 109, 125, 133, 149, 156
  causality 20, 41, 45 n.59, 46 n.63, 47, 51, 68, 75 n.249, 125, 165
  dilemma of knowability and representation 135–7
  First Mover 187
  form 47–8
  highest good 59, 176, 186
  kalokagathia 101 n.37
  natural inclinations 104, 155
  notion of *scientia* 116
  notion of *theologia* 107
  physics 46
  political nature 104, 155, 183, 186
  potency and act 9, 19, 46, 133 n.313
  rhetoric 32
  scholasticism 99 n.64
  subalternation 106
  tabula rasa 98
  transcendentals 45
Arnobius of Sicca 50
Athanasius 5, 5 n.22
atheists 123, 132

Augustine of Hippo 7, 7 n.32, 59, 70
  dictum 122
  emotions 129–132
  exchange formula 64
  hypostatic distinction 42
  illumination 100
  immediacy 27, 36–8, 42, 64, 68, 76, 77, 78, 82, 88, 140, 144, 149, 152, 154, 156, 173, 176, 188
  modification of a Dionysian account of law 58
  politics 104
  uti/frui 134
authoritarian constitutionalism 168
authoritarianism 167–8, 187, 196
autonomy 18, 42 n.39, 54, 79, 90–2, 94, 145, 148, 172, 195, 197 see also heteronomy; theonomy
autopistos 114–7, 120, 125 n.255 see also Calvin, Jean; Holy Scripture
  Holy Spirit, testimony of 117, 124–5
  origins of idea 115

Bancroft, Richard 151
baptism 5, 72–3, 110, 111, 158, 160–2 see also Christ; Eucharist; participation; sacraments
beauty 3, 45, 53, 54, 59, 61, 86, 101, 143, 144, 145 see also being; goodness; truth; medieval transcendentals
being 3, 9–11, 16–17, 20, 23, 36, 40–1, 44–7, 51–6, 150, 169, 196 see also beauty; goodness; truth; medieval transcendentals
believers 4, 5, 7, 12, 61, 63, 69, 71–5, 82, 109, 115, 135, 148, 162
Beza, Theodore 159 n.56
biblical omnicompetency 139, 145, 152, 153, 159 see also law; Holy Scripture
Bilson, Thomas 151
bishops 151, 153, 164, 170
  angels of God 170–1
  benefits of 169
  divine origin 166, 186
  image of God 150–1, 170–1
  institution 164–5
  jure divino 151
  monarchical episcopacy 164–6, 170
Bodin, Jean 184

Bonaventure 84, 107
bonum publicum 53, 56, 169, 173, 176, 181–2, 185–7, 193
books of power 33, 62, 149, 151, 188, 190
Bracton, Henry 184, 185, 187
Bucer, Martin 159 n.56
Bullinger, Heinrich 115

Calvin, Jean 7, 115, 122, 124, 154, 159
  fora 150, 154, 157–8, 175, 177–9, 181, 188–9
  Holy Spirit, testimony of 117, 124–5
  humana ratio 117, 123
  Logos autopistos 115–7, 120, 125 n.255
  probationes 122–3
Campanella, Tommaso 10
Cartwright, Thomas 145, 160, 174–5, 177, 179, 181
Catholic Church 122, 152, 167
causality see Aristotle
Chalcedonian logic 106, 150, 154, 156, 159, 162, 173–181 see also Christ
Christ see also God; Holy Spirit; Trinity
  Adamic Christology 69–70
  adoption 5, 6, 23, 27, 64, 65, 69, 70, 88, 162
  body of 4, 5, 67, 70, 73–4, 87, 153, 156–8, 161, 163, 165, 172, 180
  Chalcedonian Christology 24, 65, 173, 174, 175, 177, 180
  Christification 7, 74, 194
  deification 67–70, 78
  deiform glory 61
  divine law of Scripture 60
  exchange formula 5, 64
  headship, internal and spiritual 178
  human affectivity 147
  humanity of 5, 6, 10, 13, 29, 30, 67, 68, 159
  hypostatic union of natures 20, 37, 63, 64, 66–7, 70–2, 76, 78, 83, 106, 150, 157, 173
  immediacy of salvation 77
  Incarnation 2, 5, 64, 66–7, 78, 87–8, 144, 192
  key 12, 37, 78, 82, 87, 89, 173, 181, 188, 190, 193–7
  liturgical reception 161
  paradigm for creation 12

participation in 13, 20, 23, 24, 27, 63, 68, 70–3, 75, 76–88, 144, 154, 160, 162–3, 170, 192
political Christology 175
sole mediator of redemption 192 n.2
Son of God 20, 175
Sophia 83–7
sovereignty 178
sufficiency 37
supernatural perfection 68
union with 4, 17, 72, 76, 127, 144, 153, 157–8, 161
Wisdom of God 12, 82–4, 86–8, 105, 146–8, 191
Word (*Logos*) 10, 13, 61, 83, 87, 146, 147, 180, 183, 192
Christian affectivity 148
Christian Platonisms 27, 36, 68, 77, 140, 149, 152, 154, 156, 159, 173, 188–90
Church *see* ecclesiology
Clement of Alexandria 83
cognitive ecology 89, 92, 127, 135
cognitive participation 89–92 *see also* participation
  Christ 145–8
  desire 127–45
  natural 92–105
  supernatural 105–27
coherency 21, 24, 27–31, 193
common good *see* bonum publicum
Commonwealth 149, 152, 164, 167, 169, 173–7, 179, 182, 185, 189, 190, 193
communicatio idiomatum 66, 159, 170, 183,
compositio et divisio 113
conciliarism 167 *see also* General Councils
constitutionalism 186
Convocation 150, 153, 167, 184, 185, 187
Covell, William 162
creatio continua 10
Crown-in-Parliament 150, 167, 185–6
Crown's power 151, 167, 181, 182, 184, 187
customs 99, 99 n.65 *see also* tradition
Cyril of Alexandria 65, 66, 83

deification 2, 4–8, 5 n.23, 7 n.32, 12–17, 21–3, 33, 35, 41, 70, 75, 76, 78, 91, 108, 141, 194 *see also* methexis; participation
  apotheōsis 5

Christification 7, 74, 194
  doctrine of 6–7
  ecumenical retrievals 2, 13, 15, 19, 21
  participation, as a form of 16, 35, 74, 89, 149 n.4
  philosophical registers of 3–4
  retrievals of 2, 13, 19, 144
  scriptural registers of 4–5
  theme of 7, 195
  theopoiēsis 4
  theōsis 4–7, 14–16, 22–3, 28, 76, 195
  typology 6, 28, 71
desire 1, 19, 20, 23, 52, 129, 134, 169, 186
  Christ 68, 88, 147
  definition 52
  faith 135–9
  first-order desires 130
  intellectual 56, 90, 93
  intellectual affection of 130
  liturgical re-creation of 92, 127, 135, 139–44
  logic of 50, 52, 88, 128, 130, 134, 135, 138, 139, 140, 141, 144, 147, 148, 150, 163, 169, 170, 173, 181, 182, 186
  natural 52, 56, 58, 60, 64, 68, 108, 131
  participation of God 1, 19–20, 35, 46–52, 59, 60, 64, 75, 133, 134
  rational 56, 93
  self-warranting desire 135
  sensitive 56
  spiritual 52, 169
  vegetative 55–6
Dionysian *lex divinitatis* 36, 49, 63, 76, 78, 150, 188–9
Dionysian mediation 36, 38, 42, 68, 78, 142, 144, 149, 173, 188
dispositive hierarchy 42–4, 64, 150, 154, 189
divinization *see* deification
Duns Scotus 16, 42 n.37, 93, 107 n.128, 118

ecclesiology 25, 70, 89, 149, 153–4, 156, 160, 163, 172, 176, 185
  bishops 151, 153, 164–71
  body of Christ 4, 5, 67, 70, 73–4, 87, 153, 156–8, 161, 163, 165, 172, 180
  Calvin, fora 150, 154, 157–8, 175, 177–9, 181, 188–9
  coercive institution 160, 167–8, 187, 196

government 37, 112, 153, 158–60, 163–5, 178–80, 182–5, 196
grammar 153–72
lay supremacy 149–52, 172–87
Luther, two regiments 150, 154, 156, 157–8, 175, 177–8, 181, 188–9
mystical 61, 70, 72–4, 87, 125, 142, 150, 152–63, 171–2, 178, 188–90
political and supernatural society 142, 150, 155, 161
polity 27, 89, 105, 112, 153, 157, 158, 160, 165, 166, 170, 188–90
visible/invisible 72, 149, 153–7, 160–2, 172–8, 180, 186, 193
Eckhart, Meister 10
Edwards, Jonathan 7
Elizabethan Religious Settlement 1, 24, 38, 128, 139, 152, 182
emotions 90, 92, 127–30, 132–4, 138–9, 141, 143–5, 148 *see also* affections; passions
  communities 127
  delusion 90
  scripts 142
  taxonomies 129–31
epistemology 27, 29, 89–91, 94, 98, 128, 135, 148, 153, 163, 168, 173, 182, 190, 192
Eriugena, John Scotus 10
eternal law *see* law
Eucharist 4–5, 73–4, 88, 91–2, 144, 161
  see also baptism; Christ; participation; sacraments
Eusebius of Caesarea 83
exitus-reditus 11, 20, 50, 63, 71, 72, 76
  see also monē-proodos-epistrophē
extra calvinisticum 180

faculty-based anthropology 93 *see also* anthropology
faith 61–2, 107 *see also* hope; love; virtues
  assurance 135–7
  formed by love 139
  intellectual habit 30, 110, 138, 146
  public profession of 158
  reason 30, 90–1, 106–8, 110, 118, 126
  sola fide 26, 36, 59, 75 n.249, 117
  theological virtue 22, 110, 138
first eternal law *see* law

Fortescue, John 184
forum conscientiae 154 *see also* Calvin, Jean
forum externum 154 *see also* Calvin, Jean

geistliches Reich 154 *see also* Luther, Martin; spiritual regiment
General Councils 166–7, 185 *see also* conciliarism
God *see also* Christ; Holy Spirit; Trinity
  absolute power 43 n.49
  Creator 1, 10, 11, 14, 42, 44, 51, 69, 70, 76, 78, 79, 84, 87, 114, 116, 140, 171
  divine nature, participation of 1, 2, 4, 7, 12, 16, 20, 36, 43, 45, 49, 54, 55, 59, 64, 69, 72, 74, 76, 85, 88, 95, 97–8, 106, 108, 114, 131, 136, 139, 160, 179, 185, 187
  father of lights 38, 101
  government 40, 44 n.55, 50, 55, 57, 60 n.35
  highest good 19, 59
  intrinsic certainty 136–7
  metaphysical simplicity 43–5, 57–8
  non-contrastive community 39
  opera Dei ad intra/ad extra 43
  ordained power 43 n.49
  perfection 5, 45, 47, 53, 54, 56, 58, 69–70, 80, 84, 97, 98, 163
  primary analogate 19, 40, 42, 45, 49, 69, 77, 94–5, 173
  providence 40, 44, 51, 70, 80, 84, 86, 150, 165, 180, 183
  purus actus 46–7, 94, 98, 133
  (re)union with 20, 38, 78, 82, 89, 97, 114, 128, 192
  self-diffusive being 150
  self-disclosure in divine law 62–3
  self-subsistence 9, 16, 46–7, 52
  transcendence 6, 8, 21, 23, 30, 43, 64–6, 75, 76, 82, 88, 183
  union with 5, 7, 12, 15, 20, 36, 38, 46, 57, 58, 59, 61–3, 73, 75, 78, 82, 87, 109, 131, 135, 138, 139, 155, 169, 193
  workman 51
goodness 3–4, 9, 19, 45, 47–8, 50, 52–3, 54, 57, 59–61, 68, 70–2, 75, 81, 86, 93, 98, 101, 103, 108, 124, 127–8, 130, 132, 134–5, 137–140, 142–5,

148 *see also* beauty; being; medieval transcendentals; truth
grace 6, 12, 14, 16, 26–7, 33, 53–4, 79, 80, 81, 114 *see also* nature
  church 154, 160, 162
  common grace 56 n.129
  definition 80
  faith 75
  hypostatic union 36, 63, 67, 76
  integrity 89
  justification 127, 140, 162
  nature and glory 78
  perfects/uses nature 60, 92, 103, 105, 108, 110, 112, 122, 127, 172
  sacraments 66, 71–4, 161
  sanctification 70, 82, 106, 138
  sola gratia 36
  Wisdom 86–7
Gregory of Nazianzus 4–5
Gregory of Nyssa 66, 71, 83

habit of faith 30, 110, 138, 146
heart *see* anthropology
Hebrew Testament 83, 84, 159
henosis 4, 10
heteronomy 42 n.39, 52, 90, 93, 94, 145, 148, 195, 197 *see also* autonomy; theonomy
hierarchy *see* dispositive hierarchy
Hobbes, Thomas 18
Holy Scripture 1, 29, 37, 38, 48, 58–61, 77, 83–4, 90–1, 102, 105, 106, 109–14, 146–7, 150–2, 155, 158–60, 163, 165, 168, 183, 185, 192 *see also* autopistos; biblical omnicompetency; law
  authority 37, 114, 115, 120
  Christ 59, 146–7
  divine law 23, 36, 39–41, 48–9, 56, 58–61, 63, 76, 78, 81, 100, 106, 108, 113, 121, 146, 153, 159, 169, 172, 187, 193
  hermeneutics 112–13
  Holy Spirit, testimony of 117, 124–5
  omnicompetency 38, 139, 145, 152, 153, 159
  ratiocinative analysis 117
  scientific principium (*principium cognoscendi theologiae*) 106, 109, 111, 115–16
  self-authenticating authority 114 n.196, 115–8, 120, 125 n.255
  sufficiency 111
  teleological definition 112
Holy Spirit 40, 47, 75, 80, 82, 106, 111, 115, 117, 120–6, 148, 162, 165–6, 168, 175 *see also* Christ; God; Trinity
  internal testimony (*internum testimonium*) 115, 117, 124–5
  per se causation 101, 118, 125–6
Homer 95
hope 22, 61, 75, 130, 132, 137, 138 *see also* faith; love; virtues
hyper-rationalism 91, 102, 114, 117, 118, 126, 144 *see also* reason
hypo-rationalism 90, 94, 106, 110, 126 *see also* reason
hypostatic distinction 42, 64
hypostatic union 20, 37, 63, 64, 66–7, 70–2, 76, 78, 83, 106, 150, 157, 173 *see also* Christ

imagined community 142, 155
imitation (*mimesis*) 3 *see also* deification; participation
immediacy *see* Augustine
Incarnation *see* Christ
influence (*influentia*) 12, 47 n.68, 68, 90, 188
inner forum 154, 157
intellect 98, 102 *see also* cognitive participation; reason
  active/passive 97–101
  appetite 132
  deification 108, 141, 144
  divine 3, 94–5, 98
  faith, intellectual habit of 108, 137–8
  illumination 40, 97
  image of God 55, 94–6, 105
  logic of desire 148
  power 94, 108
  practical 56, 58, 96, 98–9, 108, 133
  speculative 57, 98, 108, 136
intelligentia indivisibilium 98
internum testimonium 117, 124–5 *see also* Holy Spirit
invisible church *see* ecclesiology
Irenaeus 66
irrationalism 91, 110, 132, 150

emotions 90, 128
grace 27, 90
sins of passion 130

Jerome 83, 165
Jewel, John 186
John of Damascus 64
Junius, Franciscus 40 n.24, 41 n.34,
justification 23, 62, 70–2, 75 n.249, 82, 138, 140, 157, 161–2 *see also* sanctification
Justin Martyr 83

law 1–2, 19, 37, 189, 192–3
  analogy 38, 40
  angelic, celestial 39, 53, 54, 161, 170
  coherency 35–7
  conceptions 26
  definition 39, 41, 42
  divine 23, 36, 39–41, 48–9, 56, 58–61, 63, 76, 78, 81, 100, 106, 108, 113, 121, 146, 153, 159, 169, 172, 187, 193
  eternal 39, 40, 43–8, 49, 51 n.93, 52, 55, 58, 59, 64, 76, 84–5, 139, 150, 154–7, 160, 164, 184
  first eternal law 43–4, 48, 71, 154, 157, 189
  ius gentium 166–7
  lex divinitatis 36, 49, 63, 76, 78, 150, 188–9
  natural 17, 19, 36, 39, 40, 55, 58, 69, 72, 79, 192
  non-coercive character 41
  positive 38, 167, 172, 174, 178, 183–4
  of reason 48, 50, 56–8, 81, 94, 95–6, 99–101, 103, 106, 112, 133, 165, 145–6, 193
  second eternal law 44, 48, 49, 64, 71, 154, 160, 189–90
  supernatural 38, 59, 112, 155
  systematic examination 37
  types 39
lay ecclesiastical supremacy *see* monarch
liberalism
  suspicion of secular 18
  theological defence of 196
liturgy
  Dionysian resemblance 142
  Dionysian sign 141
  edification 30, 89, 90, 109, 127, 139–41

  established 127–8, 142–3, 161
  mysticism 10, 70–4, 90, 92, 127, 135, 139–44, 90
  recreation of holy desires 92, 127, 135, 139–44
  union with Christ 72, 127, 144
Logos autopistos see autopistos
love 130–5 *see also* faith; hope; virtues
  beauty 53, 61
  deification 141
  divine 147
  faith 75
  goodness 127, 129, 130
  reciprocal relationship 131
  Renaissance theological retrieval 144
  theological virtue 22, 75, 137–8
  Thomistic idea of faith formed by 139
  union with God 59, 69, 75, 90, 102, 128, 130–1, 141, 148, 192
  worship 139–40
Luther, Martin 7, 65 n.189, 154 n.24, 156, 157, 158 n.50, 159, 172 n.73, 173, 177, 179, 181
  consubstantiation 73
  two regiments 150, 154, 156, 157–8, 175, 177–8, 181, 188–9
  ubiquity 66–7, 180

manuduction 30, 90, 124, 139–40, 147, 194, 196
Marsilius of Padua 26, 151, 189–90
mediation *see* Pseudo-Dionysius
medieval transcendentals 9, 45–6, 50, 53, 54, 61, 86, 101, 133, 135, 140, 142 *see also* beauty; being; goodness; truth
Meister Eckhart 10
Melanchthon, Philip 159
Mercurius Trismegistus 96
methexis 2–3, 8, 20, 35, 63, 73 *see also* deification; participation
  etymology 3
  philosophical register 4
  scriptural register 4, 20
modern individualism 16
de Molina, Luis 184
monarch 178, 187, 190
  constitutional limits 185
  divine right 151, 186
  God's Lieutenants 150, 187

image of God and Christ 151
law 184–5
lay ecclesiastical supremacy 24, 32, 38, 62, 114, 149–50, 172–4, 177, 179–82, 186, 188, 190, 193
origins 183–4, 186
parliament 150, 167, 185–6
uncommanded Commander 150, 187
monarchical episcopacy *see* bishops
monē-proodos-epistrophē 11, 46, 50, 181 *see also* exitus-reditus
monotheism 5, 45
More, Thomas 172 n.132
Mosaic Decalogue 100
Moses 146, 159, 182
multiplex intelligentia 113
mystical Church *see* ecclesiology
mysticism *see* liturgy

natural cognitive participation in God *see* participation
natural law *see* law
nature 81 *see also* grace
  definition and meanings 79
  depraved 104
  human 5, 6, 20, 23, 55, 56, 58–9, 63, 65–8, 71, 76–7, 81, 94–6, 102–3, 105, 144–6, 148, 157, 159, 177–80, 192, 195
  natural integrity 93
  need of grace 60, 172
  providence 80
  school of 147
  similitude of God 50, 80
  sincere 104
  subordinate instrument 51, 57, 66
Neoplatonic metaphysics 8, 19, 20, 37 *see also* Pseudo-Dionysius
  exitus-reditus 11, 20, 50, 63, 71, 72, 76
  influentia 12, 47 n.68, 68, 188
  logic 45 n.61
  monē-proodos-epistrophē 11, 46, 50, 181
  procession 44–5
Nestorianism 175, 179
Nestorius 65, 175 n.147
New Testament 4, 79, 83, 146
Nicholas of Cusa 10
nominalism 16–18
nomological cosmology 102

non-rational agents 49, 50 n.88, 52–4, 79

Ockham, William of 42 n.27, 107 n.128
Old Testament *see* Hebrew Testament
ordained power (*potentia ordinata*) 43 n.49 *see also* God
Origen 83
Oxford Movement 21–2

Palamas, Gregory 6, 14
participation 1, 2, 6, 63 *see also* deification; methexis
  analogy 40, 94
  Aquinas's definition 2
  architecture 2, 8, 11–13, 21, 27, 33, 35, 38, 41, 49, 61, 64, 76, 89, 92, 94, 103, 106, 122, 126, 127, 133, 148, 149, 152, 153–4, 159, 172, 177, 181–2, 185, 188, 191–7
  in Christ 13, 20, 23, 24, 27, 63, 68, 70–3, 75, 76–88, 144, 154, 160, 162–3, 170, 192
  ecumenical retrievals 2, 13, 15, 19, 21
  epistemic 146
  Eucharistic 4, 73, 91, 161
  extensive 11–12, 27, 37–61, 78, 88, 89, 92, 133, 146, 191
  genealogy 8–9
  in God 1, 2, 4, 7, 12, 16, 20, 36, 43, 45, 49, 54, 55, 59, 64, 69, 72, 74, 76, 85, 88, 95, 97–8, 106, 108, 114, 131, 136, 139, 160, 179, 185, 187
  grammar of 149, 154, 161, 162, 163, 165, 172–87, 193
  images of 2, 3, 4, 8–11
  intensive 11–12, 27, 33, 38, 49, 58, 62–76, 78, 88, 90, 92, 102, 109, 114, 128, 131, 133, 135, 139, 140, 146, 192, 194–5
  natural cognitive 10, 92–7, 102, 108, 114, 126, 140, 144
  Neoplatonic 45, 50, 128, 188
  non-cognitive 49, 50 n.88, 52–5, 79
  Platonic 2, 3, 8–11, 45 n.59, 76–88
  politics of 18–19, 149–90
  reciprocal 20, 73, 125–6, 131, 144
  retrievals of 1–34, 144, 196
  sacramental 20, 24, 35, 62–4, 160, 192
  scriptural concepts 4

spirituality 3, 22
  supernatural cognitive 90, 94 n.25, 102, 104, 105–14, 118, 126, 134–5, 138–41, 144
  theonomy 12, 42 n.39, 52, 56–8, 68, 79, 86, 94, 145, 148, 188, 197
participatory consciousness 128
participatory metaphysics 38
passions 129–32 *see also* affections; emotions
passive aptitude (*aptitudo passiva*) 105
passive intellect 98 *see also* active intellect
per se nota 107, 115, 119–21
persuasion 89, 106, 117, 123, 124, 168, 195
Plato 2–4, 3 n.13, 4 n.14, 8–9, 18, 45, 46, 51 n.93, 56 n.130, 95
Platonism 19, 27, 36, 37, 47, 49, 63, 69, 77, 82, 129, 140, 144, 149, 152, 154, 159, 173, 178, 188–90
Plotinus 10–11, 11 n.47–8, 45 n.61
polemics 37, 90, 123
political theology 149, 195
politicized metaphysics 149, 167
Pope 152, 189
power 4, 18, 22, 36, 55, 67, 189–90
  absolute power 43 n.49
  appetitive 132
  bishop 150, 155, 164, 169, 170, 171
  books of power 33, 62, 149, 151, 188, 190
  Christ 72, 179
  Church 165, 177
  eternal law 39, 51
  God 4, 17, 36, 84, 148, 150, 164, 181, 183, 188, 193
  Holy Spirit 53, 69, 87, 118, 120, 126, 148, 173–4
  monarch 150, 155, 178, 180, 182–7
  ordained power 43, 49
  reason 59, 91–105, 106–8, 114
  secularization and politicization 187
practical intellect 56, 58, 96, 98–9, 108, 133 *see also* intellect; speculative intellect
precisian 37 n.12 *see also* radical puritan
predestination 55, 78, 95 n.32, 156, 162
Presbyterian 37 n.12, 120 *see also* radical puritan
presbyterian polity 153, 166
presbyters 164
principium quod of faith 126

problem of paganism 102
Proclus 11, 11 n.50–2, 20, 181
providence 40, 44, 51, 70, 80, 84, 86, 106 n.126, 165, 180, 183
Pseudo-Dionysius 5, 5 n.20, 20, 36, 171, 187 *see also* Neoplatonic metaphysics
  angelic orders 54, 142, 170–1
  deification, definition of 5, 141
  Dionysian mediation 27, 36, 42, 68, 64, 68, 76–8, 82, 88, 140–4, 154, 156, 159, 173, 188–9
  doctrine of God 43
  episcopal orders 171
  grace 80
  influence (*influentia*) 12, 47 n.68, 68, 90, 188
  lex divinitatis 36, 49, 150, 189
  liturgical signs 141, 143–4
pure act (*purus actus*) 19, 46–7, 94, 98, 133
puritans 37 n.12 *see* radical puritans

Radical Orthodoxy 16 n.71, 18, 18 n.81, 19, 19 n.87, 196
radical puritans 27, 37, 37 n.12, 38, 90, 92, 105, 145, 147, 151, 196
  arguments 38, 62, 89, 103, 104, 111, 117, 120, 123, 127, 132, 134, 139, 153–68, 173, 175–6, 178–84, 189
  definition 37 n.12
  putative isomorphism 113, 124
Ramystry 99 n.64
rational appetite 133
rational by participation 131
rational consciousness 128
rational soul 129
rationalism *see* hyper-rationalism; hypo-rationalism
reason 27, 30, 80, 90, 92, 93–105 *see also* hyper-rationalism; hypo-rationalism
  Christ 92, 146
  definition of law 41
  elicitive principle 125
  humana ratio 117, 123
  image of God 52, 55
  instrument 57, 106, 108, 110–14, 124–5
  law of 48, 50, 56–8, 81, 94, 95–6, 99–101, 103, 106, 112, 133, 165, 145–6, 193
  right reason 44, 96
scriptural authenticity 114–27

scriptural interpretation 113-14
redemption 23, 33, 38, 41, 49, 59, 69, 82-3, 87, 92, 193
Reformation principles 37
Reformed orthodoxy 18, 114, 123, 125, 126, 135, 149, 156, 181, 196
Reformed scholasticism 51, 125 *see also* scholasticism
Reformed scholastics 51, 110, 125, 154, 165 *see also* scholasticism
Resurrection 58
reunion with God *see* deification; God; participation
revelation 27, 40, 43, 48, 56, 79, 90, 91, 95, 101, 106-7, 120, 124-5, 145, 171
Richard of St Victor 84
righteousness 59, 70-2, 75, 82, 157, 161, 163
Royal Supremacy *see* monarch

sacra scriptura 107 n.132
sacraments 2, 12, 20, 36, 62-7, 71, 72, 75, 77, 88, 144, 148, 154, 159, 161, 170, 187 *see also* baptism; Christ; Eucharist; participation
instrumentality 74, 82, 87, 180
sacred doctrine (*sacra doctrina*) 107-8, 121
salvation 5, 7, 22-4, 36, 64, 66, 68, 71, 77-8, 81, 88, 105, 107, 109-12, 115, 118, 135, 147, 158, 170, 192
sanctification 6, 70, 75, 82, 138 n.348, 154, 162 *see also* justification
Saravia, Hadrian 151, 184
satanic delusion 57
scholasticism 43-4
  medieval scholasticism 115, 125, 165
  Reformed scholasticism 51, 110, 125, 154, 165
science (*scientia*) 30, 106-7, 109-10, 115-16, 118, 120
Scotus, John *see* Duns Scotus
Scripture *see* Holy Scripture
second eternal law *see* law
sensitive appetite 132, 133
similitude 6, 12, 35, 40, 46, 47, 49, 50, 52, 76, 84, 94, 97, 101, 126, 142, 148, 177, 182
sin 23, 30, 40, 57-60, 72, 76, 78, 88, 92, 104-5, 148, 158

angelic 54
total depravity 57 n.135, 77, 104
Smith, Adam 18
Smith, Thomas 184
sola scriptura 119
Sophia 83-7 *see* Christ; Wisdom of God
soteriology *see* salvation
de Soto, Domingo 184
speculative intellect 57, 98, 108, 136 *see also* intellect; practical intellect
spiritual illumination 168
spiritual regiment 157, 174, 175, 178, 180
St Germain, Christopher 184
Stoics 51 n.93, 69, 83, 96, 129,
Suàrez, Francisco 184
subalternation 106-8, 118, 120-1
subordinationism 179
supernatural cognitive participation in God *see* participation
supernatural duties 59-61
supernatural finality of human beings 72
supernatural society 155, 161
systematic 19, 25-7, 148, 152, 176, 180, 191, 193-4
types 31-3

tabula rasa 98
temporal regiment 154, 155, 158, 160, 173, 175-7, 179, 189-90
theology 30, 107, 110
  natural 79, 119
  revealed 116, 146
theonomy 12, 42 n.39, 52, 56-8, 68, 79, 86-7, 93, 94, 96, 97, 103, 145, 148, 188, 197 *see also* autonomy; heteronomy
theopoiēsis 4 *see also* deification
theōsis 4-7, 14-16, 22-3, 28, 76, 195 *see also* deification
total depravity 57 n.135, 77, 104 *see also* sin
tradition 27 *see also* customs
transcendentals *see* medieval transcendentals
transubstantiation 73-4
Tridentine Catholicism 111, 167
Trinity 13, 19, 20, 23, 43, 47, 53, 64, 69, 71, 83, 85, 111, 141, 148, 170, 179, 192, 195, 197 *see also* Christ; God; Holy Spirit
Trinitarian participation 53, 87, 148

Trinitarian relations 14, 23, 43, 53
true society 196
truth 4, 45, 99, 110, 135–40, 143 *see also* beauty; being; goodness; medieval transcendentals
Tudor Averroism 151, 181
Turretin, Francis 125 n.255

uncommanded Commander 150, 173, 187
uninformed enthusiasm 92
union *see* Christ; deification; God; participation
univocity 16, 18

vegetative appetite 133
Vermigli, Peter Martyr 165
virtues 82, 133 *see also* faith; hope; love
   episcopal 170
   moral 53, 56, 102, 103
   public 62, 193
   supernatural 81
   theological 75, 108, 131, 139
virtuous habits 131, 142
visible Church *see* ecclesiology
de Vitoria, Thomas 184
Voetius, Gisbertus 125, 126
voluntarism 17, 18, 41, 42 n.37, 150, 181

weltliches Reich 154 *see also* Luther, Martin; temporal regiment
Wesley, Charles 7
Western Orthodoxy 22, 195
Whitgift, John 174–5, 177
Wisdom of God 12, 82, 83, 86–8, 105, 191 *see also* Christ; Sophia
Word of God 12, 82, 83, 85, 87–9, 145, 147, 191 *see also* Christ
worship *see* liturgy

Lightning Source UK Ltd.
Milton Keynes UK
UKHW051849231221
396063UK00012B/384